LEGISPRUDENCE

For Vlad Perju and Wojciech Cyrul
students in the past, colleagues in the present, and friends for a long time I hope

Legisprudence
Practical Reason in Legislation

LUC J. WINTGENS
University of Brussels, Belgium

Routledge
Taylor & Francis Group
LONDON AND NEW YORK

First published 2012 by Ashgate Publishing

Published 2016 by Routledge
2 Park Square, Milton Park, Abingdon, Oxfordshire OX14 4RN
711 Third Avenue, New York, NY 10017, USA

First issued in paperback 2016

Routledge is an imprint of the Taylor & Francis Group, an informa business

British Library Cataloguing in Publication Data
Wintgens, Luc.
Legisprudence : practical reason in legislation. (Applied legal philosophy)
1. Law–Philosophy. 2. Legislation. 3. Jurisprudence.
I. Title II. Series
340.1-dc22

Library of Congress Cataloging-in-Publication Data
Wintgens, Luc.
Legisprudence: practical reason in legislation/by Luc J. Wintgens.
p. cm. – (Applied legal philosophy)
Includes bibliographical references and index.
ISBN 978-1-4094-1981-5 (hardback : alk. paper)
1. Legislation. 2. Law—Philosophy. I. Title.
K284.W56 2012
340'.1—dc23

2011049787

ISBN 13: 978-1-138-25686-6 (pbk)
ISBN 13: 978-1-4094-1981-5 (hbk)

Contents

Series Editor's Preface

The objective of the Applied Legal Philosophy series is to publish work which adopts a theoretical approach to the study of particular areas or aspects of law or deals with general theories of law in a way which focused on issues of practical moral and political concern in specific legal contexts.

In recent years there has been an encouraging tendency for legal philosophers to utilize detailed knowledge of the substance and practicalities of law and a noteworthy development in the theoretical sophistication of much legal research. The series seeks to encourage these trends and to make available studies in law which are both genuinely philosophical in approach and at the same time based on appropriate legal knowledge and directed towards issues in the criticism and reform of actual laws and legal systems.

The series will include studies of all the main areas of law, presented in a manner which relates to the concerns of specialist legal academics and practitioners. Each book makes an original contribution to an area of legal study while being comprehensible to those engaged in a wide variety of disciplines. Their legal content is principally Anglo-American, but a wide-ranging comparative approach is encouraged and authors are drawn from a variety of jurisdictions.

Tom Campbell
Series Editor
Centre for Applied Philosophy and Public Ethics
Charles Sturt University, Canberra.

Introduction

Current legal theory is premised on the central role of the judge in contemporary legal systems. Although this evolution has contributed much to a vibrant understanding of law, it has also left the role of the legislator largely ignored and under-theorised. Legal theory routinely takes the law as 'just there', and limits its theoretical undertakings to law as a 'given'. Law, it claims, is the result of political decision-making. But once law comes into force, it can be somehow miraculously separated from politics. And the realm of politics is impure – unlike law's 'neutral' and 'objective' methods of reasoning and decision-making.

This book takes a different view on law and legislation and in this process it offers a radical shift in the theoretical thinking about law. It argues that practical reason in legislation comes to the practice of reason throughout the process of legislative law-making. It establishes 'legisprudence', by contrast to jurisprudence, as a legal theory of legislative law-making. Where does the law come from? What are the premises of a theory that considers law separated from politics? What does it mean for a legislator to be bound to the rules of a constitution throughout the process of legislation? Does the constitution consist of rules to be followed by the legislator or is its role merely confined to be a political programme?

At first glance, it may seem puzzling why contemporary legal theory fails to take legislation seriously. The quantity and quality of legislation has become a central topic in the public discourse of Western democracies. There are common complaints about the exponential increase in the volume of legislation coupled with a striking decrease in its quality. It is by no means obvious what can be done to get contemporary democracies out of this predicament. We typically think of politics as the realm of power, not reason. Decisions are made by vote, and it is political interest, rather than the force of the better argument, that determines how representatives vote. Politics is a power game, resulting in compromises that are framed into a legislative or statutory structure. This power game seems to have its own logic, the results of which most of the time outweigh any other form of logic.

This book rejects this common wisdom about the nature of politics and its outcome: legislation. It provides a new perspective, which I call 'legisprudence', the rational creation of legislation and regulation, hence, practical reason in legislation. In doing so, I use the methods, theoretical insights and tools of current legal theory and philosophy of law. But it puts these tools, which have been deployed in the past to deal with judicial interpretation and application of statutes, to a new use: the creation of law by the legislator.

Within this new approach, a variety of new questions and problems – for example, the validity of norms, their meaning, the structure of the legal system, and so on – are raised. Traditionally, these questions are approached from the perspective of the judge. However, when shifting our attention from the judge to the legislator, the same concerns arise but in a slightly different form – in what sense must the legislator take the systematicity of the legal order into account? What counts as a valid norm? – to mention but a few.

However important it is to state these questions about the role of legislation, answering them requires an incursion in the philosophical roots of legal theory. Indeed, I argue in this book that it is no accident that the legislator is the missing actor of contemporary legal theory and philosophy of law, despite the undeniable importance of legislation in modern democracies. My diagnostic is clear: the reason for the disregard of legislators are the long decades of legalism in legal reasoning. For generations, lawyers have been taught that everything happens behind the veil of sovereignty as far as legislation is concerned, and behind the veil of legality when it comes to the execution of legislative acts.

These veils teach ignorance about the possibilities of an alternative theoretical reflection on rule-making. Claims to sovereignty silence debate about alternative ways of regulating society. Sovereignty is sovereignty in silence.

Consider the familiar scenario: rules come from the sovereign; they are valid or invalid; if they are valid, they must be obeyed; the state can legitimately coerce those who disobey. In this linear scenario, questions of law's efficacy, effectivity, efficiency, or rational acceptability are not in order.

The time has come to move beyond this simplistic, albeit influential, account of the fundamentals of political power. We must rethink legislative prerogative and articulate a new conception of sovereignty.

This book explores the contours of a theory of legislation called 'legisprudence' as a rational, principled theory of legislation. Rational legislation focuses on the role of practical reason in the creation of legal norms upon which norm givers are considered not merely political actors but legal actors as well.

I said that legalism in legal reasoning is responsible for the disregard of legislators in the legal theory. We cannot, however, uproot legalism without reaching further into the philosophical assumptions on which it is premised. Early modernity provides the privileged spectrum to explain why the lack of a theory of rational legislation that gives a place to law in a social context is not an accident. We cannot shift the paradigm that underlies legal thinking unless we explore in more detail the deeper roots of law's basic concepts and core assumptions about the nature of the subject, rationality and freedom, as well as law's authority.

In this respect, the argument of the book provides a larger view on what is generally considered the Modern period of philosophy, exploring these basic concepts and assumptions. While there is general agreement that Descartes is the initiator of what is called 'Modern' philosophy, this view is supplemented with a brief outline of these concepts in pre-modern philosophy, mainly focusing on the nominalist position of the impossibility of the existence of universals outside the mind.

Upon this position, the nature of law shifts from insight into the nature of justice to a normativist characterisation of law as a command including a moral obligation to obedience. This transition is briefly illustrated on the basis of the major claims of the work of some representative doctrines. These doctrines support the view that law mainly consists of norms containing rights and duties externally imposed on subjects having to follow them. This is initially typified as 'legalism', presenting law and law-making as an a-contextual expression of a sovereign's will.

A more fundamental analysis and critique of this legalistic pattern of thought is preceded by a contextual interpretation of individualism, rationalism and freedom that paves the way for a legisprudential understanding of law and legislation. Put differently, the idea of law and legislation in context requires us to revisit their a-contextual understanding rooting in pre-modern and Modern philosophy. The critique of legalism builds on the idea that a proper understanding of the concepts of the subject, rationality and freedom must proceed by putting them in a context of participation.

To begin with, the contextual interpretation of the subject proceeds on the basis of a critique of the solipsistic cogito, thus enlarging the 'conception of the self' in the cogito to the idea of a subject having a self-conception. The latter approach is elaborated on the basis of the theory of symbolic interactionism, according to which the subject emerges throughout interaction with others. The subject's self includes a social as well as an individual pole. By articulating these two poles, an attempt is made to take seriously the subject as an autonomous moral actor.

Secondly, the contextual interpretation of rationality criticises Descartes' idealisation of it, that is, its decontextualisation that obscures the fact that it is historically situated. This situatedness shows rationality to be rather a matter of contextual argumentation referring to reasonableness than self-revealing rationality that operates as demonstration or calculation.

Third, since legislation is about rules, and rules are about individual conduct, they impact on freedom. Legisprudence as a theory of rational rule-making therefore needs a theory of freedom, that relies on a contextual interpretation of it. The contextual interpretation of freedom then joins the contextual interpretation of the subject and rationality. Freedom as a practical concept allows for different conceptions or concretisations. Conceptions can be conceptions *of* freedom or conceptions *about* freedom. The former are the subject's own concretisations of freedom, while the latter are someone else's to which the subject is submitted. Conceptions of freedom relate to the social subject's moral autonomy upon which they can frame their interactions with other.

In order to take the social subjects' moral autonomy, I argue that norm-givers have to provide arguments for why their conceptions about the subjects' freedom have priority over the subjects' conceptions of freedom, thus diminishing the latter's autonomy. At the background of this duty to provide arguments lies the idea that the social subjects should be taken morally seriously, and cannot be expected to surrender their capacity to act on their conceptions of freedom to the state. The further elaboration of legisprudence follows upon this approach to freedom.

Upon the contextual interpretation of individualism, rationality and freedom, the argument proceeds with a focus on the characteristics of legalism the origin of which is sketched in the beginning of this book. The main critique of legalism is that it has impeded the emergence of a principled theory of legislation in that it limits, generally speaking, law to orders or commands of the sovereign. It obliterates practical reason in legislation. The separation of law and politics as the main strategy of legalism takes law to be a-contextual. Here as elsewhere this view on law and legislation is shown to rely on a foundationalist approach to thinking. The main characteristics of what is called strong legalism take law to consist of norms of the state that have a universal form providing them with unquestionable legitimacy.

As a critique of legalism, legisprudence builds on the contextual interpretation of rationality, subject and freedom in order to focus on practical reason in legislation. The articulation of practical reason in legislation proceeds on a distinction between legitimacy on the one hand and legitimation on the other. Legitimacy is an a-contextual aspect of norms issued by sovereigns that are considered *ipso facto* irrefutably rational.

This idea is proper to strong legalism. Legitimation for its part refers to a process of active justification of norms by the sovereign, thus arguing why it is more rational to organise freedom on these norms than on the subjects' own self-regulative interaction. This is the basic premise of legisprudence. Legisprudence distinguishes between legislation as a product and legislation as a process.

The distinction between legitimacy and legitimation is a novelty this book wants to emphasise by providing a twofold interpretation of the idea of the social contract.

The first is the proxy version of the social contract upon which subjects give a proxy to the sovereign to issue subsequent limitations of their freedom or norms. From the 'moment' of the contract onward, the sovereign is *ipso facto* legitimated in substituting conceptions about freedom for conceptions of freedom. On the proxy version, the sovereign can legitimately, that is, without further legitimation, transform any propositional content into a true norm.

The second interpretation of the social contract is labelled the 'trade-off' model. On this model, the subjects trade off conceptions of freedom for conceptions about freedom. This comes to saying that the substitution of conceptions about freedom for conceptions of freedom must be justified by the norm-giver. No rule can be held legitimate if this justification or legitimation is lacking.

Legisprudence as a theory of rational legislation builds on the latter model, and can be taken to rely on three major intertwined points: freedom as principium, that forms the basis for principles of rational legislation, that finally can be concretised in duties of the norm-giver.

The principle of coherence is the first principle of legisprudence. It requires that norms make sense as a whole. The principle of coherence thus identified is elaborated in a theory that I propose to call the 'level theory of coherence'. The minimal level of coherence$_0$ requires that norms are not self-contradicting. The level of coherence$_1$ requires norm-givers to give reasons why norms are changed or not changed, thus installing coherence over time. Third, legislators are to argue on the level of coherence$_2$, or the level of coherence of the system, in that their rules must make sense as a whole within the system. Finally, the level of coherence$_3$ refers to the fact that a legal system depends on theories that are not themselves law, but to which legislators must refer in order to justify their norms.

This level of coherence, typically, refers to theories like the rule character of norms, the separation of powers, and others, all of which, so it is argued, refer to freedom as principium. In this sense, the level of coherence$_3$ has a recursive impact on the other levels of coherence, as well as on the three other principles of legisprudence. This impact is elaborated by arguing that the principles of legisprudence, upon their connection to freedom as principium, constitute each other's context. In that respect, it is argued that they are not to be taken in a lexical order but in a contextual setting.

Social subjects are initially free and capable to rationally organise their freedom in a context with others. It follows that they are primarily to act on conceptions of freedom. A substitution of a conception about freedom for conceptions of freedom can only be legitimate if it is legitimated or justified as an alternative for failing social interaction. This is the second principle of legisprudence, called the principle of alternativity.

The third principle of legisprudence is the principle of temporality. The limitation of freedom on a conception about freedom must be justified as 'on time'. Any justification is, however, embedded in a context, because rationality as reasonableness is context related, and therefore historically situated. This involves that if the justification of a norm is successful it will only be temporarily so; that is, norms can become obsolete. The principle of temporality then requires an ongoing justification over time, and not only on the moment that a norm is issued.

The fourth principle of legisprudence is the principle of necessity of the normative density. Rules should not automatically contain sanctions as the strongest from of normative density. If sanctions are included, this requires a specific and supplementary justification why weaker alternatives (information campaign, incentives, labelling, covenants and so on) are not withheld.

While the principles of legisprudence are concretisations of the idea of freedom as articulated earlier, they can still be more concretised as duties of the norm-giver. Upon the requirement of the justification of norms, the duties that are identified in this respect include: the duty of relevant fact-finding, the duty of problem formulation, the duty to weigh and balance alternatives, the duty to prospection or the duty to take future circumstances into consideration, the duty to monitor the issued norms, the duty to retrospection, and the duty to review. The fulfilment of these duties comes to showing how a norm-giver arrived at the concrete norms he or she is issuing.

The requirement of the justification of norms, the principles of legisprudence, and the corresponding concrete duties of the norm-giver, so the argument ends, support a rationality control by constitutional and administrative courts. This process of rationality control does not however affect the political or value choices made through legislation, but focuses on the concrete argumentation of the norm-giver upon the principles of legisprudence.

This approach to the rationality of legislation opens a new perspective on the problematic exponential increase of legal systems and the decreasing quality of legislation in most European democracies. Upon the requisite that a norm-giver considers more seriously his way of creating norms and the requirement to show how he did by justifying his norms legisprudence has the potential to contribute to an improvement of the quality of legislation. The improvement of the quality of legislation as the main purpose of legisprudence may be expected to result in a decrease of legislative norms, since better norms need less corrections, adaptations and changes.

In addition to the involvement of practical reason in legislation in line with the requisite of its justification, norm-givers show that they take legal subjects as moral agents more seriously, since they support legal obligation with justificatory reasons. In doing so, legisprudence expands the realm of legal theory so as to include legislative activity that is submitted to a rationality control. In this respect, the legisprudential approach advocated in this book provides legislation with a deeper justification by subtracting it from political law-making as a power game, and by connecting it to the legal theoretical model of argumentative justification calling the legislator to account for his rule-making. In this respect, the project of legisprudence has a practical bearing on the predicament of contemporary democracies by stressing the legislator's responsibility for legislation that goes beyond mere political accountability.

Books are rarely the product of the author's solitary cogito, and so it is with this one. I have generously benefited from interaction, intellectual and otherwise, with many. Numerous are the friends and colleagues who have contributed to it in one way or the other. I will not enter into a detailed description of their contribution which would be an impossible enterprise. Suffice it to mention their names with the hope that they will recognise some of their thoughts, reflections, critiques and encouragements somewhere in the book. Since the regime of strict liability applies to the content of this book, they are not responsible for its final content.

The persons that come to my mind are Aulis Aarnio, Maurice Adams, Robert Alexy, Bruce Anderson, Jacques Andreu, Manuel Atienza, Koen Baeten, Zenon Bankowski, John Bell, Samantha Besson, Tadeus Biernat, Jes Bjarup, Guido Calabresi, Tom Campbell, Emilios Christodoulidis, Herman Cousy, Wojciech and Aga Cyrul, Martine de Clercq, Erwin Depue, Adeline Desegher, Johan Desmet, David Dhooge, Guillaume Drago, Timea Drinoczi, Hugues Dumont, Philip Eijlander, Michiel Elst, Imer Flores, Åke Frändberg, Benoît Frydman, Tito Gallas, John Gardner, Philippe Gérard, René Gonzalez, Linda Gröning, Guy Haarscher, Jaap Hage, Cyril Holm, Mark Hunyadi, Tatsouo Inoue, Eerik Lagerspetz, Mark Lambrechts, Sheldon Leader, Juha Karhu, Maria-Isabelle Köpke-Tinture, Daniel Lalana, Francesco Laporte, Luzius Mader, the late Neil MacCormick, Frank Michelman, Charles-Albert Morand, Dwight Newman, Francois Ost, Richard Parker, Trinie Parker, Stanley Paulson, the late Aleksander Peczenik, Vlad Perju,

Marcin Pieniazek, Kauko Pietilla, Pasquale Policastro, Patricia Popelier, Daniel Priel, Pekka Riekinen, Thomas Roberts, Geoffrey Samuel, Giovani Sartor, Woomin Sim, Jerzy Stelmach, Andreas Takis, Jyrki Tala, Gunther Teubner, Benoît Timmermans, Hannu Tolonen, Michel Troper, François Tulkens, Stamatios Tzitzis, François Vallançon, Koen Van Aeken, Mark Van Bellingen, Wibren Van der Burg, the late Michiel Vandekerckhove, Michel van de Kerchove, Frederik Vandendriesche, Rob van Gestel, Claude Van Reeth, Scott Veatch, Roger Vergauwen, Amaryllis Verhoeven, Wim Voermans, Jeremy Waldron, Marcin Weisbrot, Kenneth Winston, Willem Witteveen, Helen Xanthaki, Wojciech Zadurski, Mauro Zamboni and Marek Zyrk-Zadurski.

Thomas Roberts considerably helped me with the linguistic corrections of the text, including the translations of foreign quotations where necessary.

I am indebted to the *Fonds voor Wetenschappelijk Onderzoek Vlaanderen* that has generously funded this project, as well to the University of Brussels (HUB-KUB) for leaving me the time to carry it out. Paul Wouters was very helpful and efficient in the financial administration of this project for which I owe him special thanks.

Luc J. Wintgens
Florence, Easter 2011

Chapter 1
The Metaphysics of Legalism

Introduction

In an attempt to characterise the nature of Modernity, Hans Blumenberg (1983) has argued that there is something irreducibly original about it, while Karl Löwith (1970) claims that its intellectual *Gestalt* is a secularisation of Christian theology. Both seem to have it at least partly right. Descartes' *cogito* is prima facie an irreducible novelty, while 'sovereignty' in a Modern context is no doubt related to late mediaeval divine omnipotence. Following the latter, the claim that Modernity is a radically new period in history, in that it comes up with new problems, needs to be qualified. It is a different way of 'understanding understanding', a new form of consciousness of the perennial problems of philosophy.

As far as legalism is concerned, which is the main issue to be explored in this chapter, it is usually related to Weber's articulation of the relation of capitalism and Protestantism (Weber 1992). On his contraction of legality and legitimacy, Weber is held to be the initiator of legalism in that all norms that have the form of rules are therefore legitimate. It combines the rational organisation of labour with rational book-keeping, both of which are freed from any religious or superstitious beliefs. For capitalism to flourish, a stable and predictable legal system is needed. The easy conclusive step would be to assert that capitalism is 'caused' one way or the other by Protestantism, the combination of which calls for a rational legal system consisting of predictable rules. Legalism can be characterised as 'the ethical attitude that holds moral conduct to be a matter of rule following and moral relationships to consist of duties and rights determined by rules' (Shklar 1986: 1), no matter where these rules come from (Bankowski and Schafer 2007: 34). I will most of all dwell on the first part of the expression, that is, that normativity is a matter of rule-following. The content of these rules and the determination of moral relationships as rights and duties require a different study which will be a matter for the future.

The main claim of this chapter is that legalism is not an invention of Modernity. On the contrary, it is a metaphysical concept that has its roots in late mediaeval theology. For legalism, it is rules that are important, not where they come from. From there it spreads into political and legal philosophy going along with both jusnaturalism and positivism.[1] Far less is it the spin-off of positivism. The opposite

1 Haggenmacher (1983: 472–3) identifies a type of jusnaturalism that is both legalistic and positivistic in the *Decretum Gratiani*. The *Decretum* (twelfth century) was part of the *Corpus Iuris Canonici*, that retained legal force until 1917, when it was

is true. Whilst legalism may give rise to positivism, it is not, however, conceptually related to it.

I will not enter into the discussion sparked by the Weber thesis. Protestantism and capitalism may have met upon some favourable historical circumstances, so that the former may have strengthened the influence of the latter, both combining into legalism.[2] More interesting for our purposes however is the exploration of one of the basic roots of legalism, that is, nominalism.[3] In this respect, I propose to explore nominalism as the metaphysical setting for legalism, in which mediaeval nominalism in both its philosophical and theological versions plays a key role.

Nominalism has many variants and articulations (Largeault 1971: 7–43). The revival of the interest in it, combined with its positive assessment since the middle of the last century, is at odds with the critical evaluation of nominalism as a degeneration from late mediaeval scholastics, more specifically Thomism.[4]

While the renewed interest in nominalism saw its importance in the focus on logic rather than metaphysics, Heiko Oberman has drawn attention to the fact that 'Nominalism is not a doctrinal unity, but a common attitude, on some points at least, of remarkably different strands' (Oberman 1960; see also Michalski 1927; Vignaux 1948). An aspect of this common attitude which is crucial is the interpretation of

replaced by a new Code. Haggenmacher's interpretation of Grotius for its part considers his jusnaturalistic theory as both legalistic and voluntaristic (ibid.: 520). As regards legalism in contemporary natural law philosophies, see Johnson 1987. Shklar for her part (1986: 106) argues that 'The argument between natural lawyers and positivists is thus essentially a family quarrel among legalists.' She adds to that that both the positivist and the natural law program are equally legalistic (ibid.: 123).

2 Max Scheler (1964) has suggested an intellectual relationship between Franciscan rationality, hence nominalism, and the emergence of capitalism. On the relationship between nominalism and economics in the classical era (Hume, Smith et al.) see Largeault 1971. For an empirical test of the Weber thesis that Calvinist Protestantism induced capitalism or adherence to individualistic free-market principles, see Barker and Carman, 2000.

3 The aspect of mediaeval religion and Protestantism is often neglected in Weber's scholarship; see Kaeler 1996.

4 For the renewed interest in mediaeval thought last century, see the excellent overview of Knowles 1947. A survey of the most important scholarly work is found in Courtenay 1990: 11–24. On nominalism as a reaction *vis-à-vis* mediaeval Thomism, see Villey 2003: 204 ff. On the idea that late mediaeval philosophy is a disintegration and decline of philosophy in general, see among others, Gilson 1955: 489: '… the consequence of Ockhamism was to substitute for the positive collaboration of faith and reason which obtained in the golden age of scholasticism, a new and much looser regime in which the absolute and self-sufficient certitude of faith was only backed by mere philosophical probabilities.' See also Gilson 1999: 25–72. This position is criticised in, among others in Oberman 1978: 80–93 (pointing to the myth of the 'Thomist phalanx'); Moody 1958; Ginascol 1959; Leff, 1956; Lindbeck 1959. For a recent view on the decline or disintegration of post-Thomist metaphysics, see Bastit 1997.

God's omnipotence, from the thirteenth century onwards (Oberman 1960). This new interpretation had a particular influence on the position of the Church, as well as on Christian metaphysics. Protestantism, with legalism in its wake, may be considered a conceptual offspring of nominalism. What are usually held to be the characteristics of Modern philosophy as Descartes initiated it – individualism, rationalism and freedom – are actually products of late mediaeval theology in which nominalism takes root. They are, as I will argue throughout this chapter, conceptually related. In chapters 2, 3 and 4, I will come back to individualism, rationalism and freedom respectively and offer a contextualised interpretation of these concepts.

Nominalist Metaphysics

On a rough characterisation, a nominalist metaphysics deals with language and discourse while realistic metaphysics deals with things themselves.[5] The latter therefore claims to provide a direct access to reality while the former only provides an indirect one; I will call them 'direct access' and 'indirect access' theories respectively. The difference between direct and indirect access theories is the location of concepts, that is, as being respectively outside or inside the mind. This involves adopting a metaphysical position in that it affects the whole of reality and its ontological status.

Like its realist mediaeval forerunners, nominalism considers the relationship between theology and philosophy to be a hierarchical one. In this respect, philosophy includes the belief in God as the highest cause, that is, the source of being of all beings. The *credo in unum Deum omnipotentem* is capable of different rational explanations, depending on the relationship between intellect and will in the Supreme Being. The realists' interpretation boils down to God's unique access to the *lex aeterna* containing the order of the world. Upon revelation, God has made part of the *lex aeterna* accessible through the *lex divina* expressed in the Scriptures.

On Aquinas' view for example, *ens et bonum convertuntur*: what is is at the same time what it ought to be.[6] This is at its maximum in God or the *Ens realissimum* on whom all being depends. Any being forms part of the totality, the

5 This stems from the first version of nominalism in Abelard; see Vignaux 1931: 717–33; Largeault 1971: 79–93. A reference work in the history of philosophy is Coppleston 1993a for the controversy concerning universals up to Duns Scotus, and Coppleston 1993b after that period. See also Cranz 1974: 95. Referring to Abelard's positions, Cranz writes: ' … the mind 'legislates' concepts through which it can think *about* things' (italics in original). For a similar position, see Ozment 1974: 78.

6 Aquinas, 1898: q. XXI, a. 2 ('Utrum ens et bonum convertantur secundum supposita'), 8: ' … impossibile est aliquid esse bonum quod non sit ens; et ita relinquitur quod bonum et esse convertuntur.'

relation with which provides its *telos*. The order of totality is the harmony God created. He does create what he creates because it is the best possible world he could create. Whether he created the world according to a first plan or *lex aeterna*, or whether he first developed a plan on the basis of which he then started creating, is of the utmost philosophical importance.

If the order of the world coexists with God it is therefore true. What matters in a realist – mainly Thomist – metaphysics is that God acts according to a plan that, logically speaking, precedes action. If God creates the world without a pre-existing plan, or when he acts according to a plan resulting from his own will – this is roughly speaking the version adopted in Spanish Scholastics in the sixteenth century – the status of reality is fundamentally different. Creation without a pre-existing plan is generally speaking what characterises the nominalist approach.

A fundamental metaphysical issue related to this point concerns the relationship between God's intellect and his will. It is a philosophical evergreen *par excellence*: is what God orders good because he wants it or does he order it because it is good? This problem is known as the Euthyphro problem (Plato 1943: 35 ff.) to which I will return later in this chapter. This question again articulates an aspect of the difference between nominalism and realism. If God wants what is good, he wants it because it is good. This is what the realist position comes to. If, on the contrary, what God wants is good, and it is good because he wants it, we face the nominalist position.

Apart from the distinction between direct access and indirect access theories, and the Euthyphro problem, there is yet another way of characterising the differences between realism and nominalism. This consists in saying that what the faithful believes in – that is, God – can turn into the object of rational thinking. The faithful believes in God as a matter of revelation and tradition, including the authoritative interpretation of the content of faith by the Church. Another perspective is that the faithful believes in God and recognises his dependence upon God as a matter of irrational submission to the source of all Being.

Both positions can be combined with a rational inquiry into the nature of God. This is different from the religious perspective and the personal relationship this involves between God and the faithful. From the nominalist perspective, the two perspectives are not only compatible; they are mutually dependent. The realist may however object that an inquiry into faith apart from authority and tradition is heretical.

What characterises nominalism at this stage is the articulation of thinking as a purely *human* experience. It involves the unfolding of the rational capacities of a limited mind. It is limited because it is created. Without creation it could not exist unless it is God's; and because God is unique, only he can be as he ought to be, that is, perfect. Nominalist metaphysics therefore takes a critical attitude toward human reason, the speculation of which in scholastics is no longer considered rationally warranted. The revealed truth of Christianity in other words should no longer be obscured by speculation.

Nominalism involving the human perspective in the metaphysical project does not, however, therefore alone slip into subjectivism. Both realism and nominalism stick to the objectivity of ideas. Realism is not more objective because it holds that concepts exist 'out there'. When focusing on man as a knowing agent, the distinction between both can be considered a matter of emphasis or simply a matter of belief.

In this respect, Aristotle's realism heavily stresses the belief in the existence 'out there' of universals, while the extension of what is 'out there' is much more limited for nominalists. The objectivity of concepts, however, is not affected upon their location inside or outside the mind.

Upon this general outline of realism and nominalism, I will now enter into more detail in order to show how nominalism operates as the metaphysical basis of legalism. In the following pages, I will begin by exploring in greater depth the philosophical version of nominalism and clarify the status and role of 'distinctions' and 'universals' as they operate in nominalism. After pointing to some ontological consequences of this, I will turn to the theological version of nominalism. This is not to say that there are two different versions of nominalism, one philosophical, the other theological. Rather, nominalism consists of a differentiation of two perspectives on reality, one philosophical (or logical, as we will soon see), and the other theological. Because I hold that nominalism like realism is a metaphysics, and hence deals with the totality of the world, including its own status and God, both perspectives are not mutually exclusive.

Philosophical and Theological Version of Nominalism

Philosophical Version of Nominalism

The combination of Aristotle's problem of the unification of the one and the multiple with Christian revelation opened up a new type of questioning after the high Middle Ages: is there more in reality than our experience of the multiple? (Aristotle 1984c: 1056 b, 3 ff.). The negative answer to this question is the hallmark of nominalism's criticism of mediaeval realism. It prepares Descartes' search for certainty, that is, the certainty that reason provides without the help of Revelation, with a critical investigation of the arguments which show how God, Being, the world and the human person form a unity. This position shows nominalism worthy of the qualification 'metaphysics'.

The issue may have been obfuscated by the fact that many scholars have considered nominalism merely as a matter of logic. There is a good deal of truth in that. It leaves however unanswered the question as to why philosophers, who are as a matter of fact first of all theologians, would all of a sudden begin to focus exclusively on logic. Logic on its own has nothing 'metaphysical' in that it gives a rather thin view of reality. It would be silly to believe that mere logic was going to explain the world as it was, including the position of God. The position of God as the omnipotent Creator of the world however was at stake in the confrontation with the universal ideas or essences that were imported from Greek philosophy. 'Divine freedom' and 'universal ideas', so the nominalists thought, were at odds, or at least difficult to reconcile.

The first attempt at a synthesis of the stoic inheritance with Christian faith has Augustine's Neoplatonic stamp. The stoic *recta ratio* governing the world is reinterpreted as the Christian *lex aeterna* existing in God's mind.[7] On the Neoplatonic basis of this thought, human understanding of the world involves a divine illumination of the human intellect or a participation of the human mind in the divine intellect. What this approach, in short, suggests is that we can look upon the world through God's eyes. The Augustinian view on the question of universals is that they are located in God's intellect in which we participate.[8] Under this doctrine, divine freedom in creation is absolute, not bound by any antecedent form or norm.

The Augustinian theory, in combination with the rediscovery of Aristotle in the West in the early thirteenth century, is critically interpreted by Aquinas. This critique strongly resembles Aristotle's appraisal of Plato; that is, human knowledge addresses the material world. Universals or ideas do not exist separately from the world, as Plato holds, and the understanding of which follows does not exist separately from participation in or illumination from God's mind, as we read from Augustine. What there is to know, according to Aquinas, is the universal, which is only *intelligible* by the method of abstraction. The universal in each thing represents the permanent form that pre-exists in God's mind. According to Aquinas, our intellect only understands by abstracting this form, universal, or essence, upon an investigation of nature, from the material thing which leads back to divine unity. Beings thus exist as *materia signata*, matter marked by the form resulting in individuation.

In direct relation with Aquinas, Duns Scotus (1893: d. 3, q. 6, n. 1) argues that the essence or universal is extended into the individual and is seized by intuition. A universal is differentiated, according to the process of *haecitas* or individuating difference, into different individuals. This ontology preserves the dynamics of Being in terms of 'becoming' as in Aristotle's metaphysics. It suggests however that intellect is related to the individual rather than to the universal.

The core of Scotus' version is the ontological passing over of a common nature into an individual. Intuition reveals a number of universal formalities inside individual things, upon which the unity of the universe is guaranteed in its dependence on God, from where these formalities stem.

For all the realism that is his, Scotus brings to the fore an issue of great importance in connection to nominalism. In his interpretation of the classical unity

7 Augustine 42: Book XXII, ch. 27, col. 418: 'Lex vero aeterna est ratio divina vel voluntas Dei … .' The theme recurs in later chapters (28, 30, 43)..

8 Augustine 40: q. 46, 2, col. 30: ' … sunt namque idea principales formae … quae in divina intelligentia continentur.'

of the four causes, he introduces the 'Christian cause' of the universe, that is, the omnipotent God. Reserving a further exploration for later in this book, it is crucial to notice that in his omnipotence God can create matter without form. Matter and form could exist separately *de potentia absoluta Dei* (if God wanted it). This is not necessarily a conclusion based on experience. In other words, it need not be actually the case that both are separated. It however shows the possibility of a different world, containing other beings ordered in another way.

Scotus' position is focusing on *things*, on what there is, even if only hypothetically. This *metaphysical* position is fine-tuned from a *logical* point of view by Ockham. Under the latter position, it is no longer possible to focus on things directly. Any rational discourse in other words must be preceded by a rational critique of discourse. On this point, Ockham's 'second' version of nominalism respects Abelard's 'first' version. Ockham's logical theory, as we will soon see, carries with it a metaphysics. It explores not only what there is but also what reality could be if God had wanted it that way.

Ockham's rational critique of human discourse explores conditions of possibility. The investigation of the conditions of the possibility of rational discourse is a matter for philosophy, under which access to reality is no longer direct but indirect. It is, I venture to say, an exercise of Kantian transcendental philosophy *avant la lettre*. This critique contains the seeds of a straightforward and thorough attack in showing the absurdity of realism, a critique according to which a universal is not a thing and to hold a different opinion is wrong and absurd. Universals are not things other than names (McCord Adams 1987: 13–69).

The crucial point in realist theories is the ontological status of the idea, the universal, or the essence. Realists hold that it exists in reality. Universals create order that is reality. The order 'out there' is the object of Ockham's critique. Over against the authority of tradition, Ockham takes sides of the philosopher's 'God's eye' and investigates reality from a logical perspective. Logic connects philosophy and its object, the world as a whole, to how the human mind thinks. The belief that logic exists in reality as Aristotle claims is compatible with the investigation into how it operates in the human mind. This approach results in the detachment of philosophy from theology, in that it no longer focuses on direct access to unqualified 'truth'. Apart from 'what there is', philosophy investigates 'our way of dealing with what there is', what it means 'for us', in short, what knowledge is and how to acquire it. Theology operates 'a Deo', while philosophy as it is differentiated from it operates 'a homine'.

The shift of the focus from 'what there is' to 'how can it be known' is a philosophical proof of modesty as it were, in that the unwarranted direct access of realism is submitted to a critical assessment. This suggests that it is the human perspective on what there is, and no longer God's eye or a 'view from nowhere' that is at stake. In order to grasp this shift, three aspects of Ockham's position require clarification in order for us to be able to get a better grasp of nominalism. The first is Ockham's critique of the scholastic method of distinctions. This involves, secondly, a reassessment of the ontological status of universals and relations, which has, thirdly, an important consequence for his theory of reality.

Ockham's Critique of the Distinctions and the Method of Philosophy

The Aristotelian tradition that is dominant throughout the Middle Ages uses two types of distinctions: the real distinction and the rational distinction. Distinctions can be considered 'aspects' of a thing.

A real distinction is a manifest distinction between real beings (*entia naturae*). A real distinction involves the absence of real identity between two things or their components. X is really distinct from Y if X exists without Y. A rational distinction is a distinction of the mind between 'beings of reason' (*entia rationis*), the objects of logic, for example. A distinction of reason or rational distinction is made by the mind, and has no *locus* in the things.

Within the distinction of reason, Scotus sees an even more subtle distinction. While a real distinction is a manifest distinction of things and a rational distinction is a mental distinction having no *locus* in reality, Scotus points to the formal distinction *ex parte rei*. It is a formal distinction, hence made by the mind. It is however made of a thing in that it is located 'at the side of the thing'. The formal distinction *ex parte rei* precedes the intellectual grasp by the mind (like the real distinction) and so is related to a real thing as an aspect of it. In addition to that, it can be distinguished within a thing without however necessarily being separated from it.[9]

The originality of Scotus' on this point is striking. The formal distinction *ex parte rei* involves an interpretation of divine omnipotence. Under the realist interpretation, God's omnipotence means that only he has creative power. Scotus qualifies this power saying that God has not only this power; he can also create all things that are not in contradiction with his nature. The crucial point is the distinction of matter and form. This is, so Scotus argues, a formal distinction *ex parte rei*. If God wanted to separate matter and form, then matter could exist without form. This is a breach into the classical theory of the four causes of being that are necessarily related to each other, matter being one of them (Aristotle 1984b: II, 7, 338–9). Matter is also the subject of substantial mutations, and for this reason it does not receive being from its form (Duns Scot 1893: d. 12, q. 1, 11). Matter that is has a certain positive reality outside the intellect and outside its cause. It is by virtue of this reality that it can receive the substantial forms that are acts *tout court* (ibid.: d. 12, q. 1, n. 13). Matter can be known separately[10] and could exist separately (ibid.: d. 12, q. 2, n. 3) if God wanted it.[11]

9 A standard reference to this problem is Gilson 1952: 432–77. See also Jansen 1929. For a historical and doctrinal analysis, see Coppleston 1993a: 508–17; Wolter 1962: 725–36.

10 Duns Scot 1893: II, d. 12, q. 1, n. 20 ('Dico igitur quod materia, secundum se in sua essentia cognobilis … ').

11 Ibid.: II, d. 12, q. 2, n. 4: '[materia] potest virtute divina esse sine forma.'

Ockham attacks his predecessor on this point. Scotus argues that a distinction need not be real in order to make sense. This, says Ockham, is absurd. The absurdity boils down to this. A distinction is real or is not. If it is real, it really exists. If it is not real, it does not exist at all. The reality of a distinction has the potential to cause theology to implode, while it looks as if it is a simple exercise of logic. I will come back to this at a later stage.

Ockham also takes sides on the formal and the rational distinction. He claims that only a real distinction between individual beings makes sense. Any other distinction flows into absurdity. We know, that is, only propositions, and they are about things. Propositions are true or false in the logical sense. We do not know things themselves, as the nominalists – with Kant in their wake – claim.

Ockham's philosophical method also involves a logical interpretation of the principle of non-contradiction that according to Aristotle's metaphysical interpretation is of an ontological nature.[12] Under the latter interpretation, the principle of non-contradiction forms part of reality in that it is impossible for the same attribute to belong and not to belong at the same time, and from the same perspective to the same subject.[13] The metaphysical interpretation holds it *logically* impossible to affirm and to deny at the same time a predicate to a subject on the *ontological* impossibility of the coexistence of these contraries.[14] Under a realistic ontology, that is, the principle of non-contradiction is a law of reality.

According to Ockham's nominalist interpretation, the principle of non-contradiction no longer forms part of reality. The ontological status of beings follows from a logical argument, and not from an ontological one. Under the former argument, all beings are singular, and inside the singular, no distinctions can be made. We know therefore that only individuals exist, and exist outside the mind, while universals cannot (Ockham 1970: d. II, q. 6, 196).

According to this interpretation, everything can exist on condition that it is not contradictory. Since anything exists as a consequence of creation, God's creative power is constrained by the principle of non-contradiction in that he cannot create what contradicts his nature. What there is therefore is what is logically possible, although what really exists does so because God wants it. The radicalisation of the logical interpretation of the principle of non-contradiction, including its application to God, results in Ockham's nominalism.

---

12 Aristotle 1984c: 995b, 5–10; 1061b, 34-35; 1062a 1: 'There is a principle *in things*, about which we cannot be deceived, but must always, on the contrary, recognize the truth, – viz. that the same thing cannot at one and the same time be and not be, or admit any other similar pair of opposites' (italics added).

13 Ibid.: 1005b, 16–20: 'Evidently such a principle is the most certain of all; which principle this is, we proceed to say. It is, that the same attribute cannot at the same time belong and not belong to the same subject in the same respect.'

14 As for an indirect demonstration of the principle of non-contradiction, see ibid.: 1006a–1009a, 5.

Ockham could claim to be faithful to Aristotle in the logical approach to his theory (Moody 1935). His faithfulness to Aristotle however, including his realistic ontology, turns out to become much more complex, if not impossible, when it comes to the integration of Christian theology and Aristotelian metaphysics, according to Ockham's application of the principle of non-contradiction to God. His interpretation of the principle of non-contradiction then unavoidably and irreversibly affects the nature of universals, transforming them from real things into objects of the mind. Universals, that is, are no longer located in extra-mental reality. This calls for closer exploration.

The Ontological Status of Universals and Relations

The ontological status of universals is what divides realists and nominalists. Plato locates ideas or universals in the world of ideas. Objects existing in the world are only a pale imitation of these ideas. Aristotle for his part considers essences to be very part of concrete beings, thus criticising the Platonic theory.[15] According to Augustine's Neoplatonic theory, ideas exist in God's mind. They order reality in that they are models or archetypes of what can be created as God thinks them before creating them.

Realists suggest that a universal is common to a plurality of singular beings ('humanity' is common to 'Wojciech' and 'Vlad'), while it is at the same time one in number and distinct from them (Ockham 1970: d. II, q. 4, 99–101). Concrete beings participate in these universals, in Plato's view. In Augustine's Neoplatonic theory, our understanding of them occurs through participation in God's mind.

According to Ockham's view, however, there is no need to presuppose the existence of these rational models, since belief in the existence of God and his creation of the world as points of faith are sufficient in order for the world to be intelligible.

In line with his logical interpretation of the principle of non-contradiction, Ockham criticises the existence of universals outside the mind. Their existence outside the mind as one of the characteristics of metaphysical realism is denied on logical grounds and is embedded in his theory of *suppositio*.[16] Under this theory, terms signify things and stand for them in discourse. Depending on its function in a proposition, a term has a *suppositio personalis* ('this man runs'), *suppositio materialis* ("'man' is a noun"), or *suppositio simplex* ('man is rational'). In the latter proposition, the term does not refer to a concrete reality, but to a universal reality that is nothing but a concept.

A term can only refer to a concrete reality or an individual. A universal does not qualify as a concrete reality because universals are not substances. A substance is a singular thing, which a universal is not. If it were, 'man' would at the same time be a singular *and* another singular which is absurd. Under this contradiction, a universal

15 Ibid.: 990b–993b. Aristotle's critique of Plato spreads throughout the whole of his metaphysics in general, and more specifically ibid.: 1076 a, 8 ff; 1087 a, 29 ff.

16 The theory of '*suppositio*' is exposed in Ockham 1974: lxii, lxiii, lxiv and lxviii.

substance is but a series of singular beings and no universal is a real thing or a substance.[17] If a universal were real, and if it were shared by concrete beings, then each time God annulled a concrete being, this would have to have an effect on other beings, *quod non*. In the next section, it will be clarified that universals cannot exist because what exists is created by God, and God cannot create universals according to the nominalist interpretation of his omnipotence. This shows a fundamental connection between Ockham's philosophy and his theology.

Under Ockham's view, therefore, if Socrates is real, nothing that belongs to Socrates escapes this singularity. Put differently, whatever is of the singular is singular (Ockham 1970: d. II, q. 5, 158–9). Between individual beings, there can only be real distinctions. Distinctions cannot exist within things, since things are what they are; they exist *en bloc*. What is more, if the formal distinction were a genuine distinction, it would be identical to the real distinction; otherwise any real difference between beings would be abolished (ibid.: d. II, q. 6, 173–4). A universal or 'common nature' is therefore an *ens rationis*. If the singular is real, which cannot be denied, the universal must be an *ens rationis*. Universals then have only a logical meaning. Logic is a logic of names or signs rather than a logic that expresses the real relations between things.

Relations between things, like universals, have no extra-mental existence, since in reality only absolutes exist. Absolutes are metaphysically separated from each other and are isolated. Any 'relation' between them is not essential in that an essential relationship between two beings would form part of their very essence. Relations are merely contingent or accidental facts of beings, and that is what the mind can express. As a consequence, *ordo* in reality is not intrinsic. Any 'whole' is just an aggregate of absolutes that are juxtaposed, but are not essentially related to each other (de Lagarde 1946: 216). Like universals, relations are signs or names that are produced by the mind. Because relations between beings are no longer real, they cannot make an 'order' out there, because 'order' precisely presupposes a relationship between beings.

Ontological Consequence

Under this logical deconstruction of the reality of universals and relations, that is, their existence outside the mind, Ockham holds that the mind operates using concepts. Concepts are 'triggered' by what exists out there, without however having a necessary relationship with it. On the one hand, concepts are signs for things that he calls 'natural universals'. Things trigger the formation of concepts in the mind as a result of experience. That is, the mind cannot but produce universals. On the other hand, the deconstruction of realistic ontology on the basis of his theory of distinctions gives a schematic view of Ockham's theory of reality.

Under this theory, universals are a form of discourse and not objects existing in reality. As a consequence, when singular beings resemble each other, this is not

17 Ockham 1974: I, 15, 5–6, 50: 'Quod enim nullum universal sit aliqua substantia extra animam existens evidenter probari potest.'

because they share a common nature, but only because we label them with the same name. Names or concepts are signs produced by the mind, with the help of which we signify singular beings. Put differently, concepts are artificial, arbitrary, or conventional signs imposed on singular beings where they resemble each other.

Because any being is singular, the singularity of beings logically excludes that universals exist outside the mind. The proposition 'A singular horse and "horseness" exist outside the mind' is a contradiction. Therefore there cannot correspond any reality to universals outside the mind. Universals, including relations, are signs that signify concrete singular beings. Singular beings are radically simple in that there exists no distinction inside a singular. What you see then is what there is.

The logical interpretation of the principle of non-contradiction has shown that universals and singulars cannot exist together. What looks as a mere logical approach to reality is in fact a new ontology. The logical exclusion of the existence of universals and particulars outside the mind reflects the structure of reality. If something exists that is, it must be created by God. It all depends then whether God can or cannot create something.

A result of this projection of logic into ontology, as Tornay (1936: 246) calls it, is that the logical theory is accompanied by a metaphysics because Ockham holds that God cannot create universals. Taking his existence as a point of faith, philosophy contributes to a rational articulation of the content of the *credo*. More specifically, the application of the logical interpretation of the principle of non-contradiction to God affects the extension of his omnipotence. According to this interpretation, God's omnipotence necessarily means that he can only create individuals. On this point, the philosophical version of nominalism intersects with the theological version that I will comment upon in the next section.

The Theological Version of Nominalism

The theological version of nominalism is not the philosophical version as applied to theology. I venture to say that, on the contrary, a specific aspect of theology, divine omnipotence, triggered the use of logic in theology. The philosophical version fits with the theological version in the metaphysical whole. While the nominalists were logicians, they were first of all theologians. Their logical interpretation of divine omnipotence, as we will see in this section, is driven by the larger extension of the latter. In doing so, they suggest an understanding of God's power that better fits its magnitude.[18] In other words, the perfection of God as the first cause is no

18 On this aspect of Franciscan theology and philosophy, see, among others, Villey 2003: 204–7; Oberman 1960: 50: 'Nominalist theology is not merely an automatic conclusion drawn out of its philosophy; but, on the contrary, Nominalist philosophy is the reflection and echo of its theology, and, in particular, of its concept of God's *potentia absoluta*.' I disagree on this point with Lindbeck (1959: 60), suggesting that it was the very success of the nominalist philosophy that led the nominalists astray into theology. For the same reason, I disagree with Moody (1935: vi, 307) that Ockham is remarkably free from

longer measured by what he has done, but by what he could do (Celeyrette and Mazet 2005: 39).

The theological version of nominalism articulates a different perspective on reality than the philosophical. Nominalism involves a way of looking at the world from the human perspective and not merely from God's eye as Augustinism claims. In contrast to the philosophical version focusing on man and his access to reality, the theological version's centre of attention is God. In line with the nominalist method, the multiple attributes of God (justice, goodness, wisdom, intellect and will) are considered to be identical with his essence. God's essence coincides with all his attributes. Two conclusions follow from this.

First, because of his radical unity, it must necessarily be concluded that his attributes are only names or signs of God. The expression 'God is justice' is correct, but it does not exhaustively encapsulate his essence. Moreover, none of the distinctions – that is, either real, formal, or rational – applies to God. The real distinction does not because there is only one God as the essential point of faith. Since the formal distinction and the formal distinction *ex parte rei* are impossible, they do not apply to God, just as they do not apply to any other being.

Secondly, according to the theory of *suppositio*, the attributes of God are only signs. 'Intellect' and 'will' are taken for the object they designate, and so are identical to God's essence. Signs and concepts however are not real as 'intellect' and 'will' are. What signifies God is not identical to God, since a sign is different from what it signifies.

In view of the fact that his will and intellect are both real and perfect, God's nature is of a radical simplicity. Due to God's radical simplicity, any order of succession or hierarchy between his intellect and his will is impossible. Because God is a perfect being, there is no internal distinction between the attributes, nor are there any degrees of being in Him. God is simply *perfect* as it were (Vignaux 1931: 754–69).

The metaphysical articulation of God and more specifically of the relationship between his intellect and his will on Ockham's merciless logical interpretation of omnipotence marks a breaking point in the history of philosophical problems. More specifically, it enables the emergence of philosophy as an autonomous discipline. The importance of this problem and its consequences will be discussed in the following pages.

Divine Omnipotence and the Possibility of Autonomous Philosophy

Questions that deal with the problem of God's omnipotence necessarily raise the problem of freedom (Courtenay 1990; Geach 1973; de Muralt 1993d). It is not because of the mere occurrence of something that we know the reason why God acts, and why he acts the way he acts. The foundation of God's action cannot be

---

the theological preoccupations of his Scholastic predecessors, which makes him a secular philosopher when compared to them.

a point of reflection since God owes us no justification just like, more generally speaking, God owes nothing to his creatures.

An essential point of belief is, however, that he is good. He cannot, that is, want to do something bad. The crucial point thus concerns the relationship between what God wants and what is good. This is a variant of the Euthyphro problem referred to above. The belief in God's goodness is different from the rational investigation into what this actually means from the perspective of natural reason. It is this shift of perspective, from faith to natural reason, applied to divine omnipotence, that ultimately changes the relationship between theology on the one hand and philosophy on the other.

Historically speaking, the questions that the problem of divine omnipotence has triggered are numerous. It was dealt with for the first time in *Magistri Petri Lombardi Sententiae in IV libris distinctae*, one of the first systematic treatises in Christian theology. It was written in 1155 and provided the basis for some 1,400 commentaries over the course of the following centuries. Some of them, like Aquinas', Scotus' and Ockham's, have reshaped the very structure of Western philosophy. This shows how philosophical thinking crystallised around a theological problem and triggered questions on the limits of human thinking. It provokes, what is more, an unexpected emancipation of philosophy from theology.

In distinctions 42–44 of Lombardus' *Sentences*, we find the discussion of God's omnipotence. The three main ideas are as follows: (1) if there is something God cannot do, this would be incorrectly understood as a limitation or a lack of omnipotence; then it is asked (2) whether God could have created a different world or created the world differently, or even created a number of possible worlds or chosen from a number of possible worlds to create one of them. Finally, the question is raised (3) as to whether God could have made things better than he.

Obviously there are things that God cannot do, for example, undo the past. Nor can he lie or die since this would contradict his nature. The discussion of omnipotence relates to the structure of the created world in the wake of Duns Scotus' questioning of the relationship between matter and form. The combination between matter and form in hylemorfism has been an topical issue since Aristotle. For Scotus as we saw, form can be thought of separately from matter, since form is added to matter. As a result, matter can, but need not, exist separately or independently from form. If God had wanted it, matter and form could have been separated. We may call this the 'separability thesis', that is, the meaning of the formal distinction *a parte rei*. It is a distinction the mind can make upon the logical interpretation of divine omnipotence. In order to understand the separability thesis, we do not need any form of experience. It is an a priori claim. The fact therefore that matter and form are not actually separated or that we have no experience of them does not exclude the a priori possibility of conceptualising them as distinct *de potentia absoluta Dei* (de Muralt 1970, 1974). As a result, matter and form are separable *ex parte rei*.

A 'case study' on divine omnipotence which sparked discussion among theologists from the eleventh century onwards deals with the question over whether God could restore a woman's virginity after she had been raped. Would it not be a clear sign of his omnipotence that God could intervene in reality and re-establish the situation? As a result of this, the raped woman would unite the status of 'virgin', 'non-virgin' and 'again virgin' in one person, which sounds rather counter-intuitive without microsurgery.[19]

This question however opens a larger perspective on the belief in one omnipotent God. Even if he is omnipotent, he cannot change the course of time.[20] If he were omnipotent, he could make that the consequence of the rape be undone. The more precise point is that God could have done it, if he had wanted it. After all, his son was born from a virgin, so why could he not restore a raped woman's virginity?

The perspective shows some aspects of the problem of the omnipotence of God. God could have prevented the act from occurring in the past. If he did not do so, this means that he did not want to. The world may have looked differently had the act not occurred. It did occur though, and God did not prevent it while he could have. You may also say that it occurred because God did not prevent it. As a result of this latter connection, God's omnipotence shows the radical contingency of his creation. If something happens, it happens because he wants it.

Omnipotence Elaborated: Autonomous Philosophy

The separability of matter and form as it shows up in Scotus' work has an important consequence. At the background of the separability thesis we observe the Aristotelian problem of the relationship between the one and the multiple (Aristotle 1984c: 1056 b, 3 ff., 1669 ff.). This problem is reshaped from a Christian perspective in that the existence of reality depends on the will of its creator. The creator is omnipotent as a point of faith. Upon the dependence of the world's on an act of will, there are a number of different perspectives from which it can be dealt with: what God wanted, what he could have been wanted, what *we* observe, and the way *we* understand, to mention just a few.

The human perspective in the experience and understanding of the world is precisely articulated by the logical method in philosophy. It is this method that allows for the articulation of different perspectives on reality, depending from which position the question is asked. Ockham suggests that this question can be asked from the human point of view, which is different from the Augustinian 'view from nowhere'. This in turn opens up the way for a further distinction between 'what there is', or truth unqualified and the human way of dealing with it. One of these ways is knowledge.

While this seems unproblematic, it triggers a main philosophical problem, again as a consequence of the logical interpretation of divine omnipotence. In the

---

19 Damianus 1972: 'Vtrum Deus posit reparare uirginem post ruinam.' The case study opens the argumentation on God's omnipotence.

20 A point already observed by Aristotle 1984d: 1139 b, 10–11: 'For this alone is lacking even to God/To make undone things the have once been done'; Aristotle refers to a text of Agathon, author of Greek tragedies of the fifth century BCE.

next section, I shall briefly deal with two aspects of this problem that are two sides of a coin. One is the certainty of knowledge as one of our ways of dealing with the world. The other concerns action and the problem of freedom and indifference to values as a consequence of nominalism. Both aspects, as we will see, will allow a better hold on the problem of normativity and legalism.

Before moving on to this point, I propose to explore a bit further the status of autonomous philosophy involved by nominalism. Autonomous philosophy can be characterised as reflexive. As a human activity, it can take itself as the object of reflection, thus articulating its possibility conditions. The reflexivity of philosophy is the result of a critical investigation of reason by itself which culminates in the general outline of Kant's synthesis of philosophy. The self-determination of reason shows up as the mere result of thinking itself as independent of any *authority*. Autonomy counterbalances authority, and so gives rise to a new philosophical problem: freedom. As a philosophical problem, it is not a product of the seventeenth century. It is the result of the logical interpretation of God's omnipotence initiated by Scotus and culminating in Ockham (Boulnois 1994: 9–68).

Theological discourse operates as a top-down argument, starting from the *belief* in God towards *rational conclusions* following from that belief. A theological argument locates reason within faith (*a Deo*) (Gilson 1960: 61 ff.). Philosophy for its part works as a bottom-up argument, starting from natural reason and then 'climbing' as far as it can using its own force (*ab homine*). Philosophy goes over the edge and melts into theology as a requirement (irrational) of completeness from a metaphysical perspective. Metaphysics necessarily comprises the whole of reality, including, as Kant holds, the determination of its own limits. Up to that point, belief in God is simply irrational from the philosophical point of view, though not unreasonable or in contradiction with human dignity.

The pivotal point allowing for and provoking the distinction between philosophy and theology is, here as elsewhere, the principle of non-contradiction. On the one hand, it keeps theology and philosophy together as rational activities. Neither can waive it. In philosophy, the principle is articulated as the basis of any rational demonstration as part of the science of being. Because of the inclusive nature of metaphysics, the question arises as to whether it applies to God, apart from applying to a theological discourse about God. The self-revelation of God in Christian religion did call for a recombination of Antique philosophy and theology. On the one hand, the hierarchical order of the world proper to Antique philosophy can be thought of in a theological top-down model, that is, starting from faith and which includes reason.

On the other hand, it can be articulated as a bottom-up model. In this model, natural reason elaborates a rational explanation for the world, climbing up to its own limits from within mere reason. Both models share the necessity of complying with the principle of non-contradiction. No rational discourse about God, in whose existence the faithful believe, or about the world can include a proposition that something 'is' and 'is not' at the same time. From this perspective, it does not matter whether it is faith or natural reason that is at the basis of the discourse.

Apart from these two types of discourses, the question arises as to whether the principle applies to the Creator himself? Can God in other words determine that something is while at the same time it is not? Would this not be the best sign of his omnipotence as the essential point of Christian faith?

God's omnipotence and its different potential investigations are, as I said before, a pivotal point in late mediaeval metaphysics. As the essential content of Christian faith, it is a matter of belief. Because of his omnipotence, God can do everything that corresponds to his essence, that is, justice, goodness, intellect and will. Because of the perfection of his being, the acts of his intellect and will are the best possible.

Further, what exists, exists because God wants it to exist. He is the cause of all beings, the source of Being. On the rational connection between 'what there is' and the ontology of creation, a differentiation of two aspects of God's omnipotence is made. While his power is one and unique, a distinction is made between what God could make and what he actually makes or has made. The latter articulates the naturalistic dimension of the world as Aristotle investigates it. The former explores the modal dimension of the world, and examines whether what there is, is constrained by any necessity.

Therefore this approach inverts the relationship between what there is and its cause, in that Aristotle presupposes an unmoved mover as a first cause from a bottom-up perspective. Christian belief ends up adopting the opposite position, that is, a top-down perspective on the belief that the first cause of things is God. The first mover as a possibility condition of what there is, becomes the necessary cause of the world. The origin of nature, that is, is not of the same nature as nature itself.

The conjugation of pagan philosophy and Christian faith generates a problem of compatibility that, roughly speaking, comes to this. If the world must necessarily exist, it was necessary for God to create it. If the world necessarily is what it ought to be, God had no choice to create it – and to create it as it is – so that he was not free. If he is not free, he cannot be omnipotent, which contradicts the axiom of faith. The position that God is not free to create or not to create a world refers to Averroës' necessitarianism. Aquinas' adherence to this version of Aristotelianism resulted in condemnations of his work in 1270 and 1277 respectively (Van Steenberghen 1966: 413–93). From a historical point of view, it is on these condemnations that nominalism took the wind from realism in stressing God's freedom. Nominalists asserted the belief in the contingency of the world as a result of divine omnipotence. Having warded off the jeopardy of a not-so-omnipotent God, nominalism could start flourishing (Courtenay 1990: 95; Bastit 1990a: 176–80). God's absolute freedom and the radical contingency of the world are two sides of a coin.

In order to safeguard God's freedom, it is necessary to articulate two dimensions within his omnipotence, that is, the *potentia absoluta* and the *potentia ordinata*. These are two aspects of power, not two different powers. *Potentia absoluta* operates *ex nihilo*, which again is a philosophical absurdity, although a theological necessity. *Potentia ordinata* in turn refers to what there is as the normal course of events. This again is a matter of perspective. The latter is connected to the human perspective, that is, the experience human beings have of the world. The former refers to the divine perspective, in that it relates 'what there is' to God's will.

In the next two sections, I shall briefly explore the consequences of the nominalist interpretation of divine omnipotence for human cognition and human action.

Omnipotence, Contingency of the World, and Human Cognition

Under Ockham's logical method, God's radical simplicity and the fact that it is impossible for universals to exist are two sides of a coin. Because in God everything is equally perfect and simple, he is not the source of universals that he first conceives before creating individuals (Scotus). Nor is his intellect the locus within himself where he finds the eternal form of the things he is going to create (Aquinas). Aquinas' God binds his power upon his own decision to a *potentia ordinata*. Ockham on his turn more strongly emphasises will as autonomous power.

Intellect and will are equally perfect in God. From God's perspective, therefore neither has priority over the other. A priority of intellect over will would involve the former directing the latter which is, as a result, less perfect. Creation therefore is radically contingent or undetermined. Due to his omnipotence, God even has no reason to create. Due to the world's radical contingency, only what logically cannot be created also ontologically cannot exist. Even if God is omnipotent, his will must respect the principle of non-contradiction. Conversely, anything that is not logically contradictory could exist. Anything that is logically possible God is free to create. This is not an incidental piece of the doctrine of nominalism, but is connected to its very philosophical centre.

An important consequence for the purposes of this chapter is that the order in the world exists *depotentia ordinata Dei*, that is, as his concretised *will* and not, as in realism, as the realisation of a pre-existing eternal *order*. Because of God's radical simplicity, there logically exists no eternal law, nor any order of priority between his intellect and his will. Creation in other words is stable because of the immutability of God's will.[21]

The method of logic applied to divine action brings about a world of singular beings created by an omnipotent God. Like his creatures, God is a singular being. Unlike his creatures, however, he is radically simple in that he is not composed of two or more things. Because of this radical simplicity, both his will and intellect

21 This is Descartes' interpretation of divine omnipotence. God could have created a plurality of worlds, indeed, he could have created a mess. Because of his goodness though, he created a world that we are able to understand. The principle of non-contradiction that makes human knowledge possible is an arbitrary creation of God; see Descartes 1996b: 118–20; 1996i: 232–3 (answers to the sixth objections). (God has no idea of the world before creating it. It depends on his mere will what the world will be. God's indifference is the best proof of his omnipotence.)

are equally perfect. Due to this perfection, there cannot be any order before God creates it, and the order that exists after creation exists because he wants it like that.

It should be pointed out in this respect that the *philosophical* version of nominalism rigorously keeps pace with the *theological* version, the essence of which is the nominalist interpretation of divine omnipotence. The philosophical version of nominalism is backed by the theological version. Under the philosophical version, universals cannot exist outside the mind because this would involve a contradiction. Under the theological version, God as the omnipotent creator of the world can however not create a universal first, and individuals later on, because that would limit his omnipotence.

Even if this were a self-imposed restriction, it is logically inconceivable. It would indeed be contradictory because omnipotence logically involves the impossibility of self-limitation. The very possibility of the existence of a plan for the creation of the world would be a limitation of God's omnipotence. This interpretation of omnipotence therefore is nothing less than sheer blasphemy. God creates whatever, whenever, and however he wants, on the mere condition that he respect the principle of non-contradiction.

Beings share their 'being created'. For reasons mentioned above, similar beings however do not share any common nature because God's omnipotence prevents him from creating common natures, essences, or universals. Universals, that is, would determine God's will in subsequent creation which contradicts his absolute freedom. Divine omnipotence therefore equals God's absolute freedom that is freedom not bound by anything.

The crucial point is that God's omnipotence entails that everything that can be caused by an observable secondary cause God can cause immediately.[22] For example, under the normal cause of events, the birth of a child is preceded, and therefore caused, by the sexual intercourse of his parents. Parents are God's creation and so are the secondary cause of the existence of the child. God as a primary cause, however, can create a human being without the intervention of this secondary cause. Using the technical terminology mentioned before, under the normal course of events, he acts *de potentia ordinata*. When he acts immediately or as a primary cause, as is the case with miracles, he acts *de potentia absoluta* (Freddoso 1991).

The immediate action of God, that is, action as the primary cause, can be traced back to the epistemological dimension of nominalist thought. Our intellective knowledge, following Ockham, is twofold. In the absence of universals as intelligible species and as the means of informing the intellect for knowledge, we have *cognitio intuitiva* and *cognitio abstractiva*. Under the former, we have evidence of a contingent truth, the object of which actually exists. Under the latter,

22 Among other references, Ockham 1981, II, q. 3–4, p. 63, q. 15, 350: '… quia [Deus] cuiuscumque potest esse causa partialis, potest esse totalis.' See also Pernoud 1970.

it cannot be known whether the object really exists or not since abstraction is made of the existence or non-existence of the object.[23]

According to the principle that God can always act as the primary cause and 'jump over' any secondary cause, so to speak, *cognitio intuitiva* or *abstractiva* is connected to divine omnipotence. It is therefore possible for God to cause in our mind an intuition of a non-existent object. Put differently, God sees all creatures even if they do not exist. Yet as an act of grace, he can create an understanding in man, making him participate in this divine intuition.[24] Intuitive knowledge is necessarily true, since an 'erroneous evidence' is a contradiction. He can also cause this knowledge today and stop causing it tomorrow. Furthermore, he could cause it in A's mind, but not in B's. Or he can cause it not at all, or always. Due to the nominalist interpretation of divine omnipotence, we may have certainty of knowledge, though not of its correspondence with reality.

Truth is therefore no longer the natural goal of the intellect. As a result of this, the relationship between *subject* and *object* 'explodes'. The object itself no longer causes intuitions in our mind that then are 'processed' into concepts that are related to reality. As noted above, the object as a secondary cause of intuitions can be replaced by God as the primary cause of everything, and hence also intuitions. The active role of the object in the process of cognition however can be short-circuited by God as the prior cause of everything, including knowledge. This knowledge *a priori causa* competes with knowledge 'a secunda causa', so to speak as the 'real' cause of knowledge.

The problem of the possibility of intuitive knowledge of a non-existent entity, as many authors debate,[25] is not necessarily whether God can cheat us or not. On the assumption that God could cheat us, a radical scepticism arises. But even if God were not cheating us, and merely substitutes *ex potentia absoluta* his power for the secondary causes, the scepticism would remain. We do in fact not know when God interferes *ex potentia absoluta* and when he does not. It is a free decision of his absolute will. The consequential scepticism is not due to anything like cheating. God's omnipotence and his power to substitute for any secondary cause involves a radical uncertainty of his creatures. It is the uncertainty about the *real* cause of knowledge, that is, God or the things, which involves nothing less than scepticism. This uncertainty negatively affects the status of autonomous philosophy, that is, human science *ex puris naturalibus* or knowledge gathered on mere rational grounds.

---

23 Ockham 1967: I, prol. q. 1, 38: 'Potest haberi notitia intuitiva de re non existente.'

24 For this Augustinian interpretation of intuitive knowledge of non-existents, see, for example, Vignaux 1948: 36; Pernoud 1970: 89.

25 For an excellent overview of this problem, see Pernoud 1970. For a radically sceptical interpretation of Ockham, see, among others, Pegis 1944; de Muralt 1966; Scott 1969. For a critique of the sceptical interpretation, see, among others, Putallaz 1983 (criticizing de Muralt's skeptical interpretation of Ockham, and suggesting that historians claiming an identity between Descartes' evil spirit and Ockham's God are wrong).

In this respect, as I have argued elsewhere (Wintgens 2006a), Modernity in philosophy does not start with Descartes. Descartes' philosophical search for certainty is inspired by the scepticism that Ockham and his followers left behind. There is unfortunately not sufficient space here to show the similarities between Ockham's and Descartes' view, so that Descartes, despite the careful concealing of his sources, can be considered to be working in the same line as Ockham. His *cogito* is an attempt to overcome the uncertainty caused by the theory of dual causality and the subsequent scepticism.

Omnipotence, Indifference of the Will, and Human Action

Divine omnipotence has a rigorously parallel effect on human action as it has on human cognition. For the very same reason he cannot create universals, God is indifferent as to values in the world. Indifference means that all values are equal when it comes to creation. The reason is that according to the nominalist version of divine omnipotence, any teleological interpretation of nature is contradictory with God's essence, because this involves a preliminary creation of the telos preceding concrete beings whose telos it is. If the natural telos of man is happiness, this must be part of a universal or essence that determines human action. Man then strives towards the realisation of his telos or nature and becomes happy. However, this telos can no longer exist for a logical reason, as said before. In the absence of a telos, there is nothing to strive towards.

I have already mentioned the fact that the nominalist or logical interpretation of God's omnipotence was triggered by the critique that any other interpretation limits his freedom. Paradoxical as it may sound, divine freedom involves an equal freedom for humans. The more God is free, the more man is free. This is the normative *pendant* of the radical contingency of the world, the consequences of which lead straight to legalism. This is what I propose to explore in the following pages.

As mentioned above, realism and nominalism differ as to the nature of the good. The former holds that God creates or commands something because it is good; the latter claims that something is good because God creates or commands it. The nominalist may object to the realist that his position unduly limits God's omnipotence. The realist for his part may criticise the opposite position which argues that nominalism destroys the order of the world and that it is contradictory.

From the realistic perspective, as in Aquinas, for example, God creates the world according to the plan contained in the *lex aeterna*.[26] What we know of *lex*

26 Aquinas 1910: I–II, q. 91, a. 1 ('Est aliaqua lex aeterna, ratio videlicet gubernativa totius universi in mente divina existens … Et ideo ipsa ratio gubernationis rerum in Dio sicut in principe universitatis existens legis habet rationem … Si igitur aeternus divinae legis conceptus habet rationem legis aeternae secundum quod a Deo ordinatur ad gubernationem rerum ab ipso praecognitarum.' Ibid.: I–II, q. 93, a. 1: ' … lex aeterna nihil aliud est quam ratio divinae sapientiae, secundum quod est directiva omnium actuum et motionum.'

aeterna is what God has revealed to us in the *lex divina*. By using our rational capacities, we can discover in ourselves the *lex naturalis* that participates in the *lex aeterna*.[27] The idea of 'participation' stresses reason rather than will in law. Any law is a dictate of practical reason.[28] The former leads man to his supernatural end, the latter to man's natural end (Aquinas 1910: I–II, q. 91, a. 4). It can be summarised as 'Good should be done and sought after; evil is to be avoided.'[29]

The conceptual move therefore from realism to nominalism unsurprisingly involves the erasing of the *lex aeterna*, even if one were to conclude that God has created or decreed it. If it exists, it must be identical with his essence. As a result of that, it must logically precede creation so that it is a binding norm for God. He shows his omnipotence as *potestas ordinata*, since he is bound by his own nature, and his rationality.[30] Here as elsewhere, the difficulty of reconciling Greek naturalism and Christian revelation becomes apparent. The Augustinian standard of reconciliation of both throughout the Middle Ages had been that divine ideas and divine will are one in God's mind, which makes Augustine a special case from the very beginning.

It is no coincidence that the nominalists get along well with Augustine's contraction between divine intellect and will, as compared to the short Dominican tradition with Aquinas on top. The latter is grafted upon the rediscovery of Aristotle in the first quarter of the thirteenth century which provided the conceptual basis for the development of Christian theology. The revival of the Augustinian line of thought in the fourteenth century quite clearly shows the consequences of the attack on realism from within theology.[31] It considers creation to be an act of divine will. Divine will is related to divine intellect. Under the Augustinian tradition, God

---

27 Ibid.: I–II, q. 93, a. 3: 'Quioniam, teste B. Augustino, in temporali lege nihil est justum ac legitimum quod non sit ex lege aeterna profectum; certum est omnes leges, inquantum participant de ratione recta, in tantum a lege aeterna derivati.' See also Finnis 1982: 398–403.

28 Aquinas 1910: I–II, q. 91, a. 1: 'Utrum lex est aliquid rationis.' Aquinas' theory of the natural law (*lex naturalis*) as a rational discovery by human creatures gives raise to the theory of rational natural law of Grotius. Grotius' theory for its part is considered the beginning of the school of modern natural law, upon which man by the use of reason alone can find out what his duties are. See, on this interpretation, Haggenmacher 1983: 475–9. This is not identical to saying that natural law is secularised, as the expression of Grotius (2005: § 11) 'etiamsi daremus … ' is often interpreted. See Haggenmacher 1983: 496–506; Edwards 1970; Novak 2000; Sève 1989: 36–9.

29 Aquinas 1910: I-II, q. 91, a. 2: 'Est in hominibus lex quaedam naturalis, participatio videlicet legis aeternae, secundum quam bonum et malum discernunt.' And further, ibid.: I-II, q. 94, a. 2: ' … bonum prosequendum, et malum vitandum esse … .'

30 Aquinas 1910: I, q. 25, a. 5: 'Cum autem potentia Dei, quae est ejus essentia, non sit aliud quam Dei sapientia, convenienter quidem dici potest quod nihil sit in Dei potentia, quod not sit in ordine divinae sapientiae … .'

31 See, on this theme, the path-breaking work of Gauchet 2006, who argues that due to the over-estimation of God's omnipotence, Christian religion contains the germs of

creates reality according to a scheme. Unlike within the preceding stoic tradition, however, this scheme or *lex aeterna* is said to exist in God's mind, not in reality (Augustine 42: Book XXII, ch. 27, col. 418).

In Aquinas' version, divine intellect takes a priori-ty over will. The existence of the *lex aeterna* can be observed within the order of reality, as a sign of God's wisdom. According to this version, God is free to create, but not free to create whatever he wants. Were he free to create whatever he wants, then he could destroy the order of reality as it is contained in the *lex aeterna*. This would involve a contradiction which even God's will cannot afford because he is bound by the principle of non-contradiction.

The priority of intellect over will in God, as Aquinas pointed out,[32] may itself be hard to grasp, because it limits God's freedom even if this is understood as a self-limitation of God. In other words, even if God were the author of the *lex aeterna*, this very act of creation would be a self-imposed restraint on his omnipotence. *Any* theory that limits God's freedom is in contradiction with faith. The world therefore must be interpreted as entirely created by God, in such a way that order is the result of divine will, and not of the intellect. This is the reinterpretation that Duns Scotus offers of Aristotle's legacy in combination with the Christian eschatology as it was reconsidered from the perspective of faith.

Here as elsewhere, Ockham suggests a more radical interpretation which argues that normativity can only be the result of an act of will or command. Because God can only create individuals, they do not share a common nature as a source of normativity. The individual therefore no longer finds in nature his *causa finalis*, because this no longer exists. Creation, that is, is uncaused in *this* sense, and does not therefore require a pre-existing model.

In this respect, the separation of subject and object in cognition – as mentioned above – has a rigorous parallel in action. Universals, under a realistic ontology, contain the normative pattern that rational beings are to realise as their *causa finalis*. According to the nominalist interpretation of God's omnipotence, normativity no longer belongs to reality where it can be observed. In a consistent line with this interpretation, God's will is not bound to any good. If it were, this would involve him first knowing the good and then acting upon it, viz. commanding it. This is a contradiction, even on the assumption that he first created the good which then

---

its own end. It is in Gauchet's terms the 'religion of the exit of religion'. It is regrettable though that Gauchet does not mention his sources, which, I guess, are of a nominalist brand.

32 Aquinas 1910: I, q. XIX, a 1. Answering the question 'Utrum in Deo sit voluntas' Aquinas writes: 'Conclusio. Cum voluntas intellectum consequatur, opportet in Deo voluntatem esse, cum in eo sit intellectus. Respondeo dicendum in Deo volutatem ess, sicut in eo est intellectus. Voluntas enim intellectum consequitur.' Instead of the literal reading 'will follows the intellect', which would correctly expresses the rationalistic view of Aquinas, a nominalistic reading of the Blackfriars reads: 'As there is mind in God, so there is will; the one involves the other.' This reading excludes any priority of the intellect over the will which according to good nominalist logic stresses God's radical simplicity.

binds him. His will therefore is – and must logically be – indifferent. That is, God's will is freedom because of its radical indeterminacy. It cannot be bound to what is good, because this would contradict his omnipotence.[33]

The normative emptiness of reality because of God's radical omnipotence brings about a new pattern of normative thinking. If normativity exists, it can only be imposed by God upon his creatures as an obligation. An act is morally good because of its correspondence to an external norm imposed on freedom. If it were morally good because of its intrinsic goodness, we would be again on the track of realism. Morality therefore is conformity with a norm expressed as an act of will or command that is addressed directly to man's freedom.

Under the nominalist interpretation, God's will is indifferent because it is no longer 'informed' by his intellect. To create and to command are two qualitatively different acts, although they may occur at the same time. Identifying justice with divine will suggests that as a logical consequence of God's radical simplicity and omnipotence, the content of his commands is arbitrary.[34] Arbitrariness of divine commands has a twofold consequence. First, their content merely depends on God's will. He therefore commands whatever he wants. Secondly, as a consequence of the first, he can change his commands whenever he wants to, for example, by

33 This is a variant of the Euthyphro problem in Plato, see Plato, 1943 and a *locus classicus* throughout the history of philosophy, see among others: Aquinas (adopting both positions) Aquinas 1910: II–II, q. 57, a. 2: 'Sunt enim in lege divina quaedam praecepta quia bona; et prohibita, quia mala; quaedam vero bona, quia praecepta: et mala quia prohibita.' Ibid.: I-II, q. 71, a. 6: 'Sed non omnia peccata sunt mala quia prohibita, sed quaedam sunt prohibita quia mala. Non ergo in communi definitione peccati debuit poni quod sit contra legem Dei.' Duns Scotus 1894: II, d. 22, q. 1, n. 3: 'Sed omnia peccata, quæ sunt circa decem præcepta, formaliter non tantum sunt mala, quia prohibita, sed quia mala, ideo prohibita, quia ex lege naturæ oppositum cujuslibet fuit malum, et per naturalem rationem potest homovidere, quod quodlibet præceptum ex illis est tenendum.' Ockham 1984: q. 8, 442, 446; Ockham 1977: d 17, q. 3: ' … [Deus] quia eo ipso vult, bene et iuste factum est'; Leibniz 1953: 5: 'Also, by saying that things are not good by any rule of goodness but by God's will alone, it seems to me that one unthinkingly destroys all love of God and all his glory. For why praise him for what he has done, if he would be equally praiseworthy in doing just the contrary.' Where then will be his justice and his wisdom, if there only remains a certain despotic power, if will takes the place of reason, and if according to the definition of tyrants, what pleases the most powerful is just by that alone?'; Descartes 1996i: 233 (there is no priority of knowledge in God and nothing is good prior to the decision of God to make it that way); Pufendorf 1994c: I, ch. 6, § 4; Spinoza (1965b: 121–21) for his part holds that it does not 'matter whether God is believed ... to govern things freely or by natural necessity; to lay down laws as a ruler or to teach them as eternal truths.'

34 This is a general outline the purpose of which is to show the main *logical* consequences of the nominalistic interpretation of divine omnipotence. These consequences have also been denied, for example, by Hans Welzel (1962: 149), who claims that the interpretation is wrong, because no voluntarist from Scotus to Pufendorf has ever excluded divine goodness which excludes arbitrariness. See, however, Haggenmacher 1983: 482 and Edwards 1970: 802.

commanding Abraham to kill his son, contrary to the general norm that one should not kill. God's indifference to the good means that it does not exist independently of his will since it is his will that makes something good.

The only thing God cannot command is 'X' and 'non-X' at the same time. In addition to the arbitrary nature of divine commandments, there is no reason accessible to the human mind why 'X' rather than 'non-X' is commanded. God may have his reasons for doing so, though he owes no justification to his creatures. From their perspective, this is identical to the absence of a reason. His commands are therefore arbitrary acts of will; they are good because he commands them, and not the other way around.

The arbitrary content of the divine commands means that the normativity of a proposition depends on revelation without which God's will would remain unknown. What we know of God's will is thus what he has commanded and revealed in the Scripture as the Ten Commandments. The metaphysical consequence of this interpretation is that the *lex divina* and the *lex aeterna* coincide or that the *lex aeterna* steering the content of the *lex divina* no longer makes sense.[35]

An exemplary although paradoxical issue in this respect is the command of God to hate him or the problem of the *odium Dei*.[36] In the first Commandment, God has ordered the faithful to love him. The love of God entails the requirement that the faithful do anything which they or the ecclesiastical institution believes pleases God. As a matter of duty, the minimal implication is not to violate God's commandments. As a matter of aspiration, the sky is the limit, as it were. Duty or aspiration are normative motives for following his commandments. The deeper

---

35 Bastit 1990a: 186 and 189. On the identity of the *lex aeterna* and the *lex naturalis*, and the comparison with Grotius' 'etiamsi daremus', see Rommen 1948, esp. 447.

36 Ockham 1981: q. 15, 348: 'Si igitur actus odeindi Deum potest fiery a solo Deo sine peccato et potest etiam fieri a voluntate create, igitur potest Deux praecipere voluntati ut odiat Deum.' The theme of the *odium Dei* is a recurrent one and it divides the realists and the nominalists. According to Duns Scot (1894: IV, d. 28, 6) the love of God is the only act that is good in view of its only object; to hate God is the only act that is wrong in view of its only object, and there is no circumstance that could make it good. See also Aquinas 1910: II–II, q. 34, a. 2: 'Ergo odium Dei est pessimum peccatum hominis … Cum per Dei odium per se homo avertatur a Deo, ipsum Dei odium inter peccata gravissimum esse consequitur.' In his conversation with Burman, Descartes (1996g: 160) replies to Burman's question: 'Sed an ergo potuisset Deus imperare creaturae ut se odisset, et hoc bonum ita instituisse?', 'Jam non potest; sed quid potuerit, nescimus; et quidni creaturae hoc imperare potuisset.' (But does it follow from this that God could have commanded a creature to hate him, and thereby made this a good thing to do? God could not now do this: but we simply do not know what he could have done. In any case why should he not have been able to give this command to one of his creatures?' (translation from Cottingham 1976: 22). The idea is a logical consequence of the nominalist interpretation of divine omnipotence, though not necessarily an ethical one. Yet it may be contradictory to hold on the one hand that one has to hate God in order to be saved, yet to love him in order to follow that commandment, see on this Bastit 1997: chapter 9.

inspiration is the love for God. According to the love for God throughout his life, the faithful *can* then be admitted to eternal salvation. The basic idea is that the love for God determines one's chances to get access to salvation, since God is good and just.

However, according to the logical or nominalist interpretation of divine omnipotence, the content of God's commandments is considered arbitrary. God therefore could as well command that he be hated. The hate of God, like murder, adultery, or theft, are logically possible contents of a divine command and may serve as the basis of justification and salvation. The belief that God is good and just is not determinative as to the content of his commandments. Thus the commandments are no longer related to the *causa finalis*; that is, the good, like knowledge, is no longer related to what there is. Knowledge, as mentioned above, is possible of a non-existent thing. Since good is what he commands, it is possible that he commands that he be hated, on the basis of which those who hated him most will be saved. Or maybe not, because again God owes nothing to his creatures.

The result of this is that the faithful do not know what must 'really' be done as a matter of 'good' found 'out there'. All that must be done is to obey the commandments of God as they are revealed, without any hope of salvation. Because of the arbitrary nature of divine commandments, not only their content but also the consequences of following them are undetermined. Because there is no necessary connection between obedience and salvation, it is therefore possible that murderers are saved and Samaritans are damned despite the commandment to love God and vice versa. Here as elsewhere the basic premise that makes the command to hate God rational is his omnipotence.

The reason why normativity is logically connected to a commandment is not hard to find. Because God cannot create essences, to act according to our nature no longer makes sense because 'human nature' or 'human essence' no longer exists. The normative emptiness of the world must therefore be compensated by commandments imposed on otherwise free creatures. What is more, everything which he wants to be done must be commanded, because what is not forbidden is permitted. This is yet another consequence of nominalism.

The moral goodness of an act is therefore no longer a result of the realisation of the good as the *causa finalis* of the commandment. Its goodness follows from the compliance of the act with the norm that is imposed. Morality, that is, stems from the imposition of norms on human freedom. Compliance with these norms is what makes an action morally good. Following norms imposed by God is all man has to do.

The Metaphysics of Legalism

The Nominalist Concept of Obligation

Due to God's omnipotence, he can no longer create universals. Natural law in its classical version is therefore erased because nature no longer has any universal value. The Thomist version of natural law also disappears under the subsequent interpretation of Suarez. According to Aquinas, God creates the world according to the *lex aeterna* which contains the plan of creation. Within this general framework law is an *ordinatio ad bonum commune*. However, teleological thinking disappears due to the intervention of nominalism. In the absence of essences, a *causa finalis* no longer makes sense. After a short analysis of the concept of obligation according to nominalism, I will briefly explore the characteristics of the metaphysics of legalism as they appear in the work of Suarez, Pufendorf and Kant respectively.

Suarez's reinterpretation of Aquinas, combined with Ockham's nominalism results in a new definition of law. Law is a command of a superior, and first and foremost God. Law as a command is imposed upon the creature's freedom, and compliance with this command is the essence of morality; that is, law undergoes a 'moralisation'. What Aquinas called the *Decalogos*, inspired by the *lex aeterna*, thereafter takes on the shape of the Ten Commandments, the content of which merely depends on God's free will. Remember in this respect that it was Ockham's opinion that God could equally command that he be hated as well as loved.

Commands link norms with freedom, and at the same time determine moral action. Legal thinking undergoes an important shift within this new constellation. Michel Villey in his studies on Roman law and legal obligation has repeatedly argued that law is an object ('*id quod justum est*') and creates a relationship between the creditor and the debtor. It is a *horizontal* obligation between two individuals according to objective law. The *vinculum juris* extinguishes once the debt is paid, the thing given, or the action performed.

Following the transformation of law into a command, the horizontal obligation is supplemented with, or made dependent upon, the *vertical* obligation that comes to a submission to the will of the superior. In that respect, the moral obligation to obey the law precedes the creation of legal obligations based on the will of agents. The vertical obligation is of a moral nature since submission is an act of will. It is not extinguished with the fulfilment of the legal duty; it is on the contrary a perpetually enduring obligation due to God, the natural law, or the state (Sève 1985).

The vertial obligation that results from the submission to a superior is, as a matter of fact, a-symmetric compared to the horizontal obligation between creditor and debtor. This creates a problem of legitimacy, to which both Max Weber and Paul Ricoeur refer. The claim to legitimacy and the belief in or acceptance of this claim by those under an obligation is dissymmetric or asymmetric (Ricoeur 1986e: 310). The nominalist metaphysics that lead to legalism as I have explored in the preceding pages involves as a major thesis divine omnipotence in its logical interpretation. As a radicalisation of Scotus' formal distinction *ex parte rei*

Ockham and subsequent nominalists hold that what is not logically contradictory is ontologically possible if God wants it. What is contradictory for its part is ontologically impossible because God cannot want it.

Under this view of obligation, authority refers to the source of norms qualified to impose limitations of freedom. God's authority in this respect is a necessary element of nominalist metaphysics because without the existence of common natures or universals, the only source of normativity is God's will. Under the nominalist interpretation of divine omnipotence, the Ten Commandments are read from a new perspective as they are considered as mere acts of will by God. Their content is subordinated to their source; it is the source and not the content that endows them with authority.

The Commandments are the ultimate source of normativity addressed directly to human freedom that must be exercised by the will. Normative action therefore is no longer mediated by grasping the intrinsic goodness of the end but is confined by the extrinsic norm that frames its normativity. To choose according to right reason is to will what is dictated by reason because it is dictated.

The above comments, read in connection with what I have said regarding knowledge and action according to nominalism, schematically summarise the pattern of normative thinking embedded in the metaphysics that we currently label 'legalism'. The normative emptiness of reality as an upshot of the nominalist interpretation of God's omnipotence relates normativity to an external source with the power to impose its will. This source can be anything as long as it has the authority to act in this way. Authority in this respect equals power that can be recognised by its external property or its form. That source then combined with the normative category of obligation is constitutive of law.

The transition from Aquinas' rationalistic tradition into the new voluntaristic approach of normativity following Ockham involves the substitution of a binary deontic code, for example, 'right/wrong', 'moral/immoral', 'legal/illegal' for a gradual achievement of a virtue in terms of 'excellence'.[37] Normativity as superimposed on existing creatures therefore adds something to the world without changing it. It is a different world, the world of 'ought' separated from the world of 'is'. The world being itself without values, norms are to be imposed upon human creatures. Any act, therefore, is normatively indifferent, unless commanded otherwise.

---

37 As a result of this transition, metaphysics itself is transformed into a legislative system, under which what exists is created and what ought to be done is commanded or imposed, cf. Bastit 1990a: 180. Lon Fuller, for example in his effort to articulate the two types of morality, on the one hand highlights the morality of excellence, aspiration, or virtue associated with the Aristotelian tradition. On the other hand, he points to the morality of duty, referring to Kantian deontic morality. Both types of morality combine in what Fuller has called 'the morality of law', thereby stressing the impact of a morality of excellence or aspiration, far less known than the morality of duty under the auspices of legalism; see Fuller 1969: 3–32; Brochard 1954: 489–503.

It follows that what is not forbidden is permitted, because normativity is expressed in relation to a norm, and a norm must be ordered and promulgated. Normative action and its subsequent evaluation in terms of morality therefore needs an explicit and extrinsic norm. The normative assessment of an act, so it must be concluded, is no longer a matter of the goal in view of which it is accomplished. It is rather its correspondence to a norm issued by a superior to whom the actor is submitted. The normativity of an act and its legality, therefore, are one and the same. The correspondence of norm and action determines the latter's moral quality.

The scepticism to which nominalism had given rise, combined with the Reformation that was at least partially rooted in nominalism, formed a counterweight in Counter-Reformation theology and philosophy. At the beginning of the seventeenth century, Spanish Scholastics took up the thread of mediaeval Scholastics, while merging it to its nominalist successors. The result of this merger was a synthesis of the rationalist tradition following from Aristotle through Aquinas on the one hand and the voluntarist tradition connecting to Augustinianism and its Franciscan followers throughout the fourteenth century.

Suarez

The lead is taken by Suarez whose work marked the beginning of a century-long standard interpretation of Aquinas known as 'neo-Thomism' (Ross 1962: 737–8). This interpretation was part of the Counter-Reformation in which the Jesuits took the role of *ecclesia militans*. It culminated in the encyclical *Aeterni Patris* of Leo XIII in 1879, urging the restoration of Scholastic philosophy. This resulted in the celebration of Suarez's brand of Thomism, as a combination of Scholasticism's intellectualism and nominalism's voluntarism, of which the following observations are relevant for the metaphysics of legalism.

In his etymological account of the term '*lex*' at the very outset of his *De Legibus ac de Deo Legislatore*, Suarez refers to what can be interpreted as the opposition between realism and rationalism on the one hand, and nominalism and voluntarism on the other. On the one hand, Suarez observes that '*lex*' is etymologically related to '*legere*' (to collect, to read), thus pointing to a realist or rationalist component. On the other hand, he suggests a different origin of '*lex*', that is '*ligare*' (to bind), thus stressing the nominalist or voluntarist aspect of law.[38] Suarez admits that the etymology is somewhat spurious and of a lesser importance (Suarez 2003: 97–9) and there is good reason to believe that he borrowed this idea from Gabriel Biel, one of Ockham's pupils (Courtines 1999: 99; Bastit 1990b: 211–20.

38 Suarez 2003: book I, ch. 1, nrs 8–9, referring on the one hand to Aquinas 1910: I–II, q. 90, a. 1c: 'dicitur enim lex a ligando … ', and on the other to Cicero 1999: book I, 20, p. 112, connecting '*lex*' to '*legēre*', to select, while '*nomos*' according to him is derived from '*nemô*', to divide); Augustine 35: II, q. 15, 2395: 'Lex a lectione dicta est, ut de multis quid eligias scias.'

However, Suarez's attempt to conjugate Greek rationalism and Christian revelation on the one hand, and nominalism on the other, summarises different aspects of a long-standing tradition. The rationalist or realist tradition holds that legislation is preceded by a cognitive grasp of reality, and hence judgment precedes decision. In this respect, the 'intellect' has priority over 'will', according to which for Aquinas all laws (divine, natural and human) participate in the eternal law.

However, absolute indifference as the core of the nominalist interpretation of God's omnipotence means that God can only command, and not create norms essentially belonging to individuals' 'common nature'. God first creates individuals using his *voluntas creativa* and then imposes his will upon them using his *voluntas imperativa*. In this respect, nominalist metaphysics sheds a different light on the Decalogue. Under the realist view, it can be considered a (partial) revelation of the eternal logos or *lex aeterna* governing creation. Under the nominalist view of God's radically simple nature, reason no longer has a priority over will, since both are equally perfect within God. However, unbounded will has absolute priority over this equality, so that decision is no longer preceded by judgment. In view of this, the Decalogue can be labelled the Ten Commandments, stressing more their imperative than their rational nature. They consist of norm externally imposed on the creatures. Suarez's theory of law as a command cuts off Aquinas' definition of law's finality. It is the source as *causa efficiens* that defines law's authority, thereby erasing the realist *causa finalis*.

In his synthesis of Thomist intellectualism and nominalist voluntarism, Suarez finds his way out of the problem raised by the conjunction of Greek rationalism and Christian revelation. On the one hand, God creates the world. This involves the creation of natural laws as well as rational creatures. The latter are to understand the former, which explains man's obligations towards God. On the other hand, God can not pack his norms into human nature, because this would limit his creative power, and hence involves a contradiction with his omnipotence.

The result of Suarez's definition of law is that natural laws do not prescribe as long as they are not commanded. Therefore, in order to preserve God's freedom – a problem that much troubled Aquinas in following Averroes' Aristotelianism – Suarez has added a prescriptive element to natural laws. However, creation and prescription are split or differentiated without being dissociated as a purely nominalist approach would have involved. In creating man as a rational being capable of knowing good and bad, God could not have wanted not to forbid intrinsically bad things and not to prescribe intrinsically good things. Nevertheless, the 'necessity' of a 'prescriptive will' is a consequence of having exercised his 'creative will'. It follows that man is obliged by the laws of nature that contain 'the good' – this is Suarez's realist intake – and obligation results from a supplementary act of will, a commandment, of God which articulates Suarez's nominalist side.

Normativity, therefore, is conceptually related to commandment, so that Suarez can be said to have initiated the distinction between the realm of '*Sein*' on the one hand and the realm of '*Sollen*' on the other, a distinction that later inspired Pufendorf and, much later, Kelsen. With this distinction we have identified an essential aspect of legalism, that is, the external imposition of norms or the external limitation of otherwise unlimited freedom. The roots of this are God's omnipotence and his radical and absolute indifference as acknowledged in Ockham's nominalism. Of his articulation of '*lex*' as '*legere*' and '*ligare*', it is the latter that obviously fits in better with his position as a nominalist. The normative force of a law inevitably stems from an act of will of a superior, and so Suarez rather qualifies as a nominalist than as a realist, despite his attempts to combine the best parts of the two.

Normative theory as it is initiated in this new form by Suarez holds that normativity is a matter of following norms, an approach that closely fits with Shklar's definition of legalism. The morality of an act no longer merely consists in realising what is good per se. A result of the preceding nominalist interpretation of divine omnipotence and the subsequent normative emptiness of the world is that the realist ontology no longer holds. Instead, the morality of an act follows from its compliance with a norm that is externally imposed. Legalism in this respect is a variation on the Euthyphro theme.

A number of Suarez's successors elaborate his theory of normativity as compliance with an externally imposed norm in that they incorporate it into political philosophy. Rule following in this respect takes on a political dimension in addition to its moral dimension. Both the moral and the political dimension of rule following are related to 'freedom' in the nominalist reading as 'indifference'.

As for political society, the main consequence of nominalism is that there is no longer exists a natural or universal model like Aristotle's *polis*. Since universals have no ontological value outside the mind, the universal or concept of 'society' must be thought of differently. It consists of a conjunction of ontologically separated and free individuals owing obedience to divine commandments to begin with, and following commanded norms of the state or sovereign as their duty. Here again, Suarez's is a conjunction of Aquinas' rationalism and nominalist voluntarism and pre-echoes the tradition of the social contract. Normative theory, as it was established in this new form by Suarez, asserts that normativity is a matter of following norms, an approach that closely fits in with Shklar's definition of legalism. The morality of an act no longer merely consisting in achieving what is good per se. A result of the preceding nominalist interpretation of divine omnipotence and the subsequent normative emptiness of the world is that the realist ontology no longer holds. Instead, an act is considered as a moral act where it complies with a norm that is externally imposed. Legalism in this respect is a variation on the Euthyphro theme, since the commands are valid due to the authority of the commander, not their content.

A number of Suarez' successors elaborate his theory of normativity as compliance with externally imposed norms in that they incorporate it into political philosophy. Rule following in this respect takes on a political dimension in addition to its moral dimension. Both the moral and the political dimension of rule following are related to 'freedom' in the nominalist reading as 'indifference'.

As for political society, the main consequence of nominalism is that there is no longer a natural model or a universal like Aristotle's *polis*. Since universals have no ontological value outside the mind, the universal or concept of 'society' must be conceptualised differently. It consists of a conjunction of ontologically separated and free individuals owing obedience to divine commandments from the outset, and obeying commanded norms of the sovereign as their duty. Here as elsewhere, Suarez' theory is a mix of Aquinas' onto-theological rationalism and nominalist voluntarism. More specifically, it pre-echoes the social contract tradition of which he provides an embryonic version.

Since God cannot create universals like a 'state', a state's existence depends on the union of a people into a community by common consent. This union is not a simple multitude or juxtaposition of individuals, according to the nominalist device '*totum sunt partes*'. It is, on the contrary, a moral or quasi-political unity or *corpus mysticum* (Suarez 1944: 375). Since all power comes from God (Romans 13:1), he immediately bestows it upon the group as a whole. A result of this conferral is that it becomes an 'original democracy' (Suarez 1944: 380). The original democracy is a perfect community which exercises political power as a whole (ibid.: 364, 375), although it is mere matter (the people) without form (a government). This is reminiscent of the Scotist distinction *a parte rei de potentia absoluta dei*, or the logical possibility of the separation between matter and form if God had desired it.[39]

Yet, since God or nature does anything in vain, endowing the perfect community with original political power means that there must necessarily be some power governing that community, since God does not govern human societies directly, but only through secondary causes (ibid.: 365–6). The *potestas dominativa*, the *ius imperandi*, or the power to rule should therefore be vested in a human government, without which the community would be less perfect. Its perfection, that is, consists in realising the common good (ibid.: 375), which necessarily means that the people (matter) must be endowed with a form (government).

It follows that God's conferral of political power as a natural attribute of a perfect community must necessarily be followed by a voluntary act of the people transferring its power to a government as the seat of authority (ibid.: 380–81). The body politic is a unity with the common good as its finality. The proper preservation of this unity therefore requires subjection to one and the same rule and to some common superior power (ibid.: 375). The *pactum unionis* supplemented with a *pactum subjectionis* completes the institution of the perfect community and it sketches out the contours of the subsequent social contract tradition.

As regards the institutional form of the commonwealth, although Suarez expresses a preference for monarchy, men are free to choose the form of government they desire (ibid.: 383). As regards the nature of the transfer of power

39 Rousseau (1997a: 49) espouses this idea of the original democracy, referring to Grotius: 'A people, says Grotius, can give itself to a king. So that, according to Grotius, a people is a people before giving itself to a king.'

or the *pactum subjectionis*, Suarez leaves no doubt: 'Accordingly, the transfer of the said power from the state to the prince is not a delegation but a transfer (as it were), that is to say, an unlimited bestowal of the whole power which [formerly] resided in the community ...' (ibid.: 391).[40] The transfer is an irreversible gift (*donatio*) in that the power holder cannot be deprived of his power which is under his true ownership (*dominium*), unless he lapses into tyranny (ibid.: 387). Political power vested in the sovereign is absolute, although it is mediated by human agency, and the laws of the sovereign are morally binding upon the divine source of the original power conferred on the commonwealth (ibid.: 387).

Hobbes

Hobbes is the first to clearly draw the consequences of nominalism in connection to politics, and for this reason he can be said to be the initiator of 'political nominalism'. Confronting freedom as a new philosophical problem, he offers a new conceptual framework the contours of which will be briefly articulated in the following sections.

Three Dimensions of the State of Nature

In the state of nature, there is no power independent of or external to individual subjects. Therefore, the operationalisation of the *ius naturale*, the right of all to everything, merely depends on the subject's own judgement. In the state of nature three dimensions – the normative, the epistemological and the anthropological – can be isolated.

The first, normative dimension, in the state of nature, is governed by the laws of nature.[41] The laws of nature are built on the duty and the corresponding right to stay alive, as Locke later argues (Locke 1963c: (Second Treatise) chapter 2), According to the fundamental law of nature, man ought to seek peace and follow it. If peace cannot be obtained, we can by all means defend ourselves (Hobbes 1966c: 117).

From this definition of a law of nature result a number of laws, the second of which reads 'that a man be willing, when others are so too, as far-forth, as for peace, and defence of himself if he shall think it necessary, to lay down this right

40 The Latin version is clearer: 'Talis translatio potestatis a republica in principem non est delegatio, sed *quasi alienatio*, seu *perfecta largitio* potestatis quae erat in communitate': (Suarez, 1856: 186, italics added).

41 Hobbes 1966c: 116–17: 'A law of nature, lex naturalis, is a precept or general rule, found out by reason, by which a man is forbidden to do that, which is destructive of his life, or taketh away the means of preserving the same; and to omit that, by which he thinketh it may be best preserved.'

to all things and be contented with so much liberty against other men, as he would allow other men against himself' (ibid.: 118).[42]

Apart from being found out by reason, they are also commanded by God (Hobbes 1966b: 49–50; 1966c: 147). As commands of God or dictates of reason, the natural laws are eternal and unchangeable (Hobbes: 1966c: 145) and their knowledge is what the true moral philosophy consists of. They are identical with the moral law (Hobbes 1966b: 47) and confirmed in the Scripture (Hobbes 1966b: 52; 1966c: 147).

Three related reasons exclude the possibility of peaceful coexistence in the state of nature. The first is that the duty to survive is owed to God as the author of the laws of nature. They are of an individual moral nature, not a social one. This clarifies the nature of the *ius naturale*: it is a permission to do everything in order to fulfil the duty. The second reason is that because the duty is only owed to God, the connection between the right and the duty to survive is of a logical nature. If A has a duty to survive, it logically follows that he has a right to act accordingly. However, A's right does not correspond to a duty of any B to respect it (Hart 1955; Warrender 1962: 355).

The third reason is related to Hobbes's nominalism. Since only individuals exist, relations between individuals lack ontological status. Relations between individuals lack support in reality because the opposite contradict Hobbes's nominalism and subsequently individualism. As a result, the philosophical articulation of relations between individuals is pointless.

This brings in the second, epistemological dimension of the state of nature. The ontological status of the laws of nature does not allow any conclusion as to their meaning. Concepts, like relations, lack any ontological status even when they figure in the laws of nature; they are just words. The meaning of words is conventional, not natural or ontological. Since the laws of nature oblige the subject to God, their meaning is merely 'private'. The individual subject's meaning is a necessary and sufficient condition to fulfil his duties to God. Apart from the practical impossibility for the laws of nature to be socially operational on that basis, private meaning is in any case absurd. Both the source and the nature of the obligations in the laws of nature create a partition between their existence and their meaning as a consequence of Hobbes's nominalistic ontology. It makes the laws of nature unfit for implementation in social interaction.

The third dimension of the state of nature focuses on Hobbes's anthropological view. For Hobbes, passions, equality and reason are the basic anthropological elements. From their mixture follows an explosive cocktail. Indeed, man's goals are framed throughout the process of deliberation. It results in the sum of desires, aversions, hopes, and fears (ibid.: 48).

---

42 Hobbes 1966c: 118. The other natural laws affect the way social interaction, in the absence of any organised political space, could pass off quietly. Accordingly, the third law of nature requires that man respect his covenants, the fourth that one not be ungrateful, the fifth that man be compliant with others, the sixth that one be merciful, and so on.

In framing their goals on deliberation, all men cherish an equal hope of getting what they want. Since the product of physical strength and speed of mind turns out to be constant as Hobbes suggest, men are of equal ability (ibid.: 111). Competition, diffidence and pride complete the picture of the anthropological dimension of the state of nature. They make men attack each other for gain, safety, or reputation respectively. The resulting situation of war involves the absence of industry, arts, science, letters, and so on. Worst of all, however, is the 'continual fear, and danger of violent death' (ibid.: 113), all of which makes 'the life of man, solitary, poor, nasty, brutish, and short.' (ibid.: 113).

The Three Dimensions Combined

The three dimensions of the state of nature are interrelated and corroborate each other. Under the nominalist dimension, the concepts in laws of nature have no meaning of their own. They are, as I mentioned, semantically empty. No wonder that everyone fills in these concepts as he thinks fit. Social life on the basis of the laws of nature turns out to be impossible because, within the epistemological dimension of the state of nature, there is nothing like 'true meaning'. The anthropological dimension only makes things worse.

The normative dimension ties in with the epistemological one. The endeavour to comply with the laws of nature, an 'unfeigned and constant endeavour' as Hobbes (1966c: 145) calls it, is sufficient to fulfil them. What does good will, however, add, since it is impossible to know their true meaning? This seriously qualifies Hobbes's opinion that they may easily be observed. This is only correct with regard to their *moral* aspect and consequently the mere endeavour to their performance.

The anthropological dimension again reinforces the normative dimension of the state of nature, as the epistemological dimension also did. However, it does not essentially affect the normative character of the laws of nature. These laws are norms upon God's command. Their impracticability, therefore, does not in principle affect their normativity.

Therefore, when an A would like to externalise his 'desire [that the laws of nature] should take place' he makes himself prey to others, thus procuring to his own ruin (ibid.: 145). As with the theory of the covenant as we will soon see, any transaction except a performance on the spot is a violation of the first law of nature, and therefore forbidden. A's desire therefore that men perform their covenants made should not be externalised by his performing first. Any conventional lapse of time between the two performances is not only naïve; it is at the same time a violation of the first law of nature as well. So, A's desire to show his gratitude to a benefactor, for example, risks being misunderstood, and maybe even taken as a sign of contempt. In addition to that, the duty 'that every man acknowledge another for his equal' (ibid.: 141) may conversely lead to gross misunderstanding, as positive discrimination sometimes shows.[43]

These problems do not necessarily flow from wickedness or bad will. They mainly occur because the terms of 'covenant', 'gratitude' and 'equality' are not universals. They are just words that do not have any ultimate, that is, real meaning. Their meaning is conventional, not real. From their lack of real or ultimate meaning it follows that the laws of nature in which they appear lack operative effect.

Here as elsewhere, the anthropological dimension may make things worse since passions only rarely contribute to smooth social interaction. Put more strictly, compliance with the laws of nature entails *being* moral. Acting on them, however, as an externalisation of the 'desire they should take place' involves a contradiction with the definition of the natural law *tout court* and may turn out to be immoral. To be moral and to act in a moral way are two different things.

This paradoxical interpretation shows that the anthropological dimension of the state of nature is not the primary cause of the ineffectiveness of the laws of nature. It may, however, strongly contribute to it, not to mention reinforce it. The deeper root of the trouble in the state of nature consists of its epistemological dimension. Because the terms figuring in the laws of nature have no real meaning, the laws of nature are semantically empty. Good will or bad will does not essentially matter, since Hobbes makes interaction under the laws of nature epistemologically impossible. This epistemological impossibility is Hobbes's version of the epistemologisation of philosophy, inaugurated by Descartes.

The difference between the existence of the laws of nature on the one hand, and their semantic emptiness on the other, frames freedom as a new, philosophical problem. Since political space has no longer a root in reality, it must be thought of as a rational construction. The foundation of this construction is the fundamental law of nature as a command. Using his rational capacities received from God, man must act according to right reason, which Hobbes combines with the state of nature resulting in the social contract.

Theory of the Covenant

The third law of nature ' … is this, that men perform their covenants made … ' (Hobbes 1966c: 130).[44] A and B make a covenant. A performs, while B regrets his decision since the object of his act is not 'some good to himself' any more.[45] B tells A that their arrangement is not a covenant, so that he has not to perform. A

---

43 The procuring of a benefit to members of a minority group simply because they belong to that group may be misunderstood as a confirmation that the beneficiary really has the negative qualities that the benefit wants to diminish or abolish.

44 In the following, the bracketed numbers refer to page numbers in Hobbes 1966c.

45 Hobbes 1966c: 120 (object of voluntary act is some good to himself). The determination of whether an object is good depends on man's appetite or desire for it. 'For these words of good, evil, and contemptible are ever used with relation to the person that useth them: there being nothing simply and absolutely so': ibid.: 41.

presumably disagrees with B, since he has already performed. B holds that what A calls 'performance of a covenant' is nothing else than, say, A's providing B with a sample version of a new variety of strawberries. A and B disagree on what a covenant is. They disagree, that is, on the meaning of the third law of nature, not on its existence. In order for the semantic disagreement to stop, the semantic emptiness of the laws of nature must be remedied by a theory of meaning. This is the theory of the covenant. This theory is exemplary for the solution of the semantic disagreement in the state of nature due to Hobbes's nominalism.

A contract consists of a reciprocal transfer of rights (120). Hobbes distinguishes between four hypotheses. First, the transfer of rights can be accompanied by an immediate transfer of the thing itself (type I) (120), and so there is a mutual exchange. Secondly, both parties can contract and delay the transfer of the thing (goods and money, for example) (type II). Under that hypothesis, the right is transferred while the actual delivery of the external goods is postponed (121). Third, in the event that only one party actually performs while the other's performance is delayed, the former must trust the latter (type III). Fourth and finally, both parties may contract to perform later, in which case they must trust one another since performance on both sides is postponed. For the party who has yet to perform, the contract is called a pact or a covenant (type IV) (121). The lapse of time during which no performance takes place but is expected is covered by trust and the corresponding duty is to maintain a promise or faith (121).

On a different classification, (I) and (II) belong together. In (I), everything is performed on the spot, so no trouble could arise as to the performance of both parties. In (II), both parties agree to deliver later; they transfer the right at $time_1$ and postpone delivery to $time_2$. Under a strong interpretation, this hypothesis can be understood as involving no contract at all. There may be a contract in some theoretical sense. Yet, if both A and B have a right to all, and if they proceed to a mutual exchange of part of, it can be asked whether they do not transfer to each other something that they already had, that is, the right. Didn't they have a *ius in omnia*, so that the question arises as to what the object of the contract is?

The common denominator of types (I) and (II) is delivery, present or postponed. In (III) and (IV), it is performance in another form. In this class of contracts, a different type of performance comes – called 'keeping of promise' – that is, the characteristic of contracts called covenants or pacts. Hobbes argues that within the class of covenants, making a promise is equivalent to a transfer of rights; therefore, covenants are contracts (as we knew already from the definition). Since a promise transfers a right, a covenant is obligatory (123). The obligatory force of a covenant finds its basis in the third law of nature, holding that man must perform their covenants made (130).

So far, the theory of contract taken as such looks pretty analytical. However, when it is placed within the larger context of the theory of society that Hobbes depicts in Chapter XIII of his *Leviathan*, the validity conditions of the contract become somewhat thicker. The systematic reading of the theory of contract in the light of the theory of the *ius naturale* and subsequently the theory of society gives rise to a qualification of the theory of validity.

Despite the fact that a covenant is obligatory (123) (under the third law of nature), a covenant of mutual trust – that is, in which neither party presently performs (type IV, 124) – is invalid where there is 'a fear of non-performance on either part' (131). This equally (and a fortiori) applies to a covenant where one party performs (type III, 124). This is the case because the contracting parties violate(s) the first law of nature. According to this law, 'a man is forbidden to do that, which is destructive of his life, or taketh away the means of preserving the same; and to omit that, by which he thinketh it may be best preserved' (116–17). A man knows or should know that he cannot trust his fellow. Since a covenant, like all contracts, is a voluntary act, this act contradicts the first law of nature. As a consequence 'he which performeth first, does but betray himself to his enemy … .' He is exposing himself to prey which no man is bound to (118, 145). Even stronger, it is 'contrary to the right he can never abandon, of defending his life, and means of living' (125).

Because this type of contract violates the law of nature, it is invalid. In other words, obligation is a consequence of validity in that the latter conditions the former. Did not Hobbes however say that the covenant is obligatory, while at the time it is invalid? It would be silly to presuppose that Hobbes was not aware of this paradox. How can the paradox be solved?

The third law of nature contains a general moral norm that men perform their covenants made (130). Here as elsewhere, Hobbes's nominalistic stance is important. Not every covenant made is to be performed. Therefore, it can be asked what kind of covenants are to be performed? Only those 'where no other law, as in the condition of mere nature, forbiddeth the performance, the covenant is valid' (126–7). This is a necessary condition for the consistency of the whole: only covenants that do not violate the laws of nature are to be performed.

The Laws of Nature Interpreted

The nominalistic premise underpinning the epistemological dimension of the state of nature excludes the existence of an objective semantics required in order for the laws of nature to be effective. Under this semantics, the laws of nature could have a 'natural' or 'real' meaning. In the absence of this semantics, the theory of the covenant is called in.

This theory attempts to neutralise the negative effects of the state of nature. These effects can be summarised as the *bellum omnium contra omnes*. The war of all against all is triggered by conflicts of meaning of the concepts in the laws of nature. The possibilities of conflicts are abundant. Under the fourth law of nature, for example, gratitude comes to 'he which giveth … have no reasonable cause to repent him of his good will.'[46] The fifth law of nature states 'that every man strive to accommodate himself with the rest' (138), while the eighth law says 'that no man by deed, word, countenance, or gesture, declare hatred, or contempt of another.'[47] It is easy to see that 'reasonable cause', 'good will', 'to accommodate oneself with the rest', or 'contempt' are that much open to conflict that they are of no practical use.

The laws of nature could be considered a set of rules of thumb allowing for a peaceful social interaction. Prima facie, if everyone were actually to live according to the laws of nature, there would be peace. None the less, the laws of nature are fulfilled when man is *striving towards* their performance.[48] The striving towards peace, though, is not identical with the achievement of peace.

One way of putting the problem of social life draws on the anthropological dimension of the state of nature. Because man is inclined to follow his own selfish preferences rather than taking his fellows' interests into account, his egoism prevents him from being moral. A different way of putting this problem combines the three dimensions into a different sequence. It brings the nominalist dimension to the fore, and takes in the anthropological and the normative premise as an additional support to Hobbes's construction.

The Politics of Freedom

The three dimensions of the state of nature culminate into Hobbes's theory of political society. Political society emerges as a natural process on the following grounds. First, for Hobbes, unlike for Rousseau, there is no social space preceding political space. Social space and political space are coextensive.

Secondly, Hobbes does not take man as an *animal rationale* that is different from other animals. It was noticed that both man and animals dispose of the capacity of deliberation, according to which both are said to have a will. The will is nothing but the end sum of desires, aversions, hopes and fears after deliberation. Will itself is the last appetite. Appetites are not rational, and hence that qualification 'rational' is not a *differentia specifica* of 'man'.

A result of this, third, is that the end sum of deliberation composed of passions, desires, hopes and fears weighed and balanced against each other is not miraculously transformed into something qualitatively different from its constituent elements. Will is an appetite, a volatile product of a process.

---

46 Ibid.: 121 and 138 (definition of gift, in view of friendship, reputation of charity, magnanimity, and so on).

47 Ibid.: 140, combined with the passion of contempt (40).

48 Ibid.: 146: 'The same Laws [of nature], because they oblige only to a desire, and endeavour … are easie to be observed. For in that they require nothing but endeavour; he that endeavoureth their performance, fulfilleth them … .'

Fourth, therefore, men are drawn into agreement upon the convenient articles of peace as reason suggests (Hobbes 1966c: 116).[49] However, these 'suggestions of reason' are not rationally conclusive. How could they be without having any meaning? They simply draw into agreement, whether they wish or not.

According to this mechanism, men are drawn to lay down their *ius in omnia*, one aspect of which deserves a brief further exploration. It is related to the epistemological premise of Hobbes's nominalism embedded in his theory of the covenant.

Despite his efforts to provide a definition of the concept of a covenant, as it appears, for example, in the third law of nature, Hobbes's definition does not make a concrete covenant exist. The definition contains the necessary, though not sufficient, conditions in order for real covenants to exist. A covenant of mutual trust corresponding to the analytical definition is obligatory; however, it is not really valid. 'Covenant', 'obligation' and 'validity' are analytically related. A conceptual analysis can detect these analytical relations.

Nevertheless, the moral obligation contained in the third law of nature does not say anything about the ontological status of a covenant.

In order for a covenant to exist, that is, to be really valid and hence in order to be really obligatory, something more is needed. As the fountain of justice (ibid.: 130), the third law of nature dictates that men perform their covenants. *A contrario*, the definition of injustice is not to perform a covenant. Hobbes once more plays his nominalist master card. It appears to be the illness as well as the cure. Since concepts do not exist, every man defines the meaning of the law of nature in his own way (epistemological dimension). This fulfils his obligations towards God.

According to the third law of nature, man knows that he is to perform his covenants made. It may seem tautological to add that 'the nature of justice, consisteth in keeping of valid covenants' (ibid.: 131). This addition, though, is just more nominalist grist to the mill. Despite the sophistication of the theory of the contract incorporated into the theory of the laws of nature, an important aspect is missing.

As result of the theory of the covenant we do still not know what a covenant *is*, or when it is *valid*. This occurs only when a covenant is made. However, making covenants that are not backed with the certainty of their performance is a violation of the duties of the law of nature. The only covenant, therefore, that does not qualify as a violation of these duties must be of a self-executing nature. This is what the social contract amounts to.

The reason is not hard to find: the social contract is a self-referential implementation of the theory of the covenant. As a contract of mutual trust according to the definition of the covenant, it is prima facie not permitted under the laws of nature. Its object, however, is 'the constitution of a civil power, sufficient to compel men to keep [their covenants]' (ibid.: 131).The civil power thus constituted by the covenant has this power because it simply *is* this power. As a self-referential implementation of the theory of the covenant, the social contract is

49 See, however, the critique of Pufendorf (1991: 132): 'It is not enough to say here that man is drawn into civil society … .'

self-executing. In addition to being self-executing, it provides the missing premise in order for any covenant to be valid.

Pufendorf

Pufendorf's theory of normativity is similar to Suarez's in that he borrows from the latter his 'double ontology', that is, the differentiation between God's creative will and his imperative will. It is Pufendorf's view that God created man as a rational and social being. Human creatures are different from others, for example, dogs, in that they are capable of changing movements, and suspending or moderating them.[50] This capacity is ingrained with the *entia moralia*, as a certain attribute that is imposed (*superadditum*) on things in order better to direct or temper the freedom of intellectual beings (Pufendorf 1994c: 100).

These attributes are called *entia moralia* because the human mores and actions directed and moderated by them thereby assume a character and aspect different from the unrefined simplicity of the brutes (ibid.: 100). The *entia moralia* – whether imposed by God or by men (ibid.: 101) – are most conveniently defined as certain modes superimposed by intelligent beings to physical things and motions for the special purpose of directing and regulating man's free, voluntary actions, and for giving life a certain order and grace (ibid.: 100). Moral entities are imposed (*superadditum*), and have no substance of their own; neither are the accidents, and they therefore need a substratum in order to make sense at all. Their 'imposed' nature reveals the intervention of an intelligent being, God or man, with the authority to do so.

Entia moralia are not natural things, in that they 'do not arise from the intrinsic substantial principles of things, but are superadded to things already existent and physically complete ... by the will of intelligent beings who alone determine their existence' (ibid.: 100–101). Since they are not natural, and emerge from the intellect in order to serve the distinctive perfection of human life (ibid.: 100), they can be called 'concepts' in the nominalist sense. The latter qualification fits their 'super-imposition', that is, imposed from outside on existing beings. They institutionalise human life in a normative manner.[51]

Therefore, Pufendorf's view is of a complex puzzle involving the classification of persons into private, moral, public, sacred, political, and so on, thus creating a classificatory conceptual network, some elements of which are of special importance for us here. He differentiates between moral entities that are similar to substances which he calls 'moral persons'. A specific sub-category of the latter is

50 Pufendorf 1994c: 100: 'By means of this special light [of the mind] he can more accurately comprehend and compare matters, infer the unknown from the known, and judge of the proper arrangements among things, so that he is not compelled to act always in the same manner but can exert, suspend, or moderate his actions as seems fit.'

51 The term is used by Seidler in his 1994 edition of Pufendorf, that I am using here. It was Jean Barbeyrac who translated Pufendorf's term '*impositio*' as 'institution'.

the composite moral person, called a political state or society. Those unified as a moral person are so united with one another that whatever they do at present or in future by virtue of that union is considered as one will and one action (ibid.: 104). I will not enter here into the detailed distinctions which Pufendorf elaborates in this respect. Suffice it to say the moral entity is that classified as 'operative active moral qualities', and that contains the concepts 'authority', 'right', and 'obligation'.

The authority over persons other than oneself is called sovereignty. 'Sovereignty' is a moral entity or 'institution' imposed by humans, while the creation of the state results from following a divine commandment.

Suarez's differentiation between '*Sein*' and '*Sollen*', discussed above, takes on a new guise, without however being essentially altered. Creation as an act of will and resulting in a specific choice does limit God's commanding power so as not to contradict the social nature of his creature. Having created man like he has, he cannot but command that they have a duty to favour social life (Pufendorf 1994b: 70; 1991: 33–8). Under this view, Pufendorf criticises Grotius' '*appetitus socialis*' because the appetite for society is insufficient in order to carry man into civil society (Pufendorf 1994c: 203–4). The social nature of man, his rationality, self-love and weakness are features of human nature that are to be read as how God must have meant them to work to the advantage of men. Therefore, the fundamental law of nature: 'Any man must, as far as possible, cultivate and maintain toward others a peaceable sociality that is consistent with the native character and end of humankind in general' (ibid.: 152).

In this respect, Pufendorf's theory is of a legalistic brand in a similar manner to that of Hobbes and Suarez. All of them elaborate a theory of political society the beginning of which refers to a divine command. Kant, as we will soon see, maintains the legalistic form in that the beginning of society consists in following a norm, namely the categorical imperative, but without any reference to a divine norm.

It is necessary in this respect to remember the nominalist normative emptiness of the world from which Pufendorf, like Hobbes, drew the consequences regarding the necessity of entering into the social contract. For both, and despite the more rational outlook of their theories, the social contract's ultimate source is a commandment of divine origin. On the basis of the existence of the state as an *ens moralis*, authority – yet another *ens moralis* – is assigned to the supreme sovereignty: ' … civil laws derive their origin from a pact because this is what establishes the supreme sovereignty to which the authority to enact laws in a group subject to it belongs' (Pufendorf 1994b: 59).

Just as political society finds its origin or foundation in a divine command, Pufendorf's legalistic theory also applies to laws. Laws are decrees by which a superior obligates someone subject to himself to direct his actions according to what the superior prescribes (ibid.: 58). The reason for a commandment is not some general or specific good; it is the mere will of the commander. Here as elsewhere, Pufendorf's theory generously draws on the nominalist source. Obligation becomes the criterion for morality. An action is morally good or morally bad depending on its compliance or failure to comply with a norm,[52] and not on realising something good or bad: 'Goodness denotes merely conformity with the law ... ' (ibid.: 31).

This reminds us of the nominalist sources of legalism as we saw in the beginning of this chapter. Like Duns Scotus and Ockham, Pufendorf argues that law is good because it is prescribed. The moral goodness of an act, as in Ockham, does not depend on the will's natural orientation towards the good, just like the act of knowledge can be independent of the existence of the thing known. He claims that 'honest' and 'dishonest', 'good' and 'bad' do not exist and make no sense 'before the law', that is, before the institution of a superior (Pufendorf 1994c: 129, § 3). Pufendorf therefore espouses the premise of an omnipotent God who is indifferent as to the external determination of his power, for example, by a *lex aeterna*. This indeed would contradict with his omnipotence and his sovereign freedom to create the world as he pleases. Pufendorf's normative theory, like that of Ockham and Hobbes, articulates a morally indifferent universe. It is this morally indifferent universe or the normatively empty world as I have called it, that connects Pufendorf's work to the new scientific presentation of a physical world without any normative dimension. This again confirms his close connection to nominalism.

The above considerations provide a better hold on Pufendorf's legalistic position. Obligation, that is, limits the will and imposes the requirement to make some performance. In the field of law, the obligation is incurred by a voluntary submission to one whose directions are accepted (Pufendorf 1994b: 59; 1994c: 119–28). The obligation to obey the law, and to act in conformity with it, preceded by the obligation to enter into a state by means of the social contract, have the same structure: they involve a vertical subjection to the will of a superior (God, the sovereign or another person to whom one is committed). Obligation is the result of a vertical subjection to the will of a superior, and not of a connection to some end.

Here the principle of legality gains its full weight. It provides the measure for the fulfilment of the obligation. Compliance with an externally imposed norm is the ultimate criterion according to which human action will be evaluated. The principle of legality, and its exclusive concern with external behaviour, pre-echoes Kant's separation of law and morality, thus articulating the very essence of legalism.

---

52 Pufendorf 1994b: 27 and 30: 'Actions in accordance with law are called good [*bonus*]; contrary to law bad [*malus*]. For an action to be good, I must be totally in accordance with law; for an action to be bad, it need only be deficient on a single point.'

Kant

While Hobbes and Pufendorf still drew on natural law in their theory of law, Kant's project is to purging law of anything like that. We learned from nominalism that only individual things exist, and that action is the result of an imposed norm. In its theological version, the norms are commandments of God. In this sense, I have proposed calling the nominalist version of Divine law the Ten Commandments, while in the realistic version they can be called the Decalogue. God's sovereign freedom gave him the power to command as he wishes. He could thus command his subjects to hate him, to steal and to rape, and so on.

Kant's position as to theoretical knowledge is not straightforward 'nominalist', in that he does not hold that 'things' do not exist. What he means by 'things' are that what makes them 'things', that is, their essence. He does not argue that essences do not exist; he only claims they cannot be known. In that respect, the result of his theoretical position is similar, though not identical, to the nominalist claim that essences do not exist '*extra mentem*'. The fact that they cannot be known is a logical consequence of his position that should throw off the shackles of dependence on revelation or religion – that is, to get rid of revelation or religion as a source of knowledge and action (Kant 1996: 35). '*Dinge an sich*' for their part can exist, but their existence is a matter of faith. Knowledge of them is, however, impossible. On this idea, Kant constructs a nominalist theory of knowledge determined by the a priori rules of the mind, and so gears it to the anti-teleological a priori method inaugurated by Descartes.

As for practical reason, Kant's position draws on the a priori morals proper to the Modern philosophical project. They were the consequence of the normative emptiness of the world according to nominalism. Kant's position is therefore of the utmost relevance for legalism.

In this respect, Kant pushes Pufendorf's position a step further. For Pufendorf, normativity or the moral quality of an act consists in its *conformity* with the law. From the perspective of moral theory, this is not enough for Kant. An action can only be moral if it is willed because of the law, that is, for the law's own sake.[53] Rational beings are capable of representing the law, not only in order to conform their action to it but as the legislators of these laws.[54] Moral actions therefore present the will that accomplishes them as the object of an immediate respect. Unlike for Pufendorf, 'imposition' is not necessary. This would, on Kant's view, be a violation of human autonomy and dignity.

---

53 Pufendorf 1994c: 129: 'It must be noted here, however, that for an action to be good it is necessary both that it agree with the law regarding all its material requisites, so to speak, and that as far as its formal aspect is concerned it be performed not out of ignorance or from some other cause, but in order to render to the law the obedience owed to it.'

54 Kant 1997: 39 (articulating the third practical principle of the will, that is, the idea of the will of every rational being as a will giving instituting a universal law).

Moral legislation involves the universalisation of the maxims of action so that I must be able to wish that my maxim could be a universal law. Moral agents, therefore, are both rule followers and legislators. As legislators, they also follow rules, in that not simply every maxim can become a law. Only maxims that do not lead into contradiction upon universalisation can. Therefore, moral action results from the dual compliance of the action with the rule thus created, and its compliance with the categorical imperative in creating this rule. This is what Kant's legalism amounts to, and I will briefly comment upon it in the following pages.

Kant's purification of the metaphysic of morals aims at a critique of pure practical reason (Kant 1997: 52). It articulates will as a type of causality, and no longer as the total sum of desires like in Hobbes. Causality has a twofold dynamics, that is, from outside to inside and from inside to outside. The former involves a determination of the will by causes foreign or external to the actor. From that perspective, the will is caught up in natural necessity. Out of natural necessity, the cause is independent of the consequence. The will is therefore heteronymous in as far as the actor himself does not determine it. This is the negative concept of freedom (ibid.: 52).

The idea of freedom is inseparably connected with the autonomy of the will or the positive concept of freedom. Just as theoretical reason does not know things in themselves, the autonomous agent has to presuppose a self 'behind himself', whatever it may be of itself.[55] The Kantian subject is a rational subject that has, like for Descartes, a capacity for representation. It does not represent his own desires or conceptions of freedom that it then tries to realise in the world. Kant's is a rather non-substantive idea of autonomy; this is because subjects are not 'real', autonomous pre-social units that are then assembled in order to make a state. Rather, their autonomy as an aspect of their rational nature allows them to represent how rational decisions are made. On this idea, their action is guided by the representation of laws.[56]

In representing himself as a transcendental subject, the rational actor must consider himself as belonging to both the sensible world and the intelligible world, of which he has no further cognisance (Kant 1997: 56). Because reason is required in order to derive actions from laws, will is nothing else but practical reason. Will is the faculty to choose that what only reason and not inclinations, far less circumstances, indicate as practically necessary (ibid.: 24). 'Good' can only be a classification of the will, not of something belonging to the external world. In this respect, Kant's approach is of a nominalist brand. The good will is what is required in order to perform a moral action, that is, an action in *conformity* with law out of *respect* for the law.

---

55 Ibid.: 56; Habermas 1996b: 158: ' … the ego qua a subject capable of moral action is a thing-in-itself and thus eludes cognition … .'

56 Kant 1997: 24, cf. Rawls 1971: 516: ' … acting autonomously is acting from principles that we would consent to as free and equal rational beings' (this again does not say what we are, but what we are supposed to be if the procedure were rational).

The moral quality of an act, that is to say, depends on its legality. This classification follows from Kant's effort to separate normative action from divine commandment, or to establish morality independently from theology. The reverse side of this operation is, however, a paradox: the subject of the act is so autonomous that it does not really exist. Not that this is a problem for Kant, since the empirical self is not the focus of his attention. The moral quality of the act as legality requires the transcendental subject as its necessary condition. The real or empirical self is an epiphenomenon or a by-product of transcendental philosophy.

In theoretical thinking, the world is narrowed to the appearance through which we receive representations of the world. Because what there is to know can only be known as representation – excluding knowledge of the *Dinge an sich* – knowledge is essentially representational. Any subject therefore would also be given through representation. The subject who represents must therefore be a transcendental condition and not a being within the world, as subject qua subject.

In practical as well as in theoretical thinking, representation does not represent self-present beings or substantive subjects with concrete interests. Subjects again are not knowable 'things' in the world, and autonomy is a feature of moral individuals rather than a description of decision making. Representation does not express a pre-existing self. In the absence of a moral nature of the subject, subjects must be represented in the political process. It is only through representation that the subject comes to its self, in that he is self-formatting through the political process. Autonomy again is the necessary condition in order for representation to operate. The knowing subject, like the autonomously acting subject, is not within the world but the condition upon which knowledge and action are deemed possible.

However, Kant's legalistic morality boils down to the fact that the morality of an act consists of the relationship between actions and the autonomy of the will, that is, the universal legislation that is made possible by the maxims of that will (Kant 1997: 45–6).

The conformity of an action out of respect for the law is the essence of legalism. The absolute good will – say, that of a saint – always acts in this manner. Therefore, says Kant, the saint always acts out of duty and does not require any constraint. Rational beings should consider themselves as belonging to the intelligible world, the virtual world (ibid.: 56), where the agent acts on the mere grounds of respect for the moral law. Agents, however, as sensible beings, also belong to the sensible world. The will of human beings who are also partially empirical beings is not always absolutely good in relation to the principle of autonomy. Given the absence of an absolutely good will, there is a need of moral constraint, which Kant calls 'obligation' (ibid.: 46). Its principles must be found a priori in the mere concepts of pure reason (ibid.: 4). Normative action out of respect for the norm is Kant's version of legalism in morality to begin with. It is extended into political space.

The foundation of political space for Hobbes and Pufendorf resulted in the establishment of the institution 'state' following a divine commandment. For Kant, on the contrary, it is based on a moral duty, an 'ought to will' in accordance with and out of respect for the moral law. The duty is structured as a categorical imperative that gives it a universal form, without however being of source of knowledge of duty.[57] Since the moral law formally and exclusively determines will, independently of its content the latter cannot be determined by any pre-existent or given norm either. As a mere form, the categorical imperative is empty. One wills, therefore, because of will itself. Will, that is, has become reflexive in taking itself as an object of willing.

The moral quality of an action, therefore, does not result from its moral content per se. It is the consequence of a formal operation of universalisation, without which the action cannot be moral at all. Put differently, if the subject wills some content, the moral character of the latter does not primarily depend on this will but on universalisablility of the content. Through universalisation, the content receives the form of a law that connects it to truth.

According to this formal theory of morality, the classical formula of the law 'suum cuique tribuere', as it is found in Aquinas (1910: II-ll, q. 58, a. 1), is expressed by Kant in an imperative form: 'honeste vive, neminem laede, suum cuique tribue' (Kant 1996: 29). This imperative form then is transformed into another imperative. To begin with, one *must* leave the state of nature, following which one *ought to* enter into a state in which everybody can be assured, as far as his 'own' is concerned, against anybody else. To leave the state of nature or the civil state and to contribute to the constitution of the State is a moral duty (ibid.: § 41 and § 49). The moral argument amounts to a moral duty of the individual to transform himself into a citizen, and so to transform his pre-legal rights and duties into legal rights and duties (ibid.: § 44). It is a duty imposed by the categorical imperative, as an a priori norm of reason. The imperative is connected to the idea of law itself, and the state can therefore only be the legal state (ibid.: § 45).[58]

According to his view of the state, the common purpose of the contract partners is a matter of duty, and not (as Kant interprets Hobbes) a matter of fact. The Kantian theory thus conceptually connects freedom with law, that has a universal form and that expresses itself in the universality of the categorical imperative. His theory of law, like Rawls', is based on universal principles of reason. In consequence,

57 Kant 1996: § 44,§ 42,§ 49, where the duty to enter into the State is related to the categorical imperative.

58 Hegel (1991: § 258) pushes the moral argument somewhat further. He argues that not only does one have a moral duty to leave the state of nature, as in Kant, but that the moral duty consists of being a member of the State. The State with its general will pre-exists individuals (ibid.: § 257) and is not the result of a social contract, but an emanation of reason itself. For Hegel, the interest of the subject, rational or otherwise, no longer counts. The existence of the State in no way depends on the subject's will, neither for its creation, nor for its continuing existence.

freedom as the *principium* of law will be universal, or *conceptual.* Freedom, according to Kant, is the 'independence' or autonomy of the individual.

The practical problem arising in the Modern philosophical project is how to reconcile the independent agents acting according to conceptions of freedom with others. This is, according to Kant, the function of the law. With regard to the moral duty to leave the state of nature, in which all men are independent individuals, the law's function is to conciliate the individuals' *arbitrium* with the others' according to a universal law of freedom (Kant 1996: 24–5). In that respect, Kant establishes a conceptual link between freedom and law. It is the law that makes freedom possible. Freedom thus is freedom according to the law (Kant 1997: 52–3), according to which we will what we ought to will.

Kant's enterprise of conceiving a metaphysics of morals including a philosophy of right is built upon the categorical imperative. The dualism he marked between the agent's empirical nature and his rationality marks out the difference between 'morality' and 'state law' more clear. Given their duty to subsume their natural inclinations under the ethical law, Kant seems to erase this dualism. If all agents were willing to bring their natural inclinations into line with the moral law, the institution of the state would be superfluous. But human agents are no saints. They are not all willing to comply with the moral law by themselves. Therefore a state is needed to force them to do what they do not do voluntarily.

While the foundation of the state is related to the categorical imperative, obedience to the laws of the state may take a different form. External compliance with the law independently of the agent's motive is what Kant calls 'legality' in legal matters (Kant 1996: 20). This marks out a clear difference between moral legalism (act in accordance with the moral law out of respect for it, and act in such a manner that your maxim can at the same time become a universal law (ibid.: 17) and legal legalism which claims that one must act externally in such a manner that the free use of one's discretion can coexist with the freedom of all others under a general law. It follows that both morality and law operate in a legalistic manner, albeit in different ways. Positive law turns out to be a fine-tuning of the categorical imperative, and both state and laws are founded on the categorical imperative (ibid.: § 45).

It can be concluded from the above that Kant's view on morality and law incorporates a legalistic mechanism in that under both following rules is what the agent has to do. Therefore, in concretising the categorical imperative, the metaphysics of morals, including the theory of right, is organised as a system in which rules take the lead in determining one's moral and legal duties. Following these rules out of respect for the moral law, or externally conforming to them, with or without external force from the state, is all the agent has to do.

Conclusion

In this chapter, I have argued that legalism is related to a specific metaphysics, viz. nominalism. Following the exploration of the philosophical and theological aspects of nominalism, it was concluded that divine omnipotence as interpreted by Ockham and his followers involves the absolute freedom of God. God's absolute freedom entails that he is indifferent as to values, and hence the world he created is normatively empty. A result of the nominalist or logical interpretation of divine omnipotence, God can only create individuals that, in turn, are also free. The freedom of human beings is externally limited by God's commandments.

This provided us with the premises of the Modern philosophical project, the beginning of which is usually associated with Descartes. Descartes, however, finds himself confronted with a theory in which rationalism, individualism and freedom are conceptually related, due to the nominalist interpretation of divine omnipotence.

A consequence of the metaphysics of legalism (that is, nominalism), normative behaviour fits with Judith Shklar's idea of legalism, that is, the ethical attitude that claims moral conduct to be a matter of rule following and moral relationships to consist of duties and rights determined by rules. The rule following attitude is embedded in the metaphysical theory that I have explored in this chapter, since human creatures must follow the norms commanded by God. Law as a commandment is what characterises the work of late mediaeval and modern philosophers, and causes a rift between classical legal philosophy under the auspices of Aristotelian realism and modern legal philosophy premised on nominalism.

In this respect, Suarez's work is of crucial importance, in that he made an attempt to reinterpret Aquinas' work in the light of Ockham's nominalism. In doing so, he tried to overcome the split that occurred in ontology between realism and nominalism. His ontology, however, in differentiating between the realm of '*Sein*' and of '*Sollen*', inspired his successors to elaborate further the nominalist premises of pre-modern (or post-mediaeval) philosophy.

This thesis is further illustrated in the work of Hobbes, Pufendorf and Kant respectively. All three take into consideration the necessity of constructing a state via a social contract. This construction in turn is itself the result of rule-following behaviour. In other words, the establishment of the institution 'state', with the help of the social contract in any of its versions as well as the internal operation of the state, involve the same mechanism of rule following.

Hobbes's nominalist epistemology ties in with his anthropology (*homo homini lupus*) and combines it with the weakly normative laws of nature. The latter are commands of God, the following of which results in the conclusion of the social contract. The laws of the sovereign in turn determine what is good and just, and the morality of human action is limited to following these rules.

Following Suarez, Pufendorf elaborates the distinction between '*Sein*' and '*Sollen*', or God's creative and imperative will. God created man as a social being, who must enter into a social contract in accordance with that. This results in following a norm imposed by God. Once the state has been created, the latter's commandments are to be followed, whatever their content. This is Pufendorf's nominalist aspect. His legalist position, on the other hand, involves arguing that obligation merely consists in the following of norms, compliance with which makes an action moral. Kant's theory for his part was called the essence of legalism, in that normative action requires not only conformity to a norm, but conformity to it out of respect for the norm.

Chapter 2
The Individual in Context

Descartes' Project

In the previous chapter, it was argued that individualism is the necessary consequence of the nominalist interpretation of God's omnipotence. Since God is omnipotent, he is radically simple. His will therefore cannot be distinguished from his intelligence. This makes God totally, that is, absolutely, free. This freedom gives rise to the radical contingency of the world. In order to understand the beginning of Modernity correctly, it is necessary to clarify the position of Descartes, who is not the only father of Modernity.

Descartes on the one hand espouses some aspects of the nominalist interpretation of God's omnipotence. In doing so, he takes sides with Aquinas and the Scholastics. Furthermore, Descartes' ontological position shows nominalist traces, for example, on the nature of numbers (Descartes 1996j: rules 58–9). On the other hand, he draws on the Augustinian notion that truth exists and is to be found within the subject. According to this exercise of introspection, as Hegel reads Descartes (Hegel 1955: 126–7, cf. Husserl 1996: 19), the subject becomes aware of his awareness; this is the establishment of the *cogito*. Descartes' *cogito* therefore is both in line with and a reaction against the nominalist view, more specifically the scepticism embedded in knowledge which was discussed in chapter 1. While the vast majority of scholarly literature reads Descartes as a realist, some of it does not exclude a nominalist influence.[1] It is the nominalist aspects that I would like to stress in the following pages, without, that is, any making claim to exhaustiveness.

Within the nominalist metaphysics, the transcendental relationship between the knowing subject and known object is erased from philosophical discourse. It must be reframed, since philosophy is no longer oriented towards the structure of reality that it seeks to decipher. Philosophy, that is, is assigned the task of structuring reality, and thus substitutes epistemology, morals, and politics for the transcendentals that belong to the structure of reality according to metaphysical realism. Structuring reality as opposed to discovering reality's structure is a dynamic activity instead of static *theorein* or vision. It requires intervention by the human mind, the importance of which has come about from both the philosophical

1 Rodis-Lewis 1971. Gilson (1987: 128–56) argues in favour of a double influence on Descartes of Scotus and Augustine, more specifically where the primacy of the will over the intellect is clear. This allows for the qualification that Descartes had at least some nominalist tendencies.

and the theological versions of nominalism. This again has already been explored in the previous chapter.

The nominalist claim regarding the inexistence of universals within an extra-mental reality requires an onto-theological repositioning of the human self. This repositioning involves a new articulation of the relationship between man and the world as well as between man and others. Because of the radical contingency of the world, this repositioning calls for a new strategy. This strategy consists of the search for an origin or self-referring beginning that provides the basis or foundation for knowledge and action.

The main line of this strategy is the exploitation of the self-referential nature of reason, both theoretical and practical. The self-referential nature of reason relates to the fact that theoretical thinking can be the object of theoretical thinking. In practical terms, it means that freedom is to be exercised in freedom, which is the upshot of the contingent nature of the world. If freedom is not exercised in freedom, there is no freedom.

Descartes takes a special place in this new strategy. He lines up with Ockham on this point. Ockham argues that after abandoning of the concept 'relation' in the ontological sense and the critique of the Scholastic theory of the reciprocal causes, it is possible to attain true knowledge of a non-existing object. Knowledge, however, can only be true when it corresponds to reality. Yet the possibility of God causing knowledge of a non-existing object is a source of confusion which leads to scepticism. Ontologically true knowledge, that is, knowledge corresponding to reality, is therefore dependent upon God's *non*-interference as a primary cause. Since it is not known whether or not God interferes – except in the case of miracles – it is not certain whether certain knowledge – intuitive knowledge is always certain – is also ontologically true. If the object known does not exist, the correspondence between a proposition and reality does not exist. Just as Augustine reacted to the scepticism of the Academics, Descartes assigned himself the task of meeting the scepticism that nominalism leaves in its wake.

In this respect, Descartes walks on the path trodden by Ockham who established the possibility of knowledge of a non-existing object *de potentia absoluta dei*. The radical contingency resulting from that can be taken to be one of the motives for Descartes' philosophical investigation. Knowledge, that is, can be true without having any relationship with reality, which is clear when the object does not exist.

The intuitions we have need not come from reality, because God can cause directly (*de potentia absoluta*) those intuitions that are normally the effect of secondary causes (*de potentia ordinata*). Whether it is caused by God or by the object, intuitive knowledge is always true.

Ockham paved the way for Descartes' epistemology with this formulation of the nominalist position, that is, the view that it is possible to gain knowledge of non-existent objects.

Descartes' method aims to provide a remedy for this scepticism. He searches for rational certainty using a method that aims to determine its origin (Wintgens 2006a). I therefore propose classifying this method as a *quaestio originis*, or quest for the origin as a certain and self-referring beginning on the mere use of natural reason. The search for an origin as a self-referential beginning provides philosophers with an anchor point or foundation for their thinking. For this reason, it is also labelled 'foundationalism', the details of which will be discussed later.

According to the standard interpretation of the beginning of Modernity, Descartes is sitting at the fireplace watching a piece of wax. The wax changes colour, odour, form and size, and hence Descartes concludes that he cannot know through vision, touch, or imagination what the wax is. Indubitable knowledge of the nature of the wax can only be conceived by the mind as 'extension' (Descartes 1996i: 26).

His search for the Archimedean point, one indubitable certainty, is accompanied by the possibility of a *malingenius spiritus* that could cheat him. The evil spirit is Descartes' version of nominalist knowledge of the non-existing object, with God as its primary cause. If some evil spirit were to attempt to deceive him while he is thinking, Descartes would still none the less be thinking. If he is right in thinking that he exists, then he exists. If he errs in thinking that he exists or doubts his existence, then he likewise exists. He can not think that he does not exist.[2] He cannot think either that he is dead. In other words, to hold that he thinks, but does not exist, is patently impossible. Therefore, if he thinks, he exists. *Cogito ergo sum*. The *cogito* resists any possible doubt and is therefore even more certain than mathematics.[3] Apart from its certainty, the *cogito* is also ontologically true. It is therefore an absolute beginning for philosophy. *Absolutus* means 'disconnected from everything'.

In addition to the existence of the subject, Descartes provides a proof of God's existence. God causes in us the idea of perfection. The idea we have of a perfect being involves its existence, without which it would be less perfect. Therefore God exists. This is a second certainty that involves ontological truth (Descartes 1996i: 27–42).

However, the possibility of error remains because we err in our judgements as to the clarity and distinction of an idea. We are, however, not systematically misled in our strong tendency to believe that an external reality corresponds to our ideas because of God's veracity.[4] While natural reason reveals no inherent necessity for

---

2 Descartes' debt to St Augustine is important, if not overwhelming. In a similar vein to Descartes, Augustine (32: II, 3) argues against the sceptics of the New Academy of his days. The one truth though of which we are immediately certain, according to Augustine, is the fact of our own existence.

3 One can indeed doubt even mathematical demonstrations: Descartes 1996j: 26–7.

4 Descartes 1996j, nrs. 5 and 29; 1996i: 42–50. If an omnipotent God exists, he has the power to deceive his creatures. And if I am the creation of a less than omnipotent being, there is all the more reason to believe that I am not perfect. However, Descartes argues that an omnipotent being has the power to deceive me, yet cannot want it, because the will to deceive is a sign of imperfection which does not fit God's nature.

external reality to exist, it is not logically impossible either. The combination of the correct use of reason and God's veracity therefore leads to truth.

Reaching truth, however, is conditional on the correct exercise of the will. Assent can only be given to those ideas that are clear and distinct. Freedom in matters of knowledge, and therefore liberation from authority, entails the possibility of withholding assent in case of doubt. These conditions, like the determination of the nature of the outside world as extension, are established on the certainty of the *cogito*, that is, inside the mind. In that respect again Descartes is close to nominalism.

Philosophy begins with a reflection on the method. Ockham's method denied ontological value to universals outside the mind on logical grounds. This logical method finds a prolongation in Descartes' methodological approach, under which philosophy is reduced to what the subject can know with certainty. Only what is certain can be relied upon; probability is no option. Only what the subject can know with certainty can have ontological value.

Descartes' is a methodological approach that withdraws intuitive knowledge from divine causation and connects it to the subject's mind. Following Ockham, intuitive knowledge is always true; yet it is not clear whether it is caused by the object or directly by God. Descartes therefore strengthens the truth condition of the intuition by requiring it to be as clear and distinct as the *cogito*. According to this condition, we know that what is certain or objectively true is also ontologically true. Certain knowledge therefore is the key to ontological truth.

This shows a double perspective in Descartes to which I referred above. He adopts a realist perspective, in that truth in the ontological sense can be reached. He also adopts a nominalist perspective, in that knowledge of truth begins with the certainty of an idea for the subject. The certainty of the subject is related to the clarity and distinction of an idea he finds within himself where it has been laid down by God. This again is the realist dimension. It is, however, the subject that finds these ideas in himself. God is the cause, that is, the reason why ideas exist in the mind, and as such he is external to the subject. The *esse objectivum* of ideas, however, is in the subject's mind. Here as elsewhere, Ockham pre-echoes Descartes' reflection on method, that is, epistemology as preceding and preparing access to reality. Despite the usual labelling of Descartes as a realist, there are reasons for considering him to have been influenced by nominalism.

Under the standard interpretation of the beginning of Modernity, reason reveals itself to the subject. The standard interpretation joins the scholastic idea of truth upon which *veritas index sui*. Truth comes wrapped with certainty. The standard interpretation is no doubt induced by Descartes' style, since he gives only a limited number of references that make it hard to discover the sources that have influenced him. According to this interpretation, Descartes' methodological doubt seems to be a radically new approach in the history of philosophy. This contributes to labelling him as 'the father of Modern philosophy'.

According to the above, and without denying the novelty and importance of his work, Descartes is thoroughly connected to the past, and his firm position on overcoming scepticism was inherited from nominalism. In that respect, it can be said that he is *searching for* certainty, which amounts to withholding a specific type of rationality. Descartes' search for certainty may be related to historical circumstances in that economic depression, religious wars, the Reformation and the Counter-Reformation triggered the beginning of the Modern philosophical project as a search for certainty (Toulmin 1990: Chapter 1).

These perspectives combine with the nominalist tradition with which Descartes familiarised himself through his reading of Suarez, into a more general framework. Descartes' thus searches for rational certainty in order to secure man's position against the omnipotent God.

Descartes' search for certainty is therefore a search for an origin, that is, a self-referring beginning for knowledge, making man, epistemologically speaking, independent of God. Having identified this origin, he set out his program for a rational explanation of reality.

According to the articulation of *veritas index sui* in the standard interpretation, certainty is logically prior to truth. Whenever an idea is clearly and distinctly conceived, it is certain. Certainty is the hallmark of knowledge, and knowledge is the key to reality or truth.

Under this reading, however, the subject is disconnected from the world. This disconnection is the price paid for the ontological truth of knowledge. The a-contextual disembedded subject (Ricoeur 1990: 16–18) and the ontological truth of certain knowledge are two sides of the same coin. If it is truth that is searched for, it may be the case that some truth is certain while other truth is only probable. Probable truth, however, is not an option for Descartes (Descartes 1996j: nr 2) as it was for Aristotle.

Descartes finds a rock in the methodological approach of doubting. It is not the rock on which Wittgenstein's spade is curbing; it is the Archimedean point to which he can anchor with certainty (Descartes 1996i: 18–26). Having doubting the whole of reality, Descartes is left with one undeniable connection that cannot be deconstructed through his doubt. That connection is so certain that it serves as the anchor point and as the criterion for the soundness of the further argument. The anchor point is 'I', connected to thinking. Doubting is a form of thinking; while doubting the certainty of the subject's existence emerges from thinking itself (Descartes 1996h: 33).

However, the application of methodological doubt involves the use of a method of problem solving that was articulated beforehand. Descartes searches for certainty. The certainty he discovers throughout doubting is that, while doubting, he exists as a thinking being. To think is the manifestation of being. From knowing *that* he is doubting to knowing *how* he is – he is thinking – provides him with the certainty of *what* he is.

Descartes' Subject

A familiar critique of the *cogito* focuses on the substantialisation of the subject. From the subject's certainty of thinking, Descartes' argument establishes the existence of the subject's existence. The argument makes a conceptual leap by claiming that it follows from the existence of the subject that it is thinking substance. In doing so, 'identity' takes over from the scholastic 'substance' as a manner of identifying beings (Hintikka 1962; Descartes 1996i: 27). Another statement of this position is to state that Descartes concludes to the nature of the self as a substance starting from one of its aspects.[5] This shift or jump is left unquestioned, with the result that it is supposed to form part of the self-evidence of the starting point.

Another line of critique follows from the connection of certainty and truth and the logical priority of the former to the latter. While truth can exist on its own, since it does not need any subject in order to exist, certainty for its part does not exist independently of the subject. Certainty that is, is certainty *of* something *for* someone. I shall return to this in the next section.

Third, and furthermore, the existence of other subjects can only be deduced from a clear and distinct idea of them. From this idea, the conclusion follows that they exist. Experience of others as an original fact is excluded.[6] This raises a problem as to the ontological status of the other.

The conclusion that the other exists can be drawn on an analogy with Descartes' own experience. The analogy, however, involves a second leap, because Descartes has no access to any other person's thinking upon which to conclude that they exist. Descartes, in other words, cannot think for the other. Avoiding the second leap must result in the conclusion that the other exists but only as an object. This conclusion again corroborates the disembeddedness of the individual as a subject.

The only philosophically relevant relationship that the subject has with others is of the same nature as his relationship with objects. He can have true knowledge of the objects to which this relationship is limited. The existence of others is analogous to the existence of objects. This type of relationship is another aspect of epistemologised philosophy. The ontological status of the other as an object within the framework of epistemologised philosophy comes together with the subject's own ontological status as a thinking substance. Because the truth relating to himself can only be based on cognitive certainty, the most that his rational capacities allow him to conclude is that *he* exists while thinking.

---

5 Descartes 1996i: 19: 'je suis j'existe' est nécessairement vrai.' See also ibid.: 20, where he argues that thinking is an attribute of the self; the nature of a substance can be known via its attributes; thinking is inseparable from the mind; therefore I am a thinking thing.

6 Since I have only representations of others resembling me, like I have of corporal or inanimated things, angels, or animals, via ideas, see Descartes 1996i: 34.

The above comments articulate the two points at the heart of this chapter. The first is a critique of the existence of the subject as a thinking substance. The second is the subject's ontological separation from others.

Both of these points coincide in the interpretation presented below. The *cogito* is a manifestation of the self, though not identical to it. The self, that is, is not a substance which gains access to itself and concludes its own existence.[7] It is only through its manifestation or performance that the subject gains access to himself and others. The self, in other words, manifests itself throughout a process (Hintikka 1962: 16). According to this distinction, so I will argue, the substantial self can be left behind, and we can explore the contours of the 'individual in context'.

Critique of the *Cogito*

It may be recalled that chapter 1 discussed the shift from realism to nominalism. According to nominalism, only the individual has ontological value. The paradoxical consequence of this shift is that only the *individual* has *universal* value. Therefore, the ontological anchoring of the individual subject in the Cartesian *cogito* requires, from the very beginning, that the subject be thought of in universal terms, that is, as a substance.

In consequence, the universalisation of the subject prevents the subject itself from being thought of within a perspective of historical situatedness, that is, from a participants' perspective or from a context he shares with others. What cannot be thought of in connection with the first certainty of the subject, the *cogito*, does, for that reason, not exist. It does not belong to the order of reason. The subject as it appears in the *cogito* is, from the very outset, ontologically anchored as an individual. The identity of the subject as an individual is based on an identification of the subject as a thinking substance as a matter of truth. Put differently, if the *identity* of the subject is a mere matter of truth, and if it is ultimately framed in opposition to the object, then this opposition can turn out to be helpful in elucidating an alternative to the subject's substantive identity.

Critical of scholasticism as he is, Descartes, however, relies on substantialist thinking in order to identify the subject as a thinking substance. This is one way of putting the matter. The identification of the *res cogitans*, however, is supplemented with a relationship of opposition, that is, the opposition between what is a 'subject' and what is not. The latter attains its identity, as a *res extensa*, as a function of what it is not, that is, a *res cogitans*. The *res extensae* are mere extensions, and lack the thinking essence that would make them a *res cogitantes*.

The identification of the subject as a *res cogitans*, so Descartes claims, is ontologically true. Once we consider this claim from the point of view of meaning,

---

7 In this sense, Aquinas (1889: q. X, 12, ad 7) : 'Nullus potest cogitare se non esse cum assensu: in hoc enim quod cogitat aliquid, percipit se esse', see also Hintikka 1962 for further references.

and not merely of truth, two additional aspects emerge. The first is that the meaning of the identity of the subject is related to what it is not, that is, a *res extensa*. The second aspect arises in terms of a question. If the subject's existence is certain, it is certain that he exists. But what is the status of others? What role do they play in the subject's life and consciousness?

Phenomenological philosophy, mainly under the impulse of Husserl, has criticised Descartes' subject on this point because it involves 'pure consciousness', that is, 'consciousness of consciousness' as the origin of philosophy and its further development. Yet, consciousness is never pure, it is always consciousness *of* something which lies beyond consciousness. Certainty for its part is certainty *for* someone. In addition to that, Descartes has endowed the individual with consciousness of his own existence, excluding the existence of others as 'thinking beings' that have some relationship with the thinking substance. In the following sections, I will focus on Husserl's critique of Descartes, and his adoption of intersubjectivity. Paul Ricoeur and George Herbert Mead, each from their own perspective, provide complements to this critique that turn out to be useful in the context of this chapter on the subject in context. I will comment on their theories after focusing on Husserl.

Husserl on Intersubjectivity[8]

Like Descartes, Husserl is of the opinion that knowledge requires an absolute and certain foundation. While Descartes included in his meditations the method of logic, the certainty of which is unquestionable, Husserl broadens the activity of the *cogito* to an unlimited range of experiences. In a similar vein to Descartes, he starts searching for a first truth (or a number of them) upon which he can build his universal science (36). This type of truth must not only be self-evident, but must be apodictic, that is, absolutely incontrovertible (37). In this respect, the existence of the world – despite our daily business with and in it – does not have the apodictic certainty required (40).

The suspension of the belief in the existence of the world leaves the subject with phenomena of the world, including his body and others. Perception is possible without presupposing that the world exists. According to this 'transcendental epochè' (46), the subject withdraws within himself and his consciousness becomes consciousness of the world as phenomena (47). The pure ego and his cogitations have priority over natural existence that is bracketed. This 'bracketing' or *epochè* involves the ego focusing on his internal transcendental and phenomenological experiences of phenomena. In this respect, the certainty provided in the internal transcendental experience is not limited to 'I am'. It enables a universal and apodictic structure of the transcendental experiences of the ego. In contrast to the sterility of Descartes' *cogito*, Husserl aims to broaden the infinite field of the transcendental experience (62).

8 Figures between brackets refer to page numbers in Husserl 1996.

As for Descartes, the evidence of 'ego cogito' in Husserl is apodictic, or absolutely certain (50). However, following George Herbert Mead, whose work will be discussed below, he takes the side of the substantive *cogito* or *ego* as 'substantia cogitans' (51). Like Descartes, Husserl deals with the problem of how other egos can be articulated, given the method of *epochè*. His point, however, is to arrive at a philosophical theory in which others are included, that is, a phenomenology of transcendental intersubjectivity (61).

Husserl's approach to consciousness is critical of Descartes' version in the following sense. My interpretation of Descartes suggested that truth can exist in and of itself, while certainty is always certainty of something for someone. However, Husserl considers consciousness to be 'intentional', that is, consciousness of something (64). Husserl therefore comes up with a thicker and richer version of consciousness, in that it involves the presence of a universe (70) that is always present within the unity of consciousness (70). The transcendental reduction accordingly involves the subject remaining in his natural attitude; however, the only objects of the transcendental phenomenologist's universal descriptive observations are the 'intentional correlatives of modalities of consciousness' (70). With consciousness being 'consciousness of something', Husserl unlike Descartes, is able to differentiate between the 'cogito' and 'cogitatum' (74). Different states of consciousness allow for a synthesis by the *cogito*, thus allowing for an identification of the experiences as the fundamental form of synthesis.

Consciousness of something through experiences of the *cogito* provides a panoply of contents. These contents are not fixed, in that the actual intention is supplemented with potentialities concerning the same object. A more penetrating consideration of the correlate of consciousness allows for a deeper insight into thinking itself (which has, unlike Descartes, many variations and perspectives – like immediate memory, pre-perceptive expectations, and so on (91), and is not limited to mathematics). In this way, the objective sense of 'cogitatum' or 'what is thought of' can be constituted for each and every category of objects which can be presented as 'the same' (91) throughout the variations of the modes of consciousness.

The constitution of an object or series of objects requires reason. Reason refers to the confirmation or verification (101) of experiences. Evidence in this respect designates a mode of consciousness, viz. the end modus. In this end modus, the thing 'presents itself'. As regards the object of intention, once its identity has been safeguarded it can be asked whether it corresponds to the mode 'itself'.

Reality then is a correlative of this (self-) evident verification. In line with the general premises of Husserl's theory, the basic concepts as indices of a universal law of (the life of) consciousness come to light. They show how truth and reality make sense to us (105).

In the Fifth Meditation, Husserl broadens the investigation to include inquiries concerning the egos of others. His theory as it was exposed in the four preceding meditations has a fairly idealistic shape, in that all the inquiries start from the *ego* that is constituted as a transcendental *ego*. The question is therefore how others who are 'not ego' can come into the picture.

Paul Ricoeur has pointed to two important aspects of the transcendental ego, on which I shall briefly comment. The first consists in the fact that the constitution of objects from experience is not creation (Ricoeur 1986d: 289), since the transcendental ego is itself not the result of a *tabula rasa* operation, or simply of a suspension of the existence of the world. The second is the fact that Husserl's critical use of 'solipsism' (ibid.) as a possible objection to his theory is to be interpreted as 'apparent'. Without others (as would be the case if solipsism were 'real'), the *cogito* would be similar to Kant's '*Ich denke*', that is, a presupposition that accompanies all of our representations, without ever coming close to what they are in the world (Kant 1929: 152 ff).

For Kant, things in themselves, whilst they may exist and are thinkable, remain unknown (ibid.: 27, 74, 87 and 149). The objection of solipsism therefore is used to show that 'others', common nature, and the community of men must be constituted. In contrast to Mead, to whom I will come in a moment, this type of constitution is a task that Husserl assigns to himself, rather than taking it is a fact (Ricoeur 1986d: 290). Husserl's task can therefore be considered as an explicitation of the *ego*, but at the same time a constitution and an explicitation of other *egos* within the *ego* itself (ibid.: 291). Under Husserl's transcendental idealism, the constitution of the other runs along the same lines as the constitution of all objectivity as the objects of consciousness (Husserl 1996: section 41; Ames 1955: 327).

As far as the constitution of others is concerned, Ricoeur refers to the use in Husserl's theory of the concept of analogy as a transcendental principle (Ricoeur 1986d: 294). In using this concept, Husserl does not intend to claim that one can compare on a homogenous platform the 'lived expressions' (of ego) and the observed expressions of others (ibid.: 292). The analogy purports to show that others are a subject just as I am (ibid.: 293) without being a prolongation of myself, far less an object of my thought as we read from Descartes. The other, that is, does not belong to my sphere of experience (ibid.: 293; Downes 1965). The subject co-posits others and so ascribes to another subject the external appearances of his expressions. This makes the other an 'alter ego'; he is 'like me' thinking, feeling, and acting (Ricoeur 1986d: 294). As a transcendental principle, the analogy of 'ego' and 'alter ego' shows that the others are also 'egos' (ibid.: 294). This principle not only operates for the ego's contemporary fellows, but also for all those who have existed, and will exist in future.

The crucial aspect of the use of analogy in Husserl's sense, that is, as a transcendental principle, opens up a wider avenue of realities and experiences that can be empirically described (ibid.: 295; Carr 1973).

Ricoeur has interpreted this as a possibility of connecting Husserl's theory to Weber's, thus taking sides and favouring the idealistic interpretation of the former. The reason is that I must be able to consider myself an alter ego, without which social interaction would lack any sense for me as well as for the other (Ricoeur 1986d: 295). Social existence is based on the constitution of a common nature, that allows for the constitution of spiritual objectivities of different degrees (like the State) (ibid.: 296).

Using this constitution, starting from the transcendental ego up to communities with their proper institutions, it can be concluded from Husserl's meditations that there are no 'social things' but only 'intersubjective relations' (ibid.: 300). The existence of others is not then a matter of inference or deduction as in Descartes, which would create the insurmountable problem of the reality of social interaction (Carr 1973: 16–17). In the Fifth Meditation, Husserl places 'ego' and 'alter ego' in relation to one another (ibid.: 19–21) – alter ego is given in experience and not within a relationship of 'representation' as Descartes suggests.[9] This reference to the consciousness of the other (as the first 'non-ego', hence as experience of 'foreignness') means that things make sense to me (ibid.: 26–7).

Husserl's critique of Descartes focuses on the substantive nature of the *cogito*. However, Husserl remains by and large on the side of idealism and feels the need to constitute the world and the others starting from the *ego cogito*. What is lacking, however, in Husserl's approach, which makes him lean towards idealism, is an empirical theory of the self. Like Descartes, he ends up with a 'conception of the self' which is an a-contextual self. Ricoeur has suggested that this connection to an empirical theory could be found in Weber's sociology as noted above (Ricoeur 1986d: 296). I will for my part focus on George Herbert Mead as a better candidate, since Weber's focus is more on social relations than on the emergence of the individual throughout social interaction.

George Herbert Mead: From a Conception of the Self to a Self-Conception

Mead's main point of critique of the Cartesian subject consists in the claim that consciousness is not an original fact.[10] It takes the subject seriously without adopting the Cartesian Olympic view. On his Olympic view, Descartes suggested that he found the truth of the subject. This view, however, isolates the subject from others as well as from reality altogether. Against the Olympic view, I will briefly explore the contours of this theory that considers the individual within context, that is, with others.

Mead's insight is different from Descartes' as well as from Husserl's interpretation of it. He does not rely on consciousness as a primary and independent fact (Mead 1962: 164; Habermas 1996b). At the same time, 'it cannot be said that the individuals come first and the community later' (Mead 1962: 189, 223) This dual claim confirms both substantive consciousness and the subject as an ontologically anchored social being. In contrast with Husserl, for whom the ego is essentially external to society, Mead takes the self to be inherently social. 'It is absurd', says Mead, 'to look at the mind from the standpoint of the individual organism' (ibid.: 133).

9 Descartes 1996i: 25. While looking through the window, it might be that Descartes only sees cloaks and coats walking in the street.

10 In a similar sense as Habermas (1996b: 158–70) reads Fichte.

Mead explores the fact that individuals are born in a society. Their relationship with others contributes to the 'emergence' of their subjectivity or 'self' (cf. Blumer 1969: 61 ff.). In doing so, he takes sides with Descartes' subject-object relationship and the associated conception of the self. He replaces the subject-object relationship with a relationship between an organism and its environment: 'The relationship then, between the individual and his world is a condition for the appearance of the relation between the subjective and the objective, but it is not coincident with it' (Mead 1972: 114–15).

The world in this respect becomes a world of experience, as against Husserl for whom the world is something 'that exists for me simply as the *cogitatum* of my *cogitationes*' (Husserl 1996: section 15).

The emergence of the subject's self is related to the triadic structure of human behaviour. Behaviour consists of gestures. A gesture by A calls for a reaction by B, and this reaction in turn again invites a reaction by A (Mead, 1962: 145). If B gets the 'idea' of A's initial gesture, he reacts with another gesture. When A in turn gets the 'idea' of B, A 'understands' that B 'has got the idea' of A.

Given the similarity of the reaction that the idea arouses in both A and B, B can see himself as A sees him and *vice versa*. When a gesture triggers the same reaction in both A and B, there is communication out of which meaning emerges.

Gestures become 'significant symbols' (Mead's term for 'concepts' or 'universals') when they 'mean' the idea that comes with them, and when they arouse this idea in the other person. 'Ideas' conveyed in a gesture are not some psychic additive to a gesture as an external event. They are not innate as Descartes held; nor are they joined to a gesture in the process of interaction. Meaning does not exist independently of any action; it emerges through interaction in terms of gestures (ibid.: 145–6).

Gestures become significant symbols because and in as far as they are understood, that is, in as far as they arouse the idea in the other person. Meaning therefore is shared meaning, because it can only emerge through interaction. As a result, meaning is from the very beginning *social* meaning.

Vocal language provides the clearest illustration of this. When A speaks to B, he can hear himself just as B hears him. Consequently, since A as a speaker can also adopt the role of the hearer, he is able to experience the same reaction as the hearer. If A, when internalising the reaction of the others, is able to converse with himself through significant symbols, A 'thinks' (ibid.: 47).

It follows from the above that consciousness is not given or prior to any social interaction. Consciousness on the contrary refers to the ability to adopt the attitude of others towards a gesture. This possibility, as noted above, does not depend on the addition of a psychological component to a gesture; it only depends on interaction itself. It is through interaction that meanings are shared and give rise to the emergence of consciousness. Consciousness then is the result of the ability to invoke the reactions of others within ourselves (ibid.: 163). On this view, there is no separation between the emergence, the existence, and the interactive operation of the human mind. Consciousness is 'the response of an organism to its own responses.' (Mead 1980: 78).

The characterisation of significant symbols as concepts or universals depends on the very same framework. It depends on the possibility of adopting the role of the other with regard to oneself. Role taking allows for the generalisation of meaning. Generalised meaning is what constitutes a concept. Concepts result from the universalisation of the meaning that resides in interaction. Universality, that is, is the result of a generalised role adoption of others towards the subject. The crystallisation out of the specific aspects of these attitudes results in what Mead has called the 'generalized other' (Mead 1962: 90). Concepts or universals depend on interaction for their creation. They are not grasped from reality, as Aristotelian realism holds. Nor are they established by God inside (Descartes) or outside (Aquinas) the mind. Universals are thus social creations and emerge out of social interaction.

According to this argument, Mead takes sides of the substantial *cogito*. Selfs are not given, nor are they creations. They emerge out of social interaction. In contrast to Descartes, with Husserl in his wake, Mead does not focus primarily on certainty. He rather claims that certainty is a form of meaning. Therefore, consciousness is not primarily (certainty of) self-awareness but awareness of meaning. For Husserl, it is only in transcendental subjectivity that any kind of meaning or that reality can be constituted (Husserl 1996: section 28). For Mead, on the contrary, it is the possibility of repeating the external interaction with others within oneself that is the basis of the emergence of self-consciousness. On this view, the subject comes to self-consciousness through the internalisation of interaction with others. It is through this process of internalisation that the two poles to the self emerge: the 'I' and the 'me'.

The 'me' aspect of the self consists of the attitudes of others or the 'generalised other' evoked within ourselves. The 'I' aspect for its part is the individual answer given to this generalised other within oneself. In contrast to Husserl's and Descartes' subject, Mead's subject has no direct experience of this 'I' aspect of his self. This experience is only indirect since it is always behind us. It is in memory that the 'I' is constantly present in experience (Mead 1962: 174).[11] It is not directly given in experience though (ibid.: 175). The dynamic interaction then between 'I' and 'me' constitutes the 'self'.

The self's dual character is the result of its interactional emergence. It is through action with, or interaction, that the self emerges. The emergence of the self is a process of differentiation. This differentiation is not associated with an opposition between thought and action. It is, on the contrary, the connection between action and thought that gives rise to the self. It can be concluded from this that the subject is not a substance that is ontologically anchored in reality; it is interactionally anchored in a context of participation with others.

---

11 Habermas (1996b: 172) suggestively calls this image I have of myself through the mediation of the gaze of others the 'memory image' of my ego.

It follows from the constitution of the self as a subject through interaction with others that he is from the very outset a social subject or an 'intersubject'. Others are essentially part of a self. They do, however, not absorb the self in that they exclusively determine his identity. The mind or the self is not, to be sure, a product of its environment. Rather, the subject's identity or self stems from an ongoing process of interaction with others. It is through interaction with others that individualisation as well as socialisation of the subject are essentially related to each other, as Habermas (1996b) has observed. His identity is of both a social and an individual nature because of the interactional process out of which it emerges.[12]

On Mead's view, to which I subscribe, the crucial point is that the 'I' cannot be conceived of without 'me'; hence separation from others is unconceivable. In addition, in line with the epistemologisation of philosophy, the transparency of the *cogito* as a specific version of the 'I' is limited to epistemological transparency. This transparency is achieved though an illusion, since the 'I' is not epistemologically accessible to the subject himself; it is always behind him, as Mead suggests. In trying to gain epistemological access to the 'I', the subject transforms himself into an object of knowledge. For the same reason – that is, without turning themselves into an object – others are not epistemologically accessible either.

The exclusion of an epistemological access to oneself or to others is not the same as the impossibility of any access. The articulation of the subject as an intersubject draws on the Modern philosophical project, in rearranging the relationship between knowledge and (inter)action. The priority of the epistemological access of the subject to himself within the *cogito* is replaced by an interactional process under which the subject and intersubject emerges. It is within this very process of interaction that the subject gains access to others and to himself. In this respect, the subject could have some idea about himself. It is, however, doubtful whether this idea will be as clear and distinct as the Cartesian *cogito* wants it to be. The subject, that is, is not a thinking substance which exists, but a conception of the self. We learn from Mead that to be a self is to have a self-conception.

Self-Conception and Intersubjectivity as a Practice: Symbolisation

As regards the emergence of consciousness through interaction with others, Mead has clearly taken sides with the substantive *cogito* of Descartes and the transcendental *cogito* of Husserl. So far we have read from Mead how consciousness emerges. However, what was referred to in the previous section – the 'intersubject' – needs a closer scrutiny. The fact that consciousness emerges in interaction with others, and that meaning is therefore 'social', does not yet sufficiently articulate the concept of 'intersubjectivity'. Therefore I propose exploring the possibility of

---

12 Ames 1955: 321: 'In Mead's philosophy we are members of one another … '; Laplantine 1999: 142: ' … Le malheur pour l'identité, c'est qu'elle soit melée d'altérité.'

a more robust version of intersubjectivity than Mead's while working on his view on the emergence of the social subject.

In a penetrating contribution, Walker Percy has drawn attention to the fact that the triadic structure of human behaviour (stimulus-response-stimulus) is nothing but a form of denotation or 'naming', and at best, symbolic denotation (Percy 1958: 635). The concept of denotation takes us to a semantic level. Denotation requires two organisms in order to be successful, with the response sequence bringing meaning to light. Symbols, however, are more than signs. In this respect, vocal or linguistic conversation is somewhat different from the adaptation of an organism within an environment mediated by signs. It is a specific kind of conversation that Mead has already pointed to.

The crucial point within the symbol/meaning relationship is that it requires at least two organisms, and so is from the very beginning tetradic (involving four elements), instead of triadic, like the stimulus-response sequence. A's calling an object a tree says that it is a tree for him and for B. Without any other person stating that the object is a tree, B would never know this. 'But not only are the two a genetic requirement of symbolisation', says Percy, '... *it is its enduring condition* ... Every symbolic formulation, whether it be language, art, or even thought, requires a real or posited someone else for whom the symbol is meaningful. Denotation is an exercise in intersubjectivity.' (Percy 1958: 636, italics added). This relationship involves (1) the namer and (2) the hearer as co-conceivers of (3) the object beheld under the auspices of (4) a common symbol (ibid.: 636).

The enduring presence of the other from the past through now transcends the relationship that obtains among data; it is itself a relationship between co-knowers, and this relationship is intersubjectivity. Intersubjectivity may not be construed as an interaction, according to Percy (ibid.: 637), although, with Mead, we recognise that it starts as interaction. Intersubjectivity moreover is not consciously constituted, as we read from Husserl, nor is it something 'given' – like consciousness for Descartes. It can only be acknowledged (ibid.: 637). In addition to Husserl, consciousness of something is at the same time symbolic, in that it is consciousness of something as being what it is for you *and* for me (ibid.: 639). Symbolisation therefore is in its very essence connected to intersubjectivity and vice versa (ibid.: 525).

Percy's view makes it possible to connect Husserl's and Mead's theories, in a similar though more penetrating way than Ricoeur has suggested for connecting Husserl's work with Weber's. Intersubjectivity is not to be constituted by the transcendental ego, as Husserl claimed; it is empirical as well. From this perspective, Husserl's and Mead's theories can be regarded as complementary. Due to the inextricable connection between consciousness and intersubjectivity, consciousness is intersubjectively constituted (ibid.: 527).

The Elusive Self

The self, so we have learned from Mead, results from a dynamic process of interaction with others. Through the substitution of the procedural emergence of the subject for a clear and distinct idea, elusiveness is substituted for certainty. The elusiveness of the self is caused by the fact that the self is not open to symbolic transformation. I remain forever unknown to myself (Percy 1958: 527).

There is a structural isomorphy between the subject's self and the society with which he interacts with others. This characterisation of the self does justice to the situatedness of the subject. The subject's situatedness connects the emergence of the self with a temporal and social context. Unlike the introspective concept of the a priori fixed subject resulting from an epistemologised philosophy, this self is replete with temporality. Conversely, meaning of and for the self is substituted for ontological truth. If there is truth, it follows out of meaning for the subject. Thus, following Mead, meaning is social.

If it is through knowledge that we arrive at truth, it is only through meaning that we arrive at knowledge. As Descartes' search for certainty affects the nature of the subject, Mead's theory of the emergence of the subject and meaning conversely affects the idea of rationality and freedom, as will be argued in chapters 3 and 4 respectively.

Following up on the insight that meaning is interactional, knowledge can be characterised as a form of action. Knowing and acting are connected in a dialectical relationship within which primarily meaning and not ontological truth is established. Meaning is no longer merged with truth. If truth exists, access to it can only be gained via meaning and meaning is achieved through interaction with others. Direct access to reality is therefore illusory.

From that perspective, certainty is a form of meaning or of making sense for the subject. The access it provides to reality is indirect. Put differently, certainty is not an index of ontological truth; it is simply an index of a form of knowledge that is preceded by the emergence of meaning through interaction.

The nature of the Cartesian self as an a-temporal thinking substance or conception of the self obliterates the subject's historical situatedness. This obliteration suggests the transparency of the subject to himself. Transparency thus creates the illusion of the subject's direct access to himself, although paradoxically, what is transparent is also invisible, and hence elusive.

Against this view, the historical situatedness of the self as it follows from Mead's work means that a self emerges through interaction with others. Interaction with others situates the subject within a context of participation. Interaction within a context of participation is constitutive of meaning that is in turn constitutive of the subject's self. It is through meaning that both the subject and knowledge are established.

The 'truth' of the subject or conception of the self is therefore mediated by meaning. Meaning is related to others with whom the subject finds himself within a context of participation. It may be the case that 'what others think of me' within this context of participation makes up part of the subject's self, but it does not however coincide with it. According to the dynamic nature of the self, the other in myself or the 'me'-aspect interacts with the 'I'-aspect. There is no 'other in myself' disconnected from this 'I'-aspect, which would amount to a sociologisation of Mead's interpretation. Because of the dynamic intertwinement of the 'I'-aspect and the 'me'-aspect, no direct access to any of these aspects taken separately is possible. This impossibility provides the locus for the subject's or the self's freedom, as will be argued in the following pages.

The 'I'-aspect of the self is not a direct datum of experience. It cannot be considered a substance without stepping into the trappings of Descartes' *cogito*. Because it is related to the adoption of the attitude of others towards oneself, it is not substantial or ready-made. It is, rather, a possibility condition for acting and thinking, as Mead argued (Mead 1962: 175).

The subject's 'I'-aspect is not a matter of substantial ontology; it is a matter of awareness. It appears to the subject himself only as past. When it comes through, it disappears at the same time. It gets through to others as they interact with the subject in the present. As an essential aspect of the self, it is a possibility condition for acting and thinking. Its reality is elusive. Therefore, it does not make sense to speak of having direct access to it. Because of that, the theory articulating it is not simply a theory *about* the subject related to a conception of the self. This indeed would annul its nature as a mere possibility condition.

The theory articulating the elusiveness of the subject's reality is a *meta-theory of the subject*. As a meta-theory, it is a theory about a theory. The theory to which it refers is a theory *of* the subject. A theory of the subject can only be a theory which the subject makes of himself. A meta-theory in turn is a theory about this theory the subject makes of himself. In other words, a meta-theory articulates the possibility conditions of this theory. It establishes the conditions under which a theory *of* the subject is possible. Only under a theory of the subject it is possible to do away with conceptions of the self and replace them with the possibility of self-conception.

It is the meta-theoretical nature of the theory of the subject that clarifies the elusiveness of the dynamic aspect of the self. It explains at the same time why the subject is not directly or immediately accessible in an epistemological manner. For the subject himself, the 'I'-aspect of his self cannot be known directly, because it is always behind him. For the others, with whom the subject is interacting, it cannot be 'known' because it does not constitute part of their own self. For them, the dynamic aspect of the other's self can only be observed from the social aspect of their own self, that is, their 'me'-aspect. Therefore, the 'I'-aspect of the self is 'unknown'; it is not epistemologically accessible to the self nor to others (Ricoeur 1986b: 109; Modell 1993: 144–5, 157). The elusiveness of the self refers to a realm of action to which neither the self nor the others have direct access. This is the realm of freedom.

The positive articulation of freedom is the possibility of choice. The negative articulation of freedom results in the absence of certainty. Both conceptual determinations combine, in that certainty excludes the possibility of choice. Conversely, the absence of certainty entails the necessity of choice. Freedom in this respect refers to both the necessity and the possibility of choice. In chapter 4, I will analyse this point in greater depth, calling it the 'circumstances of human action'. I will also reserve for that chapter the normative dimension of freedom, and it will be sufficient here to note that it consists in a distance that must be respected by others. Without any distance between others and the subject, no free action is possible. Meaningful action, because it is related to interaction, refers to others within the subject. This is what the 'me'-aspect of the self entails.

Self and Others

According to the view that the self emerges through interaction with others, we should briefly pause to consider the 'others'. From Descartes, we read that the subject is a disembedded being. More specifically, it is disconnected from the other. Husserl's attempt to constitute the other from the transcendental ego, so I have argued, lacks the empirical dimension of our quotidian existence. I have argued that Mead's theory was helpful in substituting theories operating according to conceptions of the self for a theory that allows for a self-conception. While playing a role in the subject's interactional identification, the other does not belong to my sphere of self-experience, as Ricoeur rightly stresses (Ricoeur 1986d: 293). Although he is there, he is still *absent*. We cannot, that is, take someone else's place. Perry's view for his part was instructive in that others are a necessary requirement for symbolisation that is constitutive for intersubjectivity. Others, that is, are the enduring condition for symbolisation, and hence intersubjectivity.

With regard to Perry's stress on the requirement of others as an enduring requirement for a self to emerge and subsist, it should be observed that interactionally differentiated subjects are not, at a certain moment – say, when they are 'ready' – separated from the others who contributed to their identification. On the contrary, the subject's interactional identification as differentiation from others is an ongoing process. This implies that the interactional identification does not result, at a certain moment in time, in a fixed identity (or a substance). Interactional identification, on the contrary, is an ongoing process through which the subject can and will change.

Once we disperse the ontological illusion of the *cogito* and the belief in access to reality as it is, we find a subject capable of interactionally defining himself as an 'I'. He is a subject of self-definition, as Taylor (1985c) puts it, and not just part of a theory apparently of himself, by ontologising him into a *res cogitans*. When the substantial *cogito* is abandoned, the subject *qua* subject can enter the scene, together with others.

We have already had the opportunity to draw some conclusions from the idea of the subject as a social individual. The subject, if we follow Descartes, is a *res cogitans* who thinks in solitude. While thinking, he necessarily defines himself ontologically as a substance. Some flavour of mediaeval substantialism penetrates, as appears within the Cartesian *cogito*. Given the subject's representational capacities, the *cogito* similarly conceives the other in terms of representations.

On this view, the self-identifying subject will at best have a representation of yet another thinking substance. The latter is presumed to 'be' like the subject himself is, that is, yet another *res cogitans*. In thinking that way, however, we do not attain identity as difference. If we may have some trouble in understanding meaning as difference, this is due to the idea of 'substance' which still accompanies the Modern idea of identity. On that view, identity is by very definition that which remains identical to itself; any difference is accordingly not a sign of identity, like disagreement is a sign of error.

The interactional identification of the subject as an 'I' is of a dynamic nature. More specifically, it is the result of interaction with the other with whom the 'emerging subject' is always in context. It is upon interaction with others that the subject with the meaning of 'I' emerges. What the interactional identification of the 'I' expresses is a difference from others. However, difference is not identical to separation. This is what, upon an interactional account of meaning, 'I' means. It simply *means* 'not the other'. Because of the presence of the other within the interactional setting, he is no longer represented by the solipsistically thinking subject (Descartes) that constitutes intersubjectivity starting from its own constitution as a transcendental ego (Husserl). In this respect, I disagree with Ricoeur in his claim that others do not make part of my self-experience. They do so, despite the fact that I have no *direct* experience of them.

The interactional identification of the subject is at the same time replete with absence or 'not presence'. The 'I', as I said above, is elusive for the subject himself. So it is *a fortiori* for the others. This absence or lack of full transparency can be considered the possibility condition of symbolisation. 'I' as a symbol makes something present that is at the same time absent. Nevertheless, the 'I' has significance through this absence, and this is a way to understand the significant symbol. It signifies something that at the same time is absent. And so is the other.

Whilst according to the representational view, the other is 'there' by way of a representation, in the interactional view the other is there, in turn, as an interactionally identifying self. His 'thereness' in interaction is constitutive of both his and the other's self. This self draws upon the other and takes shape in the subject's consciousness of the other as his 'me' aspect; 'me' is 'the other in me'. Here as elsewhere, the other is at the same time absent as the other, and, of course, also as 'otherness'. The subject is with others, however, in as far as the latter succeeds in symbolising the other as 'part of himself'.

However, the 'I/me' dialectics of the subject's self, which expresses a form of self-consciousness, results in a different forms of consciousness. The consciousness of the self goes hand-in-hand with the subject's being conscious of the other within his self-consciousness. This does not include identity with the other, nor radical separation from him. The other is a constitutive part of my self-consciousness as a result of the interactional give-and-take, and that is what makes a self a self. This 'presence of the other' is not any form of representation of 'otherness' within my consciousness, through which I have 'true knowledge' of him. On the contrary, his 'being there' is authentic and irreducible, not as 'otherness', but just simply as 'another'.

Interaction, Meaning and Conflict

So far, the argument on the self or the subject arriving at self-conception has had a fairy-tale flavour. Interaction, so it seems, is a smooth way to gain consciousness of oneself in a context with others. Without being devils, men are not angels either. Interaction is not always peaceful as the existence of conflicts, small and large, in daily life amply shows. Yet it is time to turn our eyes away from the sweeter side of interaction, and face the conflictual part of it.

On Descartes' view, conflict or disagreement means that none of the disagreeing subjects is right. The reason is that if one were right, he could easily convince the other of the clarity and distinction of the idea. The fact that he cannot is a sign that both he *and* the other are wrong (Descartes 1996l: 6–7).

Both Hobbes and Rousseau adopt a specific approach to conflict. For Hobbes, the subject is inherently wicked, that is, he has an imperfect nature, at least after the Fall. The Augustinian influence on Hobbes is beyond doubt. Conflicts are caused by man's imperfection after the Fall.

Rousseau for his part comes to a similar conclusion, in that the evolution of culture – mainly related to the development of economics – creates relations of dependence that result in conflict. In addition, bad governance makes man bad.[13] It is not the subject who is, like in Hobbes, of a bad nature; it is his life in society that corrupts him.

Referring to the discussion of Hobbes's theory in chapter 1, his solution of conflicts consists in repressing them as far as possible. For this, the omnipotent sovereign is called into being. The repression of conflicts is to be understood as preventing them from emerging. This prevention is the duty of the sovereign since he is required to define right and wrong or, in short, justice. Here as elsewhere Hobbes's overall nominalist theory operates in the background. Since the laws of nature are semantically empty, and since everyone has a right to everything, the definition of the laws of nature is given to the subjects themselves. It is easy to understand that everyone will define them to his own advantage, so that conflicts will be unavoidable.

13 Rousseau 1997b: 138: 'One is strongly inclinded to believe that the history of human diseases could easily be written following that of human Societies.' Rousseau 1997b: 157: ' … but quite aside from the fact that the disorders and the crimes [the laws] daily daily cause among us sufficiently prove the inadequacy of the Laws in this respect, it would still be worth inquiring whether these disorders did not arise together with the Laws themelves … .'

Once the sovereign is created, conflicts can be reduced to a transgression of a rule that deserves punishment. From the perspective of the subject, the legal order consists of duties expressed as rules that are to be obeyed. Hobbes therefore can be considered a legalist for whom the normativity of an action consists in following rules. They are limited to the category of primary rules of obligation, to use Hart's terminology.[14]

Rousseau for his part does not seek to repress conflicts, in that he wants to prevent them. He develops a way of institutionalising a proper manner of dealing with conflicts so that they can be reframed in terms of rules. If a conflict emerges, then rules will be used to solve it. In contrast to Hobbes, however, Rousseau's citizen actively participates in the creation of rules, since all citizens are members of the sovereign. His model pre-echoes Hart's in that the majoritarian principle as the object of consensus of the social contract can be interpreted as a rule for the creation of rules, their change, and their recognition as legal rules. I will return to this in chapter 8.

Both, that is, handle conflict that seems unavoidable, by subjecting it to the rules of the sovereign. Repression or prevention through authoritarian power or institutionalisation indicates a particular prospect on conflict, that turns out to be bad from any perspective. Again, the belligerent context of seventeenth-century England or the pre-Revolutionary climate of the end of eighteenth-century France could probably justify their preoccupation with conflict from their political perspective.

Consequently, given their preoccupation, Hobbes and Rousseau articulate their models of rules in order to channel conflicts. Rules bind up power, and thus limit it. Their solution, accordingly, consists of a legalisation of power, by reframing conflicts into legal conflicts. The institutionalisation or legalisation of power transforms social conflicts into legal ones. With this transformation, the solution of social problems is turned over to legal adjudication (Cyrul 2005).

The solution common to both Hobbes and Rousseau consists of withdrawing conflict from the context where it emerges, that is, social interaction. They transfer it to an instance that will resolve it, each in a specific way as it is articulated in their philosophy. From whatever perspective it is considered, the sovereign seems to be the most appropriate candidate for handling conflict, since their opinion is that any conflict can potentially culminate in war. War, that is, includes the danger of death, the fear of which they believe will be warded off by the state.

Both approaches, however, are defective in my view for at least five reasons.

First, peace does not necessarily mean the absence of any conflict. Hobbes's and Rousseau's considerations on peace may have been inspired by the historical circumstances of their time. These circumstances, however, do not contain the solution of the problem, so we must look elsewhere to find it.

---

14 On the idea of Hobbes's legal system as a set of mere primary rules of obligation, see Wintgens 1991a.

Their classification of peace as the absence of conflict, as it seems, is essentially based on the new mechanical world-view. Planets follow rules, and they do not conflict. So there is 'peace'. Following their belief that the model of rules equally applies in heaven as on earth – the premise of the mechanical world-view introduced by Galileo Galilei – they regard themselves as justified in believing that following rules is the only way to avoid conflict, that is, to repress it or institutionalise it.

Under their representational view, the model of rules represents reality, and this truth is the foundation of their theories. Conflict is a sign of imperfection, as Descartes already said from an epistemological point of view. Perfection is found in reality that is 'out there'. The cosmological pattern advocated in Aristotle's political philosophy, where the model of the planets' movement is both perfect and real, is still attractive for the Modern philosophical project. Hobbes and Rousseau are exemplary for that.

Secondly, their approach is defective because both take conflict to be of a binary character, that is, either there is conflict or there is not. If there is conflict, it has the potential to blow up into war. They fail to see, as Weber will argue later, that conflict is a matter of degree. Some conflicts are limited in nature and scope, like conflicts between two persons who are of a different opinion and 'fight' for it in a discussion. 'Peaceful conflict', as Weber calls it, leads to some form of selection, in that it can be mainly characterised as a competition. In as far as it is 'regulated' in one way or another, it includes a meaningful mutual orientation (Weber 1964: 132).

What peaceful conflict or competition aims at is selection. This form of competition, says Weber, is 'regulated' to the extent that its ends and means are oriented towards an order (ibid.: 133). Without this orientation, competition is not regulated. It is, as I interpret Weber, not *primarily* oriented towards an order. It can, however, be interpreted as being constitutive of an order, that is, an order of meaning that can serve as a meaningful mutual orientation. It is important to stress the absence of any external intervention, that is, an intervention that is external to the actual practice. My interpretation of this suggestion from Weber is that peaceful competition entails a selection of meaning, and in this sense it is 'conflict'. Since there is no pre-existing meaning that constitutes an order, meaning is to be constructed through interaction. The 'regulation' then pointed to by Weber should by no means originate exclusively from a sovereign, as Hobbes, for example, holds. Thus it can be stated that competitive conflict takes the form of self-regulation (Freund 1983: 55, 88).

Since Hobbes and Rousseau classify conflict in binary terms, they suggest that there either is or there is not a conflict. If there is conflict, it almost automatically results in war; if there is no conflict, there is peace. On that characterisation, the prudent attitude is to take care to ensure that conflict cannot break out. Prudent as it might seem, their approach raises a specific problem for two reasons. The first is that the assimilation of conflict and war is simply wrong. Not every conflict is a war, though every war is a conflict. Secondly, and more crucially, they seem to adhere to an unproblematic definition of war that is similar to the definition of the so-called *Sandhaufentheorem* (Bender 1978: 34–42). How many grains of sand are needed before the collection can be properly called a sand-heap? Similarly, how much hair should one have lost before one can be meaningfully be said to be 'bald'? And how 'strong' should a conflict be before it qualifies as a war?

No one, it may be assumed, will object to their view that the conflict they qualify as the *bellum omnium contra omnes* is a 'real' war. But can the same to be said of the proponents of the particle theory of light, as opposed to the others, who adhere to the wave theory? Although there is a conflict, which is still unresolved as far as I know, this is not going to break out into a war, as far as I expect. What the existence of this conflict shows is not that both the theories are wrong – in the Cartesian sense that neither of them can be true because there is disagreement – but that there is not yet any mutual understanding, and that meaning is 'in the making'. To be sure, the adherents of both groups know what the other 'means' in the Meadian sense. Their reaction would hardly be understandable though if, due to the fact that they do not 'understand' each other, they were to start splitting each other's skulls. Their theories make sense or are meaningful without reaching ultimate truth, nor without reaching mutual understanding for the time being.

Third, Hobbes's and Rousseau's approach to conflict is defective because their ambiguous characterisation of conflict leaves out of view its semantic potential. In criticising Hobbes, Rousseau observes that war is not a sign of the absence of a society (Polin 1971: 84). Hobbes for his part claims that, because there is no society in the absence of a state, there is a latent state of war. Rousseau, on the contrary, is of the opinion that war means that there is a society. One does not fight with somebody one does not know; if one fights with him, this is a form of interaction, and hence a social relation.

There is a fourth reason why Hobbes's and Rousseau's view on conflict is defective. This reason is that if there is conflict, it is a conflict of *meaning*. The conflict as to whether, for example, this piece of land is mine or yours does not concern the land itself, as Aristotle thought. The conflict relates to the meaning of 'mine' and 'yours'. In that sense, any economic setting is by its very nature a conflict, since both vendor and buyer have a conflicting interest in settling the price. They are engaged in an interactive process of settling meaning. They discuss, that is, the conditions under which something can be called 'mine' or 'yours'.

The price is the meaning they must agree on; otherwise the meaning of what is now 'mine' will not change into 'yours'. Meaning, like price, is neither an a priori fixed datum, nor is it probable that it will descend into war. Whilst it is correct to say that it may lead into a serious conflict, it makes little sense, however, to say that it is going to culminate in a civil war, or a war of all against all. The type of conflict described above is a form of interaction. It is also a source of meaning. And this is what makes conflict also useful. Conflict has at least some virtues.

The above example from the economic sphere illustrates my more general purpose, in that it shows the conflictual character of interaction without culminating in armed conflict. Remaining in the field of economics for a moment, Rousseau suggests that the development of economic infrastructure involves a division of labour, resulting in turn in relations of dependence that may culminate in a civil war. The 'social question' on the eve of the French Revolution amply shows that he may be right. Marx would be the first to admit it, and to classify it as a conflict between the class of capital and the class of labour, thereby suggesting that these classes are ontologically anchored. Pierre Bourdieu has rightly applauded this diagnosis while at the same time criticising Marx for giving the wrong theoretical solution to a real practical problem (Bourdieu 1994: 53 ff.).

Marx believed that the social problem is of an ontological nature, and so anchors the classes of labour and capital in an ontological way so as to hypostatise or naturalise their conflict. In doing so, he is already anticipating the proletarian revolution, from which a new and yet just social order would emerge.

Marx, Hobbes and Rousseau, each for their own reasons, embrace the ontologisation of conflict that inevitably fixes it to reality. In doing so, they blow up conflicts to an ontological dimension that serves as a justification for their specific theories. For both Hobbes and Rousseau, the ontologisation of conflict calls for the state to oppress or to institutionalise it; for Marx, on the contrary, the course of history will resolve it.

By ontologising conflicts and predicting their culmination in war or revolution, Hobbes, Rousseau, and to a lesser extent Marx, fail to see the potential of meaning that I consider is inherent to conflicts. Hobbes and Rousseau neglect spontaneous social interaction in favour of a new type of relation wrought outside the realm of conflict itself. In doing so, they may succeed in avoiding conflicts by withdrawing them from the conflict partners. They are, however, throwing the baby with the bath water.

The ontologisation of conflict therefore seems to call for a solution on the same level, consisting in the ontologisation of its solution. The solution is the creation of the state in Hobbes and Rousseau. Marx for his part believes that conflict will erase the state altogether, while Hegel argued the belief that the state was, as for Hobbes and Rousseau, the unique instance for preventing and solving conflicts.

In line with what I have argued in chapter 1, the category of a 'natural' or 'relational' place was erased by the nominalist rift at the end of the thirteenth century. Under the classical approach, the 'right' social order consists in man's insertion in the pre-existing relational order. Conflict is a disturbance of that order.

Truth and meaning are, on this approach, one and the same, which is no longer the case in the nominalist tradition, which started from Duns Scotus and Ockham. Social contract theorists are, however, eager to achieve a merger of meaning and truth. Since concepts or *universalia* lack any ontological value under their theories, the meaning of, say, justice, like any other meaning, is not 'out there' any more. Justice, like other concepts, loses its ontological value. Concepts explode into different conceptions.

Each from their own perspective, both Hobbes's and Rousseau's argument in favour of a withdrawal of the conflict from where it emerges may seem attractive. However, their approach is not consistent with their overall theories. The premise of conflict, its ontological anchoring, and its solution result in some spurious 'metaphysics of the individual', the consequences of which are not drawn out in full in their theories.

The fifth reason why Hobbes's and Rousseau's view on conflict turns out to be defective is that, given the ontologisation of conflict, social relations cannot, according to Hobbes, exist. If they do exist, following Rousseau, they lead to war. This justifies in their opinion the view that the subjects, unable to organise their interaction, should be made dependent on external limitations stemming from the sovereign. The above characterisation of conflict leaves no other possibilities. The price to be paid for that is a surrender of their moral capacity to act as free moral agents. They cannot be 'independent in interdependence' as MacCormick (1989: 188) has called it, because this results in conflict. The defect in Hobbes's and Rousseau's position here is that they fail to see that conflict is a condition for human freedom (Freund 1983: 330). Therefore subjects *should* become interdependent through their dependence on external limitations.

Hobbes's and Rousseau's preoccupation with conflict from a political perspective has an undeniable bearing on the way in which they think of the subject from a moral perspective. It includes the denial of the subject as an autonomous moral agent. This in turn affects their view of law, as I will argue in the next section. For Rousseau, only law is able to install equality and give social relations the moral dimension they are lacking outside the state. For Hobbes, only law is able to guarantee security and prevent conflicts. In short, only law turns out to be able to reduce the complexities of social life and install order.

Interaction as Conflict: Law's Alternative

Because interaction potentially turns into conflict, as both Hobbes and Rousseau hold, they invoke an instance that will prevent or regulate these conflicts. In doing so, they construct a political space that aims to provide the morality that is lacking within the social sphere.

This vision leads to a specific articulation of the relationship between law and morality. Hobbes proposes the idea that the law incorporates a morality, the one chosen by the sovereign. This morality need not be a systematically reflected, that is, rational, morality. The sovereign's will is a necessary and sufficient condition in order for a legal norm to be true, that is, morally correct.

Rousseau for his part adopts a more qualified position. According to him, propositional contents as general rules are just. No substantive morality is enforced. The moral aspect of law in Rousseau therefore appears to be separated from the law as such. Because of the law's procedural nature, it comes close to being a neutral conflict solver. Put differently, the rules express the point of view of a third party – the sovereign of which every citizen is a member – as a necessary and sufficient condition for their being law at all (Kojève 1981: 69–94).

For Hobbes, one remembers, law and morality are one and the same. This gives rise to the classification of his theory of 'juridical positivism' (Wintgens 1991b: 3–22, 40–61, 86–104). It follows from this that the subject will only be a moral agent by the grace of the law, that is, the commands of the sovereign. The commands of the sovereign set out the subject's moral duties; it is therefore pretty clear that the subject is not autonomous at all in this respect.

Things are slightly different with Rousseau. For him, the law does not create a morality that it subsequently enforces, although law is a moral fact. As a moral fact, it produces the morality that is lacking within the state of nature. In doing so, law expresses a specific view on morality. It is the morality of a morally heteronymous actor, incapable of realising freedom in freedom. He must be guided by the sovereign and act on the latter's external limitations that are his reasons for action. As a reason for action, it is exclusionary under a moral perspective, in that it is morally correct. Put differently, the law as an exclusionary moral reason for action takes over from the subject's own reasons for action. In doing so, however, law misconceives the subject's moral autonomy. I will return to this in chapter 4.

According to this approach, every external limitation of freedom issued by the sovereign confirms the social contract, in that it is based on it. At the same time, however, it confirms the moral view that the social contract expresses, that is, the inability of the subject to act as an autonomous moral agent. He is, at best, a legal actor.

Summarising the argument up until now, the previous sections of this chapter were dedicated to the exploration of a different view of the subject and his relations to others. Others belong to my world in a specific way. The relationship between subjects, as it follows from the analysis, is constitutive of meaning and their being as a subject *qua* subject. In addition to these constitutive aspects, this relationship between subjects was also, for reasons set out above, classified as conflictual.

The conflictual nature of interaction, as I will further argue in this section, contains the germs of a different moral perspective on the subject that underlies legisprudence. More specifically, legisprudence expresses a specific moral view on the subject *qua* subject. In the remaining part of this chapter, I will explore the main characteristics of this view, articulating it in relation to law. The following chapters will then be dedicated to a similar analysis of rationality and freedom respectively.

Mark Hunyadi has argued in some recent work that conflicts have some virtue. This virtue consists of activating the normativity of rules.[15] Before speaking of rules in the sense lawyers do – that is, as legal rules – we can establish the fact that subjects interact with each other. Action is social, according to Max Weber, if it takes into account the others, or other subjects in one way or another (Ricoeur 1986d: 297). Apart from the accidental collision of two bicycle riders, so Weber says, actions are always oriented towards others (Weber 1964: 113). This approach complies with that followed in this chapter, in that action that is oriented towards

15 Hunyadi 1995: 16, 17: 'Le conflit, que ce soit sous une forme exacerbée, est l'une des voies d'accès royale à la normativité de la règle.'

others is interaction. The social character and meaningfulness of an action stems from its being oriented towards others.

As was argued above in this chapter, social interaction is constitutive of both the self and meaning. The interpretation of the meaningfulness of action is not that meaning pre-exists action, and that action is then oriented towards what pre-exists in that way. Meaning, on the contrary, emerges out of interaction. From there, it follows that there *are* no meanings. Meanings can be settled at some moment, though they are never ontologically fixed. If they are settled, they can be said to become an object toward which further interaction is oriented. This, however, does not make meaning exist in any ontological sense. The 'existence' of meaning, if I may say so, is an ongoing interactive process of creation taking place in a context of participation, not in reality 'out there'. This is a consequence of the view developed in the earlier sections of this chapter.

If meanings are settled, they are temporarily fixed, and they can operate as an 'object' in the sense George Herbert Mead accords to that. They are points of reference, by no means fixed forever, in the interaction of subjects. By the very fact that they are not fixed, they can change, and this is what conflict is about. Conflicts concern meaning that is not fixed.

A result of that view is that conflicts do show at least two things. First, they show some disagreement as to meaning. Secondly, and more importantly, conflicts include a reference to *rules*. I take it that the first point goes without saying; the latter may call for some more comment.

When a conflict emerges, it refers to some rule over the meaning of which there is disagreement. I will illustrate this point with the help of two examples.

In the first, there might be disagreement as to the construction of the series of numbers by adding a new one at the end of the series '2, 4, 6, 8 … '. If the suggestion is included in the series that it is '2' that must be added, we rely on the rule 'add 2'. If it turns out to be '4' that must be added after every fourth figure, the series goes like '2, 4, 6, 8, 12, 14, 16, 18, 20, 24 … '. The rule 'add 2' or the rule 'add 2 and add 4 at every fourth number' make the series look different (Wittgenstein 1969: nr. 185; Kripke 1982: 18 ff.). Disagreement refers to a rule that may, for example, be insufficiently clear.

The second example shows a different type of rules. If a piano player is not victorious in a competition, as a loser (L) he can criticise the rule that the jury applied to the respective performances. The jury could be of the opinion that L's performance, using old instruments and following the practice as it existed at the time of composition (say, the eighteenth century), is old-fashioned. They may have been of the view that the music should have been performed in a more rhythmical manner, faster, and with more stress on the bass tones. With regard to L, the jury refers to a rule or a set of rules, according to which current music performance should be more rhythmical in order to make most sense now, that is, for a current audience. The rules referred to are rules expressing, in the jury's opinion, the *state of the art*, specifying what the canons of musical performance are (Hunyadi 1995:47).

This reference to rules is most similar to the function Hart has assigned to rules, that is, a reason for action justifying behaviour and a reason for criticism in the event that the behaviour does not conform (Hart 1994: 84, 90). In spite of the fact that the rules of musical performance are not legal rules, this does not alter their function of serving as a reason for criticism of the performance of L. At the same time, they justify the classification of the winner (W), whose playing did conform to these rules. There may be disagreement between L and W.

The conflict or disagreement refers to the rules of the practice of musical performance in view of which the player's acts are assessed, as well as to the meaning given to what counts as 'good'. If 'good' means in the jury's opinion 'making most sense now' and in that sense 'original', then L could claim in response that 'original' means 'back to the origin', and so he appeals to another canon of musical performance, say the one initiated by Nikolaus Harnancourt in the 1980s. W for his part, together with the jury, is of the opinion, that 'original' means the way he did it.

The second example illuminates at least three things. First, the jury's decision is made on the basis of some sort of rules, the canons of musical performance. Secondly, L disagrees with the jury and with W as to whether these rules are the right ones, or whether the meaning conferred upon them is the right one. Third, and in connection to that, when referring to the qualification 'original' as a requirement for musical performance, it could be argued that two sets of canons or rules compete in conferring meaning to what counts as 'original'. L says that it means 'back to the origins', while W together with the jury holds it means 'new' or 'making most sense now'.

Before beginning the contest, L or W may not have been explicitly aware of the existence of different meanings of 'original'. That is, they may have been unaware of any conflict or disagreement concerning that. If L is the first to come up with a new kind of musical performance in the contest, say, *à la Harnancourt*, this may be considered a valuable interpretation of what 'original' means.

If the contest were of a parochial size, the disagreement as to the rules involved, that is, the rules and their meaning, might quickly vanish and end in the pub over a beer. If the contest is however, say, the International Queen Elizabeth Competition, the disagreement may have some more far-reaching consequences. It may be that the rules or canons of musical performance adopted by the jury will subsequently be adhered to by national or international schools of music; it may also be that L, despite his losing the contest, is applauded for having introduced a new way of playing, say, Tchaikovsky that will be gradually appreciated and followed later on by his fellows. With that result, the disagreement as to the existence and meaning of the rules of piano performance may flow into a far-reaching change in the existence and/or the meaning of these rules.

Whatever the consequence for the future of musical performance may be, the conflict makes it clear the fact that *rules* – and not only music – are brought into play. If there had not been any conflict, there would not have been a reason to talk of rules. What the conflict does show then is that there are rules. The rules are used to decide who is going to win, and so to settle some initial 'conflict' even if it is prima facie not apparent.

Yet, it would be surprising to hear the jury declare that 'U's play was *wrong*' and that 'W's play was *right*'. This shows yet another aspect of the rules in play. They are not 'true'. L's criticism not only shows that rules exist; L's disagreement likewise shows the source of the normativity of the rules, and that source is precisely conflict.

Conflict is a form of interaction; therefore, it has also a contextual character since there cannot be any conflict in the absence of others. It is difficult to imagine how one could have in any proper sense, a conflict with oneself, which is but a variant of Wittgenstein's private language argument (Wittgenstein 1969: nrs 243 ff.). Conflict as interaction highlights the factual basis of normativity, that is, a situation of interaction in which the normativity of rules is challenged.

Hunyadi, following Wittgenstein, adopts the insightful view that rules need not be expressed in any form of promulgation; however, they must exist or be valid one way or the other.[16] Rule following consists of a practice that cannot be made entirely transparent. We may be able to articulate some aspects of the practice, in that we may be able to express the rules we are following. The transparency of that practice is, however limited. The articulation of some aspects of the practice – for example, by pointing to the rules that apply to the piano contest – leaves some other aspects in the background. This background can in turn be highlighted, but against the background of a further different background, and so on.

There is no doubt that the rules which we follow come to the surface when there is a conflict. The fact that there is conflict shows that there are rules involved. They may operate in the background of a practice, as in our example of the practice of musical performance. Although rules may be implicit in the absence of conflicts, they may be challenged. When they are challenged, their normativity is tested or activated. Put differently, while both L and W may evaluate their performance according to some rules, it will be hard to believe that they are 'following' these rules in any meaningfully conscious way. The rules, that is, and their normative dimension, come to the surface at the moment of the conflict.

In a somewhat different way, meaning, rules and conflict can be said to be intertwined. Meaning is related to rules, and this relationship is mediated by conflict. Conflict, that is, activates the meaning of rules, that is, their normative force. Here we can grasp the idea that interaction takes place in a context that is structured by rules, in so far as meaning is involved. My point here is to show the relation between meaning, rules and conflict: conflict shapes rules in that it articulates their meaning; meaning in turn shows that there are rules being followed.

This approach is similar to Hobbes', though it is in at least one way crucially different from his. Conflict for Hobbes results from the subject's inability to act on rules, in his case the laws of nature. Therefore, his theory focuses on

16 Hunyadi 1995: 50–52. The author limits the analysis of rules to the effectiveness of their validity.

the establishment of a set of rules that provide the missing link between social interaction and the laws of nature. By their very nature, the rules of the sovereign confer meaning on the laws of nature. So, even in Hobbes, who claims that there is no social space before a political space comes into being, we see that conflicts are about rules, the meaning and hence binding force of which are contested.

The above analysis corroborates the interpretation of Hobbes offered in the previous chapter. There it was argued that the laws of nature exist without having meaning, due to Hobbes's nominalist metaphysics. That is to say that they exist as commands of God; however, without intervention of the sovereign, they are semantically empty. Following intervention by the sovereign, they become meaningful. The sovereign's intervention, that is, establishes a relationship between rules, conflict and meaning.

Once the sovereign has defined the content of natural laws, his rules share in the ontological status of the latter. That is to say that they are true. The rules of the sovereign establish the missing link between the rules of natural law and conflict, that is, meaning. The rules of the sovereign *represent* the laws of nature.

In the realm of meaning, conflicts reveal meaning, and so reveal the existence of rules. As a matter of course, meanings and conflicts are not 'out there'. They are related to subjects who are the actors in the conflict. It should be borne in mind that what is understood here by 'conflict' is any form of interaction where there is no, or not yet any, mutual understanding. Under this interactional approach, meanings are related to interaction. Meaning, that is, cannot be considered to be anything but social, in that meaning is shared meaning. Meaning is not something 'out there' on which agreement can be reached over which meaning can be said 'true'. Four consequences follow from that.

The first consequence is that conflicts are not necessarily conflicts about the meaning of *legal* rules; nor is it necessary to suppose that only legal rules can solve them.

The second consequence is that rules are embedded in a social practice, in which subjects participate. This idea of participation holds that, even if rules are instruments for realising some goal, end, or value, the determination of the latter does not take place outside that practice.

The third consequence is this: from the idea that rules are created throughout interaction in a social context, it follows that they do not represent any meaning 'out there', that is, independently of any social practice. Meaning then turns out to be of a normative nature, in that it is connected to rules. Contexts are by their very definition not fixed, but are replete with temporality. So are rules. Rules are above all social rules, abounding with temporality.

The fourth consequence is that interaction in the state of nature – that is, in the absence of any rules of the sovereign, as Hobbes and Rousseau take it – is both possible and meaningful. If this interaction is conflictual, it is so by its very nature. This thesis incorporates the idea that meaning does not exist 'out there'. It starts, however, being considered like that from the time when the sovereign talks. Meaning, then, is settled in rules that are not created in any interactional sense meant above, but issued by the sovereign. The rules of the sovereign fix meaning, including the meaning of the subject. The latter then has been aptly called a 'fixed anthropologicum' (Broekman 1979: 77, 82).

Even if conflicts are suppressed, as Hobbes wants it, or institutionalised, as Rousseau has in mind, they do not disappear. However, whilst they do not disappear, they do take on a different form from the 'moment' of the social contract onwards. Conflicts, that is, are absorbed by the rules of the sovereign. They are transformed into legal conflicts, for which legal rules offer legal solutions. Legal solutions are characterised by their adjudicative nature. It is the judge who resolves the conflict by applying the appropriate rules to it. Conflicts then are conflicts that activate the normativity of these rules, in that their meaning, and so their binding force, is challenged. Interaction on the basis of legal rules does not eliminate conflicts.[17]

Following this transformation of social conflicts into legal ones, some new problems emerge. The transformation of social conflicts into legal ones does leave the nature of social interaction unaffected. This is problematic in at least two ways. First, is it legitimate to transform any social conflict into a legal conflict? Secondly, what is the consequence for freedom of this transformation?

As we will see in chapter 5, strong legalism takes these questions to be unproblematic. The consequences for legal thinking, however, are considerable, depending on their answer. If the transformation of social conflicts into legal conflicts is in itself legitimate, any form of social interaction can be moulded according to this pattern.

This view is clearly expressed by Hobbes: the subject can act freely in the absence of a legal rule. The sovereign, however, can intervene at any moment in time, on every topic or in any type of social relations. Hobbes's claim that 'what is not forbidden is permitted' is extremely fragile, if not futile.[18]

Rousseau adopts a similar position. Since any rule of the sovereign is just, no rule can be unjust. Citizens are free to act freely as long as the sovereign remains silent. However, there are no limitations on his legislative intervention. So here again, the principle that 'what is not forbidden is permitted' is delicate in nature.

It turns out that on this view, the subject can be simply 'overruled' in that his capacity to organise social interaction is denied. The subject is framed according to a conception of the self. Over against this view I have argued in this chapter that subjects are 'intersubjects' in that their self emerges within social contexts. These contexts are forms of self-organisation, and not just organisations of selves as claimed by Hobbes and Rousseau. They see the self as a 'conception of the self', while I have defended in this chapter the view that selves are agents with a self-conception, the consequences of which will be investigated later on.

---

17 Julien Freund for his part has argued for the opposite view, since legal rules, far from solving conflicts, create new ones (Freund 1974, 1983: 330).

18 Hobbes 1966c: 198–9, 206: 'As for other liberties, they depend on the silence of the law. In cases where the sovereign has prescribed no rule, there the subject hath the liberty to do, or forbear, according to his own discretion.' Cf. Kelsen 1967: 245 ff., 1934.

The problem they fail to deal with, and on which I will further focus, is the legitimacy of rule creation. This problem is different from their legitimacy *qua rules*. Hobbes, Rousseau, Kant, and the other social contract theorists have mainly focused on the second problem, thereby neglecting the first one. The legitimacy of the creation of rules for them is self-evident. Rules are issued by the sovereign, and their legitimacy coincides with their legal validity.

Apart from the neglect in the work of the authors mentioned, the creation of rules or legislation has not received the attention from legal theory that it deserves. Put differently, although current legal theory has made serious efforts to overcome some of the sharp problems involved in the interpretation and application of rules, little attention has been paid to the problem of the legitimate creation of rules. The whole of the focus has been, until now, on the creation of legitimate rules.

Chapter 3
Rationality in Context

Aristotle vs Descartes

Within the Modern philosophical project, according to the substantial identification of the subject and rationality, their common feature is that they do not alter over time. This is part of their very definition. A substance that changes is a *contradictio in terminis*; rationality that is not identical cannot lead to truth. Under the standard story of Modernity, rationality simply pops up; the subject as a substance is a logical implication of the standard story.

The proper aspect of Modern rationality is its binary nature. The binary nature of rationality means that something is either rational or not rational. The binary nature of rationality is connected to the belief in the universal nature of truth. Truth is universal because of its unity. Its unity means that it is identical everywhere and at any time the same, hence universal.

The universality of truth includes the suggestion that it is identical *for everyone*. Rationality thus articulated results in the ontological determination of the subject as a thinking substance. A substance is by definition identical to itself. Because reason is discovered (standard story), it 'comes to the subject'. It determines the subject's ontological status as the origin of knowledge. Although the subject lies at the origin of knowledge, he is not implied in the determination of rationality. Rationality is located in reality where it is to be discovered. It shows itself to be wrapped up with certainty.

Aristotle

This position is clearly different from the Aristotelian view. For Aristotle, some propositions are necessarily true, while others are only plausible, and hence uncertain (Aristotle 1984d: 1112a, 18–1113a, 14). The classical Aristotelian form of rationality articulates a way of dealing with reality. Reality is an ordered cosmos and Being shows itself through the cosmological order.

Neither the existence of the world nor its order can be rationally questioned. Only a fool or a madman would engage in this undertaking. The existence of reality is not of philosophical relevance while its order belongs to the eternal world. This ontological status of the world excludes its complete and ultimate accessibility to human knowledge. Aristotle rules out the possibility of a science as a final and fixed set of propositions concerning Being. He denies the possibility of an ultimate and perfect *theorein* of the Platonic ideas without, however, rejecting every form of transcendence (Aristotle 1984c: 997b 6 ff.; Aubenque 1972: 313–14).

Transcendence refers to the perfection of the movements of the heavenly bodies. Their movement is circular, that is, without any beginning or end. Therefore, this movement is perfect (Aristotle 1984c: 1071 b 28, 1072 a 21–5). If there is a beginning to their movement, this must come from the first or unmoved mover. The latter causes his own movement and is at the same time his own *causa finalis*. He is the ultimate form of perfection. This perfection can be perceived through observation, though it cannot be *known* in the Modern sense of the word.

This strongly Platonising interpretation of Aristotle should be counterbalanced by a 'metaphysics of separation' as Pierre Aubenque (1972: 407 ff) suggests. This metaphysics of separation throws into relief the ontological difference between the superlunary and the sublunary. The metaphysical articulation of this separation shows the ontological parting of the perfect superlunary on the one hand and the imperfect sublunary on the other.

The receptivity of man for the order of the cosmos can be expressed in rational propositions, the truth of which can be ascertained through their correspondence with reality. The existence of reality precedes its rational expression by man. Put differently, the order of being precedes the order of knowledge. According to the ontological separation of the superlunary and the sublunary, knowledge is both possible and limited. The limitation of knowledge results in the principled exclusion of a complete rational unfolding of reality.

A result of this is that we should be content with conjectural knowledge in domains where certainty is not available. For Aristotle, the method for discovering truth, that is, dialectics or argumentation on the one hand and demonstration on the other, depends on the type of *problem* dealt with (Aristotle 1984d: 1112a 17–1113a, 12). Descartes' view was that it does not depend on the problem since reason is universal.

Descartes

Descartes therefore does not withhold the approximate articulation of truth that forms part of Aristotelian rationality. Conjectural knowledge may be a beginning of knowledge, and as long as it is not certain it does not give access to truth.[1] Only certainty can. Certainty is the criterion of knowledge and knowledge is the key to truth.

Descartes' position, when considered from the perspective of the history of philosophical problems, may be understood as providing a specification of Aristotelian epistemology. This specification would entail the elaboration of the criteria of certainty that is itself the criterion of truth. It would however be grossly misreading.

Descartes' *philosophia prima* expresses a binary ontology. Any ontology is binary on an initial level, in that it draws a dividing line between what is and what

1 We can, as Descartes (1996j: nr. 44) suggests, discover truth accidentally, yet not know for sure that we have found it.

is not. On a second level, an ontology may be non-binary, in that it allows for a degree of being. Aristotelian ontology is non-binary on the second level in that it allows for degrees of being. Within Aristotelian ontology, it makes sense to say that a horse is a 'real horse' in that it has more 'horseness' than an ordinary horse on the prairie.

This makes little sense within Cartesian ontology. It would be absurd to say that a being is more a being because, for example, it thinks more or better. From this perspective, Descartes' ontology qualifies as binary on the first and the second levels. It does not allow for any degree of being.

It is important to remember the argument from the previous chapter according to which, unlike for Descartes, consciousness is not an original datum. In a similar vein, rationality is not an original datum either. Rationality, that is, does not reveal itself to a correctly thinking subject. This claim complies with the alternative reading of the standard story of the beginning of the Modern philosophical project. Variants of the standards story are that rationality is 'out there', or that rationality is a matter of discovery. Under the alternative reading, the standard story has a subject pole. On this reading, the subject knows what he is looking for. The certainty of truth is certainty *for* the subject.

In chapter 1, it was also argued that the philosophical articulation of the individual is a product of nominalist theology. Descartes combines this with the Augustinian tradition and provides a deeper metaphysical foundation for the subject's individuality. Individuality is the ontological status of all creatures. The distinguishing ontological mark of the subject is thought. Thought is a necessary condition for being, and to be is a necessary condition for thinking. Not-thinking is the status of the object. This clarifies the binary nature of Descartes' ontology: to be as a subject is to be an individual thinking substance.

This clarification opens up the way for the further articulation of rationality. The ontological anchoring of the subject relies on his rational capacity. This allows him to think of himself as a thinking substance. The self-identification of the subject in relying on rationality would result in an infinite regress if the *cogito* were a conclusion. Similarly, the argument would be circular if thinking were defined as being and being as thinking. This definition only connects thinking and being; it says nothing about the nature of thinking.

The *cogito* is neither a conclusion nor a definition. It is a truth of reason (*vérité de raison*) that is stronger than mathematics.[2] The metaphysical unfolding of the first truth shows in turn the binary character of the ontology it envelops. Under this ontology, the subject stands in opposition to the object while the distinguishing mark of rationality is certainty. Certainty is the foundation of knowledge, and knowledge is the condition for access to truth.

The binary ontology is characterised by the opposition between subject and object on the one hand and certainty as the condition for access of truth. These

---

2 Descartes 1996j: 26–7, because we can doubt the demonstrations of mathematics, not the certainty of our existence.

are two sides of the same coin. In contrast with Aristotle's ontology, Descartes' ontology does not allow for a second level. This is due to the binary character of certainty. Something is either certain or it is not. Certainty gives access to truth, while uncertainty or disagreement is the mark of error (Descartes 1996l: 6–7).

The access to truth or reality based on the certainty of knowledge obliterates the fact that truth or reality can exist on its own, while certainty cannot. Certainty is expressed in a judgement. Judgements are made by agents. The search for certainty as the main target of the Modern philosophical project involves the determination of criteria. The criteria for the certainty of an idea are that it is *clair* and *distincte*. The determination of these criteria, however, proceeds independently of any idea because certainty on Descartes' view is self-evident. Once determined in this way, the criteria for certainty are applied to an idea. If an idea satisfies the criteria, it is ontologically true.

The independent nature of the criteria for certainty is again a manifestation of the standard story. Rationality reveals itself together with its criteria. This is the same as saying that truth shows itself together with its criteria (*veritas index sui*), which is yet another remnant of scholasticism in Descartes. This means that truth comes wrapped up with certainty. This contraction between truth and certainty makes self-evidence as the mark of truth a *Perfektionsbegriff*, as Luhmann (1981: 378–9) has labelled it. However, it relies on the belief in direct access to reality. From that perspective, syllogistic reasoning is a necessary and sufficient in order to attain unqualified truth.

The interpretation proposed here argues that there is no conceptual relationship between truth and certainty. This means that it is possible to conceptualise certainty without at the same time thinking of ontological truth; conversely, truth can be thought of without being known with certainty. According to this interpretation, ontology allows for a second level. Because ontology allows for a second level, it makes sense to use expressions such as 'to know better' or 'to know with more certainty'. These expressions make no sense for Descartes, since knowledge is the path to truth unqualified by a direct access to reality.

This interpretation locates certainty on the side of the subject, and not on the side of reality. In contrast to truth, certainty needs a subject in order to make sense. Certainty is certainty *of* something *for* someone. The difference between this interpretation and the standard story is that under the latter the criteria for certainty are ontologised. The result of this ontologisation is that direct access to reality is presupposed, which is what I propose to call the 'rationalistic fallacy'.

The Rationalistic Fallacy and Epistemologised Philosophy

The Rationalistic Fallacy

The rationalistic fallacy is a variant of the scholastic fallacy that has been articulated by Pierre Bourdieu. The scholastic fallacy, according to Bourdieu, involves identifying the position of the scholar typically the sociologist or the ethnologist, observing 'reality' with the meaning that 'exists out there'. Put differently, the scholar's presupposition is that the agents he observes throughout their practices think in exactly the same way as he does. He sees them in the image of himself, without taking into account the meaning of the practices that he observes for the agent(s) engaged in them (Bourdieu 1990, 2003; Winch 1990: 87–91). Under the scholastic fallacy, the social scientist imputes to his object of study that which belongs to the scholar's way of apprehending it (Bourdieu 1994: 225).

An example of the scholastic fallacy is the belief of rational choice theorists that humans act according to rational decisions. It includes the belief that everyone has access to rationality in exactly the same way as the rational choice theorist has.[3] In doing so – most of the time unwittingly – the social scientist takes for granted a specific view on the agent, subject, or actor. This view neglects the fact that the meaning according to which the agent is acting could emerge from a process of meaning creation that is different from what the methods of scientists reveal.

A result of this is that no distinction is made between the way of knowing the object and its meaning for the subject observed. 'Truth' and 'meaning' are conflated upon the scholar's confusion between a participant's perspective and an observer's perspective (Winch, 1990: 46, 51). Where this distinction is neglected, the difference between what an observer observes and what is happening is obliterated. Meaning is therefore held to be universal. This universalistic pretension relies on a methodological presupposition, and that is the scholastic fallacy.

The rationalistic fallacy is typically a variant of the epistemocentrism – so familiar since the Modern philosophical project in which it takes root – which I call the 'rationalistic fallacy'. Under the rationalistic fallacy, the philosopher operates on the presupposition that the concepts he uses have universal validity. In taking their universality for granted, he presupposes that what is self-evident is self-evident for everyone and that rationality is identical in all rational subjects.

The rationalistic fallacy entails neglecting the distinction between a theory of reality and a theory about reality. Like the scholastic fallacy, it does not distinguish between the results of a method and what there is. The similarity between the scholastic fallacy and the rationalistic fallacy can be exemplified by the jump in Descartes' argument establishing the *cogito*. Within the act of thinking, it is concluded that the subject has certainty concerning his thinking. From this certainty of thinking, it is concluded that he exists. From this existence, it is concluded that he exists as a thinking substance. From there, it follows finally that the subject is a thinking substance. This argument, that is, makes a jump from how the subject (*cogitans*) is to what it is (*res cogitans*).[4]

The rationalistic method of the Modern philosophical project presupposes that knowledge of reality is possible. In doing so, it avoids radical scepticism that is

3 The example is Bourdieu's (1994: 228).

4 Hintikka 1962, see also Hegel (1955: 220–26) for the critique that Descartes' argument is only valid for himself.

self-refuting. The truth of the *cogito* fixes the subject as a *res cogitans*. This truth makes the subject transparent to himself. The certainty of the *cogito* is all that can be known of him by him. The *cogito* is a proposition of the subject about himself. This proposition provides him with an ontological anchoring.

A substance or essence remains ontologically identical to itself. If the subject is a substance, he is therefore identical to himself. The essence of the subject is 'thinking' that must remain identical to itself. If not, the essence changes, which is a contradiction. Since 'thinking' belongs to the very essence of the subject, it is universal.

Here the rationalistic fallacy emerges. The ontological anchoring of the subject comes with the universality of reason. Because the method of ontologically anchoring the subject results in truth, the method itself must be true. A consequence of this is that the method leads to a theory of reality. The ontological stamp is provided by God who is proved to exist according to the very same method. Given the correctness of the rational proof, the theory is a theory of reality.

An important consequence of the rationalistic fallacy is the decontextualisation of reason or rationality. Reason is universal, and it is identical for and in everyone.

While the scholastic fallacy leads Bourdieu to say that there is 'a scholar in the machine' (Bourdieu 1994: 228), Descartes' dualism leads Gilbert Ryle to his expression that there is 'a ghost in the machine'(Ryle 1988: 17 ff., 32–3). However, the rationalistic fallacy may lead to the identification of 'a Descartes in the machine'.

The Rationalistic Fallacy and Epistemologised Philosophy

A critical illustration of the rationalistic fallacy is found in Heidegger's concept of the 'world-view'. Heidegger framed the concept of a 'world-view' in order to set out the strategy of the Modern philosophical project. Under a world-view, reality appears as an image through which subject and object are opposed. The knowing subject and the known object are opposite poles, in spite of which it is believed that the subject has direct access to reality. The world-view as an intellectual construction, hence of a nominalist brand, provides the illusion of direct access to reality. This is the old philosophical dream stemming from realism.

The combination of the dream of realism, that is, direct access to reality with the nominalist ontology, shows up in the idea of a world-view. It results in the ontological illusion that I call the rationalistic fallacy: the image of reality is taken for reality itself. As a result, the world-view transforms Aristotelian qualitative physics into a quantitative theory. Quantity is considered to be the only quality of reality, resulting in what is believed to be a theory of reality.

Heidegger's view on modern science is that it is the mathematical unfolding of clear and distinct ideas. Ideas or representations are located in, or are constructions of, the thinking subject. Their clarity and distinctiveness, and hence their aptitude to become knowledge that provides access to reality and unqualified truth, depends on the mere judgement of the subject. The formation of systems for

Heidegger is co-original with the exclusivity of the Euclidean method in the newly emerging science of nature (Heidegger 1988: 59). 'System', says Heidegger, is the fundamental law of *Dasein* and the nature of the system is a *mathematical* system of reason.

Thus, systematicity as the unfolding domination of reason articulates human reason, dignity and freedom from external domination. The domination of reason as a system of mathematical reason, however, sheds a particular light on practical reason. It saddles us with a 'derivation test' which constrains rationality to what can be mathematically or logically demonstrated. What cannot be demonstrated is therefore not rational and does not form part of the system. The logic of this argument seems attractive. However, it pushes out from the realm of reason things that cannot be proven in a demonstrative manner, condemning them to the status of non-rational, if not irrational. Value judgements typically belong to this class. The unfolding domination of reason, so it proves, carries with it the unfolding domination of theoretical over practical reason. This is the essence of epistemologised philosophy.

Within theoretical thinking, the method of epistemologised philosophy idealises nature after freeing it from its theological incidences. This mathematisation of nature (Husserl 1970a: 23 *et seq.*) – or the naturalisation of mathematics (Heidegger 1962: 50–83) – follows from the conception of nature as a metaphysical idea from the middle of the seventeenth century onward. The combination of this newly developed metaphysical idea with the method of mathematics gave natural science a fresh and strong impulse, serving as a model for practical reason.

The upshot of epistemologised philosophy is that throughout the Modern philosophical project, practical problems are transformed into theoretical ones. Both types of problems are handled with the same tools. The treatment of *theoretical* problems with the help of logic and mathematics on the one hand, and empirical verification and corroboration on the other, proved to be so successful in seventeenth-century natural science that the solution of practical problems is attempted with the same method (Taylor 1995b).

Descartes' version of epistemologised philosophy involves the claim that we will have to work with a provisional morality until all the branches of science have been unrolled. Having done that, the philosopher argues, the final morality will be the fruit that grows on the tree of science: the perfect morality. This 'perfect morality' is to be constructed along the same methodological lines as were followed for the preceding elaboration for the sciences (Cumming 1955; Boutroux 1896).

Hobbes's project moves along similar lines. His discovery of Euclid strengthens his conviction that the truth of the matter in politics should be found through using this method. Rational calculation should be used in order to solve practical problems, of which Hobbes's theory of the state is a paradigmatic case. According to a rational calculation, it is better to enter into a state and surrender our freedom to the sovereign than to run the risk of a violent death.

According to Kant's approach to morality, action will be moral if it is rational. The rationality of action involves the universalisation of the maxim of the action.

Universalisation of the maxim of action does not say anything substantive about the action's morality. It only provides a form to a content that makes the latter rational (Kant 1997: 2–3, 46). The rule of universalisation makes the standard for morality indeed indubitable, yet it places practical reason on the path of scientific knowledge, constructing the practical a priori on the same footing as the theoretical a priori.

However, epistemologised philosophy as portrayed above betrays a paradox. The mathematisation of nature or the naturalisation of mathematics is all but self-evident as the paradigmatic method of natural science. Heidegger in this respect argues that 'the mathematical' is the fundamental position that we adopt towards things by which we take up things as already given to us, and also as they must and should be given. This entails the claim that 'the mathematical' is the fundamental presupposition for knowledge of things (Heidegger 1962: 50–83). This presupposition brings with it the question of the ontological status of mathematics (Wintgens 2010). Does mathematics belong to reality or is it a method applied to reality? What characterises the Modern philosophical project, according to Heidegger, is the establishment of a connection between knowledge and the mathematical *('ta mathemata')*. This connection is the expression of the search for a new relationship between subject and truth. With regard to this search, we read from Heidegger (1962: 75): 'In the essence of the mathematical, as the project we delineated, lies a specific will to a new formation and self-grounding of the form of knowledge as such.'[5]

The paradox lies in Descartes' suggestion that the connection between the first certainty and derivative propositions of science is self-revealing or self-evident, and hence brings with it its own method. What Heidegger stresses is that it is a *willed* connection between nature as the object of science and mathematics as its method of its explanation. This also throws a different light on Descartes' programme. His is a *search* for certainty, which is what he *wants* to find.[6] Heidegger (1962: 75–6) continues:

> The detachment from revelation as the first source for truth and the rejection of tradition as the authoritative means of knowledge – all these rejections are only negative consequences of the mathematical project. He who dared to project the mathematical project put himself as the projector of this project upon a base which is first projected only in the project. There is not only a liberation in the mathematical project, but also a new experience and formation of freedom itself, i.e. a binding with obligations that are self-imposed. In the mathematical project develops an obligation to principles demanded by the mathematical itself. According to its inner drive, a liberation to a new freedom, the mathematical

5 Translation of both quotations in Heidegger 1993: 295–6.

6 This interpretation is suggested in Toulmin 1990: Chapter 1.

> strives out of itself to establish its own essence as the ground of itself and thus of all knowledge.[7]

This explains the pervasive impact of mathematical method in the seventeenth century and during the Enlightenment. The belief that mathematics leads to truth is part of foundationalism itself, although it is a practical position in that it relies on choice for mathematics. We will have the opportunity to see epistemologised philosophy at work in law in chapter 5, which will discuss legalism.

The next section will briefly focus on two critical approaches to Cartesian rationality as they appear in the works of Husserl and Perelman respectively. Both authors, it will be argued, specifically criticise the mere demonstrative aspect of rationality within the Modern philosophical project. They attempt to expand the concept of rationality to a contextual version of it. The following section will draw on their view and comments on 'bounded rationality', which appears to be an interesting candidate as a conception of practical reason.

Critique of Cartesian Rationality

Husserl

Apart from his critique of Descartes on which I commented in chapter 2, Husserl's work also offers a view on rationality that is interesting for our present purposes. His view on rationality is connected to a regressive analysis of the historical roots of the concept of rationality as developed in the Modern philosophical project.

Husserl's argument suggests that demonstrative rationality in general and geometry in particular is a form of making sense that has its historical roots in tradition. It is not, however, the only way of making sense, nor is it necessarily the dominant one. In taking geometry as the paradigmatic stance of demonstrative rationality, Husserl shows that it has a historically situated beginning. A geometrical insight begins as a personal insight. This insight is an idea of a person for whom it is obvious or self-evident. The insight, however, is obvious or self-evident when it is successfully accomplished (Husserl 1970b: 356). Unlike for Descartes, it is not the self-evident nature of the insight that leads to its depersonalisation.

The depersonalisation of a self-evidentiary insight is not the work of the solipsistic philosopher; it presupposes others. Depersonalisation, as the term suggests, is a *process*. While the insight is rooted in a subject, its depersonalisation makes it objective. It does not follow that the original insight becomes detached from the subject for whom it was self-evident. In order to become objective on the

---

7 Cf. Husserl 1970a: 8: 'In the Renaissance, as is well known, European humanity brings about a revolutionary change. It turns against its previous way of existing – the medieval – and disowns it, *seeking to shape itself anew in freedom*" (italics added).

contrary, the insight has to be kept within the intersubjective world, that is, the life world or the 'we-world'. It is only on this condition that an insight can be objectified.

This process of depersonalisation presupposes other subjects who can repeat the original mental operation on their own. This gradually results in the idea that the self-evidentiary character of the insight is based on its proper internal structure, which allows others to come to the same conclusion (Husserl 1970a: § 9 a, 24 ff).

Others who achieve the same insight into its internal structure actively understand it. It does not follow from their understanding that it exists in an impersonal manner or 'out there', so to speak. In so far as the insight is externalised via signs, for example, it can be observed by anyone else, albeit in a passive manner only. The externalisation of the original insight pushes it outside of the intra-personal domain as a first step towards its objectivation.

Throughout its externalisation in language, its fixation in writing, or its expression in mathematics, it gains independence (Husserl 1970b: 358 ff.). The evidentiary insight gets anchored in language through externalisation. Due to this sedimentation, over time others may gain access to it in a material and intellectual manner, and may therefore reactivate it. Because they can reactivate it, they can repeat it, which means that they actively understand it. The original insight thus derives its objective meaning from this process.

This objective meaning can be taken into consideration from two perspectives. The first is that the insight would not cease to exist, even if no one were actively thinking of it. Geometrical insights can exist 'on their own' on the condition that they are depersonalised. However, the depersonalisation should not negate the fact that they are a cultural given constructed through human activity (Husserl 1970a: § 9a, 24 ff).

The second perspective, confirming the first, is that geometric research makes sense without referring to its historical beginning. It is not necessary to remind or repeat the whole history of geometry in order to make new additional insights possible. Any new insight can be logically attached to the original one, because of the latter's sedimentation. Although the first insight can be repeated, it need not be, since all subsequent ideas can be logically attached to it. The possibility of working back along this chain of attachment, whilst not being a necessity, is what is meant by idealisation. As a result of the idealisation, the original insight does not lose its intersubjective anchoring in pre-scientific reality from where it was abstracted (Husserl 1970a: § 9h, 48 ff).

The universal accessibility of the original insight, its transmission, and explanation through language result in the geometrist's mediated dealing with it. The geometrist's mediated dealing with the original insight means that the acquaintance with the 'how' and 'what' of its pre-scientific origin becomes unnecessary, although not impossible.

The absence of any need to go back to this pre-scientific origin does not raise serious problems. Husserl's point, however, is to show that the access to the original insight is barred, or is made impossible. The origin of the original insight is forgotten. Geometry is attached to its methodological device, and no longer to its origin. Self-evidence as a characteristic of the successful realisation of a project for the acting subject becomes detached from the horizon of human existence and lives a life of its own (Husserl 1970b: 358). This is the way Descartes uses self-evidence as a mark of truth.

The expression of geometry in mathematics easily flows into the undue extrapolation of the latter, nourishing the belief that reality is essentially mathematical. This extrapolation goes hand-in-hand with the mathematisation of nature, or the naturalisation or hypostatisation of mathematics, which is an integral part of the Modern philosophical project.

Husserl's point regarding the universality of geometry, for which mathematics is a helpful device, is that everyone can repeat the original insight. This insight *makes the same sense* to everyone who repeats it without making ontological claims. Husserl's regressive analysis is similar to Perelman's regressive analysis of the concept of justice, on which I will briefly focus now.

Perelman

Chaïm Perelman started by criticising Descartes' conception of reason and rationality in the middle of the last century. He rightly challenged the epistemologisation of philosophy, which involved the limitation of rationality to mere theoretical reason as Husserl (1970a: § 3, 7 ff.) had already done before him. From this perspective, the ontological position of the subject embedded in epistemologised philosophy is opposed to the universe (Perelman 1972d, 1972f).[8]

Speaking more generally, Perelman criticises any form of binary rationality upon which what is rational can be proved in an empirical or a logical manner. What cannot be proved in this way is therefore not rational, because logical or empirical proof is the only (binary) criterion of rationality.

Accordingly, Perelman concludes that the rational capacities of the subject are unduly limited (Perelman and Olbrechts-Tyteca 1976: 4). Logical or empirical proof as the necessary condition for rationality makes it both conclusive and impersonal. He then attempts to recontextualise reason, or to give reason back to a context, thus reframing the impersonal or universal nature of rationality.

The rationalistic fallacy takes the universality of reason for granted. Universality is considered to be included in rationality according to which it itself is believed to be rational. This belief fits the standard story under which reason is revealing itself.

8 Cf. Hampshire 2001: 13: 'Compare the institutions that have given sense to the traditional concept of reason and of intellect as opposed to imagination: they are, first of all, theoretical studies, the study of mathematics, and of logic; and the natural sciences; last, practical studies, the law and the development of legal systems. The Platonic ordering of disciplines makes mathematical proof the paradigm of reasoning and of rationality. This Platonic concept of reason is not the only possible one, and for some purposes, such as understanding the nature of justice and of morality, it has been greatly misleading.'

Perelman's view concurs in its main lines with Heidegger's idea of natural science. On this idea, natural science is based on a *willed* connection between its object (nature) and its method (mathematics). The mathematical method in natural science is primarily a matter of choice or decision, not of truth. Its choice is a practical matter, not a theoretical one. This approach draws the full consequence of the opposition between subject and object, according to which the latter is forever unknown.[9] This is simply the consequence of the self-assertion of the subject. He withdraws from authoritarian arguments and articulates his position in the world on choices relating to his self-assertion.

It follows from Perelman's position that the primacy of formal or demonstrative rationality as the only possible form of rationality cannot itself be established within this very same model of theoretical rationality. The connection between universality and rationality is not a necessary one. It has to be argued for. For this reason, rationality is embedded in argumentation that is bound to a context.

For Aristotle, the method of inquiry is determined by the type of problems that are dealt with. Perelman's originality is to relate argumentation not to a type of problem but to an *audience* that is addressed and does or does not adhere to what is argued for. Argumentation relates rationality to subjects. Subjects can be considered rational without rationality being connected to a substance or *res cogitans,* as Descartes believed. As was argued in Chapter 2, subjects are embedded in a social context as a necessary condition for their being a self. Neither subject nor rationality exists *an sich*, or independently of any context. As far as rationality is concerned, it can be asked *for whom* something would be rational, if not for the subject. He is dependent on a social context in order to be a subject at all. The subject as a self was shown to be a subject of meaning, and not merely an a priori ontologically anchored subject of truth.

The ontological anchoring of the subject as a thinking substance, and hence a subject of truth and self-revealing rationality, are two sides of the same coin. Self-revealing rationality shows itself to be self-evident. The self-evident nature of demonstrative rationality makes it a criterion for ontological truth. As a consequence, what is self-evident is rational, and vice-versa, as Descartes wants it.

Against this view, Perelman maintains that what is not self-evident is not, for that reason alone, deprived of rationality (Perelman and Olbrechts-Tyteca 1976: 4). According to this view, demonstrative rationality marked by 'self-evidence' is a way of making sense. Making sense is subject related. It follows that self-evidence as a form of making sense is self-evidence *for* a subject. Conversely, self-evidence as certainty is certainty *of* something. Upon this characterisation, demonstrative rationality is only one form of rationality involving certainty of something for someone.

This critique of demonstrative reason is supplemented with an enlargement of rationality. Taking demonstrative rationality to involve making sense for the

9 Kant 1997: 56, 1929: 82: 'What objects may be in themselves, and apart from all this receptivity of our sensibility, remains completely unknown to us.'

subject, Perelman puts forward his idea of argumentative reason or reasonableness. Argumentative reason or reasonableness is found within the practice of legal argumentation. Legal argumentation proceeds according to a dialectical presentation of arguments upon which a conclusion is reached. This conclusion – the judicial decision, for example – is in turn supported by arguments.

This dialectical model of argument takes a distance from the *more geometrico* model, predominant in the Modern philosophical project. It rearticulates the Aristotelian dialectical model of reasoning criticised by Descartes as the exemplary model for philosophy *tout court*.

A person making a decision, typically the judge, is doing two things. First, he is making a choice. Secondly, he is providing reasons for this choice. The argumentative support for the choice may result in qualifying the decision as 'reasonable'. The argumentative support for a decision is presented to an audience. An audience is particular when the speaker simply wants to persuade, as happens in advertising messages. The audience is universal when the speaker considers it to be a representation of humanity, which he wants to convince. The approval of, or adherence to, an argumentative conclusion makes the latter reasonable when the audience consists of reasonable persons. Reasonable persons form part of the universal audience; the universal audience only approves of, or adheres to, reasonable argumentation, as in philosophical argumentation.

In persuasive argumentation, the speaker only wants to obtain the approval of the audience. The audience or the addressee(s) can, but need not, be a physically present group of subjects. If it is not physically present, the audience can be called 'virtual'. This is especially the case when the universal audience is addressed. The universal audience consists of subjects who, according to the speaker's idea of rationality, represent reasonable humanity. The dialectical relationship between the speaker and his audience, especially the universal audience, is intimately related to the speaker's idea of reasonableness. This is what makes it a virtual audience.

A variant of the universal audience which deserves special attention concerns the deliberations of the subject with himself. The subject deliberating with himself provides reasons for a choice or a decision. Throughout this process of deliberation, the subject argues with others within himself. The others within himself, as in an externalised argumentation, provide the audience at which the argumentation is addressed. In internal deliberation, as in external argumentation, the audience expresses the speaker's idea of reasonableness. According to this idea, reasonable subjects should approve or adhere to the argumentation. Externalised or internal deliberation are structurally similar (Perelman and Olbrechts-Tyteca 1976: 19, 53 ff.).

Within Perelman's theory of argumentation, the question 'What is rationality?' is not answered in an a priori way. It does not embrace a definition of rationality with the help of criteria. According to his theory, rationality consists in giving reasons. When giving reasons in argumentation, others are addressed. Giving reasons, therefore, is an action for which others provide the social context. Action is of a subject. It follows that the question 'What is rationality?' is embedded in argumentation as a practice. It makes the articulation of rationality itself an argumentative issue. It is within the theory of argumentation that the question 'What is rationality?' is to be answered. This answer is an open answer because rationality is not necessarily demonstrative. On Perelman's view, argumentation is the proper method of philosophy which includes the philosophical articulation of rationality through the practice of argumentation (Perelman 1972g, 1976d; Toulmin 1990: 34 ff.).

I should like to underline the structural similarity between Perelman's theory of rationality and Mead's theory of the subject that was dealt with in the previous chapter. Mead's theory articulates an interactionally emerging self, that is, a self that emerges through interaction with others. This interaction, so we saw, shows the subject as both an individual ('I') and a social ('me') agent essentially connected to the practices into which he is engaged. While Mead stresses the emergence of the self, Perelman's theory focuses on a form of interaction, namely argumentation. The speaker has a certain idea of his audience that manifests itself in his mind. The 'real' audience, however, consists of individuals who are, like the speaker, social selves who interact with the speaker throughout argumentation.

However, the members of the audience react to what a speaker says following deliberation amongst themselves. It is the 'I' aspect of their self that allows for the adoption of a critical distance towards what the speaker says, and that can be considered as part of the 'me' aspect of the audience's self. The argumentative practice, therefore, can be interpreted as a variant of Mead's idea of social interaction of which 'role taking' is the essential aspect. Mead's 'generalised other', therefore, as the normative instance of social interaction bears a structural resemblance to Perelman's idea of the universal audience, and the internal deliberation of the subject with himself as an instance of the universal audience bears a similar resemblance to Mead's interaction of the 'I' and 'me' poles of the self (Wintgens 1993; Perelman and Olbrechts-Tyteca 1976: 18–19).

Rationality in Context: The Audience

The concept of 'audience' marks the originality of the 'New Rhetoric'. This concept allows us to deal with all kinds of problems through argument, instead of relating it to a specific type of problem. This is the case in Aristotle, for whom argumentation fits problems that cannot be dealt with in a demonstrative way.[10] Descartes exploits this distinction and turns it into a separation, which is tribute to his dualistic metaphysics. Because of this dualism, it does not allow for a second level, as noted above. A consequence of this is that rationality is a matter of all or

10 This, according to Aristotle, is due to the nature of the problem that it is ultimately due to his realistic ontology according to which it is reality that determines the nature of the problem.

nothing; it cannot be a matter of degree, nor is it connected to a context. Descartes' subject is a solipsistic individual participating in universal a-contextual reason.

Against this view, the notion of 'audience' allows for an argumentative articulation of 'rationality' itself. Challenging Descartes, Perelman rightly holds that the question 'What is rationality?' cannot be dealt with outside an argumentative context. The theory of argumentation leaves open the criteria of rationality. Rationality is not self-revealing nor does it, as a consequence, reveal its criteria. Because its articulation is embedded in argumentation, through which it establishes its reasonableness, there are no fixed criteria for rationality.

With the help of the notion of audience, rationality is brought within the context of participation. In connecting rationality to adherence of the universal audience, Perelman implements his version of the Habermassian idea of giving reason back to its contexts. Perelman's version of the context of reason is the universal audience, that is, the audience composed of reasonable beings.

In relating the philosophical question 'What is rationality?' to argumentation, rationality can be considered a matter of degree. The notion of 'audience' brings demonstrative rationality and argumentative reasonableness together on a bipolar continuum. At one end of the continuum, though not included in it, is purely emotional adherence. At the other end, and included in the continuum, is self-evidence. Self-evidence attains a maximum level of adherence and therefore is the highest degree of rationality, though not its exclusive expression. Purely emotional adherence does not involve any rationality.

Rationality being a matter of degree, disagreement is not simply a lack of rationality as we read from Descartes. Given the conjugation of demonstrative and argumentative rationality based on the common denominator of 'adherence', both are able to qualify as 'rational'. With this conjugation, Cartesian self-evidentiary rationality necessarily requires adherence. What does not stand up to rational proof, however, can turn out to be reasonable. What is reasonable can be a matter of disagreement because disagreement is not identical to irrationality or non-rationality. Reasonable persons can, however, disagree with each other without being unreasonable (Perelman 1976c, 1976d; Winch 1965).

This critique, however deep it may be, does not oppose demonstrative rationality to argumentative reasonableness. On the contrary, it allows for a rereading of Descartes' *Méditations* as an attempt to convince the universal audience. Descartes' universal audience consists of thinking substances who only accept as rational what is '*clair et distincte*'. On this reading, the *Méditations* rely on a specific rule of argumentation which claims that it is impossible to argue against self-evidence (Perelman and Olbrechts-Tyteca 1976: 42–3).

According to Descartes, where an idea satisfied this criterion it is true. Accordingly, the audience confronted with a clear and distinct idea is 'out of arguments'. Because no arguments are available, truth is reached. On the argumentative reading of Descartes, the unavailability of arguments is not identical to saying that they do not exist or are impossible.

This is precisely what Perelman points to. Against what is self-evident, no arguments are available *now*. The availability of arguments depends on the audience that encapsulates reason. Self-evidence may be a mark of truth to which the universal audience adheres. However, the adherence of the universal audience is not a criterion of truth. If it were, its adherence would be a criterion of rationality which makes the theory of argumentation collapse into a context-independent theory. The adherence of the universal audience is a mark of reasonableness, which is rationality in context. The contextualisation of rationality marks the escape from its universality, hence the rationalistic fallacy.

Who is Afraid of Practical Reason?

The rebuttal of the rationalistic fallacy throws a new light on the epistemologisation of philosophy. A result of the epistemologisation of philosophy is that practical reason operates under the auspices of theoretical reason. Self-revealing reason, so it follows from Descartes' *cogito*, is unable to deal with disagreement. Since the domain of practical reason is replete with disagreement, reason cannot be practical at all.

Perelman and Husserl disconnect truth and rationality and reconnect the latter to the subject. Under this reconnection, rationality is brought into an intersubjective context. The retrieval of the historical situatedness of a geometrical insight or the contextualisation of rationality within the universal audience prevent it falling victim to the rationalistic fallacy.

The detachment of ontological truth and rationality is carried out starting from two domains that are very sensitive to mere rational proof. In Perelman's case, it is formal logic, while for Husserl, it is mathematics. Husserl expands rationality by relating an original geometrical insight to a subject that is shared by others following idealisation. Perelman expands rationality to rational acceptability by the universal audience that is composed of reasonable subjects. Their enlargement of rationality makes it a matter of intersubjectivity and not simply a matter of the self-revelation of reason to a solipsistic subject.

As was argued in chapter 2, consciousness is not an original fact. The above analysis makes it clear that rationality is not an original fact either. It was shown in chapter 2 how Husserl's Fifth Meditation opened up the *ego cogito* to others. The relation of *ego* to *alter ego* gives rise to an articulation of a theoretical connection between Weber's sociology and Mead's social philosophy on the one hand and philosophy on the other.

From the perspective of the history of philosophical problems, this relationship between philosophy, sociology and social philosophy sheds a different light on both the subject and rationality. The decontextualisation of subject and rationality throughout the Modern philosophical project precluded any meaningful articulation of the subject *qua* subject. The rational unfolding of the a priori structure of reason leaves no place for the subject *qua* subject, that is, the subject of meaning.

Descartes' disembedded and disembodied epistemologised subject evolves towards Kant's transcendental *ego*. The transcendental ego is a disembedded and disembodied possibility condition of knowledge and action *in vacuo*. As a transcendental ego (Kant) or as a *cogito* (Descartes), the subject exists independently of others. Their existence is at the same time purified of any empirical conditions.

Husserl and Perelman are exemplary critics of the decontextualisation of reason, followed by others (Toulmin 2001: chapter 2; Taylor 1995b: 12). Their critique joins Mead's theory of the subject and its critique of rationality. Mead argues that universality is a matter of taking the role of others, with whom a context is shared (Mead 1962: 90).

Interaction and argumentation both involve others. Through interaction and argumentation, subjects adopt position towards one another. In doing so, subjects share a context of meaning, which is formative for both rationality and their selves. Husserl establishes a similar intersubjective context. It clarifies how rationality can be recontextualised by taking the subject seriously as an agent. In this respect, contextualised rationality connects rationality to the social subject and so is, like the subject, replete with contextuality.

Husserl's and Perelman's alternative to Cartesian rationality stresses its the intersubjective nature. In line with Mead's social philosophy, both strongly suggest that rationality and the subject are related to a context of participation. According to this view, the subject and rationality are primarily a matter of meaning, before eventually being related to truth. Truth is impersonal and independent of the subject. Meaning for its part can only be meaning *for* someone. Meaning makes no sense without a subject.

Speaking more generally, the epistemologisation of philosophy throughout the Modern philosophical project raises the question as to whether reason can be practical at all. According to the standard story, rationality is found 'out there'. It pops up from reality. Dealing with reality means knowing it. Knowledge of reality is the basis of truth. Truth is what the philosopher is looking for.

The place left for practical reason turns out to be a limited one. What must be done must first be known. As a result of this, normative action results from the application of knowledge, as Descartes' final moral suggests.

According to the alternative reading of the beginning of the Modern philosophical project, it unfolds as a *quaestio originis*. The basis of the *quaestio originis* is all but theoretical. The *search* for certainty is an act of freedom. We know what we want, so that the Modern philosophical project unfolds as a search *starting from* and *aiming at* freedom. This is an eminently practical position, not a theoretical one.

This practical position is, however, concealed in the further development of philosophy through the Modern philosophical project. Descartes' *Discours* and the *Méditations* set out a provisional morality to be relied upon until the final morality is established. It will only be established as the fruit of the rational unfolding of reality. This process of rationally unfolding reality involves freedom, though only in a marginal way. The subject can withhold his judgement in the event that an idea is not *clair et distincte*. Conversely, the correct use of his judgement leads to certainty, and hence truth. When truth is reached in a systematic manner, final morality can be substituted for provisional morality. The epistemologisation of philosophy transforms the philosophical problem of freedom into a theoretical one.

The domain of action will only therefore be covered by rationality in so far as it can be thought of in rational terms. The full articulation of this approach is undertaken by Kant in framing the categorical imperative, according to which action is only morally justified in so far as it can be universalised. The categorical imperative however is not a source of knowledge, since it does not provide us with any substantive answer as to what action is moral (Kant 1997: 3). It only says what makes human action rational, and that involves subjecting action to the test of universalisability.

Because the categorical imperative is not a source of knowledge, an appeal is made to an active intervention by the subject. The morality of his action does not result from its moral content per se. It is the consequence of a formal operation of universalisation, without which the action cannot be moral at all. Put differently, if the subject wills some content, the moral character of the latter does not primarily depend on this will but on universalisability of the content. Through universalisation, the content attains the form of a law that connects it to reason.

Rationality in this respect determines the subject. All he is is a subject of truth. His identity is characterised through his belonging to the realm of universality or rationality. This means that the subject is to act according to true norms. Feelings, beliefs, or convictions do not have this rational status. They are 'empirical', not universal. Unless they are universal or universalisable, they do not have sufficient dignity to deserve philosophical attention.

The analysis of rationality in this chapter links in with the conclusions of the previous chapter on the subject. The a-contextual version of rationality obliterates the subject *qua* subject. In practical matters, the transcendental ego is not in a position to relate experience to normativity. What can be known and what should be done is to be determined in an a priori manner, independently of any contact with empiricism. What Descartes had framed as the ontological anchoring of the subject is pushed right to its farthest consequences through idealism. It results in what Ricoeur (1986e: 316) has aptly called a 'discourse without a subject'. This results, according to Ricoeur, in a science of a praxis, or a science applied to the domain of the practical. Arguing against this, Ricoeur writes:

> Few ideas are today more healthy and liberating than the idea that there is a practical reason, but no science of it. The domain of action is from the ontological point of view that of things submitted to change, in the sense of what is plausible and probable. One should no doubt not blame Kant for this development that he has not wanted nor anticipated. I limit myself to saying that by constructing the concept of the practical *a priori* on the model of the theoretical *a priori*, Kant has transferred the investigation of practical reason into a domain of knowledge where it does not belong. (Ricoeur 1986c: 250)

The contraction of theoretical and practical reason led to the construction of normativity out of a theoretical model. Perelman and Husserl have shown that this need not be the case, even in theoretical reason. They substitute intersubjectivity in dealing with reality for a theory of reality in theoretical matters. Intersubjectivity is 'making sense', which is not necessarily identical to universality. In breaking down the rationalistic fallacy, they open up the way for undoing the epistemologisation of philosophy. The latter obliterates the possibility for reason to be practical at all.

The interpretation of the beginning of Modernity as a *quaestio originis* showed the practical issue behind this project. Its search for certainty was regarded as an escape from authority in theoretical matters. The elaboration of the new science of nature could be interpreted as the articulation of a new form of freedom (Heidegger 1962: 77, 1961: 141–8; Hegel 1955: 223–5). This form of freedom frames a new moral ideal for the subject, as Taylor puts it, or as an instance of self-responsibility (Taylor 1995b: 6). In line with Perelman and Husserl, Taylor holds that even when adopting theoretical stances, we are agents (ibid.: 11).

According to the standard story of the beginning of Modernity, it can only be concluded that self-revealing reason makes an abstraction of the subject. Self-revealing reason logically reveals itself as it is, and determines the subject under the auspices of universality.

As with the recontextualisation of the subject, the alternative reading of the beginning of the Modern philosophical project is of considerable help. The alternative reading primarily focuses on the practical issue of the project as the search for certainty. The search for certainty being a practical issue, the Modern philosophical project, however, lifts out the subject as an actor and makes him an object. The subject as an actor searching for certainty is made a hostage to his own thinking that turns him into an object. In order to be rational, his plan is to proceed along the same lines as those applicable to the acquisition of scientific knowledge. The subject may turn out to be liberated from ecclesiastical authority with regard to theoretical matters, although this liberation does not provide him with an alternative in the field of action.

Under the epistemologisation of philosophy, a *science* of action pushes the rationality of action outside its domain. More precisely, the rationality of action is put to the test with a theoretical criterion that is external to the action itself. Like Ricoeur, Husserl rightly criticises the dangers connected with this form of 'scientific life' (Husserl 1970b: 367).

Rationality, Reasonableness and Bounded Rationality

It may be recalled from chapter 1 that nominalism articulated God's radical simplicity. This means that no distinction is made between his intellect and his will. A consequence of this is that God's acts are no longer determined by his intellect, so that his will is absolutely free. When compared, for instance, to Aquinas' approach, God's will was related to the *lex aeterna* that contains the plan of the world. On this view, God is less free than under the nominalist interpretation of his nature.

Compared to Aquinas' approach, the metaphysical problem of the relationship between intellect and will in God is reversed under the nominalist interpretation. This reversal radically changes the outlook of reality, in that God's absolute freedom also makes his creatures free, except the fact that they are bound by his commandments. In chapter 1, it was argued that this leads into legalism, under which normativity consists of following rules.

Yet, the reversal of intellect and will as a metaphysical problem seems to apply only to God. As a matter of fact, freedom consists in the possibility of withholding one's judgement in the event that an idea was not clear and distinct. However, this only applies to the standard reading of Descartes, under which reason is self-revealing to the subject. Under the alternative reading of Descartes, as argued above, the search for certainty is an act. It is something a philosopher wants to find. On this view, and the additional fact that certainty is certainty *for* someone, it can be established that the rational unfolding of reality follows upon an act, and not on the revelation of reason.

Legalism as embedded in nominalist metaphysics takes normativity to be a matter of following rules that are imposed from the outside. Here, the freedom of the agent is limited to doing the right thing. His rationality is only involved in a limited way here. It follows that the reversal of intellect and will does not apply to the agent, but only to God. In Perelman's work, we find a convincing attempt to fulfil the promise of Modernity, in that for him practical reason prevails over theoretical reason, with meaning prevailing over truth, and argumentation over demonstration. In the following pages, I will briefly comment on the idea that conceives rationality in terms of reasonableness.

In his critique of Cartesian rationality, Perelman argued that this is an undue limitation of the agent's rational capacities (Perelman and Olbrechts-Tyteca 1976: 4; Perelman 1970c; Aristotle 1984d: 1139a, 10–15). While Ricoeur criticised the idea of a scientific idea of practical reason, Perelman pushed this critique further by rethinking the relationship between theoretical and practical reason. The first move of the strategy of his argument entails a recontextualisation of the concept of rationality as noted above, which entails a connection of rationality to the subject via the concept of 'audience'. Having connected rationality with acceptability, Perelman makes it clear that rationality is not a matter of all or nothing. Rationality is not a binary concept as it was for Descartes.

In a second move, he focuses on 'theoretical reason' as it is practiced by scientists. The role of the scientist, according to Perelman, does not simply consist in submitting oneself to self-evidence. What characterises the scientist's position is his reaction to obstacles, difficulties and unsolved problems. In doing so, he tries to reorder the field of knowledge acquired thus far, and to introduce new findings in it that had previously proved to be incompatible with it. Scientists make choices; they are no longer anonymous beings who accept the solutions that nature offers. A creative scientist is a complete being, committed to his activity, who weighs and balances, makes choices and decisions (Perelman 1950: 137; 1970e, 1972e). Under this method of scientific activity, it turns out that rationality is a matter of practice, in that it is embedded within a practice of qualified scientists.

The third move of his argument then consists in elaborating this model where decisions and choices precede knowledge. When knowledge is dissociated from necessity and a priori-ism (ibid.: 138), rationality is expanded so as to include 'reasonableness'. From there, it follows that practical reason, decision making and choosing gain the upper hand in the process of acquiring knowledge. In the absence of self-evidence, which is quite a normal aspect of scientific practice, scientists must justify their decisions in front of their audience, comprised of their peers. Acceptability then becomes part of the validity of the findings of scientific research. Acceptance following justification can be regarded as legitimation in the ongoing development of science, the results of which are no longer fixed *ne varietur* (Perelman 1972e: 130; 1970d).On this view, it seems to me that Perelman comes up with a original idea concerning rationality that will mark posterity. The point of this idea is that:

> … if for three centuries our philosophical tradition can be characterised by its particular conception of reason, of which demonstrative proof and calculus are the only manifestations, each man considers that he is reasoning when he deliberates, discusses, argues or justifies an attitude. And this fact is implicitly recognized by those who limit the competence of reason to the formal aspect of knowledge because when they want to make their point of view prevail in a debate they cannot call on the help of calculus or formal demonstration, but only on argumentation which is the only possible use of reason in this case. (Perelman 1972d: 98)

The primacy of formal (Cartesian) rationality as the only possible form of rationality cannot itself be established within this very same model of rationality.[11] If it is to be universal, universality does not necessarily by itself have a rational – that is, universal – foundation. In Perelman's view, rationality is embedded within a context-bound argumentation. The context consists of social subjects.

As was argued above, although subjects can be considered rational, their rationality is not connected to some substance, nor are they to be regarded as a *res cogitans* as Descartes believed. In order for their selves to emerge, subjects as selves must be intimately related to a social context that is a necessary condition for their being a self. This means that neither subject nor rationality exist 'as such', or independently of any context. As far as rationality is concerned, one might ask for whom something could be rational, if not for the subject. And as a subject, he is dependent on a social context in order to be a subject at all.

---

11 Simon 1983: 6 (the justification of demonstrative logic leads into an infinite regress of logics).

If the subject as a self is a subject of meaning, and not merely an a priori ontologically anchored subject of truth, the same can be said of rationality. If rationality is interpreted in this way, that is, if rationality is regarded as a way of making sense, and not merely a sign of truth, we can have it both ways. What is self-evident is therefore rational, as Descartes wants it. But what is not self-evident is not, and is for this reason alone deprived of rationality altogether, as Perelman argues (Perelman and Olbrechts-Tyteca 1976: 4–5). According to this view, we maintain the possibility of rational 'self-evidence' in the Cartesian sense, provided that it is related to the subject. Self-evidence is not standing on its own. Something then is self-evident *for* the subject. This is one form of rationality, though by no means the only one.

The relationship between theoretical and practical reason, or between knowledge and action, thus takes on a new shape. If scientists take decisions on the basis of which they acquire knowledge, the primacy of theoretical reason over practical reason will be overcome. What is more, philosophers may learn from lawyers what it means to take reasonable, if imperfect, decisions. Lawyers argue in favour of decisions that must be taken, without being able to prove their necessity in terms of rational demonstration.

> Because we cannot rely on the self-evidence of a rule, it is the 'exposé des motifs' that must show its desirability within the given political context, the values and norms that are effectively admitted providing the premises of the argumentation that must justify the promulgation of a new rule. (Perelman 1976d: 199)

In demonstrating the role of argumentation in practical matters, Perelman has opened up the way for a new concept of rationality. Practical reason as a matter of fact is no longer subordinated to theoretical reason, as the predilection for an argumentative model in science illustrated. In other words, Perelman's critique of Cartesian rationality takes sides with epistemocentrism or the view that rationality is essentially connected with an episteme.

Apart from what can be rationally demonstrated, rationality also covers a field called 'reasonable'. It follows from this that logical or empirical self-evidence is not separated from what is reasonable, but that both amount to 'ways of making sense' by rational people. This approach cuts off any 'direct access theories' holding that reality is 'out there' waiting for discovery upon the correct use of reason.

According to the view that philosophy is no longer the exclusive domain covered by a first truth (like the *cogito*), a first value or norm – in short, a foundationalist version of philosophy – rationality is dissociated from necessity. The 'rational' and the 'reasonable' are therefore located on a bipolar axis, under which rationality as a generic concept can be considered a matter of degree. 'Rational' then is what can be proven in a demonstrative or conclusive way. Logic and mathematics are therefore properly called 'rational' in this sense. What is 'reasonable', however, cannot be conclusively proven, but relies on the argumentative support for a claim or decision. This argumentative support is provided in a context. Reasonableness therefore opens up the way for a concept of rationality that is context sensitive, and is all but a dispositive concept.

Perelman's critique is instructive in that it opens up a wider avenue towards 'rationality in context'. Demonstrative rationality suggests perfection in terms of universality. It does however rest on the belief that universality is universal, so that the reduction of rationality to one of its specific manifestations excludes other, contextual variants of it. Herbert Simon for his part has focused on this problem in economic decision making which displays some interesting connections with our topic. He criticises the neo-liberal version of economics as the study of the rational allocation of scarce goods by agents who are held to be wealth maximisers. Under a narrow view of neo-classical economics, the results of rational choices are more important than the processes by which these choices are made.[12] *Homo economicus* is the twin of *homo rationalis* in Descartes.

This approach relies on the axiom that agents *are* wealth maximisers. However, the wealth maximiser is only one type of 'rational man'. A different though not unrelated type is the 'satisficer', a term coined by Simon. Optimisers act according to the thesis of profit maximisation and make the economically soundest decision in any situation. 'Satisficers' for their part stop searching for profit once they believe that every option has been explored (Simon 1997: 295–8). Remaining with the terminology used until now, optimisers act rationally, while satisficers act reasonably.[13]

According to Simon's approach, optimisers act in an optimal way according to the theory, without what is information, transaction, or deliberation costs. Satisficers for their part act on the premise that also their knowledge is a scarce good, and that a decision, all things considered, satisfies them. Optimisers are optimistic about their capacities and knowledge; their rationality is unbounded. Satisficers for their part act within a context, where costs for additional information, deliberation and transaction are weighed up against their needs or prospects, taking into account that the time to make a decision is not unlimited. At some point in time, they turn off the computers, close the economy handbooks, and make the decision with what they have. At some point in time, that is, a decision must be taken on intuitive grounds (Conlisk 1996: 687).

Satisficing agents move away from perfect, substantial, or demonstrative rationality in that their capacities are 'bounded'. Bounded rationality typically connects rationality to a context. More specifically, agents take decisions within a context. Were they perfectly rational and striving towards optimal decisions, they would be Cartesians adopting a substantive version of rationality. However, once we have put rationality back into its context, there is no superstition in the belief that the context influences the decision as well as its rationality.

---

12 Simon 1978: 2: ' … economics has largely been occupied with the results of rational choice rather than the process of choice.'

13 Korobkin and Ulen 2000: 1076: ' … we might say that satisficing behavior can be rational in a "global" sense.'

Perelman had already suggested that scientists take decisions and give arguments for them without having a full account of (that part of) the world they are dealing with. The rationality of their decisions depends on their acceptability by the universal audience that may be considered as the incarnation of reason under imperfect (because time-dependent) conditions. What Simon calls a satisficing decision, Perelman would label a 'reasonable' decision. Reasonable in this respect stands for 'rational, all things considered until now'. Rationality is thus bounded by the limited capacity of the mind, limited time (that makes the search for additional information exponentially more expensive), the limited attention of agents, the complexity of the situation or the decision-making environment, limited information about alternatives, again 'all things considered until now', uncertainty about current and future events, limited access to past events, cognitive complexity, changing environments, and the like. Unbounded (Cartesian) rationality for its part is not troubled by these kinds of boundaries or limitations.

We will return in chapter 8 to the idea of context-sensitive rationality where the focus will be on decision making by legislative rulers. That chapter will explore the possibility of evaluating the rationality of norm making according to legisprudence.

Chapter 4
Freedom in Context

Freedom and Nominalism

As argued in chapter 1, the philosophical and the theological versions of nominalism result in a metaphysical theory that articulates rationalism, individualism and freedom. Together they form the conceptual framework for the Modern philosophical project starting from the beginning of the seventeenth century. This framework is the result of the logical interpretation of God's omnipotence that denies any existence of universals outside the mind (rationalism). Therefore, only individuals can exist (individualism) that are free because of God's indifference (freedom).

God's indifference to values is the result of the radical simplicity of his nature. Due to this simplicity, his will and intellect are one. Since his intellect cannot therefore dictate his will, God can only create individuals, not universals. This interpretation of his creative power and omnipotence saves his freedom. As a result of divine indifference, normativity is absent from nature. The morality of an act, therefore, can only be evaluated with reference to a norm imposed on human will. Norms are initially imposed by God on his creatures as the Ten Commandments.

The nominalist interpretation of divine omnipotence results in a nominalist metaphysics. Under this metaphysics, normative action consists in following rules containing duties imposed by a superior. The superiority of the ruler is the basis for the authority to bind the will of the subject. This metaphysics provides the conceptual framework for normative thinking that structures the Modern philosophical project and the legalistic nature of normativity.

Of these three pillars of nominalist metaphysics – that is, rationalism, individualism and freedom – the latter deserves special attention. Because of its new philosophical articulation in connection to rationalism and individualism, it takes on a new form. Within a theological context, there can be no sin without the freedom to commit a sin. To commit a sin is to violate God's norms as a lack of submission. Transgression of God's norms logically presupposes the freedom to do so; so too does salvation as a compensation for living according to God's order. Without freedom, that is, neither sin nor salvation would make sense.

Under the nominalist interpretation of God's omnipotence, however, freedom acquires a different meaning. On the one hand, the cognitive as well as practical indeterminacy of reality liberates philosophy from its theological shackles. On the other hand, it calls on philosophy to frame the problem of freedom. Salvation, according to the nominalistic interpretation of God's omnipotence, is no longer an expected result of a lawful life. God, that is, can change his mind, and save Jesus' murderer while condemning the good Samaritan.

The characterisation of Modern philosophy as a project considers it from the perspective of freedom. From Descartes to Kant, philosophers work on the same platform, albeit from different angles that characterise their specific theories. The common focus on freedom is conceptually related to a philosophical method independent of revelation. The ontological priority of the individual characterises their philosophy as the heritage of nominalism. This heritage leads metaphysics in a new direction that turns it into a project.

As was argued in chapter 1, both the philosophical and the theological version of nominalism stress the human pole in knowledge and in individual and collective action. In chapter 2, a criticism was formulated of Descartes' version of the subject along with an alternative. According to this alternative, the agent is considered a social agent or an 'intersubject' whose self-consciousness is not a natural given. In this respect, I have argued that self-consciousness emerges through a process of interaction with others. This interaction is constitutive of the agent as a social being. The social agent has both social and individual aspects (the 'I'-aspect and the 'me'-aspect, following Mead), and in chapter 2, I have already pointed to the fact that the I-aspect of the individual is closely connected to his freedom. This point will be developed in this chapter.

Descartes' View: Freedom, Knowledge, Morality and Politics

Descartes' debt to pre-modern philosophy consists in the relationship between his thought and the main aspects of nominalism. As far as the moral consequences are concerned, Descartes limits his view to a provisional morality that will be replaced with a final morality once reality has been completely and rationally unfolded.[1] Although his theory was intended to include a moral theory, the latter was never, however, developed.[2] As for the political consequences of his thought, Descartes is prudent, because he argues that politics lacks the dignity that would make it fit for philosophical speculation. His work therefore is limited to the articulation of a new epistemology, securing the acquisition of knowledge over against the scepticism as a result of nominalism.

Freedom, however, plays an important role in Descartes' epistemology in that without freedom, there can be no knowledge. Freedom is a necessary condition for attaining knowledge and truth. Having established the certainty of the *cogito* as the

1 A systematic comment on Descartes' 'provisional morality' is provided among others by Cumming 1955 and Boutroux 1896.

2 On the unity of science, including morality, see Gouhier 1937: 169: '[la philosophie] n'inclut aucune distinction entre science et morale, ne pouvant elle-même être dite ni scientifique ni morale. Cette intuition n'est qu'une vue très simple: tout action est une idée en action.'

basis for knowledge, any additional knowledge must be as certain as the *cogito.* Only when the agent is certain of this, that is, only when an idea is as certain as the *cogito* itself, can he give his assent to it. He can also withhold his assent. Withholding assent to an idea that is not clear and distinct is an act of freedom.

It is from the perspective of freedom and the capacity of willing that man resembles his Creator most (Descartes 1996i: 41–50). The freedom of our will is known without proof (Descartes 1996j: no. 39). It is self-evident, and it is what man's most important perfection consists in (ibid.: no. 37).Because we can suspend our judgement in case of doubt, we are free. Knowledge, that is, prevents us from doing wrong. Knowledge must precede action; otherwise one is not using one's *liberum arbitrium* correctly (Descartes 1996i:47).

This articulation of divine freedom is the hallmark of nominalism. Because omnipotence prevents God from creating universals, it makes no sense to speak of human 'nature'. Nature as a concept lacks ontological, and hence normative, value. The only normativity the agent is left with is that imposed by the commands of God that are directly addressed to his freedom. These commandments can be interpreted as arbitrary acts of will or can be considered 'reasonable' in that they result from God's goodness. On the first interpretation, the world is radically contingent and divine norms can change. On the second interpretation, the ontological contingency of the world is tempered by divine goodness.

Although for Descartes, the idea of freedom is initially embedded in epistemology, and although his final morality never came to light, Descartes frames some thoughts on freedom in terms of moral philosophy. Freedom is *liberum arbitrium*. It consists in the choice over whether or not to act on what is rationally known. The rational knowledge of what ought to be done provides the basis for final morality.

Descartes' articulation of freedom through the process of establishing knowledge, and hence truth, is related to the metaphysical distinction between knowledge and the will which he learned from Scholasticism. God did create humans with both intellect and will. The quality of human and divine knowledge is identical, since truth is unique. Divine knowledge, however, is unlimited, while man's is limited in extent.[3] However, human freedom is also similar to God's in that neither divine will nor human will is determined by any object. Both, that is, are indifferent as far as their nature is concerned. It is in freedom that humans most resemble God.[4] While for God nothing precedes creation that could determine his will, humans are however submitted to divine precepts of what there is to do

3 Descartes 1996i: 45: ' … je n'en trouve aucune qui ne soit en moi très petite et bornée, et qui en Dieu ne soit immense et infinie.'

4 Ibid.: 45: 'Il n'y a que la seule volonté [*liberum arbitrium*], que j'expérimente en moi être si grande, que je ne conçois point l'idée d'aucune autre plus ample et plus étendue: en sorte que c'est elle principalement qui me fait connaître que je porte l'image et la resemblance de Dieu … [la volonté dans Dieu] ne me semble pas toutefois plus grande si je la considère formellement, et précisément en elle-même.'

('*ce qu'il faut faire*'). The radical indifference of God's will is the best proof of his omnipotence, which is worthy of Ockham.[5]

According to this relationship between knowledge and action, which results from the metaphysical articulation of intellect and will, Descartes' theory of normativity is cognitivistic. What there is to do ('*ce qu'il faut faire*') is ultimately a matter of knowledge (a clear and distinct idea). It is the sovereign good that is created by God *de potentia absoluta* (hence an eternal truth) and which must subsequently be discovered by the agent within himself. Although it is imposed externally, it is discovered internally by using reason. It is based on the love of God and of one's neighbour, which articulate two tenets of the Ten Commandments.

Therefore, there is no need for any further discussion of political matters because politics is a subcategory of normative action. This again shows Descartes as worthy of Scholasticism rather than the inaugurator of a new philosophical project. The treatment of freedom in terms of *liberum arbitrium*, thus classifying moral action as a theological problem, keeps the philosophical problem of political freedom in play. In matters relating to politics, we cannot fail to observe certain fundamental laws proposed by a unique and far-sighted legislator who has power over worldly affairs (Comarnescu 1942: 501).

As individuals, however, we are rationally free. Our freedom is rational in that it is based on the insight of what is clearly and distinctly given as the idea of our action. Human power cannot include more than our thoughts, because our intellect is, unlike God's, limited. These thoughts, however, are absolutely ours, in that they only depend on our will. Therefore freedom is rational.

Descartes' critical view on theoretical matters can be distinguished, though not actually separated, from his dealing with practical matters.[6] His critical stance in theoretical thinking is the essence of the *cogito*. Access to truth is mediated in that only knowledge provides access to it. Following the substitution of reason for authority, knowledge for its part can only be obtained by thinking an idea as clearly and distinctly as the *cogito*. Ideas that can be thought of in this manner are ontologically true, according to God's guarantee.

The search for knowledge can therefore be distinguished, though not separated from, willing.[7] However, the rational representation of an idea cannot lead to

---

5 Ibid.: 233: 'Et ainsi une entière indifference en Dieu est une preuve très grande de sa toute-puissance.'

6 Descartes 1996h: 28: ' … d'autant que, notre volonté ne se portant à suivre ni à fuir aucune chose, que selon que notre entendement lui représente bonne ou mauvaise, il suffit de bien juger, pour bien faire, et de juger le mieux qu'on puisse, pour faire aussi tout son mieux, c'est-à-dire, pour acquérir toutes les vertus, et ensemble tous les autres bien, qu'on puisse acquérir … .'

7 Descartes draws the doctrine of the reciprocal activity and passivity of both intellect (*entendement*) and will, which is not simply 'anteriority', from Scholastic philosophy as he was taught in La Flèche: see Gilson 1987: 250. Rather, the intellect 'discovers' the good that must be willed, upon which action can take place (ibid.: 248).

knowledge without the intervention of the will. Throughout the thinking process, the agent should only accept an idea that is clear and distinct. This acceptance is an act of willing. If he accepts an idea that is not clear or not distinct, the agent is induced into error. Error consists of approving an unclear or indistinct idea or rejecting a clear and distinct one.[8] Error is an inadequate use of our faculties.[9] The possibility of withholding his judgement as an act of freedom in the event of uncertainty is a necessary condition for the agent to reach truth (Descartes 1996i: 45). From the epistemological perspective, free will is instrumental for truth.

From this perspective, Descartes' epistemology is a secularised version of the Scholastic doctrine of sin. Freedom under Scholastic philosophy entails *liberum arbitrium*. It is a necessary condition for salvation. Salvation is the compensation for a decent life and is conditional on compliance with divine laws. Human freedom, therefore, is the freedom to transgress these norms. The choice it involves is the choice over whether or not to do what is to be done. What is to be done (*ce qu'il faut faire*) is an object of cognition. If known, one does it for the love of God from the Scholastic perspective, while Descartes is more inclined towards a deontic vocabulary.

The rational decoding of reality nurtures the tree of science, including all the branches of knowledge, the most important of which are medicine, mechanics and ethics.[10] On the one hand, science and its applications through inventions, discoveries and judgements will give man the ethical good. Morality, that is, is the fruit that can only be harvested after the tree has ripened. It is, in other words, the last branch that will be unfolded. Meanwhile we must be content with a *morale par provision*.[11] The maxims of the *morale par provision* allow for an elaboration of morality in addition to the philosophical articulation of the soul and the body.

---

8 Caton 1975: 100: 'Error arises from a refusal to be content with clear ideas as the sole criterion of truth.'

9 And no longer the theological dimension they had in Descartes. Descartes adopts a secularised version of sin, the theological version of which is found in Aquinas, see Gilson 1987: 274. See also Descartes 1996i: 43: 'Ainsi je connais que l'erreur, en tant que telle, n'est pas quelque chose de réel qui dépende de Dieu, mais que c'est seulement un défaut ... Toutefois cela ne me satisfait pas encore tout à fait; car l'erreur n'est pas une pure négation, c'est-à-dire, n'est pas le simple défaut ou manquement de quelque perfection qui ne m'est point due, mais plutôt est une privation de quelque connaissance qu'il semble que je devrais posséder.' Error follows from two sources – one practical, related to the needs of life producing natural prejudice, and another consisting of the tendency to neglect mathematics in favour of some obscure metaphysical considerations: see ibid. 18–28, 61–5.

10 Descartes 1996j: 14 (Preface): ' ... la plus haute et la plus parfaite morale ... présupposant une entière connaissance des autres sciences, est le dernier degré de la Sagesse.'

11 Descartes 1966h: 22 ff. On the necessity of the provisional morality, see Descartes 1996j: 15 (Preface): 'une morale imparfaite qu'on peut suivre par provision pendant qu'on n'en sait point encore de meilleure.'

As for the provisional morality, its first and most important maxim prescribes obedience to the laws of the country.[12] Because this prescription is provisional, no rational argument for it is produced. If the basis were rational, the agent would obey for reasons established through his own – rational – judgement. Moreover, any rational argument for the *morale provisoire* would be circular. Practical conformity – containing some stoical resignation – with the rules of society does, however, not engage reflective adherence. It leaves the issue of their truth intact.[13]

The substitution of the final morality to the *morale provisoire* would require a rational set of norms. These norms would have to be followed without, that is, any critical scrutiny because they have already passed the test of rationality. Given their rational nature, they constitute the true basis for human action. They could, that is, be identical to the provisional morality following the latter's passing of the test of rationality. As long it is not proved to be rational, it is not, although it could turn out that it is. This, however, will only be discovered at the end of the project.

Descartes' usual prudence also applies when he talks of politics. One of his reasons is that ruling '*les mœurs des autres*' belongs to sovereigns rather than to philosophers (Descartes 1996f: 86–8). Like Hobbes, he is aware of the religious conflicts as well as of political divergences that are the order of the day (Toulmin 1990: chapter 1). It is, rather, sovereigns which take charge of the civil order, and rule it by experience rather than by reason, because most men who participate in it are not reasonable (Descartes 1996d: 412). The final morality may have contained the solution to these disagreements, although again it was never created.

Hobbes: Political Nominalism

The political consequences of nominalism are of considerable importance. Freedom and individualism, so I have argued, are conceptually related under both the philosophical and the theological versions of nominalism. Consequential upon the nominalist interpretation of his omnipotence is that God can only create individuals. It is on these free individuals that God has imposed his commands. These commands determine the morality of actions, in that the latter must comply with the former.

As for political society, the main consequence of nominalism is that there is no longer a natural model or a universal, as in Aristotle's *polis*. Since universals have no ontological value outside the mind, the universal 'society' must be thought

12 Descartes 1996h: 22–3: 'La première était d'obéir aux lois et aux coutumes de mon pays, retenant constamment la religion en laquelle Dieu m'a fait la grâce d'être instruit dès mon enfance, et me gouvernant, en toute autre chose, suivant les opinions les plus modérées, et les plus éloignées de l'excès, qui fussent communément reçues en pratique par les mieux sensés de ceux avec lesquels j'aurai à vivre.'

13 This includes the suggestion that the provisional morality is part of the final morality, as Descartes (1996c: 265–6) indicates.

of differently. It consists of a conjunction of ontologically separated and free individuals owing obedience to divine commandments.

This is Hobbes's position. Because of the absence of any limiting norm, the individual has a right to everything. This is the expression of his freedom, that is, the absence of external barriers that prevent his actions. In addition to this, however, man ought to preserve his life by seeking peace. To seek peace is a duty imposed by the laws of nature.[14] In order to be a law, a proposition must be commanded. The laws of nature are then the commands of God (Hobbes 1966b: 49). They are the only true morality (Hobbes 1966c: 147). In order to obey these commands, the individual must transfer his freedom to a sovereign. The latter serves as an intermediate between two sorts of acts of will: God's commandments on the one side and the foundational human will on the other.

There is a similar interest in freedom from the political perspective within Rousseau's work, though without any theological relevance this time. Rousseau leaves the laws of nature outside his perspective. The creation of political space is the result not of a command of God, but the development of reason. The social contract, that is, is a rational construction of the political space out of the social. The theological impacts that were found in Hobbes have now completely disappeared, and have been replaced by a rational act of human will.

Still more than in Rousseau, freedom becomes the proper goal of political space with Kant. Political freedom is both the end and the means to achieve that end. Freedom, that is, has become reflexive. The foundation of the political space is no longer mandated by divine commandment, nor does it result from an evolution of reason in general. The construction of political space for Kant is based on a moral duty, an 'ought to will'. The latter is structured as a categorical imperative that gives the duty a universal form, without, however, being a source of knowledge or duty (Kant 1996: §§ 44, 42, 49).

The metaphysical reversal of will and knowledge reaches its pinnacle. It is the moral law that formally determines will, independently of its content. Will, in other words, is not determined by any pre-existing or given norm. The categorical imperative as the mere form of duty is empty. One ought to will because of will itself. Will, that is, has become reflexive in taking itself as the object of willing.

Freedom: Concept and Conceptions

In chapter 1 briefly discussed the status of concepts in the nominalist tradition that preceded the Modern philosophical period. Concepts, so it turned out, are man-made, and not God-made and innate (Descartes), existing in reality (Aristotle), or God-made and existing in reality (Aquinas). This section will briefly elaborate

14 Hobbes 1966c: 117: ' … that every man, ought to endeavour peace, as far as he has hope of obtaining it; and when he cannot obtain it, that he may seek, and use, all helps and advantages of war.'

the view that concepts are man-made, in that they are not metaphysical data, but intellectual or mental constructions.

Leaving aside their ontological status, concepts can be dealt with in different ways. Some concepts may be concretised, while this makes no sense for others. Some concepts require concretisation, while others do not. A concept like 'circle' does not need, and does not allow, any further concretisations. A circle is a collection of points at the same distance from a common centre. To have a 'conception of a circle' is absurd.

Other concepts, like 'justice' do allow for different conceptions. As a matter of fact, 'justice' is a vague concept, requiring concretisation in order to be operational. A conception is a concretisation of a concept without being analytically or necessarily related to it. Roughly speaking, analytical relations are elaborated in a *conceptual* analysis resulting in a proposition like 'a circle is a collection of points at the same distance from one other point.'

The distinction between 'concept' and 'conceptions' is exemplified in Wittgenstein's theory of language games. According to that theory, we are inclined to accept that what is referred to by the same word must share a number of common traits (Wittgenstein 1969: 17). This suggests that each time we use the word 'game', the objects or situations referred to share some aspects. This, according to Wittgenstein's language game theory, is not the case, which betrays his nominalist views.

What is called a 'game' can refer to a number of activities that do not necessarily share some essence. Some of these meanings have relationships with one another that do not appear in other forms of 'game'. Thus, football and chess have some resemblances, in that both are competitive. In both games, there is an intellectual component that is, however, stronger in chess than it is in football. They differ, however, in that football definitely requires more physical force than chess (Wittgenstein 1976: nr. 66).

These different activities are called 'games' because they show some 'family resemblances', a complex net of resemblances that cross or overlap, fundamental similarities here, superficial similarities there. They are not called 'games' because they share an identical substance or essence, but because of some overlapping in the way they are characterised. The concept of 'game' therefore allows for different conceptions of it.

In a similar vein to Wittgenstein, Ronald Dworkin distinguishes between 'concept' and 'conceptions'. A concept, says Dworkin, is an abstract idea that can be associated with different and more concrete conceptions (Dworkin 1986: 70–71; MacCormick 1978: 73; Rawls 1971: 7). There is not something like a 'true' conception that would be the correct translation of the concept. The more concrete a conception, the less easy it is to achieve consensus over its meaning. The more abstract a conception, the more it goes in the direction of a concept.

Dworkin sketches out the relationship between 'concept' and 'conceptions' as the structure of a tree. The trunk is what can be considered to be common to the different branches or conceptions.[15] The idea is illustrated with the help of the concept of 'courtesy', of which one can have different conceptions. Some consider that courtesy requires a man to hold the door open for a woman; others say one should also take one's hat off. Still others might hold that a man enter a venue first if the woman has never been there before. In spite of the different conceptions, everybody will agree on the fact that courtesy deals with respect. If you do not agree on that, then you are talking about something other than courtesy, and in doing so place yourself, according to Dworkin, outside the community of useful or at least ordinary discourse about the institution.

Chaïm Perelman for his part articulates a similar idea. In his theory of justice, he sums up a number of conceptions of the concept, including: giving everybody the same, giving everybody according to his deserts, giving everybody the same according to his needs, and so on (Perelman 1972b: 15; Ross 1974: 268 ff)· These conceptions are not necessarily compatible, in that some believe that justice requires that everybody should be given the same, while others hold that everybody should be treated according to his needs. Most of the time, different people will hold different conceptions.

Notwithstanding the disagreement on the level of conceptions, everybody, according to Perelman, agrees that whatever conception of justice is adopted, equal cases must be treated equally. With regard to this point, A may believe that justice means 'giving everybody the same', while B may be of the opinion that everybody should be given according to his need. Despite the disagreement over the conceptions, all As and Bs do agree, according to Perelman, that being just means treating equal cases equally. Only equal treatment according to a conception can be considered just. Any concretisation of the concept of justice results in a conception in which equality plays a predominant role.[16]

What holds for a practice like courtesy or justice also applies *mutatis mutandis* for the agent. Conceptions are concretisations of agents. To have a conception of justice refers to what justice means to the agent and can be considered one of the manifold conceptions that can be obtained of a concept.

When a conception of justice is imposed on you, it is not yours. It can be expressed as a conception *about* justice. A further differentiation is that we can establish a conception of justice on which *we* agree. It is different from where one person imposes his conception of justice on *us* (as a group), when it becomes

15 Dworkin 1986:71: ' ... the initial trunk of the tree ... would act, in public argument as well as in private rumination, as a kind of plateau on which further thought and argument are built. It would then be natural for people to regard that tie as special and in the way of conceptual, to say, for example, that respect is part of the "very meaning" of courtesy.'

16 Perelman 1972b: 26: 'Quel que soit le désaccord sur d'autres points, ils sont tous donc d'accord sur le fait qu'être juste c'est traiter de la même façon les être qui sont égaux à un certain point de vue, qui possèdent le même caractéristique, la seule dont il faille tenir compte dans l'administration de la justice.'

a conception *about* justice for us. To summarise, a conception *of* a concept is a concretisation of it which someone has as his own. A conception *about* a concept is a concretisation of that concept that is not the agent's own.

Since conceptions are not analytically related to concepts, the question arises as to how they can be operationalised? To make conceptions operational, a *conceptual* analysis can hardly suffice, as Perelman's and Dworkin's analyses indicate. A conceptual analysis elucidates the necessary internal relations of a concept from a detached perspective.

In paying attention to the different meanings one can have of courtesy and as they operate in a practice, Dworkin adopts a hermeneutical point of view towards that practice. This point of view is external in that it observes the practice of courtesy without the observer participating or engaging in it. In addition, it encompasses the internal point of view of the participants in the practice, so as to include within its description what 'courtesy' means for them. Perelman's diagnosis results in the articulation of some abstract meaning of the concept of justice. Dworkin, on the contrary, establishes what the meaning of a concept is for us, that is, from within a practice, without claiming to express its true meaning.

In summary, some concepts do not allow for concretisations in terms of a conception (for example, the concept of a circle) while others do. Conceptions *of* a concept are concretisations of a concept related to an agent as his own; conceptions *about* a concept are not.

Freedom Contextualised

Freedom as Principium : Origin and Principle

The theories briefly sketched in the above pages are helpful in outlining my view in the following way. The concept of freedom cannot be operational unless it is related to a conception. Freedom, that is, makes action not only possible but also necessary. Developing this insight, I will explore the possible conceptions that can fit in with the concept of freedom. The articulation of these possible conceptions will then unlock the gate to legisprudence, the theory of rational legislation which we are seeking.

Following the contract philosophers, we may say that before the institution of the state, there is freedom. Walking back along the line from were we are 'now' – that is, members of a state – to 'then' – that is, the situation where there is no state, something like a 'state of nature' in one of its variants – we brush away all the constructions, rules, and whatever organises our lives.

We may call this the *terminus ad quem* of the analysis. In the absence of any norm, anyone is free. In the beginning that is, there is freedom. From this perspective, freedom is at the origin of our philosophical inquiry. The 'origin' is a self-referential beginning. As a beginning or *terminus a quo*, freedom is a *principium*. As a *principium*, it is both the beginning and the principle of action (cf. Aristotle 1984d: 1139a, 31–4). Without freedom at the beginning and as a principle, action is impossible; it is mere behaviour. Action that is requires reflective or rational choice.

Freedom as *principium* is an abstract and reflexive concept. It is abstract because it has no a priori content, while at the same time it cannot have any arbitrary content. It is reflexive because freedom only makes sense when exercised in freedom. 'Freedom from freedom' therefore makes no sense.

A philosophical theory answering the question 'What is freedom?' may provide a delineation of freedom in conceptual terms. The answers differ according to the theories in which they figure. The common feature of these theories is that a limit is conceptually necessary. Without a limit or a determination, freedom is infinite, which only makes sense for God. The necessity of a limit makes freedom as *principium* a concept. Since it is an abstract concept, it has no a priori content. As long as its content is not defined, freedom is indefinite.

Consider then the following paradox. Since freedom is indefinite, it contains an unlimited range of possibilities. At each and every moment, the agent can pick up a conception of freedom on which to act. If no choice is made, freedom remains indefinite or undetermined. If no determination is made, no action is possible, because an agent must make a choice among a number of possibilities, even for the simplest action. The paradox amounts to this: no determination of freedom equals no action.[17]

As long as freedom is not determinate, it is 'complete', or 'intact'. Any action though is, by its very nature, a limitation, since not everything can be done at the same time. An A can dispose of the most complete freedom to go out of the room or to stay within. However, under a practical interpretation of the principle of non-contradiction, he cannot do both at the same time. Action X entails that action [¬ X] cannot be done at the same time.

The extension of indefinite freedom is all conceivable actions. To be 'conceivable as an action', though, is not identical to action itself. In order to be an action, what is conceived must be operationalised, that is, most of the time, externalised. This operationalisation consists in a determination of indefinite freedom. The determination of freedom is a concretisation of freedom. If there is no determination, there is no action either. Indefinite freedom in itself is mere inaction.[18] Freedom in this respect is constitutive of the circumstances of human action, as will be discussed below.

---

17 The 'more' freedom I want to keep, the 'less' action there is. You can accumulate money, and when you have a lot of it you are rich. You can imagine accumulating all the freedom you have, so that you are 'very' free. But you do not act as a free man, because you do not act at all.

18 Taylor 1985b: 213; Spinoza 1965c: 274–5: 'Nam libertas ... agendi necessitatem non tollet sed ponit'. Dauenhauer 1982: 'The object of freedom ... is not separable from its performance.'

The necessity of a limitation or determination of freedom in order for action to be possible is not itself a concretisation of freedom. It is included in the concept of freedom, that is, it ensues from a conceptual analysis of freedom. In order for freedom to make sense, the agent must concretise freedom in terms of a conception. The concretisation of freedom connects it to action. It is only when freedom is concretised that action is triggered.

The result of the necessity of freedom being limited or determined in order for action to be possible at all is the emergence of the following alternative. The first possibility is that the agent acts according to his own insights; the second is that he acts on some else's. Under the first possibility, the concretisation follows on the agent's own determination of indefinite freedom; under the second, the concretisation is related to someone else's determination.

The first type of determination is a conception *of* freedom in that it is the agent's own. Conceptions of freedom are the agent's concretisations of indefinite freedom. They express his autonomy in making the choice.

The second type of determination is a conception *about* freedom. Conceptions about freedom for their part are at odds with the agent's autonomy. They do show his dependence on another agent. This means that the agent does not carry out his conception of freedom but must act on someone else's conception *about* freedom. When this other agent is the sovereign, the concretisation is a political conception about freedom.

The foregoing alternative is reminiscent of Hobbes's theory, which will be drawn on here in order to illustrate the claim. The agent's concretisation of the laws of nature enables him to act according to conceptions of freedom. The concretisations of the laws of nature in civil laws of the sovereign are conceptions about freedom from the agent's point of view. Hobbes claims, as I have argued, that the agent violates his duties contained in the fundamental law of nature when he acts on conceptions of freedom. Since these actions jeopardise his life, they are forbidden. Any action therefore is a virtual trigger of the *bellum omnium contra omnes*. Since war jeopardises the agent's life, these actions are forbidden.

Hobbes provides the agents with the instrument to ward off the dangers of this war. This instrument is the covenant establishing civil power. It is the only possible valid covenant that can be concluded in the state of nature that at the same time marks its end. The entering into this covenant by the agents amounts to an action on a conception *of* freedom. It is each agent's rational insight that this is the best thing to do, as was argued in chapter 1.

It is important to remember in this respect that the anthropological dimension of the state of nature is only additional factual grist to the mill of Hobbes's nominalistic epistemology, and not the core of his theory. This epistemology simply makes it impossible to rely on conceptions of freedom since it is not clear of what concept would they be concretisations. The anthropological dimension adds no supplementary rational weight to the argument. If it corroborates it, it does so on a mere factual basis.

According to Hobbes's theory, the laws of nature do exist without the concepts figuring in them having any meaning of their own. They prescribe how to deal with freedom as a matter of obligation towards God. In the state of nature, action on conceptions of freedom turns out to be impossible for the epistemological reason stated above. Therefore, Hobbes argues, it is necessary to act on conceptions about freedom. Hobbes's nominalism excludes the first type of determination of freedom mentioned above, so that on this theory we are only left with the second type.

The epistemological characterisation of Hobbes's theory is therefore of crucial importance. Hobbes spares no effort to convince us that he is offering a theory of reality. When it comes to freedom, the theory holds that an agent is forbidden to act on conceptions of freedom. It is forbidden because to act on conceptions of freedom is to jeopardise one's life.

The only conception *of* freedom upon which an agent can act entails the surrender of his capacity to act on conceptions of freedom. *After* he has entered into the state, he acts on conceptions about freedom, which Hobbes's theory argues are conceptions of freedom. The technique of representation normatively connects these conceptions about freedom to the agent, who must consider them conceptions of freedom. Because of the need to abandon the capacity to act on conceptions of freedom, Hobbes's is a theory about freedom, not of freedom.[19]

The sovereign therefore has the power to determine indeterminate freedom. This power is the power of the word. It is the power of *Leviathan* or the mortal God. The sovereign, that is, defines the terms of the laws of nature, the meaning of which perfectly coincides with his positive laws. From the perspective of the agent, these concretisations of the laws of nature are replaced with his conceptions of freedom. They have, what is more, a moral duty to obey the sovereign's laws (Wintgens 1991). If agents do not act according to these conceptions about freedom, Leviathan strikes back, since it not only has the power of the word but also that of the sword.

From Origin to Principium*: Equality as the First Normative Dimension of Freedom*

According to my articulation of freedom as it was developed as the origin or the *terminus ad quem*, we can now start investigating the normative dimension of freedom and what it amounts to. Assuming no hindrances,[20] everyone has an

19 Spinoza 1965b: 228–9: '… [the state's] ultimate purpose is … rather to free everyone from fear so that he may live in all possible security, i.e. may preserve his natural right to exist and act in the best possible way, without harm to himself or his neighbour.' This pre-echoes John Stuart Mill. In the interpretation presented of Hobbes in the next section, the agent surrenders his capacity to act on conceptions of freedom, that is, to make choices and to externalise them, to the sovereign.

20 The fact that humans cannot fly like birds is a physical impossibility, not a limitation of their freedom.

'unlimited amount' of freedom. This is to be taken to mean that everyone disposes of the same indefinite range of concretisations of freedom. Freedom as the *terminus ad quem* becomes a *principium* when it is at the same time considered a *terminus a quo*. If we are all free in the sense discussed above, we must be *equally* free. It is not because we are all equal that we must be equally free; rather it is because we are all free that we are equal.

Freedom as Principium*: The Social Dimension*

The preceding section started to sketch out a contextualisation of freedom. It exposed the normative dimension of freedom as distinct from the conceptual dimension. In the following pages, the argument will focus on the social dimension of freedom, thus putting freedom, like the subject and rationality in the foregoing chapters into a context.

Apart from often being circumstantial, the contexts in which we act are social. We meet others on our way. Interaction with others, as was argued in the previous chapter, is constitutive of our self and, in consequence, a prerequisite in order for meaning to exist.

The social dimension of freedom refers to others who are, under the normative dimension, barred from imposing conceptions about freedom. As long as he has no rational argument, no A, that is, can prevent any B from acting on a conception of freedom. As a consequence of freedom as *principium*, equality puts others at distance from the agent. Since others have no initial right to impose a conception about freedom, the agent has a right to keep them at a distance. The right to keep others at a distance is equivalent to the absence on their side of a rational argument to impose a conception about freedom. Freedom as *principium* therefore involves the right to keep others at a distance.

Freedom as *principium* does not refer to any ultimate value. It does not refer to equality as a basic value. Equality is a consequence of the indeterminate extension of freedom as the *terminus a quo*. Equality thus follows from freedom, and not freedom from equality. Freedom as *principium* is not a specific conception of freedom either. Freedom as *principium* lies at the origin of action in that it makes acting on conceptions of freedom possible without itself being a conception of freedom.

The Meaning of Freedom

Freedom as *principium* is abstract, in that it has no a priori content or meaning. Therefore, the above discussion does not entail any substantial view or content. Concepts, so we learned from Mead, do not exist and do not have any content independently of interaction. It is important in this respect to recall Hobbes's theory of meaning. Since he denies the ontological value of concepts and therefore a theory of natural meaning and since he (wrongly) denies the possibility of a conventional theory of meaning, his theory of freedom turns out to be a theory about freedom. The only conception of freedom upon which an agent can act consists, as argued above, in surrendering his capacity to act on conceptions of freedom. He surrenders his capacity to act on conceptions of freedom by signing in the contract. From 'then' on, the sovereign determines the meaning of the natural laws through civil laws.

Concepts have no meaning of their own, I have argued, because meaning is meaning *for* someone. Meaning is agent-related. Agents, as was argued in chapter 2, are intersubjects, or social agents. The meaning of the concept of freedom, therefore, is meaning for the agent in a social context.

The contextualisation of freedom consists of two steps. The first considers freedom as a *terminus ad quem*, that is, as the origin of all action. Action is the operationalisation of freedom as a *terminus a quo*. This is the second step. The extension of freedom at the *terminus ad quem* is identical to its extension as *a terminus a quo*.

It follows that equality, as the normative dimension of freedom as *principium*, is context-related. Equality is not related to freedom as a *terminus ad quem* irrespective of the fact that the extension of freedom is equal for all, but follows from freedom as a *terminus a quo*. It may be inferred from this connection that equality as the normative dimension of freedom is context-related. Because of its context-relatedness, equality is relational. It refers to others. This makes the social dimension of freedom a necessary element of freedom as *principium*, and not simply one of its accidental features.

From there it is only a short step to the articulation of the meaning of freedom. Since meaning makes no sense without an agent, freedom only makes sense to an agent.[21] The meaning of freedom is agent-related. It should be remembered in this respect, as argued in the previous chapter, the agent is a social agent. To be a self or an agent crucially depends on interaction. This clarifies the social nature of the agent, as well as the social nature of meaning. The social nature of meaning and the social ontology of the agent as an intersubject justify the conclusion that the meaning of freedom must be social. This corroborates the social dimension of freedom.

Reflexivity as the Second Normative Dimension of Freedom

It follows from the interactional view on the agent and intersubjectivity resulting from interaction, that was set out in the previous chapter, that the agent is an agent of meaning and not of truth. An agent of meaning emerges out of interaction with others. The agent's self consists in a dynamic interaction between the 'I'-aspect and

---

21 Spinoza 1965b: 226–7: '… it is impossible for thought to be completely agent to another's control, because no one can give up his natural right to reason and form his own judgement about everything, or can he be compelled to.' While Spinoza (ibid.: 152–3) refers to rulers, this passage can also be interpreted as having the more general meaning, by which 'rulers and ruled alike, are men.' Cf. Berlin 1969: 126: 'We must preserve a minimum area of personal freedom if we are not to "degrade or deny our nature".'

the 'me'-aspect of his self. This is what constitutes the agent as a social being or an intersubjective agent. Neither the agent nor a fortiori others have a direct access to this 'I'-aspect. For the agent it is always 'behind him', while others have at best only indirect access to it. For this reason, the subject has been termed 'elusive'.

The 'I'-aspect of the agent's self in Mead is, however, an essential element of the agent qua agent. It is a non-speculative version of the substantive 'I' in Descartes' *cogito* or the transcendental 'I' in Kant's *Ich denke*. Their metaphysical articulation of the agent makes it a conceptual agent. Under the meta-theory of the agent, the contours of which were explored in chapter 2, conceptual agents do not exist. Only real agents exist.

However, the elusiveness of the agent's 'I'-aspect requires that others be kept at a distance. It is only on this condition that a self emerges as different though not separated from others. The meaning of the agent qua agent – that is, as a self – does not follow from his being identical to others. To be a self is to be different from others. Interaction with them constitutes the meaning of identity of the self for the self.

According to the above, the reflexive nature of freedom can be further clarified. A mere conceptual analysis may be instructive as to the reflexive nature of freedom. If freedom is not exercised in freedom, then we will be dealing with something other than freedom. When the analysis of freedom stops at the conceptual level, it obliterates the agent qua agent or the agent as a self. It neglects, that is, the meaning of freedom that is agent-related. In order for freedom to have meaning, it needs to be related to an agent who is a social being.

The contextualised version of freedom considers freedom as a *terminus a quo* to which the normative dimension is connected. From this perspective, the contextualised version of freedom combines with the meta-theory of the agent. The elusiveness of the agent's 'I'-aspect conditions the meaning of freedom as a reflexive concept. It follows that only the agent can determine its meaning by referring to his intersubjectivity that is constituted by the 'me'-aspect of his self. The 'generalised other' participates in the determination of the meaning of freedom for the agent, since it operates as the cognitive practical platform for the agent's actions.

In this respect, it is easy to see that Hobbes's agent is merely an object of the theory he provides. Hobbes's agent is an object of the power of the sovereign. As an object of power of the sovereign, he is free from fear of a violent death. This negative freedom is what the agent protects, at the price of becoming an object of the sovereign's power.[22]

22 Hobbes 1966c: 32–3: 'And words whereby we conceive nothing but the sound, are those we call absurd, insignificant, and nonsense. And therefore if a man should talk to me of … a free agent; a free will; or any free, but free from being hindered by opposition, I should not say he were in error, but that his words were without meaning, that is to say, absurd.'

Freedom is only meaningful, however, when it is related to an agent. This relationship is a necessary condition in order for freedom to make sense. The necessary characteristic of the relationship between freedom and the agent, in order for freedom to make sense, expresses the reflexive nature of freedom. Without reflexivity, freedom cannot make sense. It makes no sense because it cannot be meaningful. Freedom in short requires freedom in order to be exercised.

We have now six characteristics of freedom as *principium* that interact in the following manner. (1) Freedom is at the origin (*terminus ad quem*) and is the (2) *terminus a quo*. Under (1) freedom is an a-contextual while in (2) it is a contextualised version. Under (1) and (2), freedom is (3) of an indefinite extension. In order for action to be possible, however, a choice must be made so that the extension of freedom is no longer indefinite. Under (1), (2) and (3), freedom is a *principium*, that is, a beginning and (4) it has a normative dimension. The normativity of freedom as *principium* follows from the equality included in (2). From the relational nature of equality follows (5), the social dimension of freedom, that is intertwined with (4). The meaning of freedom finally is related to the 'I'-aspect of the agent's self, which explains (6) the reflexive nature of the concept of freedom in context.

Freedom and the Legal Framework

Freedom as Distance

I propose to call freedom as an abstract concept 'freedom as distance'. Freedom as distance is abstract in that it both allows and requires different conceptions of freedom. A more concrete conception must be connected to it in order to be operational. Freedom as distance is not itself a sufficiently concrete conception, in that it does not allow for any concrete action. Freedom as distance thus requires a concretisation of freedom. This concept will be elaborated in the following pages.

In face-to-face societies, we can imagine relatively small groups, where people know each other and can deal with each other, prima facie without expressing rules. It does not mean that there are no rules at all. It only means that the rules they are following have no separate existence from interaction itself. Behaviour can be meaningful behaviour without the rules that are followed at the same time being explicit.

Consider the case of an agent A in this small group, who has unlimited power. If an A's power is unlimited, we face something like the Hobbesian 'natural right to all', including the right to the other's life. Under that hypothesis, A's power includes the power to determine the whole of a B's life plan. B is thus his slave. On that account, B's acting on conceptions of freedom is absorbed by A's power. Apart from the legitimation questions that emerge here, and supposing that B has always been under A's power, B has no self. That is, B has never acted on a conception of freedom. On that hypothesis, he has even not chosen to be A's slave.

The 'interaction' between A and B is thus a struggle, not about what the other is going to *do* but about what he is going to *be*. What is at stake is a fusion of at least one self, A, and something else that could have been a self, but actually is not one, B. A and B are 'the same'. There are then, not two individuals, but only fused entities. If projected onto a larger group, with one A and a lot of Bs, this group would be a *corpus mysticum* in which A would be a guru.

To be an agent entails there being at least one conception of freedom on which the individual has acted. To be free as an agent is not something natural; it is not given. To be free as an agent entails limiting freedom-undetermined on conceptions of freedom. Freedom-undetermined, it should be remembered, is not operational unless it is concretised in a conception. Put differently, the concept of freedom needs a minimal critical specification, and that is called a conception.

If freedom is connected to social action, then it must also be externalised. Through this externalisation, we meet others on our way, that is, agents with their own conceptions of freedom and which are externalising them. These externalisations can conflict, in which case there is also a conflict between the underlying conceptions of freedom. It is the latter that make action meaningful in the Weberian sense.[23] As such, conceptions of freedom – and their externalisation – can conflict, though this should not be presupposed, as Hobbes and to a certain extent Rousseau do.

What Hobbes, followed by Kant, and subsequently with Rawls in their wake, invites us to adhere to is a specific idea of the agent. According to Hobbes, the agent is wicked, passionate and suspicious of others. For Kant the agent is a transcendental ego, a priori endowed with reason and will that will determine the substantive outcome of his conceptions. Rawls, finally, in a similar vein to Kant, endows the agent with a priori capacities, of which the content is barely concealed. The agent behind the veil of ignorance is supposed to know nothing in order to choose in an unbiased way. He is, however, aware of the basics of economics, psychology and politics.[24]

Rawls, in *A Theory of Justice*, and in a similar vein, Hobbes and Kant, try to convince us of the connection of the agent to a rational, *conceptual* version of the self. This agent will then, for rational reasons, adhere to an a priori universal scheme of the organisation of political space that happens to be some version of the liberal state. Their theories, therefore, concern human nature, without the agent being involved as an agent of self-determination. An agent of self-determination in

---

23 Weber 1964: 132 ff. (peaceful conflict).

24 Rawls 1971: 137: 'It is taken for granted, however, that they know *the* general facts about human society. They understand political affairs and the principles of economic theory; they know the basis of social organization and *the* laws of human psychology. Indeed, the parties are presumed to know whatever general facts affect the choice of *the* principles of justice.' On taking this knowledge in economics, politics, sociology and psychology for granted, Rawls suggests that they can be known in some natural way. It is suggested that they lack any further justification, that is, to be theories *of* reality.

the sense I take it here is an agent acting on conceptions of freedom. Their agent is an a priori, hence universal, idea, or concept, not an agent qua agent. Free agents therefore have a self-conception. Theories like Hobbes's, Rousseau's, and Kant's work with a conception of the self, as was noted in chapter 2.

Freedom and Law

As far as law is concerned it is far from necessary that the law that comes with political space should be of the type that Hobbes and to some extent Kant have in mind. They mainly think of law as rules based on a conception about freedom that is imposed and enforced by the political institutions that are constitutive of political space.

The problem with this liberal version of freedom is that it invites us to subscribe to an a priori concept of the agent or a conception of the self. As was argued above, there are no conceptual agents. Conceptual agents, like abstract relations, are nonsense. There are only concrete agents, who are endowed with a self through their interaction with others, agents in other words that have a self-conception. Agents, so we read from, for example, Charles Taylor, are to be considered agents of self-definition (Taylor 1985c), that is, agents acting on conceptions of freedom. This self-definition, relying as it does on the elusiveness of the agent himself – his 'I'-aspect – is, as was argued in the chapter 2, not a matter of the a priori, the transcendental, or anything else.

This being so, both Hobbes, Kant and to a certain extent, Rawls, connect their conceptual view of the agent with law. While for Hobbes there are theological and rational arguments to engage in the foundation of political space, for Kant these reasons are of a moral nature.

According to Kant, to stay with him for a moment, the language of freedom is translated into the language of law, and the translation is performed according to the categorical imperative. The classical formula of the law '*suum cuique tribuere*' (Aquinas 1910: II-II, q. 58), is expressed by Kant in an imperative form: '*honeste vive, neminem laede, suum cuique tribue*' (Kant 1996: 29). This imperative form is then transformed into another imperative, according to which one ought to enter into a state in which what belongs to each can be secured to him against everyone else (ibid.: 29).

This state is the legal state (ibid.: 90–91). The imperative is connected to the idea of law itself. If one does not want to deny any concept of law, one must leave the state of nature and enter into the legal state (ibid.: 89–90). It is a duty imposed by the categorical imperative, as an a priori norm of reason. As was noted in chapter 1, Kant conceptually connects freedom with law, that has a universal form, which itself expresses the universality of the categorical imperative. In consequence, freedom as the *principium* of law will be universal, or *conceptual.*

Freedom according to Kant is the 'independence'[25] or autonomy of the individual according to law.

The view I would like to present in opposition to those summarised above, is that according to legisprudence, there is no *immediate* connection between freedom and law. If there were, the balance between freedom in the political sense (action on conceptions about freedom) and freedom in the moral sense (action on conceptions of freedom) would be struck in favour of the former. This amounts to claiming that once the state comes into existence as a result of the social contract, acting on conceptions about freedom a priori outweighs acting on conceptions of freedom.

The reason why Hobbes invoked the law was precisely that the *ius naturale* does not include any distance between agents. Morality in the state of nature does not mean anything, since every one has a right to all, without limits, apart from the laws of nature that are not workable. There is no corresponding duty that safeguards the distance between free agents and which counterbalances the *ius naturale* in the state of nature. In placing limits on the *ius naturale*, the law will provide the necessary limitations on it. From then on, freedom as distance as a meta-conception of freedom starts making sense in Hobbes's theory.

It turns out, however, that the mechanism of the social contract outweighs the possibility of acting on conceptions of freedom. If we live in and by the law, as Dworkin has put it (Dworkin 1986: vii), then action according to the law or upon conceptions about freedom outweighs, as a matter of principle, action according to conceptions of freedom. If this is so, then there is no need for a theory of legislation. Law provides us with reasons for action. These reasons turn out to be exclusionary, in that they exclude any other reason for action, like acting on conceptions of freedom.

As will be argued in chapter 6, freedom as distance constitutes the basis for the first principle of legisprudence. In contrast to Hobbes, I will argue, however, that the connection between law and freedom is only *mediate.* Social conflicts or conflicts between conceptions of freedom need not necessarily be resolved by way of adjudication or legislation. Law, that is, is not necessarily the best means for realising freedom, which is roughly what the first principle of legisprudence expresses.

The requirement to look for alternative solutions that are not necessarily of an adjudicative or legislative nature makes part of legisprudence a rational theory of legislation. It relies on 'freedom as distance'. I reserve a more detailed analysis of the operationalisation of this principle of legisprudence for later in this book.

---

25 Kant 1996: 30. It seems however that Kant is confusing 'freedom' and 'equality'. Although both are of course connected, he suggests that 'equality' is innate, and that freedom amounts to independence from others on that base of equality. In my view freedom is fundamental, and it can only be limited on an equal basis because freedom unlimited is equal for everyone.

Freedom as Distance Further Explored

Generally speaking, a distinction can be drawn between four layers that express different aspects of 'freedom as distance'.

The *first layer* concerns the need for distance between agents, in order to make it possible for them to be a self. Social as they may be, there is a need for differentiation, and hence distance, in order to be a agent at all. There are four important aspects to that.

The first aspect is that, over against the conceptual, a-contextual, or a priori agent, my suggestion is that, following George Herbert Mead, the individual is a social individual agent from which his self emerges, that is, the self grows out of social interaction and is embedded therein. If agents are endowed with will and reason, this is to be considered a potential or a capacity, not an a priori determinable ensemble. As a potential or a capacity, reason and will can only take root within a social context, that is, in interaction with others. This view was set out in chapter 2.

If the agent is considered to act according to conceptions of freedom, this amounts to saying that he is defining himself in a social context, that is, with others. In doing so, the agent is not confirming how he is *identical* to others, as read in Descartes, Hobbes and, partially, Rawls, and as will be argued for Rousseau below. This point will not be developed further here. Suffice it to say here that the self-determination of an agent on the basis of conceptions of freedom entails his being different from others. To have an identity, if one may say so, is exactly the opposite of being identical to others. Identity in this sense and distance, that is, call for each other.

The second aspect of the first layer of freedom as distance is that conceptions of freedom on which the agents act require, as noted above, externalisation. This is a way of meeting others, including the possibility of conflict. The possibility of conflict is not a priori morally bad, in that it must be avoided at any price. Any form of interaction, until there is mutual understanding that is not necessary to come, is a form of 'violence', and hence conflict, or disagreement.

To be sure, legisprudence does not deny the presence of conflict in interaction. My view, however, is that conflicts do not necessarily have only a negative side. Every form of interaction has a conflictual side, in that interaction partners interact precisely because there is no mutual understanding, because they have differences of opinion and opposing interests on which to act. To presuppose that there will always be ruthless conflict, as Hobbes does, is simply another deficiency of the Modern philosophical project that was already noted in chapter 2.

The third aspect of the first layer is that interaction and conflict are very close to each other, as Rousseau had already noticed.[26] However, in order for interaction not to become too serious a conflict, others should be kept at distance. This is a logical consequence of the fact that the identity of the agent is a matter of self-

26 Conflict is a form of social relation, as Max Weber (1964: 132 ff.) and Freund (1983: 20 ff.) argue.

determination in terms of conceptions of freedom. In order to keep the conception of freedom what it was, that is, as a conception *of* freedom, others must be kept at a distance in order not to impose their conception *about* freedom.

If A agrees with B, they can be said to share a conception of freedom regarding this. If they do not initially share a conception of freedom, both can try to convince the other to do so. If disagreement persists, however, and if A imposes his conception of freedom on B, A's conception of freedom becomes a conception about freedom from B's perspective. B's resistance to that entails the possibility, and indeed necessity, of keeping A at distance in order to be able to act on his (B's) conception of freedom.

Finally, the fourth aspect of the first layer is that the keeping of others at a distance as a matter of self-definition at the same time constitutes a possible source of conflict. Because self-definition occurs within a social context, there are others with whom the conception of freedom and its exteriorisation can conflict. But this possibility must be included; if it is not, interaction is a priori excluded. It is through interaction that relationships are built – since interaction is relational – and that the agents frame their identity around conceptions of freedom. Others must be there, but they must not come too close, if it may be stated in such a general way.

Under the Hobbesian view – and to a certain extent, Rousseau's view as well, as we shall soon see – there is no relevant social interaction outside political space. There is only conflict that the law is called upon to resolve in an adjudicative manner. Each in their own way adhere to some version of nominalism, under which they are compelled to rationally construct social relations through law, since relations do not exist (Hobbes) or are deficient (Rousseau).

My claim is that these relations do exist, and that they result from the agents' interaction resulting in intersubjectivity. As was argued in chapter 2, interaction is by its very nature deficient, in that it includes the possibility of conflict. Conflict in turn has at least this virtue that it shapes interaction, and so brings social meaning to light (Hunyadi 1995). In this process of interaction, however, the others must be kept at a distance. This is the first layer of 'freedom as distance'.

The second layer of freedom as distance can be briefly articulated through the above. It shows the relationship between freedom as distance and law in another light to Hobbes.

There are essentially two aspects of interest here.

The first is this: if distance towards others is both constitutive of the agent's identity and necessary for maintaining it, it follows that freedom as distance is a matter of identity. Therefore, the agent himself must first of all master it. If not, the agent is not acting according to conceptions of freedom. He is thus from the very beginning onwards acting on conceptions about freedom. There is no reason, that is, to connect social space conceptually with political space, as Hobbes suggests. Nor is there any need to connect the construction of political space with law, as Hobbes along with Kant also holds. If this is the case, then we face the deeper roots of strong legalism, which will be discussed in chapter 5.

Law then is not a priori to be called in to organise freedom, that is, to keep others at a distance. This is a matter for the social individual or the agent himself, according to his self-conception. However, law can be called in when the interaction comes in the form of a conflict that the agent can no longer master himself. This is still a vague description of the function of law that organises the freedom from which it originally starts. This issue will be addressed in more depth in chapter 7, when discussing the principles of legisprudence at greater length. It is sufficient to mention it briefly here as the second aspect of this layer of freedom as distance.

The second aspect of the second layer of freedom as distance is that the law can be called in as a sub-routine, so to speak. By a sub-routine, I mean that law should not a priori determine social relations, at the price of destroying social interaction, and with that, the construction and the maintenance of the identity of the agents. On the contrary, law as a sub-routine enters on the scene when this process of interaction breaks down, that is, when the distance between agents risks becoming too small in order to enable them to act on conceptions of freedom. As a sub-routine or an alternative for social interaction breaking down, law can be called on in order to put the agents at a distance again. This will again be discussed in chapter 7, which will identify the principle of alternativity that refers to this aspect.

The third layer of freedom as distance concerns the relationship between law and the social agents themselves. It is so to speak a fine-tuning of both the first and the second layer. Law, on this third layer, must itself be kept at a distance from social interaction, until called upon, as it were. There are again two connected aspects that are of interest here. I will briefly mention them while reserving their further discussion for later in this book.

The first aspect of this layer is situated in legislation, or the construction of legal rules themselves. This means that, under freedom as distance, rules should be constructed in such a manner as to leave the priority of solving conflicts of interaction to the agents themselves. There are a variety of ways of doing so. One is to stipulate the necessity of reconciliation between conflicting agents prior to any intervention of the legal system, broadly speaking. Another is to posit the construction of rules that provide results in interactional terms between the agents themselves, and not, as is often the case, the fleshing-out of some interactional design accompanied by a sanction or thread with sanction. This involves, from a technical perspective, a prudent use of the technique of public order rules, in favour of private transactional mechanisms. This aspect, as will be noticed, mainly concerns the legislator's restraint from intervention.

This aspect of freedom as distance is most prominently of a legisprudential character. It translates the idea of freedom as distance into principles of legisprudence, and it includes prudence in the intervention of state power in social interaction. This point will be returned to in chapter 7.

Closely related to the first aspect dealing with the legislature, the second aspect of this layer relates to the judiciary, whose place and function the legislator frames. Under freedom as distance, the institutional design in which the judiciary operates should not permit the law automatically to structure conflicting agents' interaction.

When calling upon the judge, the interactional pattern to be activated must be as close as possible to the horizontal or social interaction. The reason for this is clear. It is through horizontal social interaction that agents frame meaning and, consequentially, their identity as intersubjectivity. Intervention by the courts, on the basis of legal rules, has the possible disadvantage of reframing horizontal social interaction into vertical interaction. As a matter of fact, the final stage of legal interaction, that is, interaction based on legal rules, is the possible coercion of one of the interaction partners or agents by the judiciary. For reasons that need to be explained further, this constraint includes the replacement of a conception about freedom with a conception of freedom.

External limitations should be constructed in such a way as to allow for this function of the courts. Instead of automatically applying rules, because they only allow for this possibility in the case of legal conflict, rules should be constructed in such a way as to include this 'feedback' mechanism. In doing so, rules do not automatically apply, but open up some space for settlement of a legal conflict, with the authoritatively enforced rule in the background. Put differently, law should not automatically come into a social conflict and solve it by way of adjudication without trying out alternative solutions. This requirement does justice to the capacity of agents to act on conceptions of freedom.

This brings us to the fourth and final layer of freedom as distance. This layer is 'equality', the first normative dimension of freedom. All legal systems seem to include a self-justifying use of general rules by a sovereign. If a rule is general, it respects equality. If the general rule is, further, also 'formally valid', the use of rules is said to be justified. That is, the substitution of a conception about freedom for a conception of freedom cannot, from this perspective, be criticised.

From the perspective of freedom as distance set out above, this replacement is not, however, self-justifying. If it were, the reflexive character of freedom, the second normative dimension of freedom, would be annulled since the agent would no longer be able to act on a conception of freedom. The justification for this replacement that was briefly pointed to in the above must keep track of freedom as *principium,* that is, freedom as a starting-point and as a *Leitmotiv* of any political and legal organisation. The limitation of freedom even within the legal limits of what the institutional design of a legal system permits sovereigns to do is not always legitimated. It needs, that is, supplementary justification. Again I refer to chapter 7 for a more detailed analysis.

Chapter 5
Strong Legalism or the Absent Theory of Legislation

Introduction

In chapter 1, it was argued that legalism relies on a nominalist metaphysics. The nominalist metaphysics on which legalism relies shows a conceptual connection between rationalism, individualism and freedom. Generally speaking, normative action turned out to be a matter of rule following.

Furthermore, in the light of this metaphysics, it was argued in chapter 2 that Descartes' philosophy was an attempt to overcome the theoretical scepticism that was involved in it. This reflects the more general thesis that Descartes' philosophy is not the beginning of Modernity, at least not when his predecessors are seriously taken into account.

The subsequent chapters formulated an alternative for Descartes' *cogito*, saying that the subject is an individual in context, that rationality is extended to reasonableness, and that freedom has to be recontextualised in turn in order to include others in a context.

This chapter will investigate more closely the characteristics of legalism. In doing so, I will first explore the contours of what I call 'strong legalism'. Generally speaking, under strong legalism, law and its construction by man is a representation of reality. In doing so, it transforms a particular perspective into a universal one. This is inherent in what chapter 3 termed the 'rationalistic fallacy'. Put differently, strong legalism makes an unwarranted use of the legitimating effects of universality. Its claim to universality, that is, the claim that law represents reality, makes a theory of legislation superfluous. It is the state that decides what is law, so any theory of legislation is reduced to a theory that justifies the authority of the state. Under this justification, the fact that rules are legal means that they are also legitimate, as Max Weber suggests.[1]

What strong legalism offers is a framework for the application of rules or principles, not for their construction. However, it is precisely because strong legalism limits legal thinking to the application of rules that it creates a limited focus on their legislative creation. In focusing on judges rather than on legislators, strong legalism misconceives the fact that legislators as well as judges do 'apply'

1 Weber 1964: 131: 'Today the most usual basis of legitimacy is the belief in legality, the readiness to conform with rules which are formally correct and have been imposed by accepted procedure.'

rules, although their dealing with rules is considerably, though not essentially, different, as will be argued in the following pages.

What the strong legalist claim amounts to is that judges should justify their decisions. They find a set of rules 'out there' that constitute a closed system. Within this system, the decision is to be found, that is, justified. In other words, first, a decision should be taken, and secondly, it must be shown to relate to the system of rules; that is what judicial justification consists of (Friedman 1966: 150–51). Because no justification is expressly required and because it does not rely on a closed set of rules, the enactment of legal rules by the legislator therefore seems to be exempted from justification (ibid.: 158 ff.).

My point is however that legislators, like judges, are bound by norms, that is, rules and principles. These norms are of a constitutional character, and must be followed by them. At least on this point, legislative activity is similar to rule-following behaviour, and so falls under the scope of legalism. According to this view, legislators should justify their decisions. However, if we require legislators to follow rules, we cannot be content with the strong legalistic model of rule following. For reasons that will become clear during the course of this chapter, strong legalism needs a qualification in order to show how a legislator can be regarded as a legal actor who is following rules. From that perspective, he is not merely a political actor taking decisions.

It is important to focus on two preliminary characteristics of strong legalism before entering into more detail. They are interrelated, and make legalism, broadly speaking, a philosophical strategy. The first is the epistemologisation of philosophy, that serves well the ends of strong legalism. The second is the separation of law and politics, which is helpful in hiding the political choices in law and in positing law as 'just there'.

Strong Legalism as a Strategy

Epistemologised Philosophy

Strong legalism, as we will soon see, operates under the metaphysical guise of representationalism. According to representationalism, the subject has 'ideas' or 'representations' of reality that have truth-values. Descartes' *cogito* is at the very heart of that. As will be argued below, however, this is only part of the truth. The rest of the truth is that representationalism quite straightforwardly results in instrumentalism, which claims that norms are a means to an end that is itself not rationally debatable.

It all looks then as if strong legalism faces a problem once it comes up against values and their discussion in politics. This problem is that politics will have no choice other than to exclude choices. According to strong legalism, politics, that is, turns into a form of zoo keeping, as Benjamin Barber (1984: 20 ff.) eloquently puts it.

Under this qualification, strong legalism starts looking much like a strategy that is a way of thinking focusing on a specific end, that is fixed in advance. However, the specific end sought after can be labelled 'certainty'. We find it in Descartes from an epistemological perspective, and Hobbes introduces it into his political philosophy under the label of 'security'.

As a matter of course, the spectacular results of natural science in the seventeenth century in terms of certainty and predictability did not remain secret or unnoticed. The mathematical articulation of natural phenomena in a sense set up a model according to which the science of man or society could reach the same or at least a comparable degree of certainty. The success of natural science was due, among other things, to the reduction of natural phenomena to what could be calculated. Secondary qualities, such as heat and colour, in so far as they were related to man, were left out of range. They were thought of as subjective, not as such, but only in as far as the subject experiences them.[2]

The 'sciences of man', so it was believed, could reach a similar degree of certainty if the experience of social life could be severed from any subjective evaluative yardstick. Put differently, if certainty could be achieved by reducing the subjective experience of man in natural science, then the same method was believed to provide similar results in the field of human action. Accordingly, strong legalism can be said to embrace this premise of scientific method.

This presupposes, however, a specific move, that was called the 'epistemologisation of philosophy' in chapter 3. The epistemologisation of philosophy consists in transforming practical problems into theoretical ones. In this respect, the certainty Descartes was searching for, as I have argued elsewhere (Wintgens 2006a), ended up delineating the realm of reason as what could be proved in a logical way. Practical problems are rather seldom of such a nature that they exclude any controversy.

However, apart from the standard story saying that one day reason revealed itself to the philosopher, there is an alternative reading of Descartes saying that he is *searching for something*, namely, certainty. Having established the certainty and the truth of the *cogito*, his project goes on as a concatenation of new certainties, following upon clear and distinct ideas that he holds true upon God's veracity. Even morality, so he believed, could thus be constituted as a set of true propositions of what we ought to do. The epistemologisation of philosophy thus means that all practical problems could (and should) be transformed into epistemological problems, thus decontextualising them and subjecting them to the methods of natural science.

The strategic character of strong legalism can best be articulated by the inherent tension it betrays between law as 'just there' on the one hand and law as 'man-

2 See Taylor 1985c: 58. The 'experience' of secondary qualities like heat becomes of course more objective when they can be measured, but measuring them does not exclude that they remain subjective, that is, in as far as they can only be experienced by a subject. See Husserl 1970a: 32.

made' on the other. This tension illustrates a symptomatic ambiguity within strong legalism. This ambiguity flows from a merger of the belief in the naturalness of law on the one hand and its artificial or man-made character on the other. It is this ambiguity that makes legalism a strategy rather than a theory.

If on the political level the strategy results in zoo keeping, on the moral level it marks a strategy of peace keeping. Conflicts, so we read from Hobbes, who was the first to put it that bluntly and clearly, are bad. They are bad in the moral sense of the word, because they go against the Christian message of neighbourly love. Man, however, is both wicked and rational. Fortunately for him, his rational capacities provide him with the insight that he should surrender his moral capacities in order to organise his life. He should, that is, surrender his capacity to live according to God's laws to the mortal god rather than running the risk of a violent death, as the second law commands (Hobbes 1966c: 118). Civil laws as the upshot of that surrender will provide man with security and, coming with that inter alia, the possibility of enjoying the fruits of his labour.[3]

The fear of death in Hobbes's work takes the place of the natural telos (Strauss 1974: 180–81), which is all but a rational argument for subscribing to the contract. What I want to make clear here is that, far less than Rousseau, to whose work we shall turn in due course, it follows from Hobbes's position that there is actually no choice. Because the choice for the contract is presented as a fully rational one, there is, as a matter of fact, no choice. The only choice man has is to enter into the contract.

From the point of view of the agent, following the rules of the sovereign is the most rational behaviour possible. Following the rules is in his own interest, which he is seeking to maximise. If this is a matter of choice, it is the most rational choice possible. Here too, strong legalism seems to have an impact on a strategic level, transforming the subject itself into a strategist. Following the epistemologisation of philosophy, man is held to be rational in such a way that his calculation necessarily brings him to enter into the contract. It is the type of rationality that Hobbes has in his mind.

The contractual construction of political space and civil laws is called in to solve conflicts that emerge in social interaction. However, contrary to Hobbes's beliefs, social conflicts do not have necessarily, and most of the time even not at all, a moral – far less a political – character. Conflicts are not always value conflicts. Hobbes, however, seems to assume, like Roberto Unger does, that every conflict can be qualified as a political conflict in that it can bring deeper social tensions to the surface. These supposed tensions, that are virtually present in every ordinary conflict, have the potential to cause the implosion of the cornerstones of social and political space. That is to say, any day-to-day conflict always has the potential to blow up into revolutionary proportions (Unger 1987: 151 ff.) Unger's therefore is nothing but an updated version of the *bellum omnium contra omnes*.

---

3 Hobbes 1966c: 116: '... desire of such things as are necessary to commodious living; and a hope by their industry to obtain them.'

Apart from its conflict-solving potential, law should also be reserved a peace-keeping function. The strong legalistic device of mere rule following provides the most successful support for this function. Peace keeping is the most appropriate way for preventing conflicts from emerging. I will illustrate this position by highlighting later in this chapter some aspects of the French codification movement at the beginning of the nineteenth century.

Before turning to that, the relationship between law and conflicting choices or politics requires some more attention. Strong legalism, as we will see, lives in tension with values. The relationship between law and politics results from the strategy of strong legalism following upon the epistemologisation of philosophy that was explored above. With this in mind, we can then further proceed with the exploration of the main aspects of strong legalism.

The Separation of Law and Politics

In line with the epistemologisation of philosophy, legalism aims to separate law from politics. The relationship between law and politics is a complex one, especially when it is considered from the perspective of strong legalism. As was argued in the previous section, philosophy emerged transformed out of the Modern philosophical project. That is, philosophy, following upon Descartes' reflective and reflexive operation of the *cogito,* did become an exercise in epistemology. Rationality is held identical to proof. Values are, from that perspective, not amenable to proof; hence, they are not rational (Wintgens 2006a).

Although it is Hume's philosophy that is most commonly associated with the separation of fact and norm, the Cartesian *cogito* is premised on the same claim, since values lack the clarity and the distinction that could make them true ideas. Hume's position is, from a different perspective, thus pre-echoed by Descartes. The similarity between the two positions is best expressed as non-cognitivism in practical matters.

While in chapter 2 the main focus was on a critical analysis of the *cogito,* this chapter will address some of its consequences. Put briefly, because values cannot be connected to clear and distinct ideas, they cannot be rationally proved, which means that they cannot be true. The absence of the possibility of rational proof makes values inherently controversial. That is where the trouble starts.

Together with the philosophical articulation of the individual in nominalism, the unsurprising but noteworthy consequence of the epistemologisation of philosophy is that the realm of politics, typically the practical domain, is drawn into that of theoretical reason. This is what the epistemologisation of philosophy results in.

Serious philosophical efforts are made to construct a *theoretical* model under which clashes of value judgements – that can all lead to the war of all against all – can be dealt with. Hobbes's suggestion involves a neutralisation of the potential conflicts, while Rousseau is rather inclined to institutionalisation them without denying them. Both then advocate a form of proceduralisation, a technique that would be worked out in the twentieth century by, for example, Niklas Luhmann (Luhmann 1983).

It is important in this respect to note the difference with the Aristotelian approach of politics. Politics in Aristotle's closed world focuses on the question of the good life and the organisation of the *polis*, typically a matter of ethics, for which dialectical method is most appropriate (Aristotle 1984d: 1094b, 12–1095a, 13; 1112a, 1–1113a, 14). A consequence of the method of the Modern philosophical project is, however, that practical questions will be dealt with by transforming them into theoretical ones.

The epistemologisation of practical problems – typically, the organisation of political space – then becomes a matter of making political space rational. It is a matter of *making*, since political space is no longer believed to be something natural. Both social space or society and political space or the state are not adjusted to each other in a natural way. This relationship also must be constructed.

Here as elsewhere, one recognises the strategic aspect that is operational in strong legalism. The impossibility of making rational value judgements, hence the endlessness of political discussion, and the absence of any help from God, Nature, or Reason, will be resolved in a strategic way. The strategy consists in presenting an ultimate or basic act of will in a cognitive dress: the social contract. In this respect Rorty claims that 'The dominating notion of epistemology is that to be rational, to be fully human, to do what we ought, we need to be able to find agreement with other human beings' (Rorty 1979: 316).

This strategy, of which Hobbes and Rousseau are undeniably the masterminds and the most important theorists, can be considered a transformation of the individual into a citizen. As we read from Rousseau (1997a: 50): 'Each of us puts his person and his full power in common under the supreme direction of the general will; and in a body we receive each member as an indivisible part of the whole.'

This transformation takes place at a hypothetical moment in time, to the analysis of which we will turn later in this chapter. From the 'moment' of the social contract onward, the citizen is everything he can be from the perspective of the system of interaction to which he subscribed by entering into the contract (Miaille 1976: 53). The contract is not, needless to say, a real event. It refers to a hypothetical moment in history, when reason has sufficiently developed, if not come to an end, and when a hypothetical 'act of will' is set to provide the fundamentals of political space.

Undoubtedly, under the above transformation, a new type of man and of society is operationalised, in which the focus is on transparency, predictability, and certainty as the most important objectives (Foqué and 't Hart 1990: 44 ff.; Arnaud 1975). Man is transformed into a citizen. As a citizen, he is conceived of as an autonomous, rational and predictable entity.

The new social and political ideal that comes with it embraces the archetype of a legal order based on rules. This idea(l) leads us to the roots of the rule of law doctrine, guaranteeing transparency through the very idea of rules itself. In doing so, revolutionary activism and uncertainty that were at the order of the day by the end of the eighteenth century in France could be blocked off.

The basic idea of the rule of law doctrine or the *Rechtsstaat*, that both the ruler and the ruled are bound to rules, can be interpreted in two ways. The first interpretation is the path of strong legalism. According to this approach, the ruler's being bound to rules is tantamount to his 'not violating' them. This is both a necessary and a sufficient condition for rules to be valid and legitimate. Under the second interpretation – which is adopted by legisprudence – the idea of following rules by a sovereign counts only as a necessary and not as a sufficient condition for rules to be valid. Legal validity on this view is distinct from legitimacy. Legitimacy for its part can only be obtained through legitimation. This issue is considered in chapter 6.

The second interpretation of a sovereign following rules according to legisprudence espouses a form of constitutionalism that answers the question as to what it means for a ruler to follow a rule. The answer to this question is encapsulated in the claim that 'not violating the rules' is a merely necessary condition for legal validity. This means that through his ruling activity, while following rules, the ruler must supply reasons for his choices.

The legitimating power of the concept of a rule itself has become far too insufficient as an implementation of the democratic ideal of freedom and equality, as envisaged in the French Revolution. The archetype of the legal order consisting of rules turns out to rely on the belief that political activism, with all the revolutionary proportions it had taken by the end of the eighteenth century, could be stopped by a transformation of the individual, as both the subject and object of power, into a citizen. According to this view, political power takes on a legal shape; that is, it is moulded into a constitution that allows for a further channelling of power through rules.

Apart from the transformation of the individual into a citizen and apart from giving political power a legal form, social interaction will be affected by these operations. Every social problem that is believed to be a conflict can take on legal form. Political space is considered appropriate for regulating conflicts through legal rules. It could be concluded that the greater the number of rules, the fewer conflicts there should be. This is however far from being true, as will be argued below.

Apart from the fact that rules do undeniably express a value judgement by their content, the concept of a rule itself is a value judgement. It expresses the value of security or it conveys the ideal of freedom, equality and fraternity. The rule character of law, in that it expresses a value judgement, however remains unquestioned. The theory of the social contract is hence a powerful device allowing value judgements to be hidden away from view. In so far as it succeeds in doing so, we are at the very heart of strong legalism. Strong legalism as the denial of value judgements is itself the expression of a value judgement.

The latter claim can be made even stronger. Under the foregoing analysis, it can be concluded that the basic motive for the transformation of the subject into a citizen, of framing political power within legal form and legalising social problems, is itself a value judgement. In other words, the transformation of practical problems into the theoretical framework of the social contract is mandated by practical reason itself that withdraws behind its theoretical 'twin'. Was it not, however, the reversal of practical and theoretical reason, rooted in theological soil, that was at the origin of Modern science? Was it not will that drove Descartes and Galilei more than revelation of truth? Here we establish one of the consequences of this reversal: the social contract as a theory of reality turns out to be a transformation of practical problems into a theoretical scheme. The operation itself conceals the fact that practical reason is at work here. Here as elsewhere, this is a form of epistemologised philosophy which was discussed in chapter 3.

If then, the mimetical relation between the science of nature and the *philosophia civilis* as Hobbes calls it is not going to be inspired by the mere theoretical success of the former, this is an argument in favour of the thesis that some value judgement operates at the background of this endeavour. And this value judgement, according to this study's analysis of strong legalism, is to be concealed behind some theoretical stance. Put differently, the construction of political space via the social contract relies on a political or practical motive, that is, it forms part of practical reason. It will, however, show up in theoretical garb. It is through this representational view as it operates in theoretical reason that we will gain access to a deeper analysis of strong legalism.

The fact that law is believed to consist of rules thus relies on a value judgement. Why rules and not something else? The answer seems to be a relatively simple one. First, according to the mechanical world-view that has been predominant from the seventeenth century onwards, it turns out that conflicts are caused by human nature. If society can be organised according to rules, like the universe is obeying rules, this must correspond with the belief that conflicts can be mastered. Planets in the universe do not fight nor do they have conflicts, since they 'follow rules'.

Secondly, rules are a fitting device for mastering and solving conflicts in a theoretical way. Rules, as in natural science, operate in a cognitive way. Thus following rules and, in case of conflict, applying them, is believed to be a mere matter of knowing them. As a cognitive operation, they do not include value judgements. As a result, the conjugation of law in terms of rules that is embedded in the grand operation of the epistemologisation of philosophy affects law as a practical matter. It transforms law into a theoretical fabric.

A consequence of this transformation of practical or political problems into theoretical ones is that strong legalism can hold that law is 'just there', as Judith Shklar so eloquently puts it (Shklar 1986: 9). It requires the judge to comply strictly with the rules, the meaning of which is supposed to be clear, in the absence of evidence to the contrary. This 'proof' is always somewhat suspicious, since it allows the judge to import his own value judgements into the law. Again, as with all value judgements, there is no method for resolving value disputes in a rational manner, so how could there be one to solve the tension between a legislative and a judicial value judgement?

If the choice for 'law as rules' is a practical question, and hence a value judgement that is left out of view as a matter of strategy, then the relationship between law and politics will be strongly affected. Not only the choice for 'law as rules' is a form of strategy, but so too is the content of the rules itself. The content of rules that are made by man is a value judgement. Given the 'thereness' of law, as the eminent expression of strong legalism, the choice of 'law as rules' and the content of the rules is concealed behind their 'being there'.

According to this articulation of the relationship between law and politics, following upon the epistemologisation of philosophy, we can now begin to explore the main aspects of strong legalism. Some of them have been briefly touched upon here previously, while others have remained latent in the analysis until now. Here, then, are the elements of what in my view strong legalism consists of. The summary below will at the same time establish the order in which they will be treated in the following pages.

We will deal with (1) representationalism, (2) timelessness, (3) instrumentalism, (4) etatism and (5) legal science respectively. Needless to say, here, as elsewhere, the intention is not to provide an exhaustive analysis. The aim is to be plausible in claiming that strong legalism consists of a cluster of theories or presuppositions, the purpose of which is to tie man-made law to reality. Put differently, under strong legalism as a strategy, law is a matter of construction that represents law as part of reality. Law that is represents reality.

Strong Legalism as a Thought Pattern

Representationalism: The Path to Strong Legalism

An initial view of how representationalism operates can be articulated in the way we question the world. As Martin Hollis has suggested, there are basically two types of questions – open and closed.

Philosophical questioning deals with problems. These problems are familiar, and attempts may be made to answer them through philosophical questioning. These answers are particularly interesting, although not because of their content. This somewhat paradoxical statement of the relationship between question and answer needs some closer observation. Martin Hollis proposes an interesting perspective on this (Hollis 1985: 5–10). This perspective consists in drawing the distinction between 'open' and 'closed' questions.

To start with the latter, closed questions are questions that can, at least in principle, receive a final answer. Two examples can illustrate this.

The first example concerns the question 'Are bachelors unmarried?' This can be answered through an analysis of the concept of 'bachelor'. This answer is valid as long as the concept of 'bachelor' exists. The second example concerns the question as to whether there is life on Mars. Until now, we do not know the answer. But we do know at least how to get it. Once we engage the necessary technical means for a thorough exploration of the red planet, there is no principled reason why we would not obtain an answer to our question. Both questions are of the 'closed' type, because we dispose of a – conceptual or empirical – framework to answer them. The answers to them are 'closed' in that the questions take a specific form of intelligibility for granted (Winch 1990 102).

Things are different however with 'open' questions. These questions are asked without a similar framework being available. In contrast to the first type of questions, the assurance that, at least in principle, we can get an answer is lacking. Questions of this type are 'What is reality?' or 'What is justice?', and at least one thing is clear with this type of questions, and that is that they are tough to answer. Why is that so?

The difficulty in answering them lies, among other things, in the fact that these questions are asked outside any frame of reference. Such a framework can at least provide some principled answer to a closed question. It is such a framework that makes it a closed question. Obviously, when questions are asked outside any such framework, they cannot profit from the advantages offered by it. Thus open questions are, like their 'closed' twins, in need of being 'framed'. This is what happens during thought. Open questions incite thinking to develop frameworks within which they can be dealt with.

Any teacher knows the rule of thumb that 'good questions contain half of the answer.' From that perspective, philosophical questions cannot really be considered 'good', though they are interesting after all. Their interest lies in the fact that they raise new questions, like questions about the framework within which they are or must be answered. And these answers, including their framework, are again sensitive to new questioning, and so on. Philosophy is then a game, and we are only players.

From that perspective, some light is shed on how the relation between philosophy and theory can be understood. As soon as a philosophical question gets an answer, like 'reality is … ', questions and answers are merged into what can be called a theory. We then seem to have knowledge of what reality is, in one form or another of *theorein.* Philosophical questions then obtain closed or theoretical answers. Closed answers take a form of intelligibility of taking the world for granted.

It looks then as if they are answerable in a final way. Again, some philosophers have the irritating habit of presenting things in this way. The framework they have set up through their thinking claims to provide direct access to reality. On this view, the question, the framework within which it is asked, and the answer to it, are fused. Through this fusion, they constitute the strong philosophical bridge to reality. In other words, on that account we walk along the *via Regis* to truth, and we are supposed to have knowledge *of* reality.

There is, however, at least one different way of looking at these answers. We may recall in this regard the distinction between questions asked and frameworks within which answers are provided. A philosophical – open – question, as I have suggested, does not have the same framework at its disposal as a non-philosophical – closed – question does. In answering the former, both the framework and the answer must be set up. It inevitably follows that the answer is dependent on a framework. The answer involves the construction of a bridge or a framework with the help of which reality is attained. It can thus be said that both answers and questions only make sense when related to a framework. Such framework then takes the name of, for example, *'Weltbild'* or 'world-view' in Martin Heidegger's work (Heidegger 1950).

A critical appraisal of the *'Weltbild'* or world-view can be considered by taming the philosophical ambitions of Modernity, and the direct access to reality believed to have been achieved. Whatever way they are labelled, the philosophical insights that are related to them by way of mediation will be referred to as knowledge *about* reality. They mediate the access to reality that is not claimed to be reached in a direct way. With this distinction between a theory *of* reality and a theory *about* reality in mind, we can again pick up the distinction that was made in chapter 1 between realism and nominalism.

Realist theories, so it follows from the discussion in chapter 1, claim to have an undisturbed view of what reality really is, while nominalist theories provide mediated access to it. Realist theories claim to provide direct access to reality, while nominalist theories use a framework or theory to operate. The former were called therefore theories of reality, the latter theories about reality.

The crucial difference between the two is that realist theories hold that truth is in the things, while nominalist theories hold that truth is in sentences. Realists tell us that we live in the immediacy of the world's presence, and that truth consists of a correspondence between a proposition and the world. Nominalists for their part hold that since truth lies in sentences, there is no direct reference to reality. Even knowledge of non-existent beings was held possible, and in this respect there is no reference to the world at all.

Things become different at the beginning of Modernity, the investigation of which was started with Descartes. Over against the scepticism that nominalism left on his desk, Descartes' approach involved displacing truth with certainty. Given God's veracity, clear and distinct ideas are certain and true. Truth then is in the ideas, or representations. Certainty as an aspect of knowledge – that, on Descartes' view, is the key to truth – is the upshot of the epistemologisation of philosophy, starting with Descartes. Knowledge, that is, amounts to a representation of the world through language. This involves saying that language refers to something real and extra-linguistic that is re-presented. Representationalism is hence the belief that our knowledge represents the world as it is, starting from an unshakeable foundation.

Preferring focus to detail, representationalism connects thinking to a foundation or an origin. It is important in this respect to remember Descartes for whom certainty is the epistemic criterion for truth. Apart from a first truth (the *cogito* and the proof of God) (Descartes 1996i: 18–42), the foundation can also be a true norm, for example, the fundamental law of nature in Hobbes (1996c: 117), the norm of sociality in Pufendorf (1994b: 70), the rule to enter in the civil state in Kant (1997: 84–5, 89–90). Another version of the foundation is a constitutive act of will resulting in popular sovereignty as in Rousseau (1997a: 49–50), a foundation of the validity of a system of positive law, that is, a thought of 'Grundnorm' (Kelsen 1967: 201–5), or a rule of recognition applied by law-applying officials (Hart 1994: 100–23). In any of its variants, representationalism is a foundationalist model of metaphysics, in which the subject's intervention in establishing truth is a necessary condition. This model is idealistic without, however, necessarily being positivistic. Legalism and representationalism are compatible with, though not necessarily related to, modern natural law theories.

According to this brief articulation of representationalism, here as elsewhere it becomes clear that Descartes espouses essential elements of nominalism, despite the fact that he is generally qualified as a realist. Nominalism and realism, however, are combined in his theory that transforms philosophy into epistemology, and so narrows our view of the world to representations thereof. It leads straight into epistemologised philosophy, as follows from chapter 3.

Representation becomes slightly more complex when we start thinking of law. It was argued in chapter 1 that legalism is the spin-off of nominalist metaphysics. This insight can now be combined with representationalism, endowing us with a promising access to strong legalism. It is representationalism that is behind the device of strong legalism according to which law is 'just there'.

On the representationalist view, law is held to be a representation of reality. In doing so, law is not mediated by politics. Hence, law is purified from value judgements or politics. Therefore, both the form – 'law is rules' – and the content of law result from a theory of reality. A theory of reality, it may be remembered from the previous sections, results from answering a philosophical question in a closed way. The answer to the question provides both a framework for answering it and the answer itself. As a result, the answer will be considered true, since it is based on direct access to reality. If the construction of the framework for answering the philosophical question is left out of view, the access to reality appears to be direct. It therefore looks as if no framework is required in order to put the question or to answer it. Truth, then, is reached and does not leave any opportunity for disagreement.

The complexity that shows up is this: law's millenary tradition is roamed through by the opposition between natural law on the one hand and positivism on the other. The emphases may be different depending on the theories elaborated, though they cannot just be erased. In this sense, representationalism as it emerged from the epistemologisation of philosophy should also be investigated from this perspective. This opens up a broader outlook on strong legalism.

In order to obtain a better hold on strong legalism, we should try to disentangle the representational view operating against its background. The distinction between a theory of and a theory about reality is again useful here. Under this distinction, we can make another one, that is, the distinction between two different approaches towards representation.

The first is a form of representation based on the structure of reality. The second, on the contrary, plays a more active role in structuring reality (Perelman and Olbrechts-Tyteca 1976: 471 ff.) The first will be called 'representation-reproduction', the second 'representation-construction'.

Representation-reproduction can be related to a theory of reality, while representation-construction can be connected to a theory about reality.

The difference between the two types of representation can be articulated as a difference between the dynamics present in each of them. 'Dynamics' is taken to mean the direction of the relationship between human thought and human will on the one hand, and reality on the other.

According to representation-reproduction, reality is re-presented. Reality is already present in that it exists, and representation-reproduction stresses that presence. Typically, this is found in both classical and modern natural law, that is, mainly, the Aristotelian and Thomistic version on the one hand, and the Modern variant on the other. The dynamics operational in this form of representation, that is, the direction of the relationship between human action and thought on the one hand and reality on the other is *from* reality *to* human thinking. Representation-reproduction is most closely connected to realism.

A further articulation of this type of dynamics leads to the identification of some of its more concrete appearances. This type of dynamics is found in models of thought according to which what exists in reality is of a *higher* value compared to the products of human activity; the latter are considered to be of a *lower* value. A variant of this is that what is *earlier* has priority over what comes *later.* If the 'earlier' is thought of 'existent', what comes later has only ontological value in as far as it is related to what exists already (Perelman and Olbrechts-Tyteca 1976: 471 ff.)

Whatever articulation is proposed, the common denominator in the dynamics of representation-reproduction is that it starts *from* something existing *to* something known or created. Human action or thought, on representation-reproduction, is subordinate to that which exists. In so far as law is concerned, the direction of the dynamics in representation-reproduction is *from* a transcendent – existing – foundation *to* positive – human – law. Positive law makes natural law present in its own particular way, that is, it re-presents what is already ontologically there. It operates, as Bluhmenberg has eloquently expressed it as 'Nachahmung' or 'Nachvollziehung' (Blumenberg 1957).

In the second variant of representation – that is, representation-construction – the dynamics of the relationship between thought and reality are reversed This dynamics operates *from* human action and thought *to* reality, and it is most closely connected to nominalism. According to the latter, concepts have no ontological value; they are, on the contrary, human constructs. The understanding of reality is affected by the dynamics of the relationship between reality and thought, since it is through the active contribution of the latter that the former can be apprehended.

It is the second variant of representation that is of most interest here. The difference is between representation-reproduction and representation-construction, which will be clarified through Hobbes's account of the relationship between the laws of nature and the civil laws of the sovereign.

In line with the comments about Hobbes in Chapter 1, for Hobbes, the laws of nature are commands of God. They are the rules that organise the social state. Given Hobbes's espousal of nominalism, the existence of the laws of nature must, however, be distinguished from their meaning. The laws of nature, that is, have no meaning of their own. Under the nominalistic dichotomy that Hobbes introduces between the laws of nature on the one hand and civil laws on the other, the latter created by the sovereign confer meaning upon the former. In that sense, the Hobbesian sovereign represents the laws of nature, though endows them with his own meaning. On this view, it can be said that the laws of the sovereign represent the laws of nature, although he actually constructs them. On this view, Hobbes can be said to hold the representation-construction view.

At the same time, however, this 'creation' of meaning is held to be the very meaning of the laws of nature, as they exist. If they exist as commands of God, they are semantically empty; they have no meaning without the sovereign's intervention. Their meaning is then imputed to them by the definitional intervention of the sovereign, so that, after all, it looks *as if* the civil laws re-present the laws of nature in the same way as human law does according to, say, Thomistic natural law. On this view, Hobbes considers representation as representation-reproduction.

This difference between the latter view and representation-reproduction amounts to a reversal of the dynamics of the relationship between thinking and reality. The dynamic of the representation-reproduction is therefore exactly the opposite of the one that can be identified in Hobbes as representation-construction. Hobbes, as a matter of fact, merges the two forms of representation. What looks like a faithful representation of the laws of nature by the sovereign, is, as a matter of fact, exactly the opposite of what takes place under a natural law theory. Without the active definitional intervention of the sovereign, the laws of nature make no sense. If they are represented throughout positive law, this is only possible through a constructive intervention of the sovereign.

While it is a construction of the sovereign, positive law is, in other words, naturalised. Natural law thinking, say, starting from the natural laws, and naturalisation of positive law may then in the end, at least prima facie, produce a similar effect. Due to the opposite dynamics that are operational under both models, they are, however, essentially different from one another.

This ambiguity at the heart of the relationship between knowledge of the natural laws and the intervening will of the sovereign can be clarified with the help of the distinction between representation-reproduction and representation-construction. More specifically, we can call this ambiguity the *naturalisation* of positive law. Other qualifications like *hypostatisation*, *ontologisation*, or *substantialisation* of law are equivalent to that. What the naturalisation of positive law amounts to is the belief that it represents reality, hence representationalism.

With the distinction between representation-reproduction and representation-construction in mind, it is only a short step to see how legalism's representation of reality is not a representation-reproduction, but a representation-construction. It is a construction that is held to be a representation of reality. While it is a construction, it is held to be reproduction. The construction, in other words, is naturalised. It looks as if it were real. The naturalisation fuses the construction with what is real or 'out there'. The naturalisation, ontologisation, or hypostatisation consists of concealing the construction, and so tries to show the representation-construction as a representation-reproduction. Representationalism in Hobbes then can be considered a merger of a 'reproduction' of the laws of nature through the 'construction' of civil laws.

Timelessness and the Validity of Law

Representationalism holds that the way we think of reality is true. It represents the world as it is. This does not essentially change following the merger of representation-reproduction and representation-construction. The opposite is true. The merger aims to conceal the constructivist intervention and takes it to be true and unqualified. However, truth is timeless. This section will investigate the effects of the merger. The thesis which will be proposed is that the merger of both types of representation amounts to a manipulation of the concept of time. This merger is a helpful device in transforming a theory about reality into a theory of reality. As a result of that, human thinking is believed to reach *universality*, hence truth, or reality itself.

In order to come to terms with the problem of the construction of political society, the social contract theorists came up with their theory of a willed social bond. Their approach sheds a specific light on the problem of time.

Since human creation has no ontological status, the problem faced in the Modern philosophical project is a dilemma. Human beings are no longer believed to be political by nature. Therefore, if it does not exist in a natural way, political space must be created. This creation, that is, will not have the same, if any, ontological status as the *polis* in antique philosophy. How then could this problem be solved?

The answer appears to be fairly simple; it is complex in nature though, as we shall see from Rousseau, on whose work I will mainly focus in arguing this point. I will concentrate the following exposé on basically two aspects, that is, the time structure of the social contract and the time structure of legislation.

Time and the Social Contract

The social contract, needless to say, marks the transition from the state of nature into a rationally organised political space. Within political space, the citizens will finally be endowed with the morality that was essentially lacking in the state of nature in both Hobbes (1966c: 253 ff.) and Rousseau (1997a: 53–4), with many others in their wake. The conclusion of the social contract as a hypothesis is a necessary presupposition for a society to take the form of a political space or a state.

The social contract marks the transition from the state of nature into a rationally organised political space. Only political space endows its members' actions with the morality that is essentially lacking in the state of nature in both Hobbes and Rousseau.

The social contract refers to a human act. While human acts are replete with historicity, the social contract has a timeless content. However, the timelessness of the contract's content seems to obliterate the fact that social life, before the contract, is embedded in time. Rousseau indicates several temporal markers that connect the conclusion of the contract with the flow of history.

One of these temporal markers is 'some fatal accident' (Rousseau 1997b: 167). Vague as it may be, it points to things that happen. These include a number of historical coincidences, such as the invention of metallurgy, the evolution of agriculture, and the increase in population (ibid.: 167 ff.; Blumenberg 1983: 221 ff.). Together, these events support the view that the state of nature is not a static situation but, on the contrary, evolves, and hence varies through time.

The basis of this evolution to which Rousseau draws attention is mainly of an economic nature. The scarcity of goods increases in proportion with the growth of the population. Given the fact that everybody strives to attain the same goods (Polin 1971: 17; Hobbes 1966c: 111), an increase in economic production is indispensable. The latter in turn, combined with the requirement of specialisation, necessitates the division of labour, for which Adam Smith provides the theoretical tools.

Finally, the division of labour is at the basis of the emergence of trade, as a consequence of which relations of dependency rise (Rousseau 1997b: 168 ff.). The emergence of relations of dependency marks the final stage of the state of nature. This final stage announces the 'moment' of the conclusion of the contract, which is again referred to with a temporal marker.[4]

Secondly, at the 'moment' of the social contract, the historical dimension of social life is neutralised. The contract absorbs the time locations and so constructs a timeless reality. This is a consequence of the universality of the clauses of the contract in space and time.[5] This universality allows for a triple interpretation.

On the first interpretation, the content of the contract exists in reality, from where it can be directly read. The existence of the true principles of public law is thus a matter of metaphysical speculation.

Rousseau explicitly rejects this interpretation. According to him, the content of the social contract is universally accepted. It need not exist in reality. This formulation suggests that the content of the contract is true *because* it is universally accepted. On this interpretation, that which all agree upon is true. This

4 Rousseau 1997a: 123: 'If, then, *at the time of the social pact* there are some who oppose it, their opposition does not invalidate the contract, it only keeps them from being included in it … ' (italics added); ibid.: 54: 'Each member of the community gives himself to it *at the moment* of its formation … ' (italics added).

5 Ibid.: 50: 'The clauses of this contract are so completely determined by the nature of the act that the slightest modification would render them null and void; so that although they may *never* have been formally stated, they are everywhere the same, *everywhere* tacitly admitted and recognized … ' (italics added).

second interpretation would make his theory a pragmatic theory of truth, which contradicts Rousseau's overall approach.

On the third interpretation, those who accept the content of the social contract belong to rational mankind, under Rousseau's idea of it. The evolution of reason brings about the true principles of public law that are in accordance with natural law. The rational organisation of political space requires the implementation of these principles.

In order to strengthen his argument, Rousseau exploits the universality of the acceptance of the principles of public law. 'What all rational beings accept as [a valid standard X] is [a valid standard]' is a logical truth, according to the following argument. A disagreement as to the standard of evaluation X means that another standard Y is invoked. Through this disagreement, a meta-judgement is needed in order to disqualify Y. Contrasting Y to X then entails measuring the fact of invoking Y by norm X. This contrast between fact and norm does not occur in cases involving universal consensus. Therefore, 'what all rational beings accept as [a valid standard] is [a valid standard]' is logically true. Therefore, X is a valid standard. Because of its universal acceptance, no alternative standard Y can be invoked. Given the universal acceptance of X, the expression 'X is a valid standard' is true from a realistic perspective because a conflict with reality exists is excluded.

Under any hypothesis, since political space is not a natural datum, it must be constructed. This construction can only occur from within the social bound. At the same time, it exists only in so far as it complies with the cognitively universal content of the clauses of the social contract, as Rousseau identifies them. As a result, political space is at the same time as it ought to be. The social contract clauses are the true principles of public law (Rousseau 1997a: 152). Despite the fact that the social contract is a human act, and hence embedded in temporality, it corresponds to reality.

The foregoing can also be put differently. In any hypothesis, political space is to be constructed from within. It exists only in so far as it complies with the cognitively universal content of the clauses of the social contract, as Rousseau identifies them. As a result, political space is at the same time as it ought to be, since the social contract contains the true principles of public law. For this reason, it can be claimed that the social contract is the result of direct access to reality. It is therefore a representation-reproduction of it. It represents the true principles of political right, hence their universal, or a-temporal validity.

Time and legislation

From the time when political space can be said to exist, a mechanism is set in motion which is similar to that which is operational in the background of the conclusion of the contract itself. On the one hand, the set of legal rules that find their origin in the contract and derive their validity from it are contingent; they are man-made. On the other hand, however, they participate in the a-temporal character or timelessness of the contract itself. This results in a similar tension between contingency and timelessness as was noticed in the analysis of the social contract. In this respect, we read from Rousseau (1997a: 109): 'Yesterday's law does not obligate today, but tacit consent is presumed from silence, and the Sovereign is assumed to be constantly confirming the laws which it does not abrogate when it can do so. Everything which it has once declared it wills it continues to will, unless it revokes it.'

From a rational natural law perspective, this idea makes no sense. Rules are either valid or they are not. When they are, they are so because they are correctly deduced from natural law. They are accordingly true, and any change to them would undermine their validity. Rousseau pushes the paradox to its very limits here: as long as rules do not change, they are timelessly valid (cf. Luhmann 1981: 374, 400).

When positive law can be changed, despite its sacred nature, this is so because its ultimate basis is convention.[6] As was observed above, the conventional, hence *historical*, characteristic of legal rules is an aspect that they share with the social contract itself. The contract, one remembers, can be legitimately broken; any law in turn can be legitimately changed. If the contract disappears, the rules based on it vanish at the same time.

This is not the only similarity between legal rules and the clauses of the social contract from which the latter derive their validity. The clauses of the social contract, so Rousseau stresses, are a matter of all or nothing; they cannot be changed without making the contract void.

When it is necessary to vote on propositional contents proposed by the legislator, citizens do not have the right to amend the proposed legal rules. Nor do they have any right of initiative (Rousseau 1997b: 116–17). The latter belongs to the legislator. He has the task of circumscribing the content of the general will – Rousseau's expression of the *bonum commune.* The general will is the will of the citizenry and it is expressed by the sovereign, of which they are all part.

The legislator for his part does not play any part whatsoever in executive power. The latter is vested exclusively in the sovereign; its majority vote expresses the general will. The vote concerns the issue as to whether the proposed propositional content of the rules does or does not comply with the general will. There are two aspects of this process that are of importance for us here.

The first is that citizens are not asked to express their own conviction or opinion. The vote does not scrutinise what the individual citizens believe ought to happen. All they do express with their vote is an anticipation of what the majority will say concerning the proposal that is put to a vote; that is, whether this proposal does or does not comply with the general will.[7] The vote is, strictly speaking, not

---

6 Rousseau 1997a: 41: 'But social order is a sacred right, which provides the basis for all the others. Yet this right does not come from nature; it is therefore founded on conventions.'

7 Rousseau 1997a: 440–41: 'When a law is proposed in the People's assembly, what they are being asked is not exactly whether they approve the proposal or reject it, but whether it does or does not conform to the general will … .'

an act of will but a cognitive statement saying whether a proposal does or does not correspond to the general will or whether it does 'represent' the general will, hence, representationalism.

The second aspect, connected to the first, is that citizens who happen to belong to the minority are logically not expected to change their opinion. Since their opinion was not asked for, why should they change something that did not matter? However, the citizens in the majority only made a cognitive judgement; they did not express any preference. So too did those belonging to the minority, only they happened to be wrong – they simply made a mistake (Rousseau 1997a: 124).

The only thing that is expected of those who happen to belong to the minority is that they adapt their external behaviour to the propositional content that was approved by the majority. Only the latter can be considered an act of will, that is, the will to behave externally according to what is standard for the majority.

Notwithstanding any appearance to the contrary, the vote on the propositional content put forward by the legislator is not an act of will. Since the minority is wrong, the majority must be right. This, however, is not an evaluative statement; it is a matter of truth. Rousseau states it in cognitive terms: the minority made an error. Therefore, the ballot of every citizen is a cognitive process, expressing in a mechanical and quantitative way the relative weight of the majority and the minority. The voting process is a cognitive process expressing a truth proposition. The general will 'exists' independently of the vote. The members of the sovereign can only recognise it. If they do so, the citizens must act according to that will.

These two observations corroborate the general line of the argument until now. It all looks as if the Rousseau mechanism is of a voluntaristic nature, that is, that will is at the basis of both the social contract and the law. The will referred to in the contract, as well as in the voting process, is human, that is, it is replete with historicity and temporality. As such, both the contract and the subsequent legislation could be considered a construct in that they rely on an act of will.

Will, however, is contingent, and so it lacks the legitimacy that universal reason includes. Rousseau's position thus consists in the merging of universal, timeless reason with contingent, historical will, up to the point that one can only 'will' what corresponds to universal reason. This, however, is not will itself, but an act of cognition. The acts of will then take on the appearance of timelessness. The historical character of political space and the rules that stem from it is concealed behind universal reason.

Concealed Instrumentalism

Instrumentalism: scientific and normative

Instrumentalism in theoretical thinking rests on the premise that theories are instruments, tools, or calculating devices that are related to observational propositions. The latter are systematised under a theory that allows for a number of derivations or predictions. The truth of the theory or its reference to reality, however, is not a relevant question for instrumentalism. From the practical perspective, instrumentalism means that a normative theory is rationally justified if actions, a life-plan, or a set of social arrangements can be shown to be the best way of achieving an agent's final ends, whatever these may be (Piper 1986: 373). Such a theory shows the means to achieve the end, without rationally questioning that end. Truth and value are detached from knowledge and action, which was, one remembers from Chapter 1, inherent to nominalist metaphysics.

In line with that approach, another aspect of the nominalist metaphysics underlying legalism as it follows from Chapter 1 is that the world is normatively empty. This means that 'justice' as the *causa finalis* of law, so preponderant in classical philosophy, no longer makes sense. Values, that is, have no ontological existence since essences can no longer exist due to the logical interpretation of divine omnipotence. Values or ends must therefore be chosen, although this choice is not amenable to rational justification. Their determination is a matter of choice or politics (in the Aristotelian sense). The rationality of action thus entails articulating the best means for achieving an end. When confining the theory to law, this means that law is a means to an end. The determination of the latter is a matter of choice, and is hence of a political nature, not rational. Generally speaking, law then becomes an instrument for social policy, the goals of which are choices that have no rational foundation. Justice, in short, is no longer the natural end of law. The law's ends are politically determined, and this is what legalism is eager to conceal.

This concealment is a variant of legalism's strategy that involves a separation of law and politics. As noted above, the nominalist metaphysics in which legalism takes root involves an epistemologisation of philosophy, and what cannot be epistemologised falls outside the scope of philosophy. Values, therefore, are left to the field of politics, and are hidden behind the universality or a-temporality of law, as shown in the previous section. Another device for the concealment of value judgements, and hence instrumentalism in law, is to withdraw into formalistic reasoning which excludes any reference to reality as well as to value choices. In the following pages, I will briefly elaborate on the main characteristics of this aspect of strong legalism.

The time dimension of Modern philosophical thinking as it appeared from the analysis of Rousseau's social contract in the above pages is an excellent introduction to the theme of this section. Timelessness and instrumentalism mutually support one another in that a-temporality conceals choice. In short, the concealing of the historical dimension of political space helps conceal the fact that values are to be chosen. Since values are no longer believed to belong to reality – they are of a contingent nature – choices must be made.

It is important to remember in this respect what was noted in chapter 1 concerning the metaphysics of nominalism. Under the logical interpretation of divine omnipotence, only individuals exist, and there is no ontological relationship between them. An ontological relationship would entail individuals belonging to the same species, which is logically incompatible with divine omnipotence. What is not individual is therefore not real, and serves only as an instrument to organise reality (Largeault 1971: 154). A consequence of this is that individuals lack any relationship of finality that connects the universe to God. God's radical freedom under the logical interpretation of his omnipotence makes him radically separated from the world. Therefore, because of the absence of a pre-existing order in the world, terrestrial activities can have their own finality, that is, 'interest' (ibid.: 152), an idea that was inconceivable under mediaeval realism.

Because values and reality in general are contingent, choices for their part are also contingent, that is, they are steered by human interest. Because of their contingent nature, they could render the organisation and operation of political space problematic. If the value judgements that articulate them can be universalised – for example, by ranging them in the domain of reason – they lose their contingent character. They become objects of knowledge. If their 'choice' can be shown to be the only possible one, it is a rationalised or epistemologised version of choice dictated by universal reason.

I began this chapter be saying that strong legalism relies on, or even is, a strategy. According to the above, this strategic character becomes clearer. Timelessness and instrumentalism mutually support one another and make values or ends lose their contingent character, failing which the whole construction would vanish under the pervasive weight of contingency. Contingency, however, is warded off by arguing that they represent reality under the merger of representation-reproduction and representation-construction.

After the transition from ancient cosmology to the Modern philosophical project, Modern natural science emerged out of the disintegration of the closed world. Unlimited space was substituted for it (Koyré 1970). Through this process, the natural place of beings was pushed aside, and replaced by the concept of the unlimited space. The Modern philosophical project, as I have argued, consists to a large extent in the metaphysical articulation of this paradigm shift and the mathematical exploration of unlimited space that comes with it.

Under this paradigm shift, place is conceptualised relative to a mathematical system of coordinates that allows for its quantitative expression. Infinite space, conceived of on the level of metaphysical thinking, derives its cognisability from mathematics. However, universality has a strong power of legitimation, connecting contingency with eternity, and showing that the 'real' operation of reason is deductive. It is in connection with this that timelessness shows up in the Modern philosophical project. A similar mechanism is at work where values are concerned, as will be argued below in this section.

With the paradigm shift of Modern natural science, order in reality loses its dynamics of qualitative 'becoming'. The dynamics is reduced to 'movement' that can be quantitatively described and explained in the language of mathematics and confirmed by experiment. Truth and certainty, as was argued above, are then related in that the latter is the mark of the former. Value judgements, since they lack certainty, fall out of the domain of truth. They do not, however, disappear for that reason.

This short presentation corroborates the nominalist beginnings of the Modern philosophical project. Since universals are lacking in the world, that has now become infinite, a new type of science, and especially mathematics must fill the gap. Mathematics in natural science describes and explains the external relations between things.[8] Scientific propositions are considered certain, an aspect that value judgements are lacking.

There is some parallel with classical philosophical thought that is revealing here. Some things, says Aristotle, can be explained with certainty, while others cannot. The latter belong to what he calls 'politics', which does not necessarily mean exclusively that which is nowadays meant by that term.[9] It mainly refers to what in current vocabulary is meant by the domain of values and their discussion, dispute and tentative articulation; in short, the things that cannot be known with mathematical, logical, or empirical precision.

Things change with the certainty claim of Descartes, the interpretation of which was presented above. If certainty is the mark of truth, value statements cannot be true. Their disputable character is the mark that they do not qualify as truth.

Instrumentalism, as noted above, appears in the wake of the emergence of natural science. Instrumentalism can be characterised by the fact that argumentation about values does not follow the same logic as mathematical, logical, or empirical reasoning. Values cannot be proven to be true; the role they play depends on a choice. Throughout the Modern philosophical project, values are no longer considered as objects of knowledge; neither are they in any hierarchical relationship. This is, here as elsewhere, a consequence of the nominalist metaphysics in which strong legalism takes root.

Instrumentalism then reduces the discussion about values to the articulation of the best possible means of realising them. The rationality of value discussions is limited to the theoretical identification of the instruments that are suitable for achieving them. The choice of the value that it is best to further is a matter of dispute; it is not susceptible to rational determination. The best that can be expected is a rational choice, a choice by which the best means for the realisation of a non-rational value can be determined. Value judgements are transformed into theoretical judgements, which is yet another version of the epistemologisation of philosophy pointed to earlier in this chapter and in chapter 3.

Instrumentalism and law: rules

Instrumentalism in law, to which I propose to limit the discussion here, relies on the idea that legal rules are instruments for realising values. Since values are subject to discussion, they rely on clashing world-views; they are essentially political in the Aristotelian sense. In consequence, if values are to be realised, they must be *chosen* without any rational justification. However, this manifestation of will as a basis of action turns out to be unbearable for rational philosophical thought. Within the context of the limitation of rationality to rational or empirical proof,

---

8 Whether it is a mathematisation of nature (Husserl 1970a: 20 ff.), or naturalisation of mathematics, as Heidegger (1962: 50–83) holds.

9 Aristotle 1984d: 1094a, 19–1095b, 12. I follow the line of interpretation suggested by Ricoeur (1986e: 303) on this point.

serious efforts were undertaken to conceal this structural deficiency of the Modern philosophical project.

Mathematics as the epistemological device of the Modern philosophical project is not fit for value discussion. Once the philosophical project sets off from the premise that reality is mathematical, mathematics is not only the epistemological *via Regis* towards reality, but it belongs to its very structure. If mathematics belongs to reality, mathematical reasoning leads to ontologically true knowledge that is embedded in a theory of reality. On this view, values cannot be known in a mathematical way; hence, they are not rational. On a second interpretation, according to which mathematics does not belong to the structure of reality, the result is the same. Mathematics as a method constructed by humans allows for a rational description and explanation of reality. The phenomena that are not fit for this kind of description fall from the pedestal of rationality. They cannot be described, far less explained, in mathematical terms. Hence, they are again not rational.

From there on, it is but a small step towards instrumentalism. According to the nominalist metaphysics that underpins legalism, values no longer belong to the world, because of God's absolute indifference to the good. It is not, however, because values or ends are no longer believed to be part of reality that their impact in life disappears altogether. What changes with the Modern philosophical project, in the wake of the underlying nominalist metaphysics is the denial of their ontological status. This denial, however, triggers a specific philosophical problem, in that values do not stop playing a role in, say, the organisation of society, or in one's personal life.

Values hence cannot be known in that they are not fit for rational demonstration. It is necessary that they be chosen or that a commitment be made to them without this operation being rational. This choice is an act of will. It is on this point, and more precisely on the necessity of decisions, that attention will be focused over the following pages.

From classical cosmology, we learn that decisions are a necessary complement to human action in the absence of full knowledge of reality. Men are not Gods; they are not omniscient and not even a majority of *phronimoi*, as Aristotle calls them: wise men resembling the Gods. Full and perfect knowledge would distract us from action because it paralyses action. Put more strongly, human action exists because man is human and not perfect.

If society is organised according to an ontologically pre-given structure, it is sufficient simply that the latter be *known* according to classical natural law or believed in according to theological natural law. If such a social structure does not exist in one of these senses, it must be created. Creation in turn is based on decisions that correspond to a choice between values.

This is what the Modern philosophical project amounts to. The social contract and the civil laws that are based on it are man-made, as was discussed in earlier in this chapter. What appears, however, as an act of will, is not therefore arbitrary. Paradoxically, as a decision it would look like an act of will; it is, however, a rationalised or epistemologised choice. If it looks like a choice, it does not follow from the determination of an alternative that consists of at least two possibilities between which a choice is to be made. Since no alternative is available, the choice is a 'rational choice', a choice that cannot be different. Rational choice conceals real choices.

Hobbes as well as Rousseau in this respect spares no efforts in showing how the theory of the social contract is a theory *of* reality. Their shared concern is to show that the *making* of the contract is an act of will fully determined by reason. One can, in other words, only will the contract; it can only be willed as it follows from their theory. The procedures that are included in the contract – for example, the majority rule procedure in Rousseau – have all the naturalness they need in order to serve as the unquestionable foundation of social order.

Here as elsewhere, it can be seen that the practical problem of the organisation of society is prima facie resolved in a practical way. The type of choice operated is, however, an epistemologised or rational choice, one that results from a mere rational calculation. The choice itself is hence rational as the best means to realise the end sought after, that is, for example, safety, peace, order, equality, or justice. The 'desire' of these values arises from human nature, so they should not be really chosen. By following one's rational nature, one rationally arrives at the 'choice' for these values. Therefore we rationally 'chose' for the contract as the best possible means for realising them.

It is thus the form of the law after the contract that dictates these characteristics. There are no substantive value choices to be made, at least not prima facie. In 'choosing' for the contract, one makes a value judgement, upon which all the other value judgements included in the rules based on the social contract are endorsed.

The concealment of instrumentalism is also clearly from Hobbes. According to him, the rules of the sovereign are just. Since they are based on the laws of nature that constitute the true morality, law and morality are one and the same. Every decision or choice of the sovereign is just. This is the same as saying that no choice is made or, put differently, that the choices made are concealed.

It follows from the above that the value of justice, typically the *causa finalis* of the classical *polis*, now becomes embedded in the very concept of the legal rule. By transforming value discussions into a cognitive position, both Hobbes and Rousseau believe that they have reached an acceptable solution for the new type of problems that emerge at the start of Modernity: the political organisation of society, for which Hobbes claims to have invented a new method, that is, *philosophia civilis* (Hobbes 1966c: 357–8).

To summarise, the above characterisation of instrumentalism shows that it is concealed as a result of the epistemologisation of philosophy. Freedom, one of the three basic tenets of the Modern philosophical project, is best realised through laws. This is a 'rational choice', in that it is a choice reframed as a theoretical matter. The choice for rules follows from there, and is also transformed into a theoretical issue. Hence, as a choice or value judgement, it is hidden behind theoretical rationality. Finally, the content of rules, which is most obviously a matter of choice, is transformed into a theoretical framework, and hence hidden behind rationality, since the choice for rules renders the latter *ipso facto* morally true (Hobbes) or just (Rousseau).

After representationalism, timelessness and concealed instrumentalism, the next paragraph will focus on the unique source of law, that is, the state.

Sovereignty, State and Etatism

Etatism as one of the hallmarks of strong legalism holds that the state is the only possible source of law. In order to get a better hold on etatism, some features of the context in which the concept of the state has emerged are important to focus on. First, I will briefly focus on the theological perspective in which etatism, in the wake of sovereignty, has taken root and which is known as 'political Augustinianism', before making some observations on sovereignty from the nominalist perspective, and finally on sovereignty in the context of legalism.

Political Augustinianism and the realist version of sovereignty

Political Augustinianism is a theo-cratic model of sovereignty and it is characterised by its top-down or descending organisation of sovereign power. The institution of the Roman Catholic Church by Christ makes it a reality, which constitutes a direct link between God and the Pope. God created the world according to his divine plan, the execution of which on earth was delegated to the Pope. Successors were thought of not as successors of the preceding Pope, but as directly ordained by God. From that perspective, he was not bound by the rulings of his predecessor, and could be said to be a sovereign.

Papal sovereignty has a second, comparative meaning, in that the Pope is superior to the Emperor. Sovereignty in the modern sense as 'supreme authority' is etymologically derived from 'superioritas' (Canning 1987: 125). A major event that is decisive for an understanding of the theory of sovereignty or *superioritas* from the theological perspective is the letter of Pope Gelasius I to Emperor Anastasius.[10] This letter is a warning to the Emperor that his power was included

10 Letter of Pope Gelasius to Emperor Anastasius on the superiority of the spiritual over temporal power: The Pope's view of the natural superiority of the spiritual over the temporal power finds a clear expression in the following remarkable letter of Gelasius I (494): 'There are two powers, august Emperor, by which this world is chiefly ruled, namely, the sacred authority of the priests and the royal power. Of these that of the priests is the more weighty, since they have to render an account for even the kings of men in the divine judgment. You are also aware, dear son, that while you are permitted honorably to rule over human kind, yet in things divine you bow your head humbly before the leaders of the clergy and await from their hands the means of your salvation. In the reception and proper disposition of the heavenly mysteries you recognize that you should be subordinate rather than superior to the religious order, and that in these matters you depend on their judgment rather than wish to force them to follow your will. If the ministers of religion, recognizing the supremacy granted you from heaven in matters affecting the public order, obey your laws, lest otherwise they might obstruct the course of secular affairs by irrelevant

in the Christian kingdom, at least as far as spiritual matters are concerned. The Emperor, in these matters, is subordinate to the Pope, while the Pope and the ecclesiastical authorities, when it comes to temporal matters, are subject to the power of the Emperor (Arquillière 2006: 117–53; Watt 1993).

It is implied in this that temporal matters are of a superior order, so that it may be concluded from that position that the relationship between the Emperor and the Pope is to be classified as 'submission' (Ullmann 1955: 20 ff.; Gérard 1986: 321 ff.), or as 'correlation' (Morrison 1960: 101–5). Louis Dumont (1983: 64–5) for his part qualifies this relationship as 'hierarchical complementarity'. Undeniably, the aspect of hierarchy points to some form of submission. The aspect of complementarity for its part refers at best to some overlapping, without being identical, that is, without the imperial power being part of the Pope's. A distinction is made between 'authority' and 'power', and it is only with the former aspect that the Pope deals in his letter. It concerns, in other words, not the power of the Emperor, but his authority as a person (ibid.: 66). Put differently, as far as temporal matters are concerned, the Church is included in the Empire, while for spiritual matters the latter is included in the former (ibid.: 66; Congar 1968).

The doctrine is plausible from at least the papal perspective. For the Papacy, the *unitas Christiana* is the basic axiom of the Pope's position. The unity of faith, like the unity of truth, is and should be expressed in a unity of power in the hands of the Pope. Underlying the distinction between authority and power, we find then the distinction between spiritual and temporal matters.

What is crucially absent, though, is something that we nowadays call a 'State'. There is only the Empire intertwined so to speak with the Church. There is no differentiated concept of a state yet, and one must wait until the very end of the seventeenth century before it emerges as a fully developed concept within the philosophical vocabulary.

When we look more closely at the vocabulary used, we may prudently conclude that the function of the Emperor is to protect the Christian Church with the sword, while the Church disposed only of the word (Ullman 1979: 89, 110). The clergy had no right to wear arms, and so had to look for protection from the Emperor. When it comes to authority, however, the Pope is hierarchically superior to the Emperor.

This doctrine may have settled the dispute between the Emperor and the Pope, were it not that the distinction between spiritual and temporal matters is by no

---

considerations, with what readiness should you not yield them obedience to whom is assigned the dispensing of the sacred mysteries of religion. Accordingly, just as there is no slight danger in the case of the priests if they refrain from speaking when the service of the divinity requires, so there is no little risk for those who disdain — which God forbid — when they should obey. And if it is fitting that the hearts of the faithful should submit to all priests in general who properly administer divine affairs, how much the more is obedience due to the bishop of that see which the Most High ordained to be above all others, and which is consequently dutifully honored by the devotion of the whole Church': translated in Robinson 1905: 72–3.

means clear. Undoubtedly, everything a Christian does on earth is related to his salvation, so that the 'hierarchical complementarity' (Dumont) may easily be taken to mean submission of the Emperor to the Pope, whose *superioritas* is in this way marked. This is confirmed by the papal coronation of Pépin the Short and Charlemagne in 751 and 800 respectively. The latter, by that fact, had, however, a calling not only to protect but also to direct the Church (Dumont 1983: 67).

The dispute between the Emperor and the Pope also has a political dimension; that is, politics interferes with theology from the time when the King or Emperor considers himself endowed with divine grace. From the theological perspective, a mundane ruler has no 'right' to power; he is only gifted power by an act of grace, for which the intervention of the Pope was procedurally necessary (hence, the development of the doctrine of submission of the Emperor to the Pope). They consider themselves however to be on the same level of sovereignty. Yet, this submission results in the superiority of the Pope even in temporal matters.

While sovereignty now refers to both temporal and spiritual matters, confined in both the Pope and the Emperor – at least under their own interpretations – we may face a dispute on the level of power. This is temporal matter, and it is the Pope who can command the temporal power using his spiritual authority (as can be noted in the crusade movement from the end of the eleventh century onward) (Villey 1942). The ecclesiastical authority then makes use of the temporal powers, including the power of the sword, like the soul of the body commands the latter.

Again, the crucial lack of a well-developed concept of a secular state is felt. As long as the descending theme of government is adhered to, that is, as long as governmental power is thought to come from God, there is not the slightest chance that a concept of that brand may emerge.[11] There are some traces of this concept with the emergence of the Papal States by 750 CE, where the Pope has authority both in spiritual and temporal matters. This, however, is not mirrored, not even in the long term, by a similar concept expressing the perspective of the Emperor. However, it is reasonable to think that this formed part of imperial ambitions although, conceptually speaking, the emperors, as noted above, were far behind the Papacy when it came to framing their aspirations into a coherent theory that could justify their claims.

The theological dispute is fused with a political dimension, which comes to a head, one might say, over the Emperor's power to appoint the clergy and bishops. This system, known as the proprietary Church, holds that the owner of a land may build a church on it, and this power includes the appointment of the personnel that will serve in it. This may be characterised as some form of the right of *accessorium*, though as a matter of course, this 'right' constitutes a direct intervention in the papal prerogative, that is, to appoint his 'own' personnel. The

11 That is, as long as the idea of the sovereign state is not connected with its territorial character, see Maine, 1834: 99 ff. For the connection between sovereignty and territory, see Hansen 2001. On the theory of power descending from God, see Ullman 1975: 277 ff. and 302 ff.; Ullmann 1979: 195–9.

theological dispute now takes on a legal form, in that its terms are borrowed from the legal vocabulary.

Sovereignty and nominalism

The emergence of nominalism at the end of the thirteenth century is of crucial importance for the emergence of the concept of the state. Under the nominalist doctrine, the Church was no longer considered a reality, but on the contrary a concept (Zuckerman 1975).

As was discussed in the first chapter of this book, nominalism's philosophical articulation of the individual can be said to have triggered two important movements in Western philosophical thought, that is, Protestantism and autonomous political philosophy based on will (Dumont 1983: 74). While the Church was fighting on the political battlefield with the Emperor, it still had to come to terms with a new concept: that is, of the individual. Lutheran, and even stronger Calvinist, freedom of conscience articulates a personal relationship with God, far less mediated by the Church than it used to be. It is conscience that dictates the will which is in turn oriented towards God. Due to the personal nature of this relationship with God, the conscience of the faithful should be free. The subject's religious convictions therefore cannot be forced by the state, for example, by punishment. Theological voluntarism means that churches should be voluntary associations, a point that will later be advocated by John Locke.[12] The secular state, in other words, has its theological roots in this form of voluntarism.

Although Luther was initially educated in nominalism, he would later criticise it, without however, abandoning its individualistic ontology (Paquier 1927: 1184–8). Subsequent Calvinism increasingly undermines the position of the Church. This contributed to its weakening situation by the end of the Middle Ages (Villey 2003: 294 ff and 303 ff.).

Of an equal if not greater importance, was the critique by Luther, and later Calvin, of the simony practices in the Catholic Church. Simony was one of the main reasons for Luther, and later on Calvin, to directly attack the institution of the Church. For Luther, the justification of man's salvation consisted in faith, and not in the orders of the Church. The doctrine of predestination, so central to

---

12 Locke (1963b) argues that religion is a matter of personal conscience. Since a church is a voluntary association (13), and no one can be forced to enter into it against his will. Neither can the church use any other power than exhortations, admonition, and advice (16) without any recourse to other punishment concerning its members (16). It can only excommunicate them (17). A fortiori, the state cannot interfere with religion. Neither the church nor the state or individuals, that is, 'have any title to invade de civil rights and worldly goods of each other, upon pretence of religion.' (20). See also G. de Lagarde (1926). In order to prevent confusion, it should be observed here that theological voluntarism is different from what the expression means in chapter 1. In that chapter, it refers to the absolute free will of the omnipotent God, while here it means that the church is a willed association of the faithful.

Calvinism, held that man had to earn his eternal life – that is, the justification for his salvation – by good works on earth because of faith, not because it formed part of his ecclesiastical duties.

This was a direct attack on the position of the Church in social life, and it would be no exaggeration to say that it strongly contributed to the crumbling of ecclesiastical power. The Church, for Calvin, was to remain invisible, and so the Catholic doctrine that the Emperor had no right to power, since it was a *beneficium* or a gift from God, now seems to turn against ecclesiastical power itself. Its power had to remain invisible, while the state was the only authority that had to be obeyed, also by the (Protestant) faithful, on religious grounds.

It is no doubt too much of a generalisation to say that the conjugation of Calvinistic Protestantism and nominalism gave rise to what we may call a state. After an initial reinforcement of the ecclesiastical institution after the Investiture contest – Henri IV had to go to Canossa in order to submit terrestrial power again to the Church – the Pope's residence in Avignon throughout the fourteenth century seriously undermined their power. As a matter of fact, the papacy was cut off from its well-documented administrative archives. At the same time, the Emperor's administrative staff generously tapped on the newly developing universities of Bologna and Ravenna that emerged from the mid-twelfth century onward.

The conflict between the *Fratri Minores* in England, the monastic order to which Ockham belonged, and Pope John XXII concerning the property rights of the former, became one of the many battlegrounds on which theologians and nominalists met. If not an immediate cause, it was at least one of the reasons that contributed to the worsening of the internal position of the Pope.

For Protestants, the relation between God and man is of a personal nature that need not be mediated by the institution of the Church, which explains at least partly a diminution in the number of sacraments in the Protestant religion. This doctrinal position may be said to have caused a rift within the conceptual scheme according to which the power claims between Papacy and Emperor were organised.

Man is reborn, not due to the effects of baptism as Catholic doctrine holds, but based on his own rational capacities, that free him from the authority of faith. The Protestant Reformation and Counter-Reformation had seriously weakened the position of the Church as the *societas perfecta*, to which other, less perfect organisations are subordinated. It is not thus surprising to find Hobbes trying to fill the power vacuum caused by the religious wars, while making use of and developing further a concept of the state that was articulated before him by Machiavelli as well as Marsilius. Both thought that the Church could be incorporated into, if not absorbed by, the sovereignty of the state.

The secular state is at least partially rooted in the Protestant criticism of the Church, and Hobbes was very familiar with Protestant writings. As a prudent man, however, he kept a low profile when dealing with them. Apart from his personal situation, his aim was precisely to establish a system of power that could keep subjects together regardless of their religious adherence or beliefs. At the same time, he contributed to the epistemologisation of philosophy in making use of Euclidian geometry to construct his state.

While under Hobbes's construction, there is still an aura sovereignty by divine right – the sovereign is called the mortal God – but this reference to religion gradually fades away. With Rousseau, religion would be reduced to civil religion, and the state would attain its full rational foundation in reason alone, and connected to a territory (Rousseau 1997a: 54–6). Reason, that is, shapes the will of those entering into the social contract that will transform them into citizens. Their choice for the state is a rational choice. The idea of the state culminates in the nineteenth century as an expression of the absolute spirit, and submission to the state is, under Hegelian theory, considered the highest form of freedom.[13]

In the Modern philosophical project, the concept of the state starts its career, however, as a construction out of the will of the subjects who, by entering into the contract, create a new entity. Despite its artificial character, the state is however considered something unavoidable and necessary. It is a product of rational thought that flavours it with some naturalness.

Following this brief sketch of some aspects of the theological perspective within which the concept of the state emerged in the seventeenth century, I will argue that the concept of the state as the unique source of law – which is the same as etatism – is closely related to individualism as one of the basic tenets of the Modern philosophical project. This aspect of the Modern philosophical project was discussed in chapter 1 of this book. In the following pages, I propose to show the consequences of this basic tenet of the Modern philosophical project for the creation of law.

Etatism

The Modern philosophical project articulates the separation of philosophy from theology. While the influence of classical theology was fading away, religion however maintained a strong hold on human life. Reformation and Counter-Reformation had not only weakened the position of the Church, but also gave rise to serious religious conflicts from the seventeenth century onward.

Locke and later John Stuart Mill pleaded for tolerance and religious freedom, which would entail the freedom of conscience as a natural right of all men.[14]

13 Hegel 1956: 39: '… the State is the actually existing, realized moral life. For it is the Unity of the universal, essential Will, with that of the individual; and this is "Morality." The Individual living in this unity has a moral life; possesses a value that consists in this substantiality alone.'

14 Locke 1963a: 10: 'All the life and power of true religion consists of the inward and full persuasion of the mind; and faith is not faith without believing.' Ibid.: 23: '… the care of souls does not belong to the magistrate … .' Yet, a magistrate, like any other man, can try to convince someone of the truth of what he himself believes. A similar view is found in Mill 1989: 16–17, 55 and 85–7.

Hobbes and Spinoza in turn offered a model in which the state regulates religion.[15] Etatism[16] shows up in the struggle between the Emperor and the Pope, and involves a submission of the Church to the state. While Hobbes's forerunners Marsilius and Machiavelli had practical concerns with their theories of the state, what was still lacking was a *theoretical* concept of the state. This is what Hobbes was to provide.

While the above has mainly stressed the epistemological issue in Hobbes, here we will consider the political impact of his theory.

This is the reading that was proposed of Hobbes in the previous chapters: the state is going to provide meaning to the laws of nature; and in doing so, the sovereign relates his own laws to the semantically empty metaphysical framework of the commands of God. It is certain that the laws of nature bind the sovereign (Hobbes 1966b: 166–7).

The state as a mortal God shares the qualities of God himself: it is omnipresent, yet invisible, the anxiety for which is, says Hobbes, the source of religion itself (Hobbes 1966c: 93). The assimilation of the state to God fits in well with Hobbes's prudent position in matters of religion. He can avoid the suspicion of atheism, yet can stave off the critique of deism, in that the state and God essentially focus and work on the same things, that is, the laws of nature. It matters little, from that perspective, that the sovereign can, under Hobbes's doctrine, define the right religion if this is necessary in order to fulfil his task, that is, providing security (ibid.: 355–6).

According to this analysis, the tension between representation-reproduction and representation-creation that was pointed out in the beginning of this chapter again emerges. While initially severing *philosophia prima* and theology, the state is a matter of definition, that is, a construction or a creation. In relating the civil laws to the laws of nature, Hobbes suggests that the former re-produce the latter, that are still of an ontological value, though have no meaning. Since the laws of the state endow natural laws with meaning, they reproduce true morality. Civil laws and the laws of nature, so Hobbes argues, are mutually inclusive.[17] The state is hence the only instance that can activate the laws of nature, thereby bestow them with meaning, and relate their binding force to the individuals that were at the basis of the state's creation. As a result, the state turns out to be the only source of binding laws.

15 Hobbes 1966c: 164, 355. Hobbes means here the determination of public worship of God, which can be considered a matter of public administration. The argument, however, goes further than that, since, if there is no uniformity in the worship of God, 'it cannot be said that there is any public worship, nor that the commonwealth is of any religion at all.'

16 Synonyms are 'Erastianism' or 'Gallicanism', see Wood 1967: 262 ff.

17 Hobbes 1966c: 253: 'The law of nature, and the civil law, contain each other, and are of equal extent.' Ibid.: 254: 'Civil, and natural law, are not different kinds, but different parts of the same law.'

The idea of etatism as one of the aspects of strong legalism can also be articulated from another perspective, mainly focusing on Rousseau.

When discussing timelessness as a characteristic of legalism, it became clear that on the one hand, the clauses of the contract are universal, while on the other, the implementation of the contract requires an act of will. An act of will, by its very nature, is historically situated, so that, after all, the construction of the state is a historical 'event', or at least a sharing in the historical situatedness of its founders, that is, the subjects in the state of nature. However, the consensus establishing the state is, as argued above, a logical truth. It is necessarily true, as the only source of legal norms.

In this respect, it can be argued that the majority rule in Rousseau is very much similar to the concept of the 'rule of change' and the 'rule of recognition' in Hart's legal theory. When this is considered from the perspective of political theory, the social contract *à la Rousseau* not only establishes political space as distinct from social space; it also establishes political space as an independent, autonomous source of legal norms, and hence a legal system. Political space, or the state, in other words, becomes yet another individual, endowed with a will of its own.

The general will, as the will of the sovereign, is therefore the only and ultimate source of law. It is both a source from which the law emanates and a source of knowledge of the law. It is the source from which the law emanates because the general *will* stamps a proposition from the legislator with a majority vote and so transforms it into a legal rule. The majority rule therefore serves as a rule of recognition of valid law in the state. In addition, the majority rule also serves as a rule of change, because no new rule can be created or any existing one changed without a majority vote, as mentioned above.

As a consequence of this, only the will of the state can serve as a device for the validity and cognition of the law, and political space becomes the unique source of legal rules, in that it is institutionalised according to the terms of the contract. The institutionalisation of political space then gives rise to the institutionalisation of law in a systematic framework, that is, as a set of secondary and primary rules. While the majority rule initially served as the only secondary rule of the system, it can be supplemented with new secondary rules based on a majority vote. No justification need be provided for that.

The majority rule, for a logical reason, can only be changed by consensus. But this, as we know, entails a change in the clauses of the contract, which cannot take place without making the latter void (Rousseau 1997a: 49–50). The majority rule, as the essential component of the social contract itself, then operates as the ultimate rule of recognition. Bearing in mind the legal character of both, it can be concluded that the legal system and the state are mutually inclusive. Hence, there is no law beyond the state and all law finds its origin in the state.

The idea of the state as the unique source of law, hence etatism, as it follows from Hobbes and Rousseau, can itself be argued as a consequence of individualism. The contract as an aggregation of will, for rational reasons, leads to the emergence of the state. Individuals, that is, rationally choose the state, as the unique source of rights and duties, as the only possible way of organising political space. The constructed state as the opposite of the natural *polis* is the image of a collection of individuals organising themselves politically.

While Hobbes and Rousseau argue respectively for a rational, calculative and historical necessity, Kant for his part framed a moral argument in favour of entry into the contract. As already argued in Chapter 1, to leave the state of nature or the civil state and to contribute to the constitution of the state is a moral duty (Kant 1996: 84–6). The moral argument amounts to a moral duty on the individual to transform himself into a citizen, and so to transform his pre-legal rights and duties into legal ones (ibid.: 89–90).

Hegel will push the moral argument somewhat further. He argues that not only does one has a moral duty to leave the state of nature, as in Kant, but that the moral duty consists in being a member of the state (Hegel 1991: 275). The latter is not a result of a social contract, but an emanation of reason itself. While for Hobbes and Rousseau, the engagement in the social contract could have been based on mere rational self-interest, and so can be mechanically explained, for Hegel, the interest of the subject – rational or otherwise – no longer applies. The existence of the state in no way depends on the subject's will, neither for its emergence, nor for its subsistence.

The state for Hegel is simply reality, the reality of the objective moral idea 'in action'. It is only within the state that the individual can realise his substantive freedom as the product of the activity of the State (ibid.: 275). Far from being a product of the imagination, as Hegel comments on Rousseau, the state has an ontology of its own. It is the realisation of the Spirit (ibid.: 281–3).

With this idea of the state, Hegel is referring to the *polis* of antiquity. The state cannot be articulated in a different manner in philosophy, that is itself an expression of the Spirit. In his view, the theories of the social contract as we find them in Hobbes and Rousseau are nothing but stages of the unfolding of the Spirit. They are some halfway realisation of it, one could say, because the contractual nature of the state is still connected to the will of the individual.

Not only does the Hegelian state require that individuals renounce their individuality in order to see their will coordinated by the state, but it also moves on to an incorporation of the individuals who can only reach true freedom by being a member of it. The state in other words does not consist of members who only want to be a member of it. If the general will emerges out of the particular wills, as Rousseau holds, Hegel's claim relies on a similar though opposed dynamics. The state with its general will pre-exists individuals, it is 'the actuality of the ethical idea' (ibid.: 275). It is only by incorporating himself in the state, not as a mechanism for guaranteeing his security, but as an organism for realising his freedom, that the individual comes to his true essence.

Again, in contrast with Hobbes, and Rousseau, the motive for the individual's renunciation is not of an individual or rational character; it amounts to surrender to the state. The law of the state is no longer opposed to the individual's freedom, in that the former limits the latter. Law is rational as the deepest expression of human freedom, as Louis Dumont puts it (Dumont 1983: 129). While it is essentially different from Hobbes's and Rousseau's construction as to its origin, Hegel's incorporation of the individual into the state results in the latter being the unique source of law.

Hobbes's, Rousseau's and Hegel's views are very close to one another in that they culminate in the idea of etatism. Some would even add that their idea of the state pre-echoes totalitarianism. From the perspective of strong legalism, however, the exclusively etatistic origin of law frames the latter into a closed system of legal rules. On this point, legal science corroborates the etatistic aspect of law. Legal science, that is, determines the cognisability of the law from the state. In doing so, legal science contributes to the confirmation of strong legalism as the dominant legal thought pattern. This is what will be argued in the next paragraph which will focus mainly on the emergence of legal science in nineteenth-century Germany.

Strong Legalism, Law, and Legal Science

Science as System: Mathematical Method

The previous sections have dealt with the major characteristics of strong legalism, as it is rooted in the Modern philosophical project. In articulating the main strategy of strong legalism as the severing of law and politics, we have pointed to the fact that law should be kept free from the contingencies of 'value judgements'. As a human construction, it is not difficult to see that law depends on value choices. Law is 'just there'. All that is to be done is to follow the rules, as argued in chapter 1. Suarez, Hobbes, Pufendorf and Kant were shown to illustrate this aspect of legalism.

However, the other characteristics of strong legalism – that is, representationalism, a-temporality, concealed instrumentalism, and etatism – all contribute to warding off the dangers of subjective value judgements penetrating the concept of law. Only from this perspective could equality, freedom, security, certainty, or justice be guaranteed over against conflict.

Legal science is quite frequently connected to the codification movement starting in post-revolutionary France, as explained above. It is an often an unduly neglected aspect of the codification movement that its breeding ground is not only the French Revolution. The codification of French law gave rise to a new type of legal science, known as *L'Ecole de l'exégèse*.[18] I will not elaborate on this school but instead focus on the emergence of legal science in the Historical School in German throughout the nineteenth century.

In that respect, German legal science was to a certain extent influenced by different revolutions throughout the nineteenth century, to which I will refer occasionally. Of equal importance for its development, however, was

18 I will not further develop this type of science here. See the excellent study of Bouckaert 1981.

Enlightenment philosophy and more specifically its celebration of 'systematicity' as the unfolding domination of reason (Heidegger 1988: 62) (*Vernunftherschaft*). Taking the domination of reason as the characteristic of Modern rational thinking, it is reason that determines the criteria of rationality within its own realm. The subsequent reorientation of thinking, anchored in the subject, articulates the authority of reason as human dignity and autonomy.

Autonomy is the hallmark of the Modern philosophical project. Throughout this project, three important axes can be detected: epistemology as built up in Descartes' work, political philosophy as developed mainly in Hobbes's and Rousseau's, and moral philosophy in Kant's critiques. Regardless of their different specific preoccupations, they generally converge upon articulating a conception of autonomy. Knowledge, politics and morals are founded upon reason as the ultimate aspect of human nature they represent (Wintgens 2006a, 2006b).

The authority of reason as autonomy and human dignity carries with it the metaphysical dimension of the Modern philosophical project. Based on the premises of representationalism, rational thinking is held to represent reality. What is more, as Heidegger suggests, what there is can be thought of in terms of a rational system as real *and* vice versa. Heidegger has proposed an interesting summary of this project in the following manner.

The mathematical conceptualisation of infinity from the seventeenth century onward articulated the transition from philosophy of nature into a mathematical science of nature. The ontological foundation of the subject in Descartes' *cogito* is the self-foundation of a new type of knowledge granting priority to certainty over truth. For Descartes, certainty located at the subject's side is at the same time his access to reality, and thus to truth unqualified. This access is mediated by clear and distinct concepts and their exclusively rational – that is, mathematical – unfolding is what science consists of.

The crucial point is that representations are located in, or are constructions of, the human mind. They have no existence outside the mind. In thus liberating the subject from external domination, philosophy has opened up the way to the subject's domination of the world.[19] What there is can be thought of as a rational system, Heidegger holds, in that the system is a mathematical system of reason. The 'system' is in other words the ontological law of modern 'Dasein'.[20] As we

19 Heidegger 1988: 59, thus showing that the formation of systems is co-original with the emergence of modern science. This reminds Descartes' saying that his scientific method and the results it sparks is going to make us masters and possessors of nature.

20 Ibid.: 58: 'System is *Seynsgezetz* des neuzeitlichen Daseins … ' (System is the law of being of modern Dasein) (italics in original). See, in this respect, Berlin 1969: 147: 'All true solutions to all genuine problems must be compatible: more than this, they must fit into a single whole: for this is what is meant by calling them all rational and the universe harmonious.' Cf. Perelman 1972g: 251: 'Une autre objection à l'absolutisme résulte de notre conception même de la connaissance comme ensemble de propositions liées systématiquement. Mais ceci est incompatible avec la thèse de l'existence d'un critère

will soon see, a scholar like von Savigny as one of the founders of legal science considers 'system' the ontology of human society (Coing 1989).

The philosophy of Enlightenment, however, has a deeper historical and conceptual root in the Modern philosophical project. In that respect, thinking in terms of a 'system' closely resembles the method of natural science that started developing from the beginning of the seventeenth century. The fundamental belief that grounded natural science was the possibility of using mathematics to explain the universe. Galilei argues in this respect that philosophy was written in the grand book of the universe in the language of mathematics (Galilei 1957: 237–8). Mathematics provided the scientist with a reliable method, the conclusions of which were certain.[21]

It is important to remember the comments made above on the belief in the systematicity of law. Systems are of a mathematical nature. Seventeenth and eighteenth-century natural science developed the connection between nature and mathematics. Under its strong philosophical version, mathematics was held to belong to reality. Under a weaker theoretical version, mathematics was a method of science applied to the object 'nature'. The mathematical systematicity of natural science is transposed to the study of law, on the all-pervasive belief that mathematics provides access to truth. This belief is part of foundationalism or representationalism itself in both its theoretical and its practical version, for reasons that cannot be further explored here. Suffice it to say that throughout the seventeenth century, mathematical method, and more specifically geometry, penetrated practical philosophy. Its effect on law was to transform it into a demonstrative system (Cassirer 1966, 1902: 425 ff. and 449 ff.).

Grotius, for example, announces his adherence to rational methodology in referring the proofs in matters of natural law to certain fundamental conceptions which are beyond question. The principles of law are in themselves manifest and clear, almost as evident as are those things which we perceive by the external

absolu de connaissance qui, parce qu'absolu, ne peut concerner que des propositions isolées, dont tous les éléments sons clairs par eux-mêmes et ne dépendent, comme des substances, d'aucun autre élément.'

21 For an overview of the relationship between mathematics and philosophy, see Kennedy 1942. Elsewhere (Wintgens 2011), I have argued that there are basically two approaches can be held in this respect. According to the first, the method of science is supposed to be part of the object. This position entails the belief that nature is intrinsically of a mathematical nature. As a result, any theory that takes nature as its object of study results in a theory of reality. On this approach, the conclusions of mathematical natural science are not only certain, but also ontologically true. On the second approach, the method is not necessarily part of the object but external to it. On this view, mathematics is a method with the help of which natural reality is explored and explained. The theory resulting from that is a theory about reality.

senses (Grotius 2005: § 39).[22] The method of mathematics and its demonstrative approach are stressed at several occasions.[23]

In a similar vein, the rational constraints inherent in the theory of the social contract in both Hobbes and Rousseau follow from the truth of their insights into the nature of the contract. Hobbes's fascination for mathematics upon reading Euclid is a strong argument in favour of his belief that mathematics is inherent in nature. His logic of *computatio* and comparison of 'volumes of power' in society may lead to the conclusion that he adhered to the mathematical nature of reality (Strauss 1974: 165 ff.) Rousseau's method of differential equations to calculate the general will, for example as exposed in his *Social Contract*, expresses the same methodological concern (Rousseau 1997a: 59–60). There can be little doubt that both hold their theories to represent reality as it is, on the use of mathematics determining the concept of law.

Pufendorf, in the introduction to his *Elements of Universal Jurisprudence* (Pufendorf 1994b: 31), declares his adherence to the method of mathematics in deducing the fundamental law of nature. This law of sociability thus deduced, all the other principles of law can be demonstrated upon it (Cassirer 1966: 242; Dufour 1991b: 100–103 (Grotius), 103–6 (Hobbes), 106–10 (Pufendorf); Dufour 1994).

Given the pervasive impact of epistemologised philosophy, law is regarded as a science built upon the model of natural science. Legal reasoning ends up using the same method as in science, that is, deduction. Leibniz for one is a convinced advocate of this method upon his belief that the method of Roman law was the science of mathematicians and geometricians (Grua 1956: 239–40). Truth that is reached through their unshakeable demonstration, and its material realisation coincides with Roman law. On this interpretation, Roman law simply coincides with law according to its nature, upon which true law is still established,[24] a coincidence of the ideal and the real as it were, as Savigny would later put it.

Nineteenth-century Legal Science: The Importance of Roman Law

Apart from the mathematical method, the ideal of a rational science of law was nourished by the persistence of the model of Roman law as the archetype of legal thinking throughout the twentieth century. The systematic, scientific and logical nature of Roman law once it is related to the method of the new natural science provoked the emergence of a new type of legal science.

---

22 He is therefore recognised by some scholars as the father of modern doctrinal writing; see Simmonds 2001.

23 Grotius 2005: § 59: 'For I profess truly, that as Mathematicians consider Figures abstracted from Bodies, so I, in treating of Right, have withdrawn my Mind from all particular Facts.' See also Cassirer 1966: 241.

24 In this respect, Leibniz writes in a letter to Hobbes of July 1670 that in his endeavour to reduce Roman law to its general principles, he had found that a clear half of it consisted of 'pure natural law'; see d'Entrèves 1961: 32.

Grotius points to this new approach in the introduction of one of his main works, saying that he tries as far as possible to reduce the matter of law to a coherent system as in Justinian's *Institutes*. He insists on ordering the legal rules in accordance with concepts as they are defined (Wellschmied 1952).

Leibniz for his part is critical of Roman law to begin with, since Justinian's *Institutes* were corrupted by Tribonianus' *post factum* interventions. However, having purged the *Institutes* from these corruptions, Leibniz compares the method of Roman law with that of mathematicians and geometricians. Like the latter, the Roman jurisconsults are 'interchangeable'. Any of their findings in law could as well have been made by any other,[25] just as mathematicians and geometricians need not know the history of or their predecessors in their discipline (Grua 1956: 239–40).[26] A well-informed Romanist and philosopher of law criticises this position saying that it is nothing more than a projection of an ideal deductive system based on Roman law, thus creating the myth of Roman law (Villey 1961: 101; Pringsheim 1944; Hoeflich 1986: 97).

In *Nova Methodus*, he proceeds with the definitions of fundamental concepts, simple rules and general rules, as well as the axioms of legal science (Hoeflich 1986: 100). In doing so, he follows his teacher Pufendorf, mainly his *Elements of Jurisprudence*, using a similar method of definitions and axioms, followed by a number of observations drawn from them (Schneider 1966). What is important for the purpose of this contribution is, as Grua observes, that Leibniz's project as a systematisation of law following 'the anonymous words of right reason' shows what there is to know of law *without* legislation (Grua 1956: 240, 242). The will of the legislator is a matter of fact. This will is imperfect, so the systematicity of law should not be expected to emerge from there.

The move that was started here, and that would spread its effects throughout the twentieth century, was this: seventeenth-century jurisprudence relied on the possibility of treating (mainly Roman) law *as* a science, as their natural science colleagues held that nature could be described and explained according to mathematical method.[27] What fascinated lawyers in the seventeenth and eighteenth centuries was that Roman law allowed for generalisation and deductive reasoning, and so they projected the geometric paradigm onto Roman law (Dufour 1994: 157–62; Hoeflich 1986: 98). However, in its further development throughout the nineteenth century, jurisprudence would defend the view that law *is* a science (Hoeflich 1986: 102).

---

25 Letter to Kestner, quoted in Dufour 1994: 148.

26 Husserl for his part holds a similar view on logic and geometry. It is indeed not necessary, he writes, to know the whole history of geometry or logic in order to be able to add something new to it; see Husserl 1970b.

27 The same holds true for the common law in England, where Francis Bacon in the seventeenth century advocated the belief that law was a science like astronomy and chemistry; see Kocher 1957: 4–6; Hoeflich 1986: 111.

Legal System and Legal Science in the Nineteenth Century

Nineteenth-century jurisprudence inherited from the preceding ages the *ius commune* or Roman law that was in force in western and central Europe (except in England) following its reception from about the fifteenth century (Coing 1989: 9). It owed its authority not to legislation but to its qualities as a rationally organised system of legal materials and its development continued without a European legislator (ibid.: 10). This *ius commune* formed itself until the eighteenth century under the influence of systematic thinking in philosophy, as mentioned above. This aspect of systematicity was pushed one step further from the beginning of the nineteenth century onwards. Instead of only drawing solutions and arguments from the *ius commune*, lawyers from then on started to distil *rules* from that corpus, thus contributing to the creation of a *system* of private law (Freund 1890).

von Savigny and the 'Volksgeist'

In this respect, the controversy between Anthon Thibaut (1814) and Friedrich von Savigny (2002) on the necessity of a codification of German law in 1814 is a landmark.

Thibaut had argued that, in line with the codifications of French, Prussian and Austrian law, German law was in need of a codification of the otherwise fragmented laws of the different German states. Savigny's reaction in his *On the Vocation of our Age* comes to refute this position on the view that this opinion is due to the lack of historical sense. In addition to that, he claimed that this belief went hand-in-hand with the exclusive ability of the State to create law and legal science as the knowledge of law thus created (von Savigny 2002: 21). Apart from some partial codifications in Germany, Savigny was of the opinion that the age of a general codification had not yet dawned.

From his own perspective, Savigny argued that law emerges from popular consciousness (*Volksgeist*)[28] and he ardently argued in favour of the importance of Roman law (von Savigny 2002: 43–52) and its reception in Germany (ibid.: 53–60). The point of his argument against codification of private law was that his epoch lacked the technical means and the language to proceed towards a codification (ibid.: 61–9), meanwhile stressing the flaws of the French, Prussian and Austrian codifications (ibid.: 69–130). Without being opposed to the idea of a codification, he claimed it was better to have no codification than to have a bad

---

28 Von Savigny 2002: 24: 'That which binds (i.e. a people's language, its morals, and its constitution) into one whole is the common conviction of the people, the kindred consciousness of an inward necessity, excluding all notion of an accidental and arbitrary origin'. With the latter, Savigny means, among other things, legislative ruling. For an analysis of the origin of the concept of 'Volksgeist', see Kantorowicz 1912; Wieacker 1995: 283–6.

one.[29] A codification was conditional upon the scientific mastery of the leading principles of law and their relationships to one another.[30]

For nations with codified law as well as for nations without, he however argued that legal science was the same for both types.[31] As for Germany, Savigny argued that its unity could be favoured, not by codification, but by scientific study at the universities. As for the method of this scientific study, the scientist is to abstract the principles from positive law, without, that is, contemplating universal rational natural law. Philosophy as a matter of fact was not necessary in Savigny's approach. Rational natural law as it was elaborated by Leibniz, Pufendorf and others was speculative, and no longer in vogue since Hegel.

As Riemann observes, rational natural law is fact-independent, a-historical metaphysical, while positive law is stable in its growth (Reimann 1989–90: 879–80). Law is the fact that legal science works upon, and that material is Roman law (ibid.: 879). While he sings the praises of Roman law, Savigny takes sides with the natural law of which Leibniz believed Roman law was the perfect materialisation. What he borrows from the rational natural law school was its method. The geometric paradigm went well with natural law, and Savigny only kept the sources (Roman law) and the method (geometrics) of the school, disregarding its metaphysical underpinnings.[32]

Herein lies a paradox. While criticising the abstract rationalist method of natural law of the preceding century (von Savigny 2002: 21), as well as an etatist or legislative conception of legal sources, Savigny however strongly champions a science of law. Law has a 'political' life inasmuch as it expresses the realities of a given social structure. Like Leibniz (and Blackstone and Bentham in England) however, Savigny was not very keen on legislative interventions in the 'system'. Positive law in Savigny's view is not legislative law, which he considers arbitrary (von Savigny 2002: 63; 1815b; Puchta 1845: § 15). It is Roman law, together with the organically grown customary law. Apart from this political moment, he heavily stressed the law's 'technical' life, which begins at the very moment it undergoes its 'scientific' elaboration at the hands of the jurist (Rückert 2004) What justifies

29 Von Savigny 2002: 65: ' … I deny our capacity for the production of a good code'; von Savigny 2002: 66: ' … I maintain that, in our age, a good code is not practicable'; von Savigny 2002: 66: 'If then, we have really nothing which is necessary to the formation of a good code, we are not to believe that the actual undertaking would be nothing more than a disappointment, which, at the worst, would merely not have advanced us.'

30 And in that sense a codification required serious scholarly preparation, which was lacking at his time, von Savigny 2002: 66. See also Gale 1982: 132–4.

31 For nations without a code, see von Savigny 2002: 130 ff. As for nations with a code, see von Savigny 2002: 156 ff.

32 Von Savigny 2002: 45: 'For this reason, [Roman law's] whole mode of proceeding has a certainty which is found no where else, except in mathematics; and it may be said, without exaggeration, that they calculate with their notions.'

Savigny's position is that he saw no difference between theory and practice in Roman law.[33]

While the origin of law is the *Volksgeist*, the study of law must be a scientific study. The object of this science is positive law which is regarded as given, or in legalistic terms, it is 'just there'. From this perspective, under a rough approach, the method of the Historical School gave rise to both *Begriffsjurisprudenz* and analytical jurisprudence.[34]

Savigny's dualistic approach between the *Volksgeist* as the historical source of law on the one hand and the law's scientific study on the other can be explained by the fact that the Historical School initiated by Savigny started from the assumption that there is reason in reality. Yet their almost exclusive preoccupation with the science of private law made them nearly insensitive to Hegel's influence because of the latter's strong focus on public law. Neither did the school support the ontological premises of historicism, which they simply regarded as a method.

Savigny's ideas did not fall on deaf ears. 'The "historical" characteristic of German legal science, Riemann writes, could thus have very different meanings. It could signify a more or less classicist or romantic veneration of the past, a belief in the organic nature of historical development, or it could constitute the postulate for a positivist form of science.' (Reimann 1989–90: 880). It was the third option that became real in the minds of Savigny's successors who initiated the method of *Begriffsjurisprudenz*.

Begriffsjurisprudenz

The decisive step towards *Begriffsjurisprudenz* starting from Savigny's approach is made by his successor Georg Puchta.[35] Puchta's view on the history of law is a development from original simplicity towards its 'scientificity' ('Wissenschaftlichtkeit') in its mature period.[36] Once this point is reached, the *Volksgeist* as the source of law is replaced by the 'Geist' of scientific lawyers who further develop law in a rigorously conceptual and systematic manner (Puchta

---

33 Ibid.: 47: 'Thus, properly speaking [Roman lawyers'] theory and practice are the same.' Cf. d'Entrèves 1961: 99: 'The Historical school had begun by stressing the growth and development of law, it ended by fostering its scientific study. I began with an apology for history. It ended with an apology for jurisprudence.'

34 It is interesting to note here that the founder of analytical jurisprudence, John Austin, was very familiar with the German Historical School. While preparing his classes for the chair of jurisprudence to which he was appointed in 1827, he spent the year 1828 in Germany (mainly in Heidelberg and Bonn), where he came under the influence of the German Pandectist movement; see Hoeflich 1985: 38–9; 1986: 111–12; Gagner 1960: 96–107.

35 For some rare criticism on Savigny's work as the basis of *Begriffjurisprudenz*,see Mollnau 1989: 82–3.

36 Puchta 1851. Like von Savigny, Puchta (1845: §§ 15, 19) criticises the role of the legislator in the development of law, which he believes causes a delay in the evolution of law, in that legislative law loses contact with the life of the people.

1845: § 18).[37] Law finds its origin outside the state (ibid.: § 11), as the immediate conviction of the member of the people or as the product of scientific deduction (ibid.: § 12).

Legislation can be a source of law, as the expression of the general will (ibid.: § 15). Like Savigny however, Puchta is not really a convinced adept of legislation, the validity of which is only taken into account as the formal expression of the general will. Beyond legislative law, however perfect and complete, there exists a mass of convictions maintaining themselves (ibid.: § 14). The dissonances thus produced are mainly caused by imprudent legislation, hasty and improvised work, as well as arbitrary interventions. What really counts is the scientific elaboration of the law that he qualifies as the third source of law (together with popular conviction and legislation) (ibid.: § 18 ff.).

This particular science of law is different from legal philosophy in that that latter shows law as a part of a universal organism ('Weltorganismus') (ibid.: § 32). The philosopher is in this respect a visionary or a seer, while the scientist is to provide knowledge of the law, both with regard to its historical and its systematical aspects.

However, when it comes to scientific knowledge of law as he conceives legal science, the historical aspect attains a rather confused status in Puchta's method (the temporal dimension in law). As will become clearer below, the role of history in legal science was gradually receding, up to the point that it became separated from it by the end the nineteenth century.

For Puchta, as for Savingy, the historical aspect of legal science did not simply mean that the scientist should study law in its historical evolution. History provides the matter of law in a simultaneous and a successive diversity.[38] However, legal science is systematic knowledge, that is, knowledge of the internal cohesion of the different parts of law that are supposed to be elements of a living organism in all its diversity. The science of law operates according to the principle of systematicity, and knowledge of law thus acquired is complete from an internal point of view *because law itself is a system* (an organic whole) (ibid.: § 33) that is capable of itself generating new law.[39] Following Savingy, Puchta considers that once the

---

37 The substitution of the lawyer's consciousness for the 'Volksgeist' is paradoxical. The solution of the paradox lies in the interpretation of Savigny's idea that law was part of a people's culture in the intellectual sense. "Culture' was not, as Mathias Riemann finely articulates, 'the totality of the habits of a people, but the characteristics of its intellectual life. When this life grew more sophisticated over time, the ideas of intellectual elites in their respective fields shaped it more and more. In respect to law, therefore, the jurists represented the nation as a culture.' Reimann 1989–90: 854.

38 Puchta 1845: § 33. This idea is reminiscent of von Savigny's idea that 'The given variety of law … is twofold, namely in part contemporaneous, and in part successive, which necessarily requires a twofold scientific treatment. The reduction of the contemporaneous variety to its inherent unity us the systematic method … The treatment of the successive variety, however, is the truly historical method.' See von Savigny 1815a: 395.

39 In this, Puchta followed von Jhering (1857: 3). See also Wilhelm 2003: 76. Legal science then becomes a third source of law, apart from customary law and legislative law.

principles of legal science have been isolated from positive law as its leading ideas, they will co-evolve with law itself, thus allowing for an organic recreation of the order inherent in law (ibid.: § 33).

The concepts that operate within legal science, Puchta further argues, are not simply a scheme of definitions; they are 'living beings' with a proper individuality distinct from their ancestor.[40] This idea relies on the conviction that the concepts of legal science and their systematic coherence reflect the basic structure of reality. Puchta calls this the 'genealogy of concepts'.[41] The method of the genealogy of concepts leads back to Roman law as the common root of all the European peoples, which makes it possible to transcend the findings of the national legal order. Roman law is the law of one people and the universal law of civilised nations (Puchta 1845: § 35). What is important for the purpose of this chapter is that legal science thus conceived, cuts law from its origin, more specifically the legislator, and closes itself off from the contributions of non-legal disciplines like sociology and economics (Gale 1982: 123) and puts it in the hands of learned lawyers (Dufour 1991c: 61; 1991d: 188–94).

I have just pointed to the ambiguous status of history in Puchta's idea of legal science. Legal science should be spared from unilaterality, that is, from too strong an emphasis on history or on science (Puchta 1845: § 33). This, however, is what happened nevertheless. Despite their claim of faithfulness to the Historical School as Bernard Windscheid (1904: 72) declared in 1878, legal science gradually took sides with the progressive growth of law from the *Volksgeist*. Pursuing the disconnection of law from its historical development, and the abandonment of the philosophical underpinnings of the Historical School – mainly its philosophy of history, but also its 'organicism' – led into the ongoing logical purification of the law.

While popular conscience (*Volksgeist*) flowing into customary law and legislation were considered sources of law as Puchta had mentioned, he pursues his elaboration of legal science as a system. This system of legal science (*Rechtswissenschaft*) is not a mere auxiliary to lawyers. It becomes, on the contrary, a new and higher source of law. Legal science is productive in that it generates new law because law is believed to be 'system'. Scientific law thus developed is one of the organs of the 'Volksrecht'.[42] Puchta pushes this view still further, arguing that scientific law in the strict sense is neither common popular conviction, nor legislative enactment, but the product of scientific deduction.[43]

40 Puchta 1845: § 33. This idea is also found in von Jhering (1857: 10) and von Savigny (2002: 45). See Jouanjan 2005: 226. Wilhelm (2003: 83) calls this a 'conceptual hypostasis'.

41 Puchta 1845: § 33 (the genealogy of concepts is illustrated by the right to enter on someone's property). The 'genealogy of concepts' is again very close to an idea of von Savigny (2002: 45).

42 Wilhelm 2003: 75, referring to both Savigny and Puchta.

43 Puchta 1845: § 15, stating that rules only become visible as the product of scientific deduction, which gives rise to the law of science ('Recht der Wissenschaft'). As

More than ever, the position of the legislator as a source of law is threatened, in that law is either scientifically legitimated or it is not.

Scientific legal positivism is replaced with 'source positivism' or 'legislative positivism' in which the legislator has the last word. The task of legitimating law, instead of being the legislator's, is increasingly assigned to legal science. The criterion for legal truth lies within the legal system, and true law therefore is scientific law, not democratically legitimated law.[44] In this respect, Puchta and his followers relied on the Kantian conception of science advocated by Savigny – that science is not merely receptive, but also productive.[45]

Productive legal science operates as a source of law and brings law to a higher lever, that is, a seamless, complete system of concepts.[46] It should be noted in this respect that while the source positivists of the nineteenth century (Austin and Bentham) had a poor sense of system, their German counterparts on the contrary had a poor sense of 'sources'. Despite the fact that they extensively elaborated on history and popular conscience as sources, towards the middle of the nineteenth century, this theory of sources had been nearly completely replaced by legal science: a science, that is, without a legislator.

'Productive' legal science and scientific positivism

The middle of the century was marked by the Revolution of 1848. It was around this time that Gerber started his scholarly activity. Gerber was a 'Germanist' focusing on German law as opposed to the mainly 'Romanist' initiators of the Historical School, who were almost exclusively addressing Roman law. In addition to that, Gerber considered that, apart from Roman private law, which had been the main focus of legal science, German private law and public law should also be treated according to the rigorous method of legal science.

The Revolution had destroyed the political world-view, while after Hegel's death in 1831, the influence of German idealism abruptly broke down. The protagonists of the Historical School were to be sure no adepts of Hegelianism,

---

this law is produced by lawyers, he calls it 'lawyers' law' ('Juristenrecht'). See also von Jhering (1857: 8) (legal production creates absolutely new legal material).

44 In this respect, law is 'true', and true law is scientifically deduced, not democratically legitimated; see Wilhelm 2003: 77–9. In a similar sense, see Reimann 1989–90: 897.

45 As von Jhering (1857: 3) already said. For two recent studies, see Mecke 2008; 2009.

46 Reimann 1989–90: 865–6: 'The law would be vastly more intelligible and manageable. Furthermore, as a logical system containing all the fundamental principles, legal science could achieve gaplessness and completeness. This would make legal reasoning comfortably predictable and independent of considerations outside the legal system. And finally, the conceptual method could even create new law out of the system itself. The fulfillment of these promises of economy, gaplessness, and self-reproduction was the agenda of legal science of the second half of the nineteenth century.'

but from the middle of the nineteenth century onward, there were no serious competitors to the scientific approach advocated by the School.

Just as in the seventeenth century, the scientific world-view attained its full weight by relying on physics, chemistry and biology (as the work of the young Jhering testified). The naturalist world-view provided the drive to organise law along the lines of these new sciences, thus trying to achieve systematic coherence of the whole body of law.[47] This formal process, as we read from Jhering, had a substantive effect on the subject matter, transubstantiating the maxims of law to a higher level than commands and prohibitions. Law, that is, became a natural science within the realm of the intellect.

I have just pointed to the ambiguous status of history in Puchta's idea of legal science. Legal science should be spared from unilaterality, that is, from placing too strong an emphasis on history or on science (Puchta 1845: § 33). This, however, is what happened nevertheless. Despite their claim of faithfulness to the Historical School following Windscheid, legal science gradually departed from the progressive growth of law from the *Volksgeist*. The pursuit of the disconnection of law from its historical development, and the abandonment of the philosophical underpinnings of the Historical School – mainly its philosophy of history, but also 'organicism' and natural law – led into a purified science of law. This is, in a way, the ironical fate of the Historical School.

To begin with, within the hands of Gerber, and later Laband, legal science carried out an ongoing purification of legal dogmatics, thus obliterating the historical dimension of law. Secondly, Gerber's focus on public law and his effort to unify the whole of private and public law, however, led to a preponderance of public law, a tendency that was already announced in Kant and Hegel.[48] Third, the purification of legal dogmatics went hand-in-hand with the progressive belief that the concepts of legal science were real. The scholars, in others words, believed in the existence of a world of immutable concepts. A result of this was, fourth, that the original programme of the Historical School of dealing with law in both a historical and a scientific manner was gradually abandoned. The historical dimension of law became slowly but surely erased in favour of the method of the natural sciences and mathematics. From treating law as a science, law itself now became a science.

I will briefly draw on the two last points, in order to show that the science of law, more than ever, also tried to erase the legislator from the scene. I will begin with the last point.

---

47 von Jhering 1968: vol. 2.2, 361: 'Die Naturhistorische Methode bedeutet die Erhebung des Rechtsstoffes in einem höheren Aggregatszustand.' See also Reimann 1989–90: 862; Wilhelm 2003: 112–16.

48 As a matter of fact, both Kant and Hegel construct their theory of law starting from private law. Public law is attached at the end of their work, thus suggesting that their focal point is on private law. However, their work betrays a more important place for public law than the structure of it prima facie shows.

An A-historical Science

As noted above, thinking operates under the auspices of systematicity. This became the ultimate device of the Historical School (Wilhelm 2003: 45), thus sublimating 'organicism' and the '*Volksgeist*' into purely formal concepts. Organicism simply serves to articulate the immanently systematic nature of law, upon which law is elevated to the level of an autonomous science. The entire law is subordinated to the method of science which involves the isolation of a single principle from which all the concepts can be deductively derived. Generally speaking, for Gerber (loosely following Puchta), this first principle is the 'power of the will' upon which the legal system becomes a 'system of rights' or a 'system of free possibilities of the will'.

What must be stressed however is the approach to law and legislation to which this method gives rise. Despite their critique of seventeenth- and eighteenth-century jurisprudence (mainly because of its adherence to rational natural law), the method of the scholars' of the nineteenth-century Historical School pretty much resembled Leibniz's 'ars combinatoria' (Villey 1961: 100–101; Grua 1956: 246; Schneider 1966; Viehweg 1965: 52 ff.). Starting from the definition of the fundamental notions of law, simple and general rules, and the axioms of legal science, Leibniz's method of 'combining' these elementary units into a fully developed legal system has more than superficial resemblances with legal science from the second half of the nineteenth century. From their combination of concepts scientifically elaborated, all legal solutions could be derived from the system thus conceived.

The Nature of Legal Concepts

The science of law – unlike Leibniz's method – worked on the materials that were provided by the legislator. This suggests that the type of legal science thus constructed was a form of legal positivism, reducing law to the will of the legislator. Legal science for its part would then simply undertake to describe and systematise legislative law. This view of the matter, however, does not reflect the intentions of Gerber. True, positive law is the material on which the scholar works, but the mere description and systematisation would hardly produce effective knowledge of the law. The early scholars of the Historical School, as mentioned above, were not keen on legislative law. This position was subsequently maintained, since positive law was considered arbitrary, imprudent, incomplete, contradictory, and often the result of hasty and improvisatory legislative work.

Therefore, legal science intervened for the purpose of scientifically elaborating the primary material into a closed system, genealogically retracing law to a set of superior concepts. This genealogical retracing can be found in Puchta, as mentioned above, and his followers have systematically deepened this method. Puchta – in line with Savigny and the early Jhering – strongly believed that the concepts of legal science were 'living beings', living their life independently of their progenitors.

In order to gain a better hold on the impact of legal science on law, it is important to have a closer look at the ontological status of the concepts operative within legal science. The independence of the concepts from their progenitors suggests that the genealogy of concepts should be understood in a logical and not in a diachronic sense. This view coincides with, for example, Puchta's idea that law is a system (Puchta 1845: § 33). The genealogy of concepts means that the system is *internal* to law, and not simply a form imposed on it externally. Legal thinking, according to the science of law, involves calculating concepts in a logical manner. This approach exceeds a mechanical application of positive law under which German legal science could be qualified as legal positivism. We rather face here the positivism of legal science (Wieacker 1995: 341 ff.), or positivism as a method of legal science.

Irrespective of the classification, what is striking, however, is that the concepts operational in this positivist science or positivist methodology are supposed to be real. They exist in the world 'out there', a world that is conceptually structured and has an order independent of the human mind. It is important in this respect to remember the comments made at the start of the study on representationalism. Representationalism is committed to the view that true knowledge represents the world as it is.

The representatives of the Historical School, especially since the 1850s, were conceptualists in that they believed that science is constructed on a mathematical basis. However, after gradually leaving the historical dimension of legal science, they push their view quite a bit further by holding that the concepts they work with are 'real'. Concepts, so we read from Wieacker commenting on the Historical School, 'must represent instantiations of permanently valid propositions of legal justice such that their logical application, like that of a rule of mechanics or an accurate formula in physics, necessarily leads to a decision which is correct, i.e., just' (Wieacker 1995: 343).

On this view, science does not produce the concepts that describe and explain reality. Quite the opposite is the case: science grasps the concepts from reality. What science then 'produces' is nothing less than truth unqualified, which is a surprising exaltation of science that wants itself purely deductive.

It is the reality of legal concepts or rather their hypostasis or naturalisation that provides the science of law with its specific nature. Jhering himself stated the principles of this science in the introduction to the *Jahrbücher* für civilrechtliche Dogmatik which he co-founded with Gerber.

The raw material of legal science are rules and principles. This is what the legislator provides through his legislative production. But as I have said already a couple of times, the scholars of the Historical School were not very keen on legislative law. Therefore, the description of legislative law is considered an inferior form of jurisprudence ('niedern Jurisprudenz'), mainly dealing with the interpretation of legislative law (von Jhering 1857: 9; Wilhelm 2003: 112). The transition of inferior to superior jurisprudence is brought about by legal construction ('juristische Konstruktion') (von Jhering 1857: 9). According to this elaboration of the raw material of law, the totality of law ('Gesammtmasse') no longer appears as a collection of propositions and thoughts, but as the prototype ('Inbegriff') of legal existents, living beings and serving ghosts ('dienenden Geistern'). In operating in this way, legal science aims to reduce legal relations to their underlying concepts, thus constructing specifically legal objects ('spezifisch juristische Körper'). The systematic classification of the legal objects then resulted in a system (ibid.: 10–11).

The view thus produced is rather paradoxical. On the one hand, the legal scientist holds that the concepts with which he works are 'real', whilst on the other hand the view prevails that they are constructions that represent reality. The legal mind as the successor of the *Volksgeist* seems to be considered a mirror of reality, while at the same time it constructs it throughout. On the first view, law 'represents' reality, whereas on the second, it becomes a 'representation-construction', or scientific law. While constructing law on the basis of concepts that were held to be 'real', the latter are so to speak 'naturalised', or hypostatised. This naturalisation may resolve the paradox mentioned, though it does, however, stress all the more the constructivist nature of legal science (Wilhelm 2003: 83). Savigny's 'artificial process' has evolved from a 'reconstruction' of existing law into a pure construction of new law (ibid.: 118) and so legal science becomes fully 'productive' in the Kantian sense, instead of remaining at the receptive level.

The system becomes disconnected from the real life of law, and becomes, again in the Kantian sense, an autonomous discipline. The consequence of this operation is a logical discipline, that is non-teleological and value-free, or detached from political, economic and sociological influences. Logical proof becomes more relevant than practical use (ibid.: 122). It follows from this that legal practice relating to legal science is a matter of deduction, rather than decision (Jouanjan 2005: 226). In this respect, democratically legitimated law could be supported or brushed aside on the strength of a decision maker's political preferences.

In Paul Laband's work, the status of concepts becomes still more mysterious given his idea that legal science's aim is to establish certain facts and phenomena that are legally relevant and to set them in order according to universal concepts. As regards their nature, Laband holds that no method other than logic is required, without any ontology (Laband 1980: 616–17). The validity of the concepts of legal science is intuitively self-evident, without any further foundation (Schönberger 1997: 89).

This is a rough and elementary sketch of the situation of German legal science around the turn of the century. It mainly deals with Roman private law. With Gerber, a couple of new moves are made on the field. The first move is this: Gerber is a 'Germanist' who believes in German law instead of giving all the priority to Roman law as the 'Romanists' – including most prominently Savigny – do. However, by the middle of the century, Gerber changed his mind, and sought a rapprochement with the Romanists, mainly with Jhering. Secondly, Gerber made an attempt to go beyond private law and incorporate public law into legal science, a '*montage théorique de l'Etat allemand moderne*' as it was aptly called (Jouanjan 2005: 196). I will briefly comment on some aspects of both these moves below.

Merger of Roman Law and German Private Law

As noted above, Gerber conceived of the legal system as a 'system of free possibilities of the will'. This was, according to him, the basic principle of the legal system. Like Jhering, he considered law along the lines of chemical or biological analysis, which is yet another way of streaming law according to natural sciences. The free combination of concepts leads him to adopt Jhering's method of 'lower' and 'higher' science that is capable of creating new law without the legislator's intervention (Wilhelm 2003: 115–16). In this way, he believes that the Historical School's method applies to both Roman and German law. However, Roman law as received in Germany is shorn of its historical roots (von Gerber 1851: 10–11). It remains foreign law for Germany. Nevertheless, Gerber holds that due to the efforts of Savigny and Puchta, Roman law was reconstructed in such a manner that their method could now be used for a similar productive treatment of German law (von Gerber 1851: 19, 23). An essential point is that law is purified from any extra-legal element that wards it off from politics. As a matter of fact, the political situation in Germany around the turn of the century was anything but stable, and the scientific treatment of law was an important element to keep private law in a stable position.

Public Law

Gerber's approach to legal science culminated in the merger of Roman and German law, following his method of science. However, at the same time, he conceived of the possibility of expanding his method to public law. Right after the Revolution of 1848, the political situation calmed down and the constitutional patchwork of the period before the Revolution had now been substantively unified. Out of this unity, an attempt could be made to construct a legal concept of the state along the same lines as the 'lower' and 'higher' jurisprudence. Just as the concepts of private law safeguarded rights from politics and legislation, so the scientific concept of the state was a legal construction aiming at stability. In a similar vein to his construal of private law in terms of 'possibilities of the will' ('Willensmöglichkeiten'), Gerber constructed the law of the state as a system of possibilities of the will, the will of the personified power of the unified people (von Gerber 1880: 4).

Paul Laband finally summarised the teachings of the Historical School as it had developed through the 1870s, and has drawn conclusions from it.[49] Legal science is what Continental lawyers understand as 'legal dogmatics', a scientific construction based on logic. It is a science without a legislator, disconnected

49 Laband has described his views on legal science in Laband 1911–14: Introduction.

from social reality, legitimating law on a scientific basis and not on democratic process. Legal reasoning is logical reasoning within a system of concepts. This approach echoes the seventeenth- and eighteenth-century method of law and legal reasoning, yet within a conceptualised state.

As was suggested at the beginning of this chapter, legal science corroborates the characteristics of strong legalism that were identified earlier in this chapter. In the rest of this section, I will briefly point to the mean features of this relationship between legal science and strong legalism.

Legal Science Corroborates Strong Legalism

Representationalism

A central element of the new developing legal science was the strong influence of natural science which reminds us of the seventeenth-century model, and its turn towards the scientific paradigm. The study of law was held to operate along the lines of a natural science. Roman law and its institutions, as in Leibniz, became the object of study of legal science, yet without any reference to natural law. More specifically, mathematical method was at the forefront and pushed legal science into a positivistic science and method ('rechtswissenschafliche Positivismus') (Wieacker 1995: sect. 23).

Begriffsjurisprudenz had given the initial impetus to this approach, in that legal science consists of a rational concatenation of legal concepts. In this respect, Puchta's disciples, mainly Carl Friedrich Gerber and Paul Laband incorporated his view on the nature of concepts into their theories. The former was a scholar of private law, whilst the latter was rather oriented to public law. Yet, as we will see, both contribute to a unified legal science, including private and public law. Puchta qualified concepts as 'living beings', thus pointing to some historical dimension in their development. Concepts, so the scholars of the Historical School held, were real.

This is not without reminding us of the mediaeval realism that was discussed in chapter 1. It brings us straight to the question as to what exactly it is that these concepts represent. Gerber and Laband, as well as Jhering and Windscheid, make no reference to an extra-legal or extra-systemic reality. On the contrary, they seek to purge legal concepts of any factual, moral, or political content. Legal concepts only have a 'juridical' content. However, concepts are mere ideas or constructions of the mind which strongly contrast with the belief concepts, as Puchta did, which are 'living beings' or 'legal bodies' (von Jhering 1857: 10).

This illustrates the attitudes of the Historical School and the development of legal science. Put in the terminology used above, there was a merger of representation-reproduction and representation-construction. This merger amounted to a hypostatisation or naturalisation of legal concepts. Legal science was thus held to be a science of reality, while it is, however, at best a science about law.

This merger of perspectives runs parallel with the purging of the historical dimension of law that was the essential characteristic of the Historical School. However, this process of the dehistorisation of legal science is reminiscent of the manipulation of time and the belief in the universality of truth discovered to which I have pointed earlier.. According to the classification of legalism as a 'strategy', it has been argued that this involves a 'turning off the time button'. A similar 'strategy', as will be argued, is at work in legal science as it develops throughout the nineteenth century.

Timelessness and Legal Validity

As already mentioned above, history has an ambiguous status in the Historical School from Puchta onwards. Three aspects are worth mentioning in this respect. After the historical research as the essential part of the programme initiated by Savigny had been concluded, material Roman private law had been brought fully into the limelight. This conviction was stimulated by the rediscovery of a palimpsest version of Gaius' nearly complete *Institutes* in Verona in 1816 by Niehbuhr (Kelley 1979).

Secondly, despite the influence of Puchta's idea of 'living concepts' as the building blocks of a legal system, the belief in the historical nature of legal concepts started crumbling in the work of one of his disciples, Carl Friedrich Gerber. The belief in the inaccessibility of the most universal foundations of private law gained the upper hand, under which history was assigned the role of an auxiliary science. Jhering's view on the matter was very explicit: time has to be driven back of the system. This amounts to saying that the operational force of history in law as it finds its expression in the 'Volksgeist' as the key concept of the Historical School undergoes a change.

The organicist approach to reality, of which law forms part, and to the changes of which it is subjected, should be conceived, as Gerber writes, in a 'sublimated form, deprived of any life'.[50] A result of this is that the fact-dependence which was one of the main premises of the Historical School turned into a fact-independence of legal science, making legal truth timeless. Historical-contingent rules, so the scholars argued, had a deeper foundation in timeless principles. On this view of law, the followers of Puchta were pretty close to the insights of the rational natural law tradition of the preceding epoch. However, they denied the transcendence of natural law that served as a critical standard of positive law.

Third, and in connection with the above, the methods of natural science, as in the seventeenth century, deeply influenced the method of legal science. On the one hand, as Savigny had already mentioned, the development of legal science had to be assigned to academic lawyers in universities. While this position of Savigny's was part of his own scientific programme, German universities during the first half of the nineteenth century tended to remove the practice-oriented curricula from

50 Quoted in Jouanjan 2005: 220.

their programmes. Lawyers who were for the most part academics were thereby forced to support a reframing of their discipline into a 'real' science in order to keep their anchorage inside the academic walls (Stichweh 1984; 1994).

On the other hand – and probably but not exclusively under that influence – natural science attracted legal scientists on its own merits. Apart from their desire to transform law into a science, they wanted at the same time to transcend the opposition between their discipline and the natural sciences.[51] Following their efforts towards the unification of both types of science, the universal nature of natural sciences again took the upper hand. Universal science by its very nature is a-temporal, just as is the much criticised theories of rational natural law (the unilateralisation so much abhorred by Puchta slips into legal science)

Concealed Instrumentalism

Speaking generally, four aspects of instrumentalism can be detected in the development of legal science in the Historical School.

The first aspect is the following. Savigny's negative attitude towards codification, discussed above, was related to his perception of the political situation of his time. Germany was a patchwork of political authorities lacking any unity or uniformity. This was expressed in *On the Vocation*, arguing that the time was not ripe for codification. This was a different situation from France, with the establishment of new political institutions that were appropriate for promulgating the French civil code. However, Savigny's instrumentalism came to the fore in his desire to protect the law from legislation and the turbulent political situation of his time. None the less, the choice for an 'a-political' legal science is not as neutral as it appears. It is a choice that is concealed behind the veil of neutrality. This coincides with legalism's separation of law and politics, which has a strong instrumental flavour.

The second aspect of instrumentalism as it is concealed in legal science is related to the first one. The protective function of legal science was pretty convenient for the bourgeoisie from 1848 onwards, considering law as an instrument for safeguarding their interests. This evolution in legal science also occurred in the United States. 'By the middle of the 19th century', Morton Horwitz (1977b: 253–4) reports, 'the legal system had been reshaped to the advantage of men of commerce and industry at the expense of farmers, workers, consumers and other less powerful groups in the society.' This reshaping of the law relied on a flexible instrumental conception of law, that from the middle of the nineteenth century was transformed into a 'science of law'. As a matter of fact, the interest groups mentioned above could only benefit from these instrumentalist approaches to law once their self-interest, that had been satisfied through the instrumentalist reshaping of the law, could thereafter be disguised in the newly established legal doctrines (ibid.: 254). The interest groups, as a matter of fact, suffered from a

51 See, among others, Kiesow 1994.

widespread fear of a legislatively authorised redistribution of wealth (ibid.: 260). There were then, Horwitz continues, major advantages in creating an intellectual system which gave common law rules the appearance of being self-contained, apolitical and inexorable, and which, by making 'legal reasoning seem like mathematics' conveyed 'an air … of … inevitability about legal decisions' (ibid.: 254; Holmes 1894–95: 7)

A third aspect concerning instrumentalism in German legal science, corroborating the first two, is formalism. Formalism indeed protects the legal system from legislative muddling with it (first aspect) but at the same time, it is a very useful approach to protect those interests that are incorporated into the law. In this respect, formalism and its neutrality leads to instrumentalism, just as instrumentalism gives rise to formalism (Reimann 1989–90: 892).

A fourth aspect of instrumentalism is again connected with the preceding ones. While the separation of law and politics as part of the strategy of legalism may be helpful in keeping law 'pure', it is nevertheless a politically sensitive position. Moreover, once the law has been separated from politics, and has been highly formalised as in German legal science, it becomes increasingly sensitive as an instrument for the protection of what interest groups were able to obtain through the law, as well as for social change. A formalised legal science can be instrumental for both a conservative as well as a progressive polity.

Etatism

While Hobbes, Rousseau, Kant and Hegel considered the state to be the sole source of law, thus leading into etatism, it is paradoxical to see how legal science in the Historical School ran in the same direction.

The original object of legal science was Roman private law as *ius commune*, a legal order that is characterised by tradition, and was elaborated for centuries by scholarly lawyers.

This systematic integration of law resounded throughout the nineteenth century and was consolidated by the generation following Savigny. Thus formalised, and purified of its non-scientific elements such as morals, politics and socio-economic circumstances – all elements that are inherently time bound – legal science underwent another drastic change in the hands of its protagonists. This change was triggered, among other causes, by the failure of the Revolution of 1848.

The purification of law in *Begriffsjurisprudenz*, and the subsequent merger of German and Roman law, culminated in the end in a conceptual theory of the state. Gerber had spared no efforts to contribute to the construction of the state on a scientific basis, that is, taking sides of the metaphysical foundations for it that were adduced by Hobbes, Rousseau and Kant. Instead, legal science developed a purely legal and scientific concept of the state as an integral part of legal science. The state then became a legal concept in its own right, lacking any political backing (especially since the revolutionary events of 1848).

As a construction on the basis of the concept of 'Willensmacht', a gradual evolution of the conception of law occurred that has already been encountered in the works of Hobbes, Rousseau, Kant and Hegel, viz that all law becomes state law from the 1870s onwards. The political situation from that moment on gave rise to the conviction that the state had to intervene in the 'social question', in which Bismarck took the lead (Haferkamp 2008: 680–86). The autonomy of private law without a state was replaced by the supremacy of the state in public as well as in private law, as had already been implicitly advocated by Kant and Hegel in the preceding century.

Chapter 6
Legitimacy and Legitimation – From Strong Legalism to Legisprudence

Legitimacy Through Representation

Under strong legalism, the form of the norm is legality. Legality as the formal requirement of a norm determines its ontology. A norm exists if and only if it has a legal form. As a necessary condition for a norm's existence, the legality of a norm at the same time involves its legitimacy. A norm is legitimate if and only if it satisfies the conditions for legality of the legal system to which it belongs. This is reminiscent of Max Weber's thesis that legality involves legitimacy.[1]

Legalism, says Judith Shklar, is an ethical attitude which holds that normative thinking consists of rights and duties embedded in rules (Shklar 1986: 1; Bankowski and MacCormick 2000).[2] Her argument in support of this thesis is both attractive and strong, and in the first chapter of this book, attempts were made to drive it home to its philosophical underpinnings. These can be summarised as representationalism embedded in a nominalist metaphysics that was addressed in chapter 1.

In this chapter, we shall focus in greater detail on the internal structure the concept of legitimacy thus provided. In general terms, this structure can be articulated as a form of 'representation'. Once this structure is sufficiently brought to the surface, some characteristics of the legitimacy flowing from this will be explored.

Under the general scheme of normativity according to strong legalism, norms exist 'out there'. Under its theological version, they are imposed by God on his creatures. In Suarez, Hobbes and Pufendorf, the foundation of normativity is a divine norm specifying that the people must transfer their power to a sovereign

---

1 Weber 1964: 131: 'Today the most usual basis of legitimacy is the belief in legality, the readiness to conform with rules which are formally correct and have been imposed by accepted procedure.' Habermas 1992: 97–8 criticises Weber's merely empirical conception of legitimacy, without an immanent relation to truth. The belief in legitimacy thus shrinks to a belief in legality; the appeal to the legal manner in which a decision comes about suffices.

2 Cf. the definition of legal formalism, the twin of legalism, in Horwitz 1977b: 252: 'There were, in short, major advantages in creating an intellectual system which gave common law rules the appearance of being self-contained, apolitical, and inexorable, and which, by making "legal reasoning seem like mathematics", conveyed "an air … of … inevitability" about legal decisions.'

(Suarez), that subjects must enter into a social contract (Hobbes), or that subjects must be social, and hence live together in a state (Pufendorf). It also fits in with a secularised version of legalism as is found in Kant by stating that we have a duty to enter into a state based on the categorical imperative.

Strong legalism, so it can be concluded from the previous chapters, holds that law represents reality. On this representation, the form of the norm, its ontology and its legality are of a timeless nature. The content of norms is the product of state activity. The state is the only institution capable of endowing propositions with legality. Given the state's uniqueness as a source of norms, etatism is yet another characteristic of strong legalism.

Under etatism, in addition to the representational nature of legality, the instrumental nature of norms is concealed. If the form of the norm exclusively determines its existence, then the instrumental relationship between a norm as a means to a contingent end, that is, is hidden from view. The instrumental nature of law means that law is an instrument with the help of which reality can be changed. The often naïve belief carried by this position has been sufficiently exposed and criticised (Summers 1977). It is difficult, however, to eradicate this view.

The representational nature of law brought about by strong legalism as an ontology shows up in legal science. The paradigmatic model of legal science, as was argued in the last chapter, is found in the German Historical School, the consequences of which were decisive for legal science until the middle of the last century. Legal science, as it developed in nineteenth-century Germany, fully incorporated the legalistic approach into law as it emerged from seventeenth- and eighteenth-century theories of the state.

The practicing lawyers' attitude towards law entails the view that valid law is legitimate law. A pedigree test as to a proposition's belonging to the legal system is *ipso facto* conclusive as to its legitimacy. The conclusiveness of this test a priori excludes any inquiry into the values, goals, or ends which the norm does or does not realise, because it is the form that makes the norm.

From the political perspective, the legislature represents the people or the nation. Without representation, 'the people' or 'the nation' does not exist. Representation from this perspective means 'conceptualisation', without which the power that is located in the people or in the nation remains invisible, that is, non-operational. Representation from this perspective is necessary in that the formalisation of power in institutions – its institutionalisation – makes it demonstrable, visible, and responsible. The institution of power, that is, the institution of the institutions like a legislature in order to represent it, is therefore not only a practical requirement, but a conceptual necessity.

The institution of an institution like a legislature or, more generally, a sovereign, is an act of a group of people. It is commonly referred to as a social contract, by which those who want to give themselves a form contractually agree with each other to do so. In this sense, the sovereign represents the founders, and his acts will be attributed to them. In earlier versions, the establishment of the institution or the representation of power is operated as a transfer (Suarez) or as a contract, either as one (for example, Hobbes, Rousseau and Kant) or two (Pufendorf).

It follows that all the expressions of power represent some original albeit invisible, fragmented, unstructured, or inefficient power that takes shape through an original act, the social contract. The bottom line of this representational mechanism is the individual subject which groups together with his fellows in establishing the institution that represents them as a whole.

The articulation of several aspects of representation gives a rough picture of the legitimacy of law from the perspective of strong legalism. The different aspects of 'representation' contribute to the legitimacy of a legal system, the products of which are considered legitimate.

The acts of the state as the sovereign's rational organisation represent the social contract, in that the products of state action are 'founded' upon it. Further executive acts concretising the sovereign's norms, and judicial decisions in which prior and/or higher rules are applied, represent the latter.

Part of this attitude is the belief that the norm is contained in a text, and that norm and text are identical. The text of the norm expresses the will of the legislator. To understand the meaning of the norm means correctly understanding the text, the meaning of which may be discovered through an exegetical or literary exercise. Reading the text of the norm correctly therefore means understanding the norm correctly. Legal decision making is therefore understood as subsumption, a logical application of a pre-existing commandment, or the application of law as a mere explanation of texts.

The rationale for this attitude is that modern democratic societies operate according to the theory of the separation of powers in one version or another. This theory holds that norm creation and norm application are separate functions. Legislation as norm creation therefore establishes the norms to be applied. Norms are created and communicated through language. The texts, therefore, contain the norms, and transport the latter over time. When they are applied, the theory of the separation of powers holds that the determination of their meaning occurs with the help of linguistic means only. This theory of interpretation is known as the plain meaning doctrine. Its characteristic is the identification of 'norm' and 'text'.[3] This includes the suggestion that the interpretation of norms is a variant of the interpretation of texts, legal or otherwise.

Because the norm is identical to the text of the norm, any other means of exploring the meaning of the norm than those appropriate for texts risks distorting the norm. More specifically, because the text represents the norm, and the norm represents the will of the legislator, through the process of adjudication its meaning is to be discovered or, if necessary, reconstructed, not constructed. The doctrine of the separation of powers can therefore be considered as yet another version of the metaphysical distinction between intelligence and will, judgement and decision,

3 For a critique on this position, Müller 1996: 175–80; Esser 1972: 124; Baden 1977; van de Kerchove 1978b.

or legislation and adjudication. Judicial judgments are the end of a chain, through which legitimacy is created. Representation legitimises every step on the basis of the preceding one.

Strong legalism suggests that once there is a legitimate state, all that follows are legitimate norms. Legitimacy, that is, is an unquestionable aspect of formally valid law. The form of the norm includes its legitimacy.

In this chapter, I want to challenge this view. More specifically, I want to argue that legitimacy is the result of a process of legitimation, and not a 'one shot' aspect of each and every norm. My claim amounts to saying that the formal validity of a norm is a necessary, though not a sufficient, condition for its legitimacy. Legitimacy is the result of a process of legitimation by the legislator, norm giver, ruler, or sovereign. On the other hand, under strong legalism, corroborated by legal science, the legislator is not a legal but simply a political actor. Based on the argument that legitimacy is the result of a process, the intention here is to view the legislator as a legal actor whose work must 'earn' legitimacy.

Legitimacy and the Chain of Legitimation

The legitimacy of law is the problem *par excellence* in legal philosophy. In order to clarify my position, I propose to begin with some rudimentary classification of some theories of legitimation.

Most of the time, theories of law are called 'positivist' or 'jusnaturalist' respectively. The opposition between the two types has been the object of a long-standing discussion that appears to be endless. For reasons of clarity, we shall use the labels 'jusnaturalistic' or 'substantive', and 'non-jusnaturalistic' or 'procedural' for models which respectively do or do not represent a substantive content. It will be argued that there is a structural similarity between the two models instead of an opposition.

Jusnaturalistic models include the classical (Aristotle), theological (Aquinas), and rational versions of natural law.[4] Under the classical version, the model exists in reality, while under the theological version, it is a divine creation according to a pre-existing plan (Aquinas), or a divine command imposed on rational creatures (Suarez and Pufendorf). In the rational version, the model is discovered by reason belonging to human nature as a creation of God.

Non-jusnaturalistic models do not rely on any substantive content whatsoever. The legitimacy of the products, therefore, must be found inside these models. More specifically, these models produce legitimate norms in a step-by-step manner, starting from the initial consent of those submitted to it. Because they do not represent a pre-existing substantive content or norm, these models must start with the establishment of an institution. They start, that is, from an initial

4 On the distinction between 'classical' and 'modern', or 'rational' natural law, see Villey 1962.

act of will of those submitted to the model's end products, and for this reason these models are labelled 'democratic' in the generic sense. A democratic model is non-jusnaturalistic in that it does not incorporate or represent any pre-existing content. It relies instead on an act of will, the content of which is not given. A non-jusnaturalistic model, that is, does not represent a transcendent and therefore unavailable normative content.

Under jusnaturalistic models, a transcendent normative content provides their normativity. According to the logic inherent in these models, a norm should not oppose this content without losing its validity. Therefore, a crucial difference between a non-jusnaturalistic and a jusnaturalistic model of legitimation is this: a jusnaturalistic model does not require an active legitimation of its norms. Compliance or the absence of conflict, with the substantive normative content providing the system with its normativity, is a necessary and sufficient condition for legitimacy; in a non-jusnaturalistic model for its part, the legitimacy of norms can obviously not rely on a pre-existing or pre-given substantive content, and so it is to be obtained through active legitimation. Legitimation, that is, refers to a course of action resulting in legitimacy.

The problem of legitimacy briefly sketched out in the preceding lines arose at the outset of Modernity with the inheritance of late mediaeval nominalism, as was argued in Chapter 1. Human beings are individuals, whose freedom God limits with a number of commandments, known as the Decalogue – more in line with a realist ontology – or the Ten Commandments – according to a nominalist interpretation. The Commandments, so the nominalist version holds, directly address man's freedom without affecting his 'nature', 'essence', or 'idea', since such 'things' no longer exist outside the mind as realists have it.

Hobbes is the first to bring forth this new constellation, with a new type of problem in its wake: man is free because 'human nature' no longer makes sense; as for action therefore, what is not forbidden is permitted (Hobbes 1966c: 206–7). What is forbidden is laid down in divine commandments, the only true morals; natural law, therefore, is permissive in that it establishes the individual's right within the context of a state that is established with God's permission after the Fall (Tierney 2002: 399–406; Hruschaka 2004). In conjunction with the nominalistic stance that the concept 'Church' has no 'real' existence as an 'institution' but only as an association, men must organise themselves anew (de Lagarde 1926: 426 ff.). With this new type of organisation, political philosophy, with the problem of the legitimacy of law in its wake, fully comes to light.

Hobbes's assumption of human freedom is adopted by his followers who concur in the construction of the theory of the social contract – a variant of the roman *lex regia* – that serves as a rational basis for the organisation of political space (Lloyd 1997: 231).

The social contract is the first step or the foundation of the organisation of political space, and the first link in the chain of legitimation. Hobbes claims that man is drawn into the contract, while Rousseau holds that it is connected to the development of reason. Locke relates it to convenience and the preservation of one's life by the protection of property, whilst for Kant there is a duty to enter into it. On the premise that the contract counts as the only possible rational organisation of freedom, it is considered the starting-point or the foundation for the chain of legitimation: without a contract, there is no legitimate use of power; when there is a contract, all the legitimate use of power refers to that original starting-point.

Contract theories, that is, articulate the social contract as the self-referring beginning of legitimacy. The contract is not a real event, only a hypothesis. Given its inevitability, it shows up, like the substantive normative content in jusnaturalistic models, as a necessity according to the rational nature of man (and hence 'rational natural law'). The contract, as was argued in Chapter 1, is a rational choice. The only 'given' upon which the subject must act is his God-given rational nature, according to which he is rationally required to enter into a contract.[5]

The legitimate – because rationally chosen – contract as the foundation of political society or the legal system establishes the authority of the norm-giver or sovereign, all of whose orders are legitimate because founded on the original contract. Further steps in the chain, like executive orders and judicial decisions, through to the authorisation of the bailiff to take away your television, share this very same foundational act.

While the foregoing pointed to the essential difference between substantive and procedural models, depending on whether or not they incorporate a transcendent norm, there is also a similarity that deserves our attention.

The similarity between the two models lies in the dynamics of the chain of legitimation. In the former, the substantive legitimating content is not available because of its transcendent nature. It simply exists or is created. Legitimacy derives *from* that pre-existent or divinely created or commanded content. A similar dynamic operates in procedural models in that all legitimacy derives *from* the contract. This similarity stems from the contract's uniqueness, and hence its necessity for the organisation of political space. Because of its necessity, the contract appears as a reproduction or a representation of reality and not as a construction added to it.

Under a substantive model, accessibility of the pre-existent or given content results from revelation or metaphysical speculation. Legislation as the specific *modus operandi* of political space is dependent on this accessibility. Under a realistic ontology, legislation as *ordinatio* (Aquinas) represents an existing order that it concretises. For a nominalistic metaphysics for its part, upon which legalism relies, a pre-existing commanded norm (Suarez, Hobbes, Pufendorf), or a rational moral norm (Kant) provides the foundation for subsequent human legislation.

While still unavailable – the command is of a transcendent nature, or can be revealed by reason – the organisation of political space and subsequent legislation is a matter of construction and not the reproduction of an existing order. The reason is

5 According to a common interpretation, Grotius's theory (Grotius 2005) is the source of a secular natural law theory. This interpretation follows from a spurious reading of the § 11 of the *De Jure Belli ac Pacis*, 'etiamsi daremus ... '. In this I with the interpretation of Edwards 1970, Novak 2000 and Sève 1989: 36–9.

that social contract theory is the twin of theological nominalism, according to which God cannot create universals, but only individuals. Because nature no longer informs human beings as to what they should do, normativity is confined to obeying divine commandments, a version of which tells them to enter into a political organisation. This is an intermediate model, between substantive and purely procedural models, as a radically democratic political organisation can be called. A purely procedural model is a voluntary association. Legitimation in this type of model represents the initial consensus. Its existence is based on an act of will.

A purely procedural model does not rely on any legitimating substantive content, the correspondence with which provides legitimacy. Natural, theological, or rationally discovered contents are no longer available. The legitimacy of norms, according to this type of model, must therefore be actively produced in that norms require the active *legitimation* of the norm giver in order to be *legitimate*.

In the absence of any substantive normative content, the initial stage of a procedural model is freedom. The point of these models is to establish norms that organise or determine freedom which in both versions entail a limitation of freedom. Any of these determinations consists of a choice between many possibilities, so that any norm is at the same time a limitation of freedom.

Substantive models for their part deal with free will. Freedom involves the choice over the ends, as well as the means to obtain it, while free will deals with what exists and what one can will or not will. A given norm or end to be realised can no longer be chosen; it can only be willed or not willed. When dealing with freedom, both the end and the means to obtain it must be chosen. Because of the reflexivity of freedom, this choice is also a matter of freedom. The reflexivity of freedom means that it must be exercised in freedom.

This necessarily rudimentary sketch makes it possible to articulate briefly the 'dynamics of legitimation'. The dynamics of legitimation is the *direction* of the chain of legitimation. The dynamics of a substantive model can be characterised as 'top-down', *from* the substantive content *to* a concrete ruling as an execution thereof. The substantive content exists or is given, and through it a concrete rule is created.

Things are similar with a procedural model. A procedural model necessarily involves several steps, the first of which is the establishment of the model. The establishment of the model – say a social contract – creates the institution(s) that will make the machine run. This institution – say a sovereign – creates norms or limitations of freedom that are legitimate because they are based upon – that is, represent – the initial institutional act. In a procedural model, the legitimacy of the limitations of freedom stems from an earlier, 'fundamental', instituting act that is represented throughout the process of creating norms.

The similarity between substantive and procedural theories of legitimation is that in a substantive model as well as in a procedural model, the dynamics of the chain of legitimation are *unidirectional*. In a substantive model, this is due to the unavailability or the transcendence of the substantive content. In a procedural model, earlier steps in the chain of legitimation must be taken for granted, without which no proposition could ever be legitimated as a norm. The social contract, for example, must be taken for granted when assessing the validity of a norm issued by the sovereign. The validity of a norm must be assumed when a judge makes his judgment on the basis of that norm. The bailiff's executive order presupposes that the judicial decision is valid. The legitimacy of earlier – higher – steps in the chain is passed down to the subsequent steps, and so contributes to the legitimacy of the latter. The direction of this chain is unilateral, in that actors in the chain have no access to the premises underlying their decisions (Habermas 1996a: 173; cf. Luhmann 1983).

Whereas norms in the substantive models represent the model's substantive content, 'lower' norms represent higher norms, including the conventional foundation of the model itself. Both models implement a similar dynamic, from what is real or true to what is artificial or conventional in a substantive model; from what is of higher normative value to what is of lower normative value (from legislative norm to executive norm, from legislative or executive to judicial norm, and so on) in a procedural model. From a more general perspective, legitimacy follows from the fact that what is represented has more value than – in that it contributes to the legitimacy of – what represents.[6]

This is the general idea. The chain of legitimation, that is, cannot be reversed, except for some steps expressly provided for in the theory, like judicial review, appeals and challenges of administrative acts, as will be shown later in this chapter. I will further elaborate on the contract versions of Hobbes and Rousseau, as examples of jusnaturalist and procedural versions of the contract respectively.

The unilateral dynamics of the chain of legitimation, as it can be observed in both substantive and procedural theories, takes earlier steps for granted. It adds to that a new content – that is yet another limitation of freedom. The concretisation of the more general limitation of freedom – typically, general legal rules – preceding executive orders, and administrative and judicial decisions connects this general limitation on freedom to more concrete situations. This calls for justification. Justification in this view connects the later to the earlier, or the lower to the higher.

---

6 The idea of procedural or step-by-step legitimation was highlighted by Luhmann (1983). Procedure (*Verfahren*) as a means of reducing complexity is a model to legitimate decisions regardless of their content. Procedure is legitimate in as far as it succeeds in excluding critique. Elections, for example, legitimate a limited number of people to make decisions, the content of which is unknown at the time of the elections. Their decisions – legislation – a priori bind the executive. Civil servants 'receive' the norms they have to apply without any possibility of critique. Court rulings in turn are justified by the fact that they correctly apply pre-existing norms, both legislative and executive. Legitimation by a procedure produces legitimacy, in that, in Luhmann's theory, the chain of legitimation is unidirectional. The chain that is consists of half-permeable barriers between the consecutive stages, from elections to legislation, from legislation to executive decision making, and from executive decision making to judicial application. The chain of legitimation is irreversible in that decisions from an earlier stage cannot be challenged at a later stage. They are sufficiently legitimated to be binding. The later stages, that is, represent the earlier.

Legislation as the limitation of freedom through legal rules is referred to as granted by the social contract; the latter is further concretised in a constitution. Elections and legislation, in turn, do not require any specific legitimation, since they stand at the start of the chain of legitimation. The entering into the social contract is based on a rational choice: it is a decision, but one that cannot be escaped. From then on, the legitimation programme starts, and can only be corrected from within, that is, on the basis of correction mechanisms that belong to the programme itself. This does not include reversals of the chain.

From this perspective, the social contract is a proxy. The parties to it agree to accept the limitations on freedom imposed 'later' on. They do abide by limitations on their freedom as yet unknown to them at the 'moment' of the contract. They enter into a programme of legitimation that is irreversible. The content of the limitations on their freedom is not available to them, just like the legitimating content of substantive theories of legitimation is out of reach. Any norm of the sovereign, provided that it is formally valid, is therefore also legitimate.

Strong Legalism and the Proxy Theory of Legitimation

The social contract can be considered a beginning of the democratic organisation of political space, even when it results from a transcendent content. The democratic organisation of political space in the Modern philosophical project, however, purports to be more radical than its classical version. Democracy, that is, is not a natural fact. Because it is a concept, it is an intellectual construction following upon both Hobbes's and Rousseau's nominalism.

The social contract, so it seems, is an act of will and could mark a radically new beginning. This view has to be qualified. The social contract is a theoretical undertaking, in that it connects legitimation to truth and to will only in a secondary order. The irreversibility of the chain of legitimation – apart from the hypothesis of giving up the contract itself (Rousseau 1997a: 120) – follows from this qualification.

Hobbes's version is based on the laws of nature that require man to leave the state of nature and to accept a series of other external limitations on freedom, that is, the norms of the sovereign. They are binding upon the subject as a result of an imputation based on the social contract. Subjects have, in other words, chosen to endure the norms of the sovereign, whatever their content may be.

There is a logical and a normative reason for this. The logical reason is that at the 'moment' of the contract, they do not know what the sovereign is going to issue qua norms because no civil laws exist yet. The normative reason is the power of the sovereign to define the natural laws' content in an arbitrary manner.[7] In the

7 Lloyd qualifies this as a 'purely arbitrary piece of legislation', see Lloyd 1981: 131.

contract, they promise obedience to what is still unknown to them. It is through the contractually expressed will that they are supposed to be the authors of these norms.

Rousseau in turn conceives things differently. According to him, the normativity of law does not stem from any external moral norm. The ultimate source of normativity is the will of those that are subject to it. Since the people have constituted themselves as sovereign, it is free to decide which propositions will have the force of law. This view in turns calls for some qualification.

Rousseau sees his theory as the last stage in the evolution from a pre-rational society to a rational state. There is nothing more rational than constructing political space that finally introduces the morality that was lacking in the state of nature (Strauss 1974: 274).

The conclusion of the contract follows from the access to the true principles of public law, as discovered by Rousseau (Rousseau 1997a: 152). Their content is not subject to the whims of history; it is fixed once and cannot be changed without making the contract 'void and without any effect' (ibid.: 49-51). As in Hobbes, the choice for the contract is based on an exclusionary reason, which is presented as an act of will. In addition, the sovereign can only validate propositions. It is the legislator who has the right of initiative (ibid.: 68–72). As a counsellor of the prince, as he has aptly been called (Polin 1971: 222 ff.), he is reason without will (ibid.: 227 ff.). He suggests propositional contents that only the sovereign can transform into law. Rousseau shows that he is not really confident in the intentions of those subjected to the laws, since he does not hold them capable of proposing or amending any of them. The people, as he says, do want the good, but do not always see it. Therefore, they need a guide (Rousseau 1997a: 66–8). This guide is the legislator, who is simply an additional link in the chain of legitimation.

It follows from the above that democracy under the Modern philosophical project, as we read from Hobbes and Rousseau, is not really radical. It is rather based on an independent, external norm for Hobbes; it results from a historical evolution that provides, according to Rousseau, inevitable cognitive standards. It is not an act of pure will, which would be necessary if democracy were to be fully democratic.

If it were, then freedom and not reason would be the *principium* of democratic organisation of political space and the resulting laws. Freedom as a *principium*, as argued in Chapter 4, has both the meaning of a starting-point and a *Leitmotiv*. In the democratic project resulting from Hobbes and Rousseau, it is only the former, although freedom in their version is only of a limited extension. Had it also been the latter, that is, a *Leitmotiv*, the philosophers would have run the risk of political space not being established at all. As a matter of fact, when using their freedom, subjects would not also be able to will the organisation of the political space.

What then both Hobbes and Rousseau are offering is a proxy theory of legitimation, not a theory of radical democracy. Their proxy theory involves the establishment of the institution 'state'. Their act of institution entails the granting of a proxy to institutions that, in an irreversible way, legitimates normative contents that will limit the subjects' freedom. Their initial consent does not relate to the content of these norms that is from the point of view of legitimation, irrelevant. This is the reason why their consent is a mere proxy.

The very proxy character of their theory of legitimation stems from its foundation in truth. The truth of the foundation in Hobbes's construction stems from the truth of the laws of nature. For Rousseau, it is a matter of reason alone. The truth of the basic framework, that is, the contract, provides a stable, indeed unshakeable, basis for the norms promulgated on that basis. They share in the truth of the framework. For Hobbes, the truth of the foundation of the contract stems from a divine commandment. For Rousseau, it is the universality of reason.

The priority and universality of reason, that is, is not a natural fact; it is a theoretical construction that is read into the head of the subject. Consider in this respect of Descartes' *cogito.* It suggests that all rational beings think in a similar way. Hegel rightly criticises this, saying that the *cogito* as *ego cogito* only applies to Descartes himself (Hegel 1955: 224). This *Hineininterpretierung* induces an erroneous idea of universality. It obliterates the very contextuality of reason, and takes universality itself to be universal. What is universal is thought of as having priority to what is not, because what is universal is true. This is, however, not due to the characteristics of universality itself, but a value judgement that is anything but universal. The privilege of the universal cannot therefore, without a fallacy, be of universal value.

As a consequence of this, what is thought of as universal, and hence rational, generates the belief in a direct access to reality. The theory resulting from this approach is presented as a theory of reality, while, at best, it is only a theory about reality.

Rousseau favours, that is, a specific conception of rationality that is supposed to be in the head of each and every subject. If citizens are to adapt their reason to 'reason' altogether, it is because the contract, the truth of which raises no doubt for Rousseau, expresses reason itself. In doing so, that is, the subject is held to be free. This articulation of freedom, however, amounts to a theory about freedom, not a theory of freedom, as discussed in Chapter 4.

A closer look under the surface of Rousseau's argument shows how it unduly neglects the interaction within social space, that is, the domain of meaning and not exclusively of truth. He intends to transform the latter into a political space under the auspices of truth. Social space, however, is not primarily the realm of truth; it is the realm of meaning from which the subject emerges qua subject.[8]

For Rousseau, the subject's natural goodness is corrupted by culture, most prominently economics, causing relations of dependence that jeopardise freedom. This is what happens in social practices, in the absence of a political space as Rousseau conceives it. This pessimistic view is at the root of the following alternative: the continuation of the shackles of the state of nature, or the transformation of the latter into a political space. There is no real choice, since the

8 As explained in Chapter 2.

construction of political space and its consequential institutionalisation of conflict must be chosen in the name of truth. The choice is based on an exclusionary reason.

The transformation of social space into a political space goes hand-in-hand with a substitution of truth for meaning. According to this interpretation, the realm of meaning in which others are recognised as part of 'us', is set aside together with the semantic potential that social interaction could engender. Put differently, the only type of interaction that Rousseau – in line with Hobbes – recognises is interaction based on legal rules. The institutionalisation of their production is combined with a proxy theory of legitimation.

The Operationalisation of Political Space: Legislation

Hobbes's and Rousseau's distrust of subjects' capacities to act on conceptions of freedom pushes them towards a theory that is helpful in avoiding the possibilities of conflict connected with the absence of any predetermined meanings. Hobbes provides us with the best starting-point for discovering what the misconception of freedom consists of.

Hobbes and Rousseau argue that the only way to endow social relations with true morality is to enter into the social contract. The operationalisation of political space involves legislation. Legislation consists in the imposition of external limitations on freedom that are conceptions about freedom. Any external limitation, according to their proxy theory of legitimation, is justified or legitimate by its very existence.

Hobbes then is correct in saying that freedom consists of the absence of any external limitations. These limitations, however, are not necessarily of a physical nature, such as, for example, gravitational force which may prevent man from flying. The external limitations, that is, must also be taken in the normative sense, as the absence of normative limitations. Because the *ius naturale* is a right to all, there is no normative limitation on any subject's rights.[9] Hobbes quite realistically suggests that any action can give rise to conflict. I disagree, however, with his overall approach for mainly three reasons.

First, in realising his freedom, any subject acts on a conception of freedom, the meaning of which is inherently social. The subject, that is, does not discover conceptions of freedom within his own mind, nor does he find them 'out there' growing in the forest. The fact that meanings are social in that they emerge from interaction is implied by their conflictual character. Hobbes suggests that any meaning, conflictual in its emergence as it is under the interpretation proposed here, can make the latent state of war break out at any moment.

Secondly, it should be remembered that I argued that it would be inconsistent with Hobbes's theory to speak of a naturally bad man. Man is not good or bad by nature, since 'human nature' as a concept has no natural existence. If the war of

9 The *ius naturale* is normative only in relation to God.

all against all is due to human nature, it is because man is imperfect. If any subject has a right to all, this right includes the right to define the meaning of the laws of nature, that is, to act on conceptions of freedom and only on them.

Third, because freedom is from the very outset framed as a right, it could be expected that any right of A corresponds to B having a duty to respect A's right. A having a general right, that is, a right that does not arise out of any special relationship or transaction between men, should then include a corresponding duty of any B not to interfere with it. From the claim that A has a right, it must follow that no one can interfere with it without justification. Put differently, unless it is recognised that interference with another's freedom requires a justification, the notion of right would have no place in morals (Hart 1955).

Hobbes's spurious anthropological theory results in some version of the might-is-right thesis. From the moral perspective, because no duty of B corresponds to the right of A, the sovereign will be called upon to frame that duty. The anthropological theory, the might-is-right thesis, and the resulting *bellum omnium contra omnes* call for some limitations. A theory of freedom, so Hobbes claims, does not work, so he turns to what was called a theory about freedom. In a rudimentary form, it is when implementing the laws of nature that the power of the sovereign introduces the necessary limitations to the *ius naturale*.

The laws of the sovereign are semantic determinations of the laws of nature. Under Hobbes's nominalistic theory of meaning, the concepts in these laws are semantically meaningless until their meaning is constructed. In the state of nature, every subject is more likely to define them in the way that best fits its own interests, including his desire for power over the other. Under Hobbes's argument that man must be willing to give up his right to all, that is, his *ius naturale*, the laws of nature become meaningful and become morally as well as legally binding.

This moral duty stems, first, from the laws of nature that are binding even in the state of nature because they are commands of God. They are, however, far from being effective. Secondly, they are binding due to the *pactum subjectionis*, that is, the promise to submit to the laws of the sovereign. To promise obedience and to withhold it afterwards is a contradiction according to Hobbes (Goyard-Fabre 1975: 133). The promise of obedience gives rise to the sovereign's right to it.

The moral duty that is added to the *ius naturale* via the social contract makes the system complete. The price, however, is not a minor one. Hobbes argues that, because subjects are unable to live according to conceptions of freedom, it is better to abandon this right, and to submit to the sovereign who will impose his definitions of the laws of nature. The latter could have been workable in the state of nature, had men not been living in the conditions of fear that define their situation. The morality that was lacking in the state of nature, that is, the duty to respect the right of others, needs a sovereign to impose it. He does so in terms of conceptions about freedom.

Freedom, as argued in chapter 4, necessarily requires a concretisation in terms of a conception in order for action to be possible. This was referred to as the circumstances of human action. However, it can be seen more clearly that the types of conceptions which the subject can act upon come in two versions, that is, a moral version and a political one. The moral version prevails in the state of nature, while the political version emerges from the contract itself.

Following conclusion of the contract, all of the choices made, that is, all of the limitations on freedom in terms of conceptions, will be conceptions about freedom, since they are the sovereign's, not the subject's. This is the core claim of the proxy theory of legitimation in Hobbes's contract.

The civil laws, according to Hobbes's argumentation, appear to be embedded in the laws of nature, the only true morality. Civil laws and natural laws are one and the same, as we read from *Leviathan*, so that truth and meaning can be presented as naturally belonging together. The truth of the matter is, however, that meaning introduced by the civil laws is imposed from the outside on the laws of nature, which provide the ontological foundation for the former. Through the intervention of civil laws, the subject finally attains an ontological definition of himself, so that his moral life will unfold under the auspices of truth, right and duty. Moral action, that is, is confined to following the rules of the sovereign, that is, to acting on conceptions about freedom.

The connection between truth and the democratic organisation of political space, as the theorists of the social contract propose it, leads straightforwardly to strong legalism. It was shown in Chapter 5 that strong legalism, including the 'thereness' of law, relies on the premise that law represents reality. The analysis of the social contract reveals how the idea of the representation of reality and the truth of the social contract flow into the idea of the 'thereness' of the law. Law represents reality in that it is based on the social contract, the clauses of which are universal, hence true. We face the problem of freedom as it is related to the representational view. The social contract is, so to speak, imposing itself in the name of truth. A similar conclusion can be drawn from Rousseau's theory of the social contract.

In placing the organisation of political space under the auspices of truth, both Hobbes and Rousseau misconstrue the reflexive character of freedom. The reflexive character of freedom includes the active intervention of the subject in the limitations or determination of freedom. Under their theories, the reflexive use of freedom is limited to the 'one shot' of the social contract. The social contract, as noted above, provides a 'one shot' legitimation for all of the laws of the sovereign.

It should be remembered that, for both Hobbes and Rousseau, conflict puts social peace in jeopardy. With Hobbes's idea of conflict, we are invited to adhere to the view that the subject is inherently imperfect, related to the Augustinian view that man's native impulses are essentially turned to evil ends. Rousseau, for his part, rather tends to the Socratic view, according to which the subject is essentially good, but his life in society has corrupting effects on him. Both, that is, conclude from this the necessity of a social contract that endows interaction with the true morality that is missing in the state of nature.

The two theorists of the social contract are in error on at least one point, that is, the historical situatedness of the subject. The need for the social contract flows from their denial of the time dimension, one of the main aspects, one remembers, of strong legalism that was discussed in chapter 5.

They ward off the risk of conflict, at its worst the *bellum omnium contra omnes*, by withdrawing the subject from his social environment and assigning him to political space. This operation is justified in their opinion in the name of truth. Consistent as this may sound, the starting premise of their argument is, however, questionable. What justifies the truth of Hobbes's anthropological premise, or Rousseau's unavoidable corruption of the subject in society? It is a questionable anthropological fixation in the former, or a spurious account of the history of culture in the latter.[10] As will be argued in the pages to come, they misconstrue freedom in the name of truth, that is, because of an epistemologisation of freedom. The resulting theory is a theory *about* freedom.

I have repeatedly referred to the idea of freedom as a *principium*, that is, freedom as (1) the starting-point and (2) the guiding idea, or *Leitmotiv* in politics and law. The distinction is an important one, and both Hobbes and Rousseau do subscribe to the first but not, or at least not sufficiently, to the second. This results in a denial of the reflexive nature of freedom, and so of freedom altogether. Any limitation of freedom on the basis of a conception that denies the reflexive nature of freedom, that is, a conception about freedom, is external to the subject. It is external in so far as the subject himself does not limit freedom on the basis of a conception of freedom.

What Hobbes and Rousseau seek is precisely the limitation of freedom in terms of conceptions about freedom, preceded by a preliminary consent to that on the basis of the social contract. Their argument essentially states that the best conception of freedom is to submit to conceptions about freedom. The imputation mechanism of the social contract makes the subject the author of these limitations. This is the essence of the proxy theory of legitimation. The proxy is an a priori limitation of freedom in that the subject does not yet know on what conceptions his freedom will be limited (Luhmann 1983: 28; 1974: 141). What he does know, however, is that it will not be his conceptions of freedom, but conceptions about freedom.

According to this idea, there is virtually no limit to the limitations on freedom that a sovereign can impose. Once the subject has consented to the contract, his freedom can be limited by the Hobbesian sovereign whose rules are morally binding, whatever their content. Rousseau's sovereign, for his part, can transform any limitation into a binding norm provided that the majority is favourable to it. Although to a lesser extent, the subject is surrendered to conceptions about freedom, in so far as he belongs to the minority.[11]

---

10 Whereas Kant (1996: 89–90) argues that we have not learned from experience that men use violence as a maxim of action in order to enter into war with each other.

11 There are some restrictions on the power of the sovereign. All the conventions on which a limitation of freedom is based must be general. And the citizen can enjoy freedom, that is, act on a conception of freedom, in so far as freedom is not limited by a

If any limitation sooner or later can become binding upon the subject, the reflexive nature of freedom risks being annulled. This is a consequence of the contractual argument, according to which it is a priori better that subjects act on conceptions about freedom than on conceptions of freedom. It seems to Hobbes and Rousseau that this is the only way to avoid the risk of conflict.

Rights

Hobbes's and Rousseau's theories include respectively a thinner and a thicker version of political rights, defined as the right to participate in the ruling of the state. The common basis for these participation rights is the social contract. By entering into the contract, they transform themselves into citizens after which they become the authors of the norms by which they abide. The detour consists in the intervention of the sovereign in Hobbes, and the legislator preceding the sovereign's legislative act in Rousseau.

Decisions of the sovereign are binding upon the citizens who are supposed, under the social contract, to have consented to this procedure when signing up to the social contract. Their political right to participation is then condensed in their consent to the contract. In consequence, every rule of the sovereign, whatever its content, will be imputed to them, as if they were its author. Their right to participation, that is, is concentrated in the proxy to the sovereign.

A result of this is that they only abide by norms to which they have themselves consented, at least by proxy, in that they have consented to the procedure for the creation or change of norms within political space. Because of the proxy nature of their consent to the social contract, these norms are imputable to them, so that they cannot be criticised afterwards for being illegitimate. No one can come up against his own action.

The proxy in both Hobbes and Rousseau is nearly complete. If for Hobbes, the *ius naturale*, or the right to everything, is to be limited for the purpose of achieving peace or self-defence (Hobbes 1966c: 118), hence it could be concluded that not all rights must, or even can be, surrendered to the sovereign.

If the right to one thing is given up, the right to *everything* no longer has the same extension and thus no longer exists as such. If, for example, the right to kill others is transferred to the sovereign, the *ius naturale* is affected in its overall character. The limit that is built into the transfer could result in the conclusion that after entering into the contract the subject finds himself left with a considerable volume of rights, that is, those rights that are not necessary for the realisation of peace and self-defence.

This conclusion is, however, not correct. 'After' the contract, when the subjects live in political space, it is up to the sovereign to define the content of their rights.

---

conception about freedom, see Rousseau 1997a: 61–4; Hobbes 1966c: 206–7; Kelsen 1967; 1934; Wintgens and Lindemans 1986

He has the power to define what is 'necessary for the realisation of peace and self-defence'. As a consequence of the Hobbesian version of the contract, the sovereign can define everything in so far as it serves peace and security. If this results in a totalitarian state ruled by a sovereign who has even the right to kill his subjects if this serves the purpose of the state, he is permitted to do so, again with their a priori consent.

There is one notorious exception to this, and that is the right to resist violence. Abandoning this right would be inconsistent with the overall logic of Hobbes's construction. If the state is founded with a view to protecting life and securing peace, the subject cannot transfer his right to survival to the sovereign. This clause of the contract would be void because it violates the laws of nature (Hobbes 1996c: 127). The right to his own life is what the subject keeps in his own hands, in that he cannot promise not to defend himself when the sovereign threatens him with death. However, as noted above, this right to resist does cancel the sovereign's right to kill you if deemed necessary for peace and security. The sovereign's right to take someone's life outweighs what may appear as a glimpse of liberalism in Hobbes's theory. Apart from the somewhat spurious right to resistance, the sovereign leaves the subject with no other rights than those he confers upon them.

Things are different with Rousseau. He also has a proxy theory of legitimation in that subjects bind themselves to all others to submit to the norms that the sovereign will promulgate. They are bound by these norms in that they bind themselves. This is a proxy, since, from the moment of the social contract onwards, the chain of legitimation turns out to be irreversible. As in Hobbes, subjects are considered as the authors of the norms they act upon.

The form of the law makes any content just. Since all citizens have consented to the procedure of the social contract, that is, majority decision, no one can contradict his own actions. Since all the citizens have participated in the contract – this is what makes them citizens – and since there is only one contract, the sovereign is not different from their personal unification with all the others (Rousseau 1997a: 50). Once they enter into the contract, they are part of the sovereign. 'The words *subject* and *sovereign* are identical correlatives whose idea is combined in the single word "Citizen"' (ibid.: 111). In keeping with the idea of the indivisibility of sovereignty, no citizen can be excluded from citizenship against his will. This provides Rousseau's approach with a version of political rights that rely on a stronger basis than in Hobbes's account.

The theory of rights, however, is limited to that. Any other right which the subject may have had within the state of nature is, through the contract itself, transferred to the sovereign, of which any subject is a member. Therefore, the rules promulgated by the latter are the citizen's own work, as a consequence of which he is ultimately only obeying himself. The rights he has must, by very definition, stem from the authority of the sovereign. Without that, they lack the normative character of a right, since everything he had was transferred to the state and since there can be no law beyond the state (Julliard 1985).

Considering the matter from the perspective of political rights, both Hobbes and Rousseau find themselves tending towards a democratic legitimation of law. They consider the participation of the citizen in the construction of the limitation of freedom – which I consider the proper definition of law – to be essential. They satisfy this democratic requirement in that all the citizens subscribe to the contract, so that, in the end, all participate in the construction of political society and its legal system.

The political right to equal participation is a necessary condition in order for their theories to be consistent. If the basic premise of their theories is freedom in the absence of any normative limitation, the starting-point of any limitation of freedom must be freedom itself. Hence the necessity of participation in the contract.

To this both Hobbes and Rousseau add a premise that affects the concept of freedom in a crucial way. The premise they add, and on which they found the necessity of the social contract, is the possibility of war. War is an essential aspect of human association, in that subjects have a right and a duty to fight for their lives, as Hobbes says. They may have become dependent upon each other due to the evolution of the economy, as we read from Rousseau. Hobbes for his part holds that war must be prevented, while Rousseau considers that the proceduralisation of conflicts is the best way of solving them.

Their argument is presented as if this premise, of a purely factual nature, affects freedom in a normative manner. Their argument, that is, focuses on the inevitability of the contract, the conclusion of which is an exclusionary reason. No reason can be good enough not to enter into it.

Everyone has an equal 'volume' of freedom in the situation where there are no limits. This is not due to basic equality, but to the absence of limitations. It must be remembered that this is freedom as the *terminus ad quem* of our *quaestio originis*. Equality comes into play with the operationalisation of freedom, not as basic equality. In the absence of any limitation, no one has an a priori right to limit anyone else's freedom, that is, to impose his conception of freedom (Locke 1963c: 339–40).

Hobbes and Rousseau – not unrealistically – suggest that this is barely workable. This is, however, not a normative claim. Their version is of a rational choice theory that frames an exclusionary reason for entering into the contract.

The question arises as to the voluntary nature of the contract itself. According to the general line of the argument until now, the contract is a species of epistemologised philosophy which transforms practical problems into theoretical ones. Chapter 5 took some time in showing the depth of this process of epistemologisation by analysing the time dimension of strong legalism. The practical conclusion is, again, that the subject is not considered to be capable of acting on conceptions of freedom and therefore is to act on conceptions about freedom.

It turns out that the consequences for freedom are drastic, if not draconian. What the subject is required to do is to surrender to the power of the state that is supposed to have been created by his own will. This power counterbalances the possibility of war, always lurking round the corner. In Hobbes as well as in Rousseau, the state determines the extent of its power, in that it can decide what limitations are necessary in order to keep the peace. In the end, for both of them, this limitation can be complete, in that anything can be forbidden by the state if it is deemed useful for that purpose.

As argued at the beginning of this chapter, the chain of legitimation that starts with the conclusion of the social contract is – leaving aside the reasons for which it is concluded – irreversible. According to the diagnosis of Hobbes and Rousseau, the reason why this is so can be articulated as follows. Because of the risk of war, that is, some total conflict, the breaking-out of a conflict must be surmised in advance. The state, so they believe, is strong enough to exorcise the demon of conflict. If the chain of legitimation were not irreversible, then some – or even most, or all – of the limitations imposed by the state could be questioned over and over again, so that conflict on the scale they suggest might reappear.

The irreversible chain of legitimation that constitutes the organisation of political space provides a straightforward justification for strong legalism, the main aspects of which were discussed in chapter 5. We shall now briefly compare the above with the conclusions from that chapter.

First, Hobbes's, and Rousseau's view of man and society claims to be true, as a representation of reality. Because of the ontological anchoring of their views, their theories are framed as a representation-reproduction of reality. However, their access to reality turns out to be an indirect one, by which their theories, far from reproducing reality, in actual fact construct it.

Politics, that is, is the source of conflict *par excellence*, and the aim of the construction of political space is precisely to allay these conflicts. Law as the spin-off of the construction of political space is the opposite of politics, the warrior effects of which it is called upon to banish. In switching the perspective from construction to reproduction, that is, in arguing that what is a construction of reality is a mere reproduction of it, we see the strategy of strong legalism at work.

Secondly, the construction both of political space and of the law is naturalised. The legitimation programme seeks to prevent conflicts from arising, and this is what would happen were the chain of legitimation reversible. Hence, it is not. In proceeding along these lines, they freeze time. The representation of reality aims at truth, and truth is eternal.

Third, the irreversible nature of the chain of legitimation fits in equally well with the instrumentalist position of strong legalism. If values are to be chosen, the risk of conflict increases. The problem becomes apparent when it becomes clear that the realisation of freedom by the subjects relies on a conception of freedom.

Because of the conflicts these choices generate, subjects are required to transfer the ability to choose – that is, their capacity to live according to conceptions of freedom – to the state. The state will provide the true morality that will frame their relationships. Since they do not know yet which limitations will be imposed on them at the 'moment' of the contract, the latter implies that the state's choices are simply substituted for their conceptions of freedom. Since these 'choices' are true, they will not appear as choices that, by their very nature, are contingent.

Fourth, as a consequence of their reliance on natural science as the apex of rationality, and because of the naturalisation of political space and the subsequent laws that emerge from there, law itself is considered to belong to reality and thus can be studied with the help of the method of natural science.

Fifth, and finally, since the organisation of political space or the state is the only purpose of the social contract, and since only the state can freely decide what limitations can be imposed, the state is to be considered the only source of law, hence resulting in etatism.

The next section will develop this last point. The naturalisation of politics and subsequently of law from the epistemological perspective goes hand-in-hand with, and is supported by, the concept of sovereignty. It is this concept, so I will argue, that contributes to the irreversibility of the legitimation chain in procedural theories of legitimation.

Sovereignty: The Black Box in the Chain of Legitimation

The irreversibility of the chain of legitimation is sealed with the introduction of a concept familiar in political philosophy since Bodin, who framed it in a version that was promised a career until the twentieth century. It is the concept of sovereignty. There is not too much exaggeration in saying that this concept is at the basis of at least as much confusion as it intended to resolve. The concept originally belonged to theology and referred to the rational interpretation of God's omnipotence. On this interpretation, God is radically simple in that his intelligence and his will cannot be separated. This necessarily entails the radical contingency of the world, as demonstrated in Chapter 1.

According to the secularisation thesis of Carl Schmitt, the concepts of political philosophy are secularised theological concepts (Schmitt 1934: 49), to which Blumenberg has added the thesis that secularisation is a legal process of dispossession or expropriation of the sacred, which I interpret as a side-effect of nominalism (Blumenberg 1983: 19 ff.) It is important to remember in this respect what was said regarding jusnaturalistic theories of legitimation under which human law is legitimate with reference to a norm that is not available in that it cannot be changed. According to the secularised version of sovereignty, the political sovereign is the ultimate source of any law. Under Austin's version, the sovereign is legally unlimited (Austin 1971: 254 ff.) and his commands count as law (cf. Bentham 1970: chapter 10).

The concept of sovereignty is helpful in confirming the irreversible direction of the chain of legitimation. In assigning sovereignty to the ruler, the participants establish an irreversible chain of legitimation for his acts. With the social contract, sovereignty comes down to earth, so to speak. Its function, so it appears, is to obstruct the reversibility of the chain of legitimation, if it were to come to mind to question the legitimacy of the power of the sovereign. This is simply impossible; since sovereignty has no limits, the power called 'sovereign' cannot be limited and therefore cannot be questioned, neither by the power holder nor as a matter of logic by those subjected to his power. Both Hobbes and Rousseau agree on that: sovereignty is inalienable and it cannot be divided (Hobbes 1966c: 167–8; Rousseau 1997a: 57–9).

The similarity between the power of the sovereign and God's omnipotence lies in the fact that God owes nothing to his subjects. The mortal God, or the sovereign more specifically, owes no justification to the citizens. His power is the highest, and therefore, as Austin suggested, is unlimited from the legal point of view. Hart's familiar critique is that the highest is always determined relative to the system within which it operates. This means that no power, not even the highest, is legally unbound.

The concept of sovereignty, therefore, releases the sovereign from the requirement to give any justification for his rulings. This is the logical consequence of the proxy theory of legitimation. Under the proxy theory, law is legitimate. The participants in the contract agreed to create an instance that holds ultimate power within the political space they are establishing. If they do, there can be no argument for criticising the outcomes of this power. A legally unlimited power only reinforces the idea that no justification is needed for its exercise. Hence, any proposition of the sovereign is *ipso facto* justified under the proxy which the participants have previously given to him.

Unsurprising but decisive is that Hobbes's and Rousseau's strong legalistic sovereign is always right. Their sovereign cannot err, since his definitions of the laws of nature are true, according to Hobbes. In a similar vein, Rousseau holds that the sovereign expresses the general will that cannot err; so his laws are unquestionable as well (Hobbes 1966c: 163; Rousseau 1997a: 59–60). They are just because they are laws.

The consequences of this view are not hard to understand. Once sovereignty has been built into political space, it operates as a black box. The ultimate source of power, as Kant later claims, is unfathomable (Kant 1996: 95 ff.). Any of its outputs is just by definition, as both Hobbes and Rousseau confirm. As a matter of logic, the magic of the black box prevents anyone questioning the outputs in any of its aspects. The participants cannot complain since they have created the sovereign and promised submission in Hobbes. They have created the sovereign and are part of it in Rousseau. As for Kant, they were under a moral duty to enter into a State (Kant 1996: § 44), so they cannot contest the subsequent duties resting on their shoulders.

Sovereignty on this view can be called upon to justify both a monarch by divine right and a totalitarian state. The monarch by divine right is the representative of God on earth, and Hobbes's sovereign is after all not far from that. Although the subjects have created him, he is called on to implement the laws of nature that are the laws of God. Under a monarchy of divine right, the monarch is exercising the divine prerogatives that are included in, and which constitute, sovereignty. On this view, the sovereign does not have the power to violate the laws of God. As a matter of logic, he has no permission to do so, although he has the power to define their content according to Hobbes.

Sovereignty also combines with the totalitarian state to the invention of which both Hobbes and Rousseau contributed. Hobbes's contribution can be found in his assimilation of law and morality, so that any law of the sovereign *ipso facto* entails a moral obligation to obey it, whatever its content may be.[12]

Hobbes for his part comes close to the totalitarian state, in that the subjects can directly appoint an omnipotent sovereign. In acting in this way, they can realise without any deviation Plato's paradox of democracy.[13] A majority can appoint one person who will decide about what is right or wrong, without any point of return inside political space, except the benevolence of the tyrant himself who may relinquish power. Here, as elsewhere, the chain cannot be reversed.

Rousseau's contribution may be said to consist in his establishing the tyranny of the majority. In contrast to Hobbes, however, he wards off the realisation of the paradox of democracy, since the majority cannot appoint a tyrant without dividing sovereignty. At least this path to the totalitarian state is barred, since this act of appointment would be void.

Taking sovereignty as a black box, we enter into the realm of absolute power that, by its very nature, cannot be legally limited, as Austin has argued. Even Kant, for whom metaphysics is only legitimate within the limits of reason, does not hesitate to connect the rules of the sovereign with commands of God, since one must act *as if* the rules of the sovereign are His commands.[14] Absolute power is disconnected from anything [ab-solutus]. If it is a source, it must at the same time be the origin, that is, a self-referential beginning.

The black box metaphor aptly throws light on another aspect of the norms that emerge from political space. Sovereignty, that is, covers all of the operations of the ruler with perfect rationality. From this perspective, the rationality of the legislator, as a premise of legal interpretation according to strong legalism, is usefully supported by the concept of sovereignty. Sovereignty, that is, plays a decisive role in the legitimation chain that is proper to strong legalism that has been analysed in this chapter. Leaving aside some weak right to resist the violence of the sovereign in Hobbes, and the right not to be excluded from the sovereign in Rousseau, the appeal to sovereignty can outweigh all other 'rights'. Under strong legalism, the rationality of the legislator, in that it reflects the irrefutable presumption of the perfection of his rules, is thus legal science's epistemological version of sovereignty.

---

12 This is a version of positivism that I have called 'juridical positivism', as opposed to 'legal positivism', where such a duty does not exist; see Wintgens 1991a; 1991b.

13 Plato 1946: VIII, 562c, 305. This 'paradox of democracy' makes Popper (1966: 123 ff.) plead for a limited version of sovereignty.

14 Kant 1996: 95 ('all authority is from God'), 108 ('the legislator is holy').Cf. Ost and Lenoble 1980: 443 ff.

What is of interest in the foregoing in relation to the theme of this book is the connection between sovereignty and the theory of law. More specifically, we should explore some of the aspects of the relationship between sovereignty and the validity of law in order to shed some more light on the possibilities of an alternative view, that is, a view that does justice to the subject qua subject.

One way of seeing the matter is as follows. Where the power of the sovereign is unlimited, it can be observed that the content of laws is a matter of choice. Since the starting-point for the construction of political space is freedom, no constraints as to the concretisation of freedom can be said to exist before that.

From the time when the sovereign comes into existence, any of his choices are legitimate in that they are imputed to the subjects who have consented to the contract. Therefore, what the sovereign says – whatever he says – becomes law. Whether this leads to totalitarianism or not is a matter of political philosophy, which is of no concern here. What is, however, of concern is that, at best according to a few formal rules of procedure, any concretisation of freedom can acquire the form of a conception about freedom, to which the subject is supposed to have consented.

When conceptions about freedom take on the form of a legal rule, they are substituted for conceptions of freedom. This is what the mechanism of political space produces: each and every conception of freedom can be transformed into a conception about freedom. When we consider this from the perspective of the subject, any of his conceptions of freedom are automatically outweighed by conceptions about freedom. Put differently, what the subject is left with are conceptions of freedom that remain at large, without any normative value. They cannot be relied on in opposition to the sovereign's conceptions about freedom.[15]

The subject-citizen is therefore under constant pressure of redefinition by the sovereign, in that any of his conceptions of freedom can, without further reason, be pushed aside in favour of a conception about freedom. The main reason is, as a matter of fact, the contract and the consent to its further procedural development within political space, without knowing in advance what the content of the sovereign's will may be.

Without necessarily leading to totalitarianism in the usual sense of the word, it installs into political space the embryo of the Trojan horse of overwhelming state action, nowadays established under the name of the 'welfare state'. If it need not result in a totalitarian state that has a right of life and death over its citizens, it does not prevent the state from playing a serious role in economic life, both as a partner and – mainly – as a regulator. This can be considered as yet another form of totalitarianism, that is, the fact that the sovereign regulates virtually every aspect of social life. This

---

15 This would amount to an act of resistance, which is a contradiction for Hobbes. The subject promises obedience when entering into the contract. To promise obedience and not fulfil the promise is a contradiction as Hobbes holds (see *supra).* On the inability of a right to withstand the rules of the sovereign and the contradiction this entails, see also Kant 1996: 438.

form of totalitarianism is founded in the belief of unlimited instrumentalism, and the ability of the law to steer virtually every aspect of social interaction.

In conferring rights and duties on economic partners, marriage partners, and citizens as claimants of social security rights, in defining the content of education by subsidising institutions that teach the 'right' contents, or by withholding recognition of degrees from institutions that in its opinion do not (to mention but a few examples), political space, and with it sovereign power, seeps into the very definition of the subject: his rights are constructed by the sovereign, so that the former is only what he is by the grace of the latter which is, in turn, as we read from Rousseau, by the very fact of being, what it ought to be.[16]

What the concept of sovereignty allows then, apart from the spheres that are nowadays protected by human rights or pre-state rights, is a redefinition of the subject in terms of rights and duties according to rules. As a result, the normative density of the external limitations of the sovereign, as we observe today, reaches such a degree as to deny any place for the subject qua subject, that is, a subject as a responsible moral agent capable of social interaction without a state looking over his shoulder – and without a subject looking over his back to check whether there is no state that is structuring, pre-structuring, or restructuring his actions on conceptions of freedom.

Any procedurally correct proposition which the sovereign makes acquires the form of law. It results not only in a permanent outweighing of the conceptions of freedom of the subjects, but also in a virtually unlimited number of limitations. According to the proxy theory of legitimation that operates against the background of political space, the participants in the contract are ready to accept any of the limitations that are imposed by the sovereign. Any proposition that recognisably has the characteristics of a rule from the sovereign is therefore a valid and legitimate law.

There are good grounds then to believe that the exponential growth of the legal system is nowadays an unintended inheritance from the Modern philosophical project. Any proposition that attains the required form is, for that reason alone, a valid limitation of freedom. Put differently, any proposition that attains the stamp of the sovereign is a valid rule. You may call this 'stamp validity'.

Stamp validity is not outweighed by rights of any sort. Rights only limit the possible content of norms, and not their volume, number, or normative density. Thus if rights reserve domains of action where conceptions of freedom prevail, they do not prevent the overwhelming growth of limitations or conceptions about freedom in the domains covered by the proxy. The tremendous impact of strong legalism induced by the proxy theory of legitimation will only be strengthened as long as no counterweight is set up against its nearly perverse effects.

---

16 Rousseau 1997a: 52: 'The Sovereign, by the mere fact that it is, is always everything it ought to be.'

Legalism and Legislation

Under the proxy theory of legitimation, any formally correct ruling of the sovereign is *ipso facto* legitimate. On this point, Lawrence Friedman's analysis of Weber's legalism is instructive. According to Friedman, legalism includes the duty for the *judge* to give reasons for his decision. Judges cannot avoid taking decisions; in addition to that, they are expected to give reasons for them and they are confined to a – more or less – closed system of rules (Friedman 1966: 150).

Legislatures for their part do not have to provide reasons for their decisions. Their decisions are, as Weber puts it, irrational (ibid.: 154). Legislation, so we read from Friedman's observations, is non-legalistic in that it cannot be deduced from any existing set of norms, like judicial rulings can and must be. This is not the same, however, as saying that there are no reasons at all for legislative enactments. What is said, is that legislation does not contain reasons in that it does not express the reasoning that lies behind its enactment.

The idea that legislators, unlike judges, need not give reasons for their decisions is, according to Friedman, the proper characteristic of legalism. Legal systems, as we read from Weber, contain within themselves a principle or several principles of legitimacy. When the logic of derivation is a closed one, it is called legalistic. If it is, on the contrary, open, it is called non-legalistic (ibid.: 158–60).

This characterisation of legalism is, in my view however, unsatisfactory. It suggests that, depending on the actor in the system, the latter is either legalistic or non-legalistic. Thus the system is legalistic from the perspective of the judge, and non-legalistic from the perspective of the legislator. On this view, Friedman draws a grand dividing line between legislative and judicial decisions. Judges should give reasons for their decisions, showing that and how they are following rules. Legislators for their part are exempt from this. They are, unlike judges, not bound by a closed set of norms.

This view easily slips into error, since it implies the suggestion that judges follow rules by merely deductively applying them. Their following rules amounts to a demonstration of how they infer specific decisions from general norms, constituting the essence of judicial reasoning. From there it follows that legislators create norms that judges apply. The former is a matter of decision, hence a form of action, while the latter is held to be a matter of application, hence a cognitive operation. This cognitive operation, as noted above, represents earlier steps in the chain of legitimation.

Both positions are in need of qualification, through which some similarity between the activities of the legislator and the judiciary can be established. Judges, like legislators, take decisions, that is, they make norms. Judges make individual norms (Kelsen 1967: 19, 72, 233 ff.), while legislators make general ones. Judges should take their decisions within the framework of the norms set out by the legislator.

This is what the separation of powers requires. In making their decisions, they should show how they act, that is, they are required to give the reasons that support their decisions. Judges, in making their decisions, do follow the rules of the legislator; they do not merely apply them. Their following of rules will become apparent from the reasons they give in support of their decisions. If they were only applying norms in a syllogistic manner, no reasons should be given because anyone could easily establish whether a decision is right or wrong, just as anyone can check whether a conclusion is correctly drawn from any given premises. This approach was mentioned in the discussion of the role of legal science in chapter 5.

My claim is that legislators in turn, like judges, do follow rules. There is no doubt that legislators are bound by the norms of the constitution. This is one of the essential points of the rule of law. It makes even less sense to hold, as with judges, that the legislator's compliance with norms of the constitution means that they apply these norms. They follow rules in making decisions, like judges do.

This means that the separation of powers points to different moments in the chain of legitimation. The legislator speaks before the judge, and the latter cannot reverse the chain without encroaching upon the legislator's domain, nor can the subject, in the absence of specific provision, challenge decisions – legislative or others – that were issued earlier along the chain.

Apart from manifest differences, the claim here amounts to an articulation of the similarity of judicial and legislative ruling, in that both make decisions while following rules. On this view of the rule of law doctrine, it makes no sense to hold, as Friedman does, that judges reason within a closed set of norms, while legislative action is open-ended. This view on both positions, in my opinion, is wrong. Judges do not reason within a closed set of norms, in that they make decisions. And legislators do not decide in an open-ended way, since they are bound by norms.

On Friedman's approach, legislative enactments reek of decisionism. Decisionism is encouraged by the idea of sovereignty, that is, the idea of the omnipotent legislator, going hand-in-hand with representationalism. According to the latter, the decisions of the legislator represent reality or they are said to be 'just there'. What we read from Friedman is thus an exemplary, though thinner, description of strong legalism than that proposed in chapter 5.

Now if both the judicial 'application' of norms and their legislative creation result from norm following, then we are in a position to direct our focus towards a consequence of this. This consequence is that, if judges follow rules and must show that and how they do this, then the legislator's following of rules will also require some justification for its issue external limitations. This position will be critically analysed further in chapter 7.

This requirement of justification is yet another reversal in the chain of legitimation. It challenges the idea of a general proxy that starts the unilateral dynamics of the chain.

From Strong Legalism to Legisprudence: The Trade-off Theory of Legitimation

Under the proxy theory of legitimation, the subject is required to give a general proxy to the sovereign via the social contract. In consequence, the subject will act on conceptions about freedom instead of on conceptions of freedom, whenever the sovereign so desires. The social contract itself is the result of one action on a conception of freedom. It could be hardly otherwise, since it must rely on freedom exercised in freedom due to freedom's reflexive character.

From that moment on, however, the reflexive character of freedom has played its role in favour of the conceptions about freedom springing from the sovereign's will. The essence of the contract then involves a switch from conceptions of freedom to conceptions about freedom as reasons for action. This switch affects the very core of freedom, that is, its reflexive character, as noted in chapter 4. Conceptions about freedom, that is, are not chosen within freedom, apart from the general proxy given to the sovereign. This proxy, as I have argued, is an exclusionary reason and therefore not a real choice.

According to this general proxy, the sovereign can regulate anything he deems fit. The Hobbesian sovereign can define the substance of natural laws. He can forbid more than the natural laws permit, though he cannot permit what natural law forbids, whatever this may mean in cases in which natural laws exist but are semantically empty. Rousseau's sovereign can regulate everything, provided that these propositional contents are approved by majority vote.

If the tyrannical aspects of their theories may be tempered by the introduction of rights that protect the citizens over against the state, it does not prevent a new form of tyranny. This new form of tyranny consists in the *overactive* sovereign that regulates everything so that, ultimately, the reflexive character of freedom is seriously affected, if not destroyed. In addition, in acting this way, the sovereign is not really confident in the capacity of the subjects to act on conceptions of freedom, and so does not really take them morally seriously. After all, the sovereign's actions are a priori justified on the basis of the proxy given in the social contract. Under this proxy, there is no requirement for any further legitimation of his increasing volume of limitations of freedom.

Over against the proxy theory of legitimation that runs along the lines of strong legalism, I will explore in the following pages the contours of the trade-off model of legitimation, and so open up the way to a legisprudential approach to legislation. As will be argued, the trade-off model theory does justice to freedom that is the *principium* of the organisation of political space.

It should be remembered that, as a *principium,* freedom is not just the starting-point of the organisation of political space. It is, and more importantly, also its *Leitmotiv*, in that it guides the elaboration of political space as a whole. What is traded off in the trade-off theory of legitimation is a conception of freedom. Any A, therefore, will act on a conception about freedom C in situation S because the sovereign has *justified* this substitution. The substitution is no longer a 'one shot' legitimation of the sovereign's ruling. Under the trade-off model, every limitation of freedom must be justified. That is the core of legisprudence: limitations of freedom must be justified.

As in the proxy theory, subjects may fail to act on their conceptions of freedom. They may fail to organise business, or education, or anything else. Failure to act on their conceptions of freedom is, however, not a priori presumed, as in the proxy theory. This failure is possible, and conflict is not excluded. Acting on conceptions of freedom does not always guarantee a successful result.

As argued in chapter 2, however, conflict is not necessarily a sign of failure. It is also a source of meaning, in that there is no binary distinction between 'conflict' and 'non-conflict' to begin with. Secondly, not every conflict is 'bad', nor will every conflict escalate into war. Some conflicts indeed are 'bad', while others, on the contrary, are 'good' or even virtuous. As a matter of fact, the seller and the buyer have conflicting interests in the good, but does this conflict escalate into war? And can it be 'prevented' without turning economics into sheer nonsense?

Unlike in the proxy theory under which the *capacity* to live or act according to conceptions of freedom is given up, in the trade-off theory the subjects only (1) give up a conception of freedom (2) for reasons provided by the sovereign.

The trade-off theory should not be taken as a challenge to the rule character of law, nor its institutional character. What the trade-off theory includes is a critique of the a priori legitimation of law under the general proxy contained in the social contract. Legislative ruling on the trade-off theory is not a priori legitimate as it was in the proxy theory. Legitimation, according to the trade-off model, consists of a justification as to why acting on a conception about freedom is preferable to acting on a conception of freedom. The legitimation of law under the trade-off theory, in short, consists in a justification of each external limitation of freedom that is a priori presumed to be legitimate or justified under the proxy theory.

According to the requirement of a justification of the external limitation of freedom, the chain of legitimation is reversed in that the unilateral nature of the proxy – that is, a proxy *from* the subjects *to* the sovereign – is to be supplemented with a justification of the external limitations *from* the sovereign *to* the subjects.

There is, therefore, some inconsistency in Hobbes's and Rousseau's concept of democracy. If the starting-point of democracy is freedom, then through its operation, freedom is replaced with something else. This amounts to saying that the *capacity* to act on conceptions of freedom is limited, up to the point of disappearing altogether. In consequence, although freedom is the starting-point of the enterprise, it is no longer its *Leitmotiv*.

Under the proxy theory, the actor does not simply give away a part of his freedom, so that, quantitatively speaking, the total 'volume' of his freedom is reduced. What is at stake here is that any limitation of freedom in terms of a conception about freedom jeopardises the moral autonomy of the actor, which amounts to a denial of the reflexive nature of freedom. Any limitation of the moral autonomy of the actor corresponds to a reduction of his capacity to act as a subject qua subject.

The articulation of the subject qua subject was, it may be remembered, the theme of the exploration in chapter 2. If strong legalism, in the wake of Hobbes's and Rousseau's theories, results in the disappearance of the subject as argued above, it will now be possible to achieve a better grasp of one of the basic reasons for this. According to strong legalism, the subject evaporates because his moral autonomy dissolves in the face of the sovereign, due to the proxy given to the latter.

As discussed in chapter 2, the restitution of the subject qua subject, that is, of the morally autonomous subject, is not to be considered identical with a claim for radical autonomy, the abolition of political space or, in short, anarchy. It does, however, call for a weighing and balancing between moral autonomy – and the possibility of acting on conceptions of freedom – and moral heteronomy – with the alleged necessity of acting on conceptions about freedom.

In line with the argument until now, the limitation of freedom to an action on conceptions about freedom cannot be *ipso facto* legitimate under a substantive model of legitimation. As a matter of fact, the latter relies for its legitimacy on a content or substance that is unavailable, correspondence to which is both a necessary and sufficient condition for the sovereign's limitations of freedom.

The democratic organisation of political space and the procedural theory of legitimation which it entails, however, is essentially a critique of these substantive models of legitimation in that it refuses to recognise any a priori content that provides legitimacy. This critique is at the basis of secularisation. Under the Blumenberg thesis, it may be remembered, it is a dispossession of the sacred. The dispossession, or 'disenchantment' in Weber's terminology, deprives any transcendent content of its legitimating power. The absence of any a priori legitimating content makes up the core of non-substantive legitimating models that have freedom as their basis.

The basic error in the proxy theory of legitimation is therefore the following. The proxy is general in that it includes submission to whatever conception about freedom may be imposed. Therefore, any conception about freedom, under the general proxy, automatically and without further reasoning outweighs any conception of freedom that competes or is incompatible with this conception about freedom. Any conception about freedom in turn, will be legitimate, that is, does not require further legitimation. The latter is, as a matter of principle, incorporated into the proxy. The proxy, so to speak, aims to achieve a general discharge of argumentation as to why a conception about freedom is preferable to a conception of freedom.

It *could* be the case that a conception about freedom is preferable to a conception of freedom; however, this, it is claimed here, cannot be presumed. If it were, this presumption would jeopardise the moral autonomy of the subject qua subject. In order to be *legitimate*, external limitations must in other words be *legitimated*. A conception about freedom must be justified, and weighed against moral autonomy. Freedom need not be justified; only its limitations need be.

Freedom as the capacity to act on conceptions of freedom is inherent in the subject *qua* subject. The subject may concretise his freedom through conceptions of freedom upon which to act. If it is a priori limited by an external organ, such as the sovereign, then in so far as the latter has unlimited power, the subject qua subject has no chance to act on conceptions of freedom. The concretisation of his freedom, that is, will be mediated by external limitations stemming from the sovereign. The general proxy of the social contract covers the latter. The proxy, then, is to be considered as a *general* trade-off of the capacity to act on conceptions of freedom. The capacity to act on conceptions of freedom is what is meant by the reflexive nature of freedom, that calls for a limitation of freedom in making use of freedom. This possibility and necessity for a limitation of freedom were called the circumstances of human action.[17] It is the reflexive nature of freedom that is expressed in moral autonomy.

The unlimited power of the sovereign in the image of the omnipotent God is, from that perspective, a reflection of the proxy, and it turns out to have the same defects as were diagnosed in Hobbes's account of the *ius naturale.* In order for freedom to have any moral dignity whatsoever, it is to be considered a right with a corresponding duty to respect everyone else's. Hobbes's account of the *ius naturale* does not include the latter. While this duty is acknowledged in principle, it is largely outweighed by the anthropological thesis (Hobbes 1966c: 110 ff.). Given the 'right' character of the *ius naturale,* it could be expected that a duty corresponds to it. It is this duty that requires that others be kept at a distance. This, however, as Hobbes argues, does not wash.

Therefore, a social contract is needed in which all the subjects submit to the sovereign. The latter, for his part, is not party to the contract, so there are no grounds for any limitation of his *ius naturale.* The sovereign, that is, remains within the state of nature, which ensures that his right cannot be limited.[18] As a matter of course, the sovereign, so it would appear, is not affected by the same inherent imperfection of the subjects in the state of nature, so that it can be expected that his way of acting will not display the same defects as the subjects' acts in the state of nature.

Hobbes inserts, as a thin normative guarantee, the right to resist the sovereign's intrusion into the subject's life. No one should abide by an act of violence from the sovereign that jeopardises his life, nor can anyone be expected to kill himself on the orders of the sovereign. Although the sovereign has no right to require the subject to act that way, he still has the power to achieve this result himself. In consequence, his power outweighs his duty, and his power is therefore unlimited.

The same argument applies *mutatis mutandis* for Rousseau. As argued in the previous chapter, the subject-citizen has a political right to participate in the sovereign. Although the majority cannot reject this right, there is no further limit to the power of the sovereign. As for Hobbes, Rousseau requires the subject to give up his capacity to act on his conceptions of freedom. He must renounce his

17 As argued in chapter 4.

18 As Locke (1963c: 392) argues. According to this hypothesis, all the subjects remain in the state of nature in relation to those who do not enter into the contract (ibid.: 393).

whole person as a subject, though he is given it back as a citizen (Rousseau 1997a: 50), thereafter remaining as free as before. What is gone for sure, however, and does not come back 'after' the contract, is his capacity to act on his conceptions of freedom whenever the sovereign has limited his freedom.

From the 'moment' the sovereign has taken over, it may be the case that the limitations of freedom have, from the material point of view, exactly the same content as that which all subjects would for themselves find out to be the best. This would, however, be a metaphysical marvel that made the contract superfluous as a whole. But apart from this theoretical possibility, the capacity to act on conceptions of freedom is removed. Each and every time the sovereign promulgates a conception about freedom, the engagement in the contract entails submission. Put differently, as under Hobbes, each and every proposition that is recognisably the sovereign's cancels any of the subject's alternative conceptions of freedom.

What both Hobbes and Rousseau invite us to do is consciously to realise a 'moral' version of the paradox of freedom. Freedom can freely be limited and surrendered to someone else, who will, from then on, exercise it. The choice not to be free is a free choice. In other words, to enter into the contract is to act on a conception of freedom. The core of the paradox lies in the transmission of the *capacity* to act on conceptions of freedom, neither in the limitation of freedom itself nor in its content. As discussed in chapter 4, in order to be operational at all, the concept of freedom needs to be limited. This is, however, different from saying, as Hobbes and Rousseau suggest, that the capacity to act on conceptions of freedom itself must be transferred.

The Trade-off Theory of Legitimation Further Explored

In this section, I will briefly point to two additional important differences between the proxy theory and the trade-off theory of legitimation.

The first difference can be articulated as follows. One might object to the trade-off model on the grounds that it criticises the proxy model and that the defects of the latter can be obviated by combining the general proxy with rights that protect moral autonomy. In that respect, we could try to make the proxy model somewhat more robust from the rights perspective. Rights, that is, can be considered moral *topoi* that serve as arguments against the interventions of the sovereign.[19] Rights, that is, could temper the transfer of moral autonomy, in that the subjects retain part of their freedom for themselves. They can, for their part, act on conceptions of freedom.

Rights are prima facie a serious candidate for tempering the overall nature of the transfer of the capacity to act on conceptions of freedom. Hobbes for his part did so with the right to resist the violence of the sovereign. Rousseau, at

19 On rights as arguments, see Perelman 1984c.

least implicitly, excluded the possibility of a limitation on the participation of the citizen in the sovereign, in that a majority cannot vote to disenfranchise a citizen group of citizens.

As regards the question as to where these rights are located, there are two hypotheses. If, on the one hand, they are granted by the sovereign, who at the same time will ensure their respect, in that he himself defines the scope of his power over against these rights, this is nothing but a mark of sovereignty itself. The rights argument is not sufficient. If, on the other hand, rights include a limitation of sovereignty though not as a grant of the sovereign, they are inconsistent with sovereignty. Again, rights will not do.

In the first hypothesis, rights are subordinated to the general proxy; in the second, they cancel out the unlimited nature of sovereignty. In the first hypothesis, rights make no sense. If they do in the second, sovereignty unlimited in turn makes no sense. The second hypothesis represents the basic premise of liberalism as advocated by, for example, Locke. In carefully avoiding most of the time the use of the term 'sovereignty', Locke can consistently argue that rights outweigh 'sovereignty', so that the latter cannot be considered to be unlimited. Sovereignty is, however, conditioned by these rights in that it cannot itself determine their scope, nor can it, in consequence, determine the scope of its own power.[20]

Only limited sovereignty that respects pre-state rights is consistent with the idea of freedom undetermined as a starting-point for the organisation of political space and as its *Leitmotiv*.

On the idea of rights as arguments, the trade-off theory shows a second difference with the proxy theory of legitimation. Not only does the proxy model entail the takeover of the capacity to act on conceptions of freedom; it also appeals to a specific form of limitation of freedom that is the law (*la loi*). Apart from the unlimited action radius of the sovereign, his means of action is unquestionably the general rule.

Rules are always and unquestionably just, so we read from both Hobbes and Rousseau. Since by their very form rules achieve justice, no alternative means seem to come to the mind of philosophers. Justice in their view does not primarily concern the distribution of goods, as it did in Aristotle. It is primarily a matter of equality. And equality, so I have argued, is parasitic on freedom that can only be limited in so far as the limitations are equal for everyone. Thus the rule characteristic of law proves to be an excellent candidate for the job of justice.

The advantage of the rule characteristic of law for Hobbes and Rousseau is twofold. Not only is a rule just according to its form, since form achieves equality, but there is also no need to discuss the ends it achieves. Any end that is formalised in terms of a general rule is by that very fact legitimate. This leads to the idea of

---

20 Locke 1963c: § 121. Since any man has these rights to property, life, and liberty from nature (ibid.: §§ 4–5) they are not created by a sovereign. Given their natural character, they cannot be withdrawn, nor can they be alienated, since the state of nature is not a state of licence (ibid.: § 6).

hidden instrumentalism, which is so characteristic of the strong legalism discussed in the previous chapter. At the same time, this approach detaches law from politics, in that politics is about values. There is no need to discuss the ends, goals, or values once they have been framed into a rule. Rules as a representation of reality, by their very nature, achieve only ends. What is more, it is precisely in order to temper the discussion on ends that the social contract needs to be established as the true foundation of political space. This was also discussed in greater detail in the previous chapter.

When law is expressed through general rules, it seems to be *a priori* justified, which puts law on the track of strong legalism. The trade-off model for its part is not a call to criticise the rule characteristic of law. It does, however, question its a priori justified character that is its main feature under the proxy model. Put differently, what the trade-off model criticises is the a priori justified end or the concretisation of freedom to be achieved, and the a priori justified relationship between the end (equality, security, and so on) and the means for achieving it.

The distinction between means and ends that is relegated to the sidelines in the proxy model throws a better light on the main characteristics of the trade-off model. Under the proxy model, the ruler determines the end, and the end comes with the rule; under the trade-off model on the contrary, what is limited is the choice of the end and the appropriate means for achieving it. This is more precisely what is traded off, since *both* the end and the appropriate means of achieving it are encapsulated in a conception about freedom. Both the end and the means of achieving it are distinct aspects of a concretisation of freedom.

Under the trade-off model, conceptions of freedom are traded off for conceptions about freedom. Both types of conceptions include a choice of means and of ends. In order to maintain the reflexive nature of freedom intact as far as possible – which is required by freedom as *principium*, in contrast to the proxy model – the limitation of freedom calls for a justification. While in the proxy model, this justification is *identical* to the proxy; in the trade-off model on the contrary, there is no general proxy. Because of this absence, every external limitation of freedom must be justified.

In answering to some critiques – mainly those who consider, like Hart, the existence of law to be a social fact – Lon Fuller has formulated an insightful idea on this point. According to him, law is a purposeful enterprise, that is, a subjection of human conduct to the guidance and control of general rules. Rules also have a purpose, and this purpose, Fuller argues, is general. It does not coincide with the purpose of the legal system altogether, which would be tantamount to a version of the proxy model.

In assigning some general, though modest, purpose to the whole institutional complex, his critiques call to mind the excesses of British and German idealism, including, among others, Hegel. This means, if I understand Fuller correctly, that he assigns a modest general purpose to the legal system as a whole – subjecting human behaviour to general rules – but at the same time does not object to the assignment of particular purposes to particular laws (Fuller 1969: 145–6).

Fuller makes an excellent point here, in distinguishing between the general purpose of a legal system and the particular purposes of laws. The general purpose of the legal system is itself related, within his theory, to some morality. The 'internal morality' of law is predominantly expressed by the rule characteristic of law and serves the moral autonomy of the agent whose conduct is guided and controlled by legal rules. The principles and inner morality encompass the generality of law, its clarity, non-retroactivity, consistent application by officials, immunity from too frequent change, and non-requirement of the impossible; they must be published properly and not be contradictory (ibid.: 39 ff.).

If there is some general purpose enshrined in a legal system, this must not be over-interpreted as meaning that the moral end which the system as a whole is serving renders any rule, by its mere existence, immune to criticism. Herbert Hart formulated an objection of this sort to Fuller's view, saying that the general morality internal to the legal system does not prevent the latter from producing morally wicked rules.[21] I agree on that, though I believe that according to Fuller's view, the chance that a rule may be morally wicked is considerably lower in an ideal system than it is in a system where no general purpose is ascribed to the legal system as a whole. In spite of the fact that legal rules may be morally wicked, the reduction of the chance that they could be so makes a legal system better.

The importance of Fuller's insight into the distinction between a modest general purpose of a legal system and particular purposes of laws is that it helps to highlight a crucial difference between the proxy model and the trade-off model that we are discussing here. If the general purpose of the legal system were sufficient to legitimate law, then no further justification for the subjection of human conduct to law would be necessary. This is precisely the essence of the proxy model.

What the legal system seeks to establish as its general purpose is the general *authority* of the legal system as a whole. That is to say that it justifies the institutional design as a whole, as a legitimate authority to limit freedom and that the system of general rules guarantees, as a matter of aspiration, some form of morality in terms of moral autonomy.

That is not, however, the whole story. It does not follow that any end is covered by the legitimacy of the authority of the system as a whole. As a matter of fact, the legitimacy of the ends, goals and values that rules seek to fulfil is not covered at all by that authority. If it were, then we would be acting under a proxy model, according to which a general proxy covered the determination of ends, goals and values.

In distinguishing between a modest general purpose of the legal system and the particular purposes of laws, the view exposed by Fuller steers a middle course that corresponds to what I mean by the trade-off model. Since ends, goals and values are not automatically justified, as the proxy model wants it, the trade-off

21 Hart 1994: 207; Rawls 1971: 59–60 (the rule of law does indeed not provide watertight guarantees for the justice of rules, but at least it provides a readiness to recognise rights and liberties of others, as well as to provide a equitable distribution of social burdens and advantages).

model requires a justification of the ends of particular laws. This means that, since freedom unlimited is the starting-point, the latter requires no justification. The fact that subjects can act on conceptions of freedom, needs no further argument on freedom as *principium*.

This points in two directions. If, on the one hand, a legal system has a general purpose, this is most similar to substantive models of legitimation, according to which law in general is connected to some normative programme. The execution of this programme, that exists 'out there' or is given, justifies the sovereign's interventions, accompanied as appropriate by sanctions. The legal system's task is to safeguard this existing normative order, and for this task, sanctions are *ipso facto* legitimate.

If, on the other hand, the general purpose of the legal system is a more *modest* one, then the relationship between law and morality is of a different nature. Under a substantive model, law should not violate morality, since this is its general purpose. Under Fuller's view, the principles of internal morality are the morality that makes law possible.[22]

In my view, however, the general purpose of law is freedom as *principium*. This means that law is to serve freedom by general rules to begin with, because of the equality requirement included in freedom. However, freedom is not only to be understood in the political sense, as freedom within political space. If it were, then the sovereign would have a proxy. As a result of that proxy, the subject qua subject would disappear, as argued above.

This, we could say, is *also* the result of the overactive sovereign who can, apart from some reserved domains covered by rights, intervene with his external limitations as he pleases, *in any other field*, with a normative density that would make any rights discourse pale. Put differently, the sovereign may issue as many external limitations as he pleases as long as he does not encroach on the domains protected by rights. This phenomenon is known as legislative inflation. Certain aspects of this were discussed in Chapter 4, which stated that 'freedom as distance' should also be interpreted as 'distance from the sovereign', that is, the over-regulating norm givers.

In contrast to this view, my claim is that any external limitation must be justified, not in general but in particular terms. This is what the trade-off theory requires. On that view, freedom as *principium* as the general purpose of the legal system is furthered by the legal system in that it *makes morality possible*. This means that the priority of the subject qua subject is to act on conceptions of freedom, and the legal system, typically consisting of conceptions about freedom, is only legitimated in so far as external limitations are justified, among other things, as an alternative for failing social interaction. This will be discussed in greater detail in the next chapter.

---

22 These principles are also labelled as: a procedural or institutional kind of natural law; the law's special morality; the principles of legality; a special morality of role; legal excellence, see, on these qualifications, Wintgens 1991b: 161 ff.

A general justification of law under the proxy model leads to a version of law as an exclusionary reason for action, that is, law as a reason for not acting on reasons other than the law itself, as has been argued by Joseph Raz (Raz 1990).

The merit of Raz's approach consists in showing that law is not merely a social fact, a point that he, like Fuller, is eager to refute. Raz infers the normativity of law from a conceptual or analytical scrutiny of the concept of law, and in doing so, like Fuller – though leaving aside some considerable differences – he assigns a general purpose to law, that is, as the provider of exclusionary reasons for action.

If I understand Raz's approach correctly, however, he adopts the perspective of rule following and not, as far as I see it, of rule creation by a legislator. Law as an exclusionary reason for action takes law from the perspective of the following of rules by subjects and their application by judges. The theory aims to establish that law as such – that is, any law – provides an exclusionary reason for action which indicates its focus on rule following and rule applying, by providing a sophisticated version of the internal point of view which made Hart famous.

When the view of law as an exclusionary reason for action is considered from the perspective of the distinction between the proxy model and the trade-off model, it follows that each rule is of and by itself an exclusionary reason for action. However, in my view, what makes a reason 'exclusionary' is not that it is a law. If this were the case, then we would be reasoning under a proxy model.

If a law is considered to be an exclusionary reason for action, it is on that ground preferable to any other reason for action. To be an exclusionary reason, according to the trade-off model, means that a rule or external norm is justified as an alternative for failing social interaction among other things, as will be argued in the next chapter.

Referring to what was argued above, it can now be said that the end of a rule, or its purpose, is to concretise the concept of freedom. The basic consideration that is excluded by the proxy model, however, is the weighing and balancing of conceptions of freedom over against conceptions about freedom. This is the case under the very proxy model itself, in that conceptions about freedom always and a priori outweigh conceptions of freedom. Conceptions about freedom are, under the proxy model, always and by themselves exclusionary reasons for action. Within the trade-off model however, an external limitation can only be considered an exclusionary reason for action if it is justified. If the justification succeeds, the law is legitimated.

This second difference between the proxy and trade-off theory of legitimation illustrates the originality of the trade-off model. A limitation of freedom is not presumed to be justified, nor is a limitation of freedom a priori legitimate. With the latter, the proxy model comes close to substantive models under which limitations of freedom are legitimate, depending on their compliance with a transcendent norm. The outcomes of the proxy model are of the same nature, in that they do not require any supplementary justification apart from the initial proxy which consists of the social contract. The proxy, as was argued above, provides legitimacy in that it is associated with an initial 'act of will'.

This is not the case with the trade-off model. Every limitation of freedom is a trade-off of a conception of freedom for a conception about freedom. According to the general premise of freedom undetermined, that is, at the basis of both the proxy model and the trade-off model, the proxy is a general trade-off. In the trade-off model on the contrary, every limitation consists of a specific trade-off.

With these characteristics of the trade-off model in mind, the next chapter will seek to explore the principles of legisprudence, of which there are four. All four principles, it will be argued, are concretisations of freedom as *principium.* Each of them articulates freedom as *principium* in its own way.

Since the principles have freedom as *principium* as their common source, in their operationalisation they constitute on another's context. They are, that is, to be read in the light of one another. This means that, since they are principles, they have to be weighed and balanced against each other. This should be kept in mind when reading the next chapter.

Chapter 7

From Proxy to Trading Off: The Principles of Legisprudence

Terminological Clarification

The term 'legisprudence', as I have developed it, is in essence a reframing of the term 'jurisprudence'. Jurisprudence is generally taken to mean legal theory or philosophy of law. The basic issue of jurisprudence is to provide theoretical insights into the judge's dealing with law, the possibilities, and limitations of a science of law, and so on. The latter is mainly conceived of as legal dogmatics. From the broader point of view, it also includes philosophical questions, like 'the nature of the law', the relationship between law and morality, and so on.

While I initially conceived of the term 'legisprudence' as a contraction of 'legislation' on the one hand and 'jurisprudence' on the other, it turned out that it had a long history of its own. Aristotle for his part refers to 'phronesis', a principle of action in politics, thus including the legislative function that leads into concrete action. 'Prudence' applied to the city then becomes 'legislative prudence' (Aristotle 1984d: VI, 8). *Prudentia* in this respect is considered to involve a steering function for human action with a stress on its prospective nature. This aspect of '*providentia*' is what Cicero in his *De Legibus* deems to be proper to legislation (Cicero 1999: I, XXII), while Aquinas for his part associates prudence with '*providentia*', a perspicacious and prognostic dealing with the future starting from the present (Aquinas 1910: II-II, q. 49, a 6).

Yet, as for the Modern period, as far as I could investigate, the term '*prudentia legislatoria*' was used, as far as I know, for the first time by Franz von Wrede in his *De Prudentia Legislatoria* published in 1622. Prudential theories become popular during the seventeenth and eighteenth centuries. One of these was presented by Conring, to name but one. Conring stresses the importance of the efficiency of law for the common good, as well as the requirement of empirical research for legislative action (Conring 2003). By the middle of the eighteenth century, attention became increasingly focused on legal science, including its scientific status, and it was within this perspective that a scientific elaboration of legislation came to the fore (Stichweh 1994; Mohnhaupt 2003a: 459–95; 2003b). More specifically, the question is asked as to whether a legislator can take decisions in an arbitrary way, or whether, on the contrary, he is constrained by principles or criteria that limit or annul his choices.

Without dwelling further on these questions than is necessary for the present purpose of terminological clarification, one scholar needs a special mention:

Johann David Michaelis, who analyses the problem of legislation from a prudential perspective. The main question he is dealing with is whether legal science is a science of legislation, or whether the legal scientist should dig deeper into the social facts, that is, should he look beyond the statutory law?

Michaelis' concern is to teach young lawyers at his university the law that will serve them in their future career. This noble concern would have passed unnoticed were it not that the class he taught addressed a specific audience or an audience who were, unlike many students today, destined for a special career. Since most of them intend to follow a political career as members of a legislature or other institutions dealing with law making, Michaelis stresses the importance of a new branch of legal science. This branch is located at the overlap of philosophy on the one hand, and '*jurisprudence*' (Fr.) on the other. He baptises it *prudentia legislatoria* (Michaelis 1973: 234–5). Yet he was preceded by Christian Thomasius (Thomasius 2003) by some decades, as well as Heinrich Ernst Kestner (2003) by half a century.

Despite the fact that Michaelis is not explicitly concerned with the contextual nature of legislation, his term has the merit of expressing well what I have in mind myself. *Prudentia* as the Latin translation of *phronesis* means 'wisdom' (Ernoud and Meillet 1994: *v* 'prudens'). The use of the term then articulates an attitude rather than a method, let alone a scientific method. Since the latter designates a model of deductive or logical reasoning, it is easy to see how *prudentia* is its opposite. Instead of deductive, or otherwise logical reasoning, it refers to a method of weighing and balancing that takes into account the social circumstances of the moment and the consequences, and hence the context, that legislative intervention will produce.

While the terminology proposed by Michaelis stems from a different perspective from the one adopted here, it shows well what is meant by 'legisprudence' as a theory of rational legislation. I shall postpone the exploration of this to the next sections.

Legislation remained largely underexposed as the object of scientific or theoretical study throughout the nineteenth century, although Bentham is a notorious exception to that. Bentham's focus was on a clear, coherent, humane and simplified legal system, thereby mainly advocating the codification of civil and criminal law. From the perspective of jurisprudence, the main line of his work consisted of the elaboration of a theoretical justification of legislation on his principle of utility (Bentham 1948).

Interest in the theoretical study of legislation revived in the twentieth century due to two path-breaking books, Sten Gagner's *Studien zur Ideengeschichte der Gesetzgebung* published in 1960, and Peter Noll's *Gesetzgebungslehre* published in 1973. Gagner's is mainly a historical exploration of the roots of what can be called a theory of legislation. Noll's *Gesetzgebungslehre* can doubtlessly be considered as the founding act of the twentieth-centurty theory of legislation.

Noll's idea is that theoretical reflection on legislation no longer belongs to philosophy, moral or any other field, but is a legal discipline. As a criminal lawyer,

Noll considers that criminology is the science of criminal legislation to which legislators appeal in their activity of creating norms. Criminology for Noll is the paradigmatic case of a *Gesetzgebungslehre* that can be expanded towards other domains of legislative intervention. He therefore adopts an approach to legal theory that mainly focuses on adjudication (what he calls *Rechtsprechungswissenschaft*) with a nearly complete neglect of legislation (Noll 1972; 1973: 29). As an alternative to the adjudicatory model of legal theory, Noll sketches out the contours of a step-by-step model of legislation, including fact finding, problem definition, elaboration of the goals of legislation and the means to reach these goals, completed with a prospective and retrospective evaluation of legislation, eventually leading to corrections (Noll 1973: 63–193).

This theoretical framework then is supplemented with principles and criteria seeking to improve legislation (Noll 1972: 164–282). Legisprudence is associated with Noll's idea of a theory of legislation in that they follow his suggestion that both judges and legislators in many respects do the same things, that is, make norms. Legislators make general norms that judges throughout their adjudicative work transform into individual norms. This functional differentiation between legislation and adjudication, however, is not identical to a simplified form of the separation of powers (Noll 1973: 48). Adjudication, that is, has some creative aspects, while legislation in turn is not a 'pure' creation.

Before exploring this issue, it is worth making two remarks. The first is again of a terminological nature; the second concerns a rough delineation of the field so as to avoid confusion from the very outset.

The term 'legisprudence' has been used within the scholarly literature, mainly in The Netherlands, to designate all the official judgments of the council of state, ministers and members of Parliament on concrete legislative proposals (Waaldijk 1994: 22, 36). From this perspective, legisprudence is a collection of the judgments of players in the legislative process concerning a concrete proposal. On this view, legisprudence is not necessarily systematic, in that a set of judgments can deal with one proposal while another set may deal with a different one. It is not theoretical in that it merely collects judgments relating to a concrete proposal; in that way, it does not include any critical reflection. From this perspective, a non-official comment, for example, from a scholar not officially involved in the legislative process, does not qualify as 'legisprudence'.

In a similar vein – though when used in a slightly different manner – the term 'legisprudence' does include the latter. Scholarly work commenting on these comments, for example, a report of the council of state on the implementation of a European directive, is referred to as 'legisprudence'(Bonnes and Florijn 1995). It is most similar to classical dogmatic legal writing, in that it describes and systematises judgments made in response to a concrete legislative proposal. It may include a critique and/or suggestions for improving the legislative process.

Most of the time, this type of scholarly writing does not include a critical reflective attitude as to its scientific, viz. theoretical character. It is in this lack of theoretical articulation that this chapter originates. Its purpose is to explore the contours of a theory of legislation that not only describes the official acts that accompany the emergence of new rules. It will be straightforwardly argued that the creation of new rules itself is dependent on a theory. This theory is a theory of rational law making that contains the critical theoretical reflection needed in order to make a set of propositions 'theoretical' in a minimal way.

The second remark seeks to highlight a possible confusion. Legisprudence, or the theory of rational law making, is to be distinguished from legislative drafting, legislative technique, or 'legistics'.

Legislative drafting, legislative technique, or legistics deal with the form of rules. Generally speaking, there may be two kinds of rules dealing with the form of rules, at least from the perspective of law making. The first are of a legal nature. These rules form part of the legal system, prescribing what form a legal rule must have. This class contains, quite obviously, the procedural rules of the constitution that deal with legislation. In addition to this, this class may contain other legal rules that have legal rules as their object. Whilst the latter concern mainly executive legal rules, they may also contain prescriptions as to the form of legislative legal rules. The second kind of rules that have legislation as their object are non-official ones. They are labelled 'legislative norms' (Viandier 1988), principles of drafting (Xanthaki 2010), *aanwijzingen* (Borman 1993), *legistische Richtlinien* (Lachmayer 1981), and so on, and they usually have no authoritative force, despite the fact that they may have been solemnly if not officially promulgated. Were they binding on the legislature, a theoretical problem might arise in that any formal requirements could challenge sovereignty. Under that perspective, the legislature would be binding itself – albeit to adhere to a mere form – which would contradict its sovereign status.

Despite the qualitative high standards of these legislative directives and their more or less solemn character, they lack binding force. That is to say, the formulation or structure of a rule that does violate one of these standards cannot be legally challenged for that reason alone. An advisory board like the Conseil d'Etat in Belgium may, however, criticise these defects. This critical advice is, however, not binding on the legislator. It is only the ruling body that decides on form, especially when it has sovereign power.

However, legistics is different from legisprudence in that the former only concerns the form of rules issued, while the latter mainly focuses on their rationality, on the conditions to be explored in the final chapter of this book. There may be factual relations between both. Obviously, directives contain the advice to formulate rules in a clear way, in order to avoid contradictions and to use concepts in a consistent manner. There is no doubt that these directives will contribute to the rationality of legislation issued under it. The clearer a rule, the easier it will be to understand and to follow. This then is an aspect of rationality. Rules that are that complex up to the point of only being accessible to experts in the field may lack rationality or even legitimacy for that reason.

Legisprudence, however, is more demanding on rationality than mere form. It deals with the rationality of law making as a whole, not merely with some formal requirements as to the linguistic or, more broadly, formal, expression of these rules.

With these terminological clarifications and remarks in mind, we can now start the investigation of the contours of legisprudence. I propose to pursue the following path of argumentation. The legal theory we are familiar with mainly elaborates the position of the judge. Current developments in the theory of judicial decision making have had the merit of incorporating practical reason into legal reasoning (MacCormick 1983). Many of these theories have focused on the coherence of legal reasoning, whilst, however, neglecting practical reason in legislation.This will be discussed in the following section.

Practical Reason in Legislation: The Principle of Coherence as the First Principle of Legisprudence

Introduction

With the incorporation of practical reason into legal reasoning, it has also become clear that judges do more than make judgments. Judgments, that is, are cognitive acts. Furthermore, judges also make decisions that are practical in nature. Here practical reason plays an eminent role.

Prima facie, however, nothing seems to contrast more with judicial norm application than legislative norm creation. Legislators are far freer than judges in their normative activity. A constitution as a legally binding norm for legislators does not affect the legislator in the same way as the law affects judges. Legislators are political actors, framing social, moral, or economic policies into law.

In order to make the contrast still more striking, unlike judicial judgments, legislative acts need not have any cognitive foundation 'in the system', since it is legislators who say what 'the system' is; their decisions are simply acts of will. On this view, a constitution is more a political programme, and less a set of binding norms, which corresponds with the view that the legislator is a political actor, and not a legal one. As a political programme, and in the absence of judicial review, in the worst case scenario the legislator can make a mess of 'the system', leaving it to the judiciary to clean it up, and keep up the appearances of rationality, coherence and legal certainty.

Judges then act *as if* the law is a rational system that protects legal interests in a more or less predictable way, while actually 'the system' as they see it from their standpoint may be just a heap of legislative commands with the only common feature that they have been commanded by the same authority.

In this chapter, I propose to explore some aspects of the position of the legislator as a legal actor whose activity is defined by the norms of the systems, mainly constitutional norms or secondary norms of power. However, following the norms of the constitution is a necessary though not a sufficient condition to create valid law in a systematic manner. Formally valid legislative norms can indeed be retroactive or can fail to make sense in different ways. Making sense has to do with the intelligibility and hence the applicability of norms.

Valid legal norms may lack intelligibility and for this reason, they are hard or impossible to apply. In this respect, they fail to make sense for the judge. There is yet another aspect to this. Valid legal norms must make sense to those whose lives they affect. The intelligibility of legislative norms is not only a matter of individual norms or norms *ut singuli*. Their intelligibility also depends on the context in which they operate, that is, the legal system as a whole. Appropriate social regulation should therefore incorporate the reasons why legal agents accept a rule as a norm. It is here that practical reason enters the domain of legislation.

Chapter 5 elaborated legalism and its main characteristics. The most important one was representationalism, or foundationalism. Foundationalism or representationalism is committed to the view that the way we think of the world tells us what it really is. It holds that our justified beliefs are justified due to the fact that they are derived from an incorrigible belief (Rescher 1974). Foundationalism or representationalism confines thinking to knowing, the certainty of which gives access to reality. This results in the elaboration of an a priori origin of knowledge (Descartes), politics (Hobbes), and morality (Kant). Representationalism in any of its variants relies on a foundationalist metaphysics. Especially in Enlightenment philosophy, it celebrates systematicity as the unfolding domination of reason.

The authority of reason as autonomy and human dignity carries with it the metaphysical dimension of the Modern philosophical project in that what there is can be thought of in terms of a rational system as real *and* vice versa. Truth, in other words, is systematic. Heidegger's view on this problem has some interesting implications for the theme of this chapter.

Summarising this view, the ontological foundation of the subject in Descartes' *cogito* is the self-foundation of a new type of knowledge that gives logical priority to certainty over truth. Certainty, in other words, is the key to truth unqualified or the access to reality. This access is mediated by clear and distinct concepts, and their exclusively rational – that is, mathematical – unfolding, is what science consists of. The crucial point is that representations are located in, or are constructions of, the thinking subject. They have no existence outside the mind. In thus liberating the subject from external domination, philosophy has opened up the way to the subject's domination of the world; Descartes had said earlier that, upon following his method, we would become 'master and possessor of nature' (Descartes 1996h: 62). What there is can be thought of as a rational system, in that the system is a mathematical system of reason. The 'system', so Heidegger concludes, is the ontological law of modern '*Dasein*'.

Apart from a first truth (the *cogito* and the proof of God's existence) leading to a system of true knowledge, in normative matters the systems is founded upon a true norm (for example, the fundamental law of nature in Hobbes (1966c: 117); the norm requiring entry into civil state in Kant (1996: §§ 41, 44). Or it can be the constitutive act of will resulting in popular sovereignty as in Rousseau (1997a:

49–51), the foundation of the validity of a system of positive law on a transcendental norm, or *Grundnorm*, as for Kelsen (1967: 205–8). or the rule of recognition practiced by law-applying officials, as advocated by Hart (Hart 1994: 100–123).

Foundationalism in knowledge holds that basic beliefs have a privileged status in that they are considered to be justified independently of any justification by other beliefs (BonJour 1985: 17). Foundationalism in law and morals holds that the elements of a normative system like law or morals are justified by their connection with the a priori validity of a norm (or value) as the unique source of all the elements of the system.

Foundationalism, thus articulated, sets out the main premise for the existence of a legal system. Hobbes, Kant, Rousseau, as well as Austin, Kelsen and Hart provide a unique norm or principle from which the norms of that system draw their validity, and hence their existence. A legal system can therefore be described as a set of normative propositions with their source in the system and any product stemming from this source is a valid law because it stems from this source. The elements of the system cohere, hence the system is coherent, due to the fact that they are derived from a single component principle or 'single source'. Call this 'source positivism'. Behind it we find a monist conception of coherence and it is supposed to lead to a *system* in law. But is this the case? I am afraid the answer is negative.

However, 'source positivism' may also lead to systematic law as it creates a mass of law. Any proposition that satisfies the criterion 'being commanded by the sovereign' or 'being decided by a judge', for example, is a valid norm, and hence belongs to the system. Without any further qualification, however, it leaves little doubt that on this mere criterion the 'system' may also turn out to be a heap of norms thrown together. This view on systematicity is dependent on Descartes' conception of rationality under which rationality is itself rational. It is conceived of as the foundation of the subject's epistemic certainty of his existence. In combination with the proof of God's existence, the subsequent concatenation of ideas that are as certain as the *cogito* results in modern science. In a postmodern sense, this conception is regarded as an undue limitation of the capacities of human reason (Perelman and Olbrechts-Tyteca 1976: 4). In line with this critique, rationality is conceived of, for example, as agent-related (Taylor 1995c), as embedded in argumentation (Perelman 1972d), as rational acceptability (Aarnio 1987: chapter 4), or as discussion free of constraints (Habermas 1973: esp. 255 ff.) What these conceptions of rationality share is 'contextuality', thus taking sides of the universality of reason, with demonstrability and certainty as its exclusive – epistemic – expression. I have referred to this recontextualisation of reason in Chapter 3, and I wish to build further on it in this chapter.

In addition to this, it should be kept in mind, as has been repeatedly stressed, that certainty is 'certainty *of* something', certainty of a belief. 'Pure' certainty as well as 'certainty of certainty' is absurd. In addition, truth can exist independently of the human mind, while certainty cannot. In addition, certainty therefore is 'certainty *for someone*'. As will be argued further, with regard to the context-relatedness of reason and rationality, consistency is a special case of coherence. Put differently, propositions can cohere in different manners, one of which is consistency. Under the latter hypothesis, coherence is used in an 'all or nothing', or dispositive mode. If propositions do not cohere in this way, they can still make sense in a different, non-dispositive use of coherence. The dispositive and the non dispositive use of coherence depends on whether reason or rationality is interpreted contextually or not, the context being comprised of those for whom something makes sense. On this view, coherence is an interpretive concept, while consistency is not. It can be interpreted that way upon considering it a maximum degree of a specific type of coherence, when *all* the propositions of a theory cohere in a contradiction-free manner. On this view, certainty and consistency are forms of making sense.

Reason's recontextualisation, it may be remembered from chapter 3, relied on the critique of a-contextual or unbounded rationality. This amounts to the claim (1) that all subjects are rational in the same way or that rationality is universal, and (2) that only epistemic beliefs are important. Apart from mathematics, however, as a framework for making sense of the world, other candidates include poetry, religion, or aesthetics.

Of Heaps and Walls: A Different View on Reason and Coherence

Speaking of arts, what qualification do André Breton's *Manifestes du surréalisme* deserve? They are not logically consistent treatises of modern art, to say the least. They, however, do make a lot of sense – at least to some of us – and so they may qualify as a theory, that is, as set of propositions cohering 'more of less in one way or another'. I deliberately put it this way, so that the connection is loose enough to throw light on the claim that consistency is a special case of coherence: a set of logical or mathematical propositions cohere in a very strong sense, up to the point of realising full consistency; the propositions in the *Manifestes du surréalisme* cohere in their own way, without realising consistency. They do not, however, *therefore* turn into sheer nonsense. Put differently, coherence is valued in art without, however, turning into vagueness. A theory of art therefore can make sense without being determined by consistency. Over-determination by consistency may make the theory disappear altogether.

This opens up the way for the further inquiry in this article. While logicians consider consistency to be identical to coherence, I will challenge this view, arguing that 'consistency is not a necessary condition for coherence' in legal systems. Having showed some aspects of the origin of this view, in the pages to come, I will propose a different view of the relationship between consistency and coherence.

Consistency is a logical aspect of a set of propositions. It means that the latter is free of contradictions. Coherence for its part means that a set of propositions 'hang together' or 'make sense'. A usual way of articulating the relationship between consistency and coherence is another logical connection, namely, that consistency is a necessary connection for coherence. However, all of the propositions from a set may cohere in a specific manner without being consistent.

In order to clarify this view on coherence, I should like to invite readers to contemplate the following comparison. When looking at a brick wall, we may say that it is a coherent collection of bricks. The bricks indeed stick together in a spatio-temporal setting. In contrast with the brick wall, a heap of bricks cohere in that they hang together in such a way that they are related, directly or indirectly, with all the other bricks in the heap. The heap is a chaotic set of bricks. Can we say it is 'totally incoherent'? Here too, I think the answer is negative.

On this view, a heap is a specifically cohering finite collection of bricks. If the position of one brick in the heap changes, we have another heap. This one change affects the position of all the other bricks on the heap. The bricks in the heap therefore cohere, though without cohering in such a way as to make a wall. The bricks may have been a wall that has been destroyed in an earthquake, or they may simply have been left in order to construct a wall out of them. Right now, they are just a heap of bricks. What is therefore lacking in order for a heap of bricks to be considered a wall is the difference in the arrangements of the bricks, that is, their arrangement according to some structure. It should be remembered that positivists tend to believe that a heap of valid norms also counts as a 'system' (cf. Heidegger 1988: 44 ff.).

As a short digression, it may sound bizarre to say that a wall is a coherent structure of bricks; but it is not silly. It would be silly to say that the coherent structure of the wall is conditioned by 'logical consistency'. The wall does not have a 'logical structure', even if we judge it coherent. There are structures involved other than logical ones to which reference is made in the coherence judgement. Therefore, the consistent application of a pattern in the construction of the wall may lead to the conclusion that the wall is coherent. Something similar occurs when we consider consistency as a necessary requirement for the coherence of symbolic systems like law. This suggests that the relations between the elements of the systems are of an exclusively logical nature, which is doubtful as we will soon see.

On a more abstract level than bricks and walls, the problem of coherence is a problem of elements or units that hang together within a larger whole. Coherence is a matter of relation. Three aspects are of importance here, that is, the relation of the elements or units to itself, the relation of the elements or units towards each other, and the subsequent relation of the elements or units toward each other.

As for the first, individual elements of a larger set are identified according to the logical principle of identity $a = a$. In a wall, the individual elements are bricks. Focusing on a legal system, the individual elements are norms, that is, general (typically legislative) and individual (typically judicial) norms. For the sake of clarity, I will leave implementing norms, that can be general or particular, out of consideration. For these single elements, only the principle of identity plays a role. A single element makes sense or is coherent if and only if it is free of contradictions or consistent. A judicial decision holding that X is the murderer of Y, but which acquits him from the charge is inconsistent and therefore incoherent. A statute requiring that cars should stop and keep on driving at red lights is vulnerable to the same charge. Here consistency is a necessary condition for coherence.

A legal system, however, is more than a logical set of propositions. Furthermore, 'law' is not necessarily identical to a legal system or that a legal system must not necessarily remain logically identical to itself in order to make sense. A legal system therefore can be considered as a body of momentary sets of general and particular norms without thereby losing its identity (Raz 1980: Chapter 8). New norms can be introduced, while old ones can be changed or repealed. In this respect, a legal order is not just 'one' set, except from the synchronic point of view, that is, when we look at it at a specific time in its historical existence. While from a diachronic point of view, a system is not a set of norms, it is rather a set of sets or a diachronic non-momentary sequence of momentary sets (Guastini 2000: 264). I will come back to this point later when I discuss the time dimension in relation to coherence.

This brings us to the second aspect of coherence as a relation. Like bricks in a heap are related to each other, bricks in a wall have a specific relevant relation to each other. It is this specific relation that is constitutive of the wall. The relation of the bricks on a heap is hard if not impossible to describe since we do not grasp the relevance of their relation to each other. Yet any change in the position of a brick makes it a different heap. Bricks making a wall have a relevant relation to each other, although this is not the only possible relevant relation that is constitutive of a wall. Stretching the image a bit further, the distance between the bricks may be unwittingly different due to mason's skill, or may be deliberately different on aesthetic grounds. This does not prejudice their coherence as a wall. However, the decrease in the relevance of their relation may rather push them towards being a wall in the Pickwickian sense, without the identity of the brick being affected.

Speaking more abstractly, for symbolic systems such as a legal system, between 'total incoherence' (which is hard if not impossible to conceive) and logical consistency exists a variety of relevant relations among the single elements. Logical consistency is one candidate amongst many others, once the legal system is considered as being composed of elementary units that are meaningfully related to each other.

The third aspect of the relation among the unitary elements of a whole is the aspect of succession. Were the relationship of a purely logical nature, then the succession of the elements would not affect their relationship. Consistency, that is, is not affected by time. When it comes to a legal system, however, it would be reductionist to withhold only this static relation between the elementary units. Legislators and judges continuously make new norms the identity of which is determined by their status as legally valid and free of contradictions. Legislative norms can be repealed or changed, and judicial decisions can differ without this resulting in the incoherence of the legal system over time. There may be good reasons for a legislator to repeal or change a norm, or for a judge to deviate from a precedent. These reasons may affect the logical relation between the unitary elements of the system, without, however, impairing its coherence.

The Level Theory of Coherence

Coherence and consistency cover a variety of meanings. Some scholars do not draw a distinction between coherence and consistency. Lalande, for example, holds that a theory is consistent if it contains no contradictions. Furthermore, he translates the French term 'consistence' by both 'consistency' and 'coherence' (Lalande 1983: 146–7, 177–8).The interchangeability of both concepts, however, leaves it unexplained why there is a need for two concepts in order to describe the same phenomenon. The existence of both terms seems only understandable as a matter of fidelity to the nuance of ordinary language (MacCormick 1984: 38).

Kornhauser and Sager (1986: 106) for their part believe that 'consistency is a necessary condition of coherence, and hence the perfectly coherent legal system would also be perfectly consistent. But in imperfectly coherent system, coherence and consecutive consistency can conflict.'

Brouwer defines coherence as a cluster of proprieties (Brouwer 1990: 25) of which consistency is one among many (ibid.: 5). In line with the latter, Gianformaggio considers consistency as a species of the more general genus 'coherence' (Gianformaggio 1990: 404–5). Kress finally shares the cluster view of coherence whereupon a theory is said to be coherent due to its consistency, comprehensiveness, completeness, monism, unity, articulateness and justified character. Interestingly, he adds that each of these properties can be considered as necessary or sufficient for coherence, while alternatively it may be claimed that the more of that property a theory manifests, the more coherent it is (Kress 1996: 533–6 ff.).

Following Brouwer, Gianformaggio and Kress in their general approach, I will explore consistency and coherence and their relation with a legal system, which entails the following fourfold claim: (1) consistency is not a necessary condition for coherence (it is only so for momentary systems, not for systems evolving over time) (Kress 1993: 650), so that (2) a set of propositions need not be completely consistent in order to be coherent, because (3) inconsistency can result in the system making more sense as a whole, so that (4) consistency and coherence are a matter of degree. Therefore, (5) 'perfect coherence' and 'perfect consistency' are rather regulatory ideals.

In arguing these claims, I will distinguish between the single units of a legal system. For the sake of simplicity, I consider a legal system to be composed of the following single units: general norms, typically legislative enactments, and particular norms, typically, judicial decisions. I leave aside other types, such as administrative norms, international norms, and the like.

Jurisprudential theories most of the time have devoted their energies to the relationship between these two types of norms, in the light of the separation-of-powers doctrine. There is, however, more to be said once we have incorporated the legislative norm creation into the picture. This expansion of the scope of inquiry is specific for legisprudence as the theory of rational law making (Wintgens 2006). I will explore the relations between these individual units of a legal system in the light of consistency and coherence, and then move on to articulate the relation between coherence and consistency. The account of this relation within the 'level theory' of coherence focuses on the coherence of legal reasoning and on the coherence of the legal system. The former typically refers to the judge, while the latter refers to the legislator. According to the view set out above, both actors are creating norms, general and particular norms respectively. These types of norms are different, though not separated.

According to the claims underpinning the level theory of coherence, I will identify four levels of coherence. These levels are: the level of coherence$_0$ (internal or synchronic coherence), the level of coherence$_1$ (diachronic or rule coherence), the level of coherence$_2$ (compossibility or system coherence), and the level of coherence$_3$ (environment coherence). From the level of coherence$_0$ to the level of coherence$_3$ the theory allows for more complexity in accounting for the legal system's contextuality. Contextuality sheds a new light on the systemic character of law and legal certainty, as will now be argued.

The Level of Coherence$_0$ or Synchronic Coherence

The level of coherence$_0$ refers to the most elementary level of coherence of a discourse. Imagine an observer attending a meeting of the drunken poets' society. One of its members is mumbling words which the audience cannot understand. Despite the applause of his fellows, an external observer deems the discourse to be incoherent because the words that our poet mumbled have no identity in the language with which he is familiar (semantic identity). Yet even if the words were pronounced clearly, and have semantic identity, when the drunk says 'poetry blue in the sky shopping bank to go', the observer may justifiably conclude that our poet drank too much beer. He cannot however make sense of what he says despite the fact that the words have a semantic identity. The poet's discourse is therefore incoherent this time, because it lacks the syntactic structure of the language the observer is familiar with. *Semantic* and *syntactic* coherence are lacking because the observer fails to grasp the relevant semantic and syntactic structure of the language he is familiar with. Coherence therefore depends on intelligibility.

As for law, these elements are norms, that is, general or particular norms. A norm can only form part of the legal system if it is valid according to the system's norms. The identity of a norm, however, is not only a matter of its being correctly produced according to the secondary rules of a legal system. It must at the same time satisfy the requirements of semantic and syntactic identity, without which a norm may be formally valid but incoherent because it makes no sense as a standard for conduct or for judgment.

A contradiction at this level normally affects the broader part of the system of propositions, legal or otherwise, in which this element operates. Coherence$_0$ therefore, is for any form of discourse a necessary condition for its soundness or for making sense. What determines the elementary parts of a discourse and the level of coherence$_0$ is the principle of identity. Whether or not we believe that the life of law is more than logic, that is, whether or not law is more than a static collection of valid norms does not affect the level of coherence$_0$.

Non-contradiction is a requirement for any of the elementary units of a system, whether static or dynamic. The absence of contradictions as a requirement for coherence at the level of coherence$_0$ allows us to conceive of a legal system as a heap of non-contradictory valid units, without any other relevant relation than their being legally valid. In this regard, it is important to remember the bricks on the heap, and the relation of coherence between them. All the commands of a sovereign that are legally valid at the same time therefore form a system. We may call the type of coherence at the level of coherence$_0$ 'synchronic coherence'.

It would be tempting to conclude that synchronic coherence as the relation of the unitary elements towards themselves – that is, their identity – is of the same nature as the relation of coherence between the elementary units. To regard the coherence of a legal system 'as a whole' as conditioned by consistency is, however, to misconstrue the relations between the elementary units. Such relations can be logical, in that judicial norms in some cases can be logically deduced from general legal norms. If so, the relationship is a logical one; if not, it is of a different nature, without however losing its relevance. It would be too hasty to say that only logic is relevant to this relationship.

If the relation between the elementary units of a legal system had to be logical, then the perspective has been implicitly shifted. It is no longer legislative and judicial norms that are the elementary units, but the legal system 'as a whole' which is considered the 'elementary unit'.

To see coherence of a legal system 'as a whole' as conditioned by consistency is to misconstrue the different nature of both types of relations. It must be remembered in this respect that consistency is the epistemic twin of certainty, that operates as the index of truth in Modern philosophy. If truth indeed is systematic, then systems as a whole must be consistent in order to attain truth unqualified. This may be taken to be another expression of epistemologised philosophy, thus neglecting the differences between a theoretical, formal system of propositions and a practical set of propositions like law. Deductive closure of a system like law may enhance a practical value like legal certainty. However, to make deductive closure a prerequisite for legal certainty is symptomatic of epistemologised philosophy, in that, as discussed in Chapter 3, a theoretical solution is imposed on a practical problem.

This becomes all the more clear once we consider the legal system as a whole within a different sense. Legal systems are not operating in a vacuum. They are operating in a spatio-temporal setting, of which the temporal dimension is more important for the purpose of this chapter. As noted above, coherence between the elements of a system involves grasping a relevant structure between them. In this respect, coherence is more demanding than mere coherence$_0$. Once we go beyond the level of coherence$_0$, and start exploring the relations between the elementary units, we will notice the importance of the agent for whom something is coherent. The logical principle of identity does not require an agent in order to be correct. To consider the whole of a legal system as being determined by coherence$_0$ amounts to claiming that the agent's relationship to the system is not important, or that the agent must organise action along the lines of consistency if he wants to act in a practically rational way. This again is reminiscent of the non-contextual approach to rationality that was criticised in Chapter 3.

The Level of Coherence$_1$ or Diachronic Coherence

Things are different when the subsequent relation between elementary units is taken into account. Legal systems typically are not static. Judges add individual norms to the system, and legislators add new general norms and change or repeal old ones. It is important in this respect to remember the heap of bricks. They cohere in some sense although we may be unable to grasp a relevant structure binding them together. In that respect, 'total chaos', like 'total incoherence', is hard if not impossible to conceive. A change in the position of one brick a priori affects the whole of the heap, which could not be said if chaos were total (even if we are for the time being unable to grasp a relevant structure). In dealing with the level of coherence$_1$ as well as when dealing with the more complex levels of coherence, I will briefly deal with the judicial perspective on the matter before focusing on the position of the legislator.

Generally speaking, a judicial decision is a concretisation of a general legislative norm. Not all judicial decisions are made on the same day, nor are they made by the same judge, nor are all the facts to which a general norm is applied identical. The succession of the elementary units or judicial decisions, however, is submitted to the norm of fair treatment or of formal justice that requires an equal application of the general norm to essentially similar cases (Aristotle 1984d: 1131a–1131b; Perelman 1972b; Hart 1994: 157–67; Coons 1987; Dworkin 1977c: 113). Formal justice, or the principle of equality, refers to fair treatment and it reflects the rule characteristic of law and this is what is meant by coherence$_1$, diachronic coherence, or horizontal continuity. On this account the unitary elements, c.q. judicial decisions at the level of coherence$_1$ show a linear connection with the preceding ones. This connection can, but need not, be of a logical nature in order to be preserved.

If norms are applied unequally to essentially similar cases, they are changed during the game. This entails judicial norm making, which involves not only a presumption of reflecting the judge's own political morality (Dworkin 1984c: 86). In addition, judicial legislation involves retroactivity since 'the losing party would be punished, not because he violated some duty he had, but rather a new duty created after the event' (ibid.; also Kress 1984). Norm change by the judiciary is equivalent to a usurpation of legislative power, hence a violation of the separation of powers. On the opposite side of this, strict *stare decisis* entirely realises the idea of formal justice upon which equal cases should be treated equally. From the logical perspective, this would require that cases in turn are identical, while at best they are similar.

In between the judicial creation of general norms and strict *stare decisis*, judicial norm making may depart from a precedent, or from a legal norm, or a long-standing practice of a norm's interpretation. If judicial norms were to follow deductively from general legal norms, all subsequent judicial norms would have to be identical. Deductive judicial norm making therefore requires no specific justification. The rules of deductive inference, that is, provide necessary and sufficient justification. These rules are, however, of an epistemic nature, while formal justice is of an eminently practical nature. None the less, they prima facie resemble each other, which is yet another aspect of epistemologised philosophy: a practical value (justice) is reframed in a theoretical way (equal rule application). As for the problem we are focusing upon here, epistemologisation involves obliterating the temporal dimension involved in the succession of elementary units of the system.

Deviation from a general norm, precedent, or settled practice of interpretation may jeopardise coherence at the level of $coherence_0$. The level of $coherence_0$ deals with the identity of the single entities of the system. A single entity must be non-contradictory according to the principle of identity. Historical and grammatical interpretation are in this respect of a conservative nature, in that they stay close to the 'original intent' of the legislator as revealed, for example, in the *travaux préparatoires*, or the 'plain meaning' of the text of the law. Judicial interpretation or the statutory construction of a general norm may, in deviating from the plain meaning of a text or its original intent, affect the level of $coherence_0$ of the single entity.

Deviation from a general norm or a precedent requires a specific justification, that articulates a different relation of relevance between the successive elementary units. Were it required that the relationship between judicial decisions be one of inference, logical or otherwise, from precedent or general norm, then deviation would simply be inconsistent. The inconsistency, however, can also be considered as too loose a connection between successive elementary units (including applicable general norms). This loosening of the connection can, however, be remedied in supplying argumentative support including justification, analogy, probabilistic and comparable evidentiary connections.

For reasons that I will point to below, the degree of $coherence_1$ is lowered by this type of decision but it can increase coherence at a different level. As a matter of fact, judges only rarely apply one norm at the time, since situations of fact are complex.

What about the legislator? He has the power to create and change norms without any accompanying duty of justification apart from the norms that enable him to do so (Friedman 1966). Most legal systems nowadays have witnessed an exponential growth of legislative norms. As long as these norms are legally valid, each of them belongs to the legal system.

At the start of the 1960s, the problem of joyriding emerged in Belgium. Youngsters stole a car and drove it until the fuel tank was empty, after which they abandoned the car. This could not be qualified as theft under existing law which required (1) taking away an object against the will of the owner, together with (2) the *animus domini*, that is, the intention of becoming the owner (article 461 of the

Belgian Criminal Code). Because the car was abandoned after use, the *animus domini* was not proved, and therefore the offender was not convicted of theft. Roman law knew this type of theft as *furtum usus*. The offender could, however, be convicted for the theft of the fuel, since its consumption was the convincing proof that the delinquent had the *animus domini*. The theft of the mere use of the car could not, however, be punished. In 1964, the Belgian legislator expanded the scope of theft in order to cover the theft of use, thus making the general norm prohibiting theft more coherent.

While the example shows how legislative norm creation can enhance the coherence of the legal system, things have become different following a change in the legislator's perception of his role. Under this different role perception, the legislator can act in a codifying and in a modifying or steering manner (Koopmans 1970). The example given on *furtum usus* is one of codifying legislation. Punishing murders is another example. If on the one hand, a legislator were only ordering society by codifying legislation – for example, punishing murderers – it would not really matter whether the tariff for murder became higher or lower.

If on the other hand, a legislator becomes a steering actor and is elaborating a housing policy – for example, by way of a tax relief with respect to interest payments on home loans – he steers society and raises the legitimate long-term expectations of those affected by his ruling.

Pure formal injustice or lack of coherence_1, from the perspective of codifying legislation or legislation that does not affect the distribution of desired goods, may be called pure formal injustice. The lowering of the degree of coherence_1 through legislative amendments when the legislator engages in steering legislation in turn creates expectational formal injustice, since it frustrates legitimate expectations and thus may clash with fair treatment (Campbell 1973: 116).

Against the background of the level of coherence_1, the legislative perspective endorses the idea that any norm change has an aspect – however slight – of retroactivity and is therefore – at least prima facie – immoral. This goes without saying when retroactivity is clear, say for a retroactive tax law. Less manifest or 'implicit' retroactivity is implicated in norm change that entails expectational formal injustice or 'ripple effects' (cf. Kress 1984: 377 ff.). A result of the prima facie injustice of any norm change is that the legislator has a duty to provide arguments at the level of coherence_1 that outweigh it (pragmatic arguments; change in circumstances, and so on).

When legislative norm making becomes more of a steering nature, diachronic coherence will be affected accordingly. Put simply, legislatures only rarely create one norm at a time (like the norm punishing *furtum usus* or changing the period of prescription of a right).

The increasing weight of steering legislation due, among other things to the emergence of the welfare state, makes legislative norm creation crucially dependent on policy programs (Zamboni 2007: 130 ff). Housing, health, education and sports have become too complex a matter to be left to a couple of simple general legislative rules (for example, Meijer and MacFarlane 1996).

Since policy programmes most of the time cover a long time span, they may induce changes of the norms that originally sprang from them. I will, however, limit myself to some easy examples that show the complexity of the matter as it affects diachronic coherence.

Most legislators nowadays are committed to what I roughly characterise as a policy of equality. They strive, for example, towards the realisation of equal rights of marriage partners (patrimonial, personal), allowing same-sex marriages, assimilating forms of cohabitation to marriage, giving the same rights to one-parent families as to married or cohabitating partners, progressively erasing discrimination between labourers and employees, promulgating rules creating equal payment for equal work, and the equality between children independently of whether they are born from married parents or not. In short, the legislator's commitment to equality pushes it to abolish existing discriminatory rulings and treatments.

To stay with the last example, in creating equality between so-called 'legitimate' and 'illegitimate' children by abolishing the connection between legitimate descent and marriage of the child's parents, legislation pursues the ideal of equality between persons. While the legislator is the only body competent to promulgate these new norms, it is doubtful whether he really can also change them at will. This is an instance of far-reaching expectational formal injustice, going beyond the term of a mortgage reimbursement, so to speak. They immediately affect the subject qua subject, and not only the subject as a bundle of rights and duties that can be created and abolished *ad libitum*. While only the legislator has the right to make and change these norms, he may be limited in doing so by the legal system he created.

According to the above, we can take one further step. Under the heap theory, there is no need to create a 'system', the coherence of which goes beyond the level of coherence$_0$. That is to say that the formal validity of the elementary units is a necessary and a sufficient condition for their existence and for their 'hanging together'. Remember in this respect Heidegger's idea that heaps are also 'systems'.

The formal validity of a norm is at the same time a relevant relation among all the norms of a set in order for them to have a structure that can be called 'legal system'. From this perspective, formal validity in other words guarantees the identity of the individual constituent elements together with the unity of all of them as a legal system.

Unlike the heap theory, however, and in the absence of a duty to legislate in a systematic manner, existing norms may prevent the legislator from making a mishmash of the system. The system of existing law may require a legislator to refrain from implementing change. This brings us to a yet another more complex level of coherence.

The Level of Coherence$_2$: System Coherence and Compossibility

As noted above, judicial legal reasoning only rarely applies one single norm at a time. In addition to that, norms are not self-imposing, nor are they self-interpreting. Even if this were the case, then the applicable norm would be selected by –

hypothetically – taking into consideration all the norms of the system. Applicable norms do not jump out of the code onto the judge's desk; they must be chosen. Norm choice, therefore, is the division of all norms into the applicable and the non-applicable. If only one norm applies, that one is selected. Most of the time, a judicial decision involves procedural norms governing the way in which to decide the case, rules of evidence and how to prove the relevant facts, while rules of interpretation provide directions as to how to determine the meaning of other norms. If penalties are involved, they may be contained in a separate code of criminal law.

In addition to that, even if only one norm applies, this is not necessarily clear in itself as the plain meaning theory holds. There are no clear norms because the clarity of a norm depends on an interpretation. The plain meaning theory therefore turns things upside down. It holds that clear norms should not be interpreted (*in claris non est interpretandum*). The clarity of a norm, in other words, is the result of an unconscious or an ongoing settled interpretation. A norm, in other words, can be clear now while it may become unclear in the future. A better way of expressing this is to say that *in claris* cessat *interpretatio* (plain meaning as a starting-point in interpretation).

Judicial argumentation on the level of $coherence_1$ typically involves the grammatical and historical interpretation of norms. These methods of interpretation stay 'close to the text' as it were, to the 'original intent', or the norm's 'plain meaning' – if any – and are of a more conservative nature. Teleological and systematic interpretation for their part engage the judge in a more creative activity. Unlike grammatical and historical interpretation, systematic interpretation distinguishes between the norm and the text of the norm and dismisses the legislator as the unique and privileged producer of meaning (Müller 1996: 177–80). Reconstructing the telos of the norm(s) or combining norms in different settings is therefore typical for argumentation on the level of $coherence_2$. These methods of interpretation free up law from the dead hand of the past and promote responsiveness to contemporary concerns (Kress 1996: 536; Raz 1992: 292). I will elaborate on this while focusing on systematic interpretation, suggesting that a similar approach is at work *mutatis mutandis* in teleological interpretation.

Systematic interpretation implies that a norm is read in the light of one or more other norms, and hypothetically all the other norms of the system. According to that claim, all judicial decisions rely on systematic interpretation, in that any law suit involves – *idealiter* – the whole legal system.

The following case illustrates the point. A defendant had acquired a house, one of the walls of which had been built in good faith over the plaintiff's property. The space thus occupied was 6 cm over a length of 20 m, which made a total of 1.2 sq. m. Many years later, the plaintiff discovered the fact and requires the wall's demolition. The demolition of the wall, however, would have destroyed the rest of the house. According to the classical interpretation of the Belgian property norm (Article 544 of the Belgian Civil Code), within legal doctrine, property is the most absolute right, the exercise of which can only be limited by law. The plaintiff claimed that he was limited in the use of his property by defendant's wall on his land. According to the classical interpretation no tort can arise in using one's right since *nullus videtur dolo facere qui suo iure utitur* (no one is considered to have committed a wrong who exercises his legal rights) (Justinian 1962: book L, 17, 55 (Gaius).

The Belgian *Cour de Cassation* changed this doctrine in the case from 1971. In its ruling, the Court held that the use of a right is constitutive of a tort – even within the legal limits of the right – whenever any reasonable person cannot recognise this use as reasonable. In that case, the use is an abuse, and qualifies as a tort, on the basis of the tort norm (Article 1382 of the Belgian Civil Code). The plaintiff, in claiming the demolition of the wall, was abusing his right, since the small advantage for him was unreasonable compared to the damages that would be caused to the defendant. The court, however, awarded the plaintiff damages compensating the loss of this small piece of land.

Under the classical interpretation, a property right is considered an absolute right. Furthermore, under the plain meaning theory, both the property norm and the tort norm are clear, and therefore need no interpretation. In relation to this doctrine, the French doctrinal writer Planiol for his part had labelled the interpretation of the property norm leading to the idea of abuse of rights a '*logomachie*' (Planiol 1909: 286). His point is that you either have a right or you do not have it. If you have a right, you can use it. If you do not have a right, and you cause damage to a third party in a negligent manner, then you are liable in tort. *A contrario*, if you have a right, the damage caused is legitimate and cannot be constitutive of a tort. Planiol is right in so far as the text of the property norm – when read *ut singuli,* that is, in isolation from the other norms of the legal system – does not allow for any qualification in terms of 'abuse'.

Both the property and the tort norm satisfy the requirements of the level of coherence_0 in that they are non-contradictory individual units of the system. They qualify as members of the system since they are legally valid. Argumentation on the level of coherence_1, or diachronic coherence, requires that property claims be decided on the mere basis of the property norm. Any claim attempting to limit this right would be dismissed due to the absolute nature of property. So far, the relationship between the property norm and the tort norm can be considered a logical one, in that they are mutually exclusive. If defendant has a right, he cannot be barred from exercising it even if this damages the plaintiff.

As noted above, the degree of diachronic coherence can be lowered, when the judge deviates from a legal norm, a precedent, or an established practice of interpretation: in this case, the interpretation of the property norm as conferring an absolute right. In doing so, the successive relationship between successive elementary units, c.q. two judicial decisions, is affected. The result of this interpretation is a tempering of the extension of the property right and an expansion of the scope of the tort norm. In earlier cases, the plaintiff was (given the right to require demolition), so in this respect the new interpretation of the court was inconsistent with its earlier rulings.

The case at hand is an illustration of how argumentation on the level of coherence$_2$ can provide a compensatory justification for the lowering of the level of diachronic coherence or coherence$_1$. The compensation adds argumentative support as to why a reading of the property norm in light of the tort norm is preferred to the mere application of the property norm, all things considered.

The *Cour de Cassation* framed its theory of abuse of rights on this combination or reconstruction of both norms. This theory results from a reading of the property norm in the light of the tort norm. This systematic interpretation led the Court to formulate a principle that any *manifestly unreasonable use of property* is a tort pursuant to Article 1382 of the Belgian Civil Code. Judges interpreting these norms systematically argue on the level of coherence$_2$. Systematic interpretation in this case outweighs argumentation on the level of coherence$_1$ favouring linear norm application.

Judges argue on the level of coherence$_2$ in relying on the systematic nature of the legal system they operate in. Reliance on the systematic nature of a legal system, however, may be deceptive. This deception may be remedied at the level of coherence$_2$. First, under the heap theory, all unitary elements of the system cohere in the sense that they are legally valid, and hence form a system. However, diachronic incoherence between general valid norms as single unities do appear. In this case, judges solve them with the help of the *lex specialis*, *lex posterior* and *lex superior* techniques. Interpretation in accordance with the Constitution is another technique. The rationale legitimising the use of this technique is the background assumption of a unifying intention on the part of the legislator. This background assumption is commonly called the presumption of the rationality of the legislator.

On this presumption, the legislator is considered to have acted in a rational manner throughout his legislative activity. This amounts to saying that he is presumed to have followed the rules of the Constitution, to have aimed to use unequivocal terminology, to avoid contradictions and redundancies, to adhere to a coherent set of values, and to circumvent absurd, iniquitous, or useless ruling. Furthermore, it is also presumed that he has respected the requirement of proportionality between means and ends and that he has not been fundamentally unpredictable (Ost and van de Kerchove 1987: 100–101; Ost 1978: 163 ff.; Ziembinski 1970: 177–8; Nowak 1969; Carbonnier 1972: 271 ff.).

The exploration of the contours of a theory of legislation properly so called requires us to move beyond presumptions. The presumption indeed lays the task of making the legal system coherent on the shoulders of the judge, thereby limiting jurisprudence as the theory of law to what I have already called '*Rechtsprachwissenschaft*'. It is at the level of coherence$_2$, or system coherence, that we attain a privileged outlook on the legislator's impact on the coherence of a legal system. While judges make sense of the legal system through systematic interpretation, the legislator's contribution amounts to systematic legislation. I will begin with an abstract case, from where I will propose some generalisation.

Suppose that, according to norm N_1, unemployed persons receive an unemployment benefit U according to criteria of distribution fixed in N_1. Some time later, the legislator issues N_2. According to N_2, companies who employ a person qualifying for U under N_1 in turn qualify for a premium to promote the employment of the economically inactive. Both premiums are paid by the state. An employer qualifying for the premium on N_2 offers a job to an employee qualifying under N_1 for U. Both employer and employee have an interest, in that the latter gets a job and a salary S and the former gets the premium. However, if the employee's salary only slightly exceeds his U, he may be entitled to think that he is paid only very little for his work. He may believe that what he 'really' earns by working is [S – U]. The smaller [S – U], the more employee will be encouraged to think that way. This problem is known as the 'unemployment trap'.

Both N_1 and N_2 are valid legal norms. In addition to this, they satisfy the requirements from the level of $coherence_0$ that they not be self-contradictory single entities. Further, the simultaneous application of both does not involve contradictions, that is, the simultaneous effects of N_1 and N_2 are not in contradiction. They can be applied whilst respecting the requirements of the level of $coherence_1$. What is at stake, however, is that they may simply largely annul each other's effect. They do not, however, satisfy the requirements of the level of $coherence_2$.

Their combination impairs the systematic character of the legal system. Their simultaneous existence, for example, causes a lot of administrative bother, procedures in court, and the like, for an effect that is close to zero. N_1 and N_2 are not effective in that they do not realise the goal the ruler had in mind. N_2 – supposing this is issued after N_1 – then needs a supplementary justification in order to show that it fits in with the system as a whole. While respecting the requirements of $coherence_0$ and $coherence_1$, the ruling becomes deficient at the level of $coherence_2$ in adding norms that are legally valid though sociologically speaking ineffective and economically speaking inefficient. $Coherence_2$, from the perspective of the legislator that is, requires it to take the systematic character of the system as a whole into consideration. That is however easier said than done (remember the heap theory!).

Legally valid norms satisfying the requirements of $coherence_0$ and $coherence_1$ may fail to make sense at the level of $coherence_2$ because they are not *compossible*. Pulling in different directions, they annul each others' effect; following both norms will entail a (practically) zero effect. It is not hard to see that this amounts to incoherent ruling.

Speaking more generally, compossibility means 'what is possible together'. Unlike $coherence_0$, $coherence_2$ as compossibility is a positive requirement. $Coherence_0$ restricts the possibilities of ruling on mere logical grounds. Not everything is possible at the same time. This is a requirement of reason. In that sense, it is universal or abstract, without determining therefore what must be done *in concreto*. It negatively tells us what cannot be part of a discursive segment (a judicial decision, a legislative norm) at the same time. $Coherence_0$, or synchronic coherence, is negative in that it excludes possibilities.

$Coherence_2$, or compossibility in a more general formulation, involves the practicability of choices, not their logical excellence. The content of a legislative norm is a matter of decision, and is hence political. The legislator's position, however, is defined by the legal system, the content of which consists of his decisions. On this interpretation, the legislator is a *legal* actor mainly taking *political* decisions. His position as a legal actor is defined in the Constitution.

Taking political decisions does not prevent the actor from being bound to legal norms. He is bound by the procedural norms that constrain his status and competence. In addition to that, under coherence$_1$, or diachronic coherence, the legislator is bound to the norms he created in as far as their change requires justification according to legisprudence. Under coherence$_2$, or system coherence, norms must be compossible at the operational stage, in that they must respect one another's effect. Compossibility or coherence$_2$ requires norms to be formally valid and not materially incompatible (Dewey 1930: 153–4; Perelman and Olbrechts-Tyteca 1976e: 262–76).

The Level of Coherence$_3$ or Embedded Coherence and Theory Dependence

When judges run out of norms, they face a hard case. Since there is no norm to 'apply', they can make no cognitive judgments, but must make a decision or practical judgment. They are obliged to do so under penalty of denial of justice. On the level of coherence$_2$, they can find an anchoring point for norm combination or systematic interpretation which is not a purely cognitive operation either. What justifies this type of arguments, since candidates for systematic interpretation do not hop on the judge's desk? According to uncontested legal methodology, the available interpretation techniques (historical, grammatical, systematic, and teleological) are not self-imposing. Judges, that is, can more or less freely determine which of these techniques to use in order to connect their judgment to the existing body of law.

Theories of interpretation suggest that these techniques – unavoidable as they may be in order to determine the historical, textual, (more or less) systematic, and teleological characteristics of law – are helpful in establishing the solution that best fits the case and makes sense of the legal system as a whole (for example, MacCormick 1978: 100 ff., 152 ff.) My view on the matter is that judicial freedom at the same time appeals to judicial responsibility, which is not necessarily expressed or expressible in a specific legal norm. The strong legalistic judge may claim to have done his duty, even if this amounts to the nonsensical application of a norm. The weak legalistic judge for his part aspires to more. He strives to come up with a coherent solution, that is, a solution that follows from a rational reconstruction of the norms of the legal system as a principled whole taking into account its consequences.

Dworkin has suggested that such a solution activates the principles that are dormant inside the legal system. According to law as integrity, coherent solutions in hard cases fit these principles. Are these principles then the rock on which the judicial spade is blunted? If I understand Dworkin correctly, he offers an interesting reformulation of the theory of the separation of powers: policies are the exclusive territory of the legislator, whilst principles are the judge's. Policies transform facts into legal norms. Legal norms work themselves into coherent wholes steered by principles. Principles do the job when judges run out of norms, so Dworkin argues.

However appealing this insight may be, it obliterates the fact that judges also make policy decisions and that legislators should keep an eye on principles as well as on previously enacted norms. If no one can profit from his own wrong, excluding murderers from inheriting, there may be serious doubts as to whether a legislative exception for tax crimes could pass constitutional muster. If the principle of equality is not explicitly laid down in the Constitution, it is obviously not a binding norm. This does not make it less relevant, though, for the legislator. A *norm* of equality holding that like cases ought to be treated alike is redundant for the administration of justice. It is conceptually connected to the rule character of law and need not be explicitly formulated. In addition, the rule character of law, like theories of interpretation, is not itself law. Such features are to be located outside the legal system, that is, on the level of coherence_3.

The level of coherence_3 is a necessary complement for the lower levels of coherence (Wintgens 2000: 131–8). It is the complement that in scientific research operates as the searchlight theory upon which observation depends (Popper 1974). Observation is steered by a theory that makes us see what we are looking for, since no direct access to reality is possible. This problem is known in scientific research, both in natural and human sciences, as 'theory dependence'. Theories depend on other theories as their 'foundation'. Foundationalism however – and its idealistic undertones – is the very problem that theory dependence is called upon to overcome. To my knowledge, the problem of the theory dependence of a legal system and its connection with legislation has not been dealt with until now.

Legal dogmatics, like any discipline, cannot resolve its methodological problems from inside the discipline. The methodology of legal dogmatics has its standpoint outside the discipline it is investigating since it seeks to clarify issues that concern the status of the discipline as a whole. However, 'classical' legal dogmatics, as noted above, is not conscious of its methodology in this way. It dissipates through the 'law', thus legitimating evaluative propositions as to the correct, if not 'true', application of legal norms in legal practice.

My view is that legal science is a theory not *of* law, but *about* law. Its methodology is not a natural aspect of the object. It does not mysteriously abide within the legal system, awaiting discovery. It is located outside the legal system. Its operationalisation is a matter of choice, not of knowledge. Yet, from the perspective of strong legalist legislator, this choice is concealed behind naturalness, and contributes to the instrumentalist view of law (Wintgens 2006).

The methodology of law is a matter of theory and not something natural. In this respect, the methodology of law allows for a theoretical investigation, an investigation that does not appear on the screen of the classical legal scientist because of the so-called 'naturalness' of the method, as the analysis of German legal science in Chapter 5 amply showed. As in natural science, as argued above, the connection between object and method is a matter of choice or decision. It is not different in legal science, and this pushes the discussion outside of the domain of law properly so called.

According to the level theory of coherence, equality in norm application, equality as the requirement of non discrimination as well as the rule character of law are not law. Nor does the separation of powers necessarily form part of it. Finally, freedom as a *principium*, that is, freedom as the beginning and as the *Leitmotiv* of law does not necessarily belong to it. They need not be expressly identified within the legal system. On the contrary, it is freedom as *principium* that identifies the legal system as a legal order. The qualification 'legal system' and 'legal order' may seem arbitrary to a large extent. Yet, 'legal order' suggests that what a legal system is for the heap theorist, a formally identifiable set of norms according to the source theory of the system itself, can be accredited as a legal order or a coherent set of legal norms from the perspective of legisprudence.

The above explorations into the level theory of coherence suggest that the methodology of the creation and application of law is embedded as a last resort in the same theory. This is a background theory in which the legal system is embedded, and on which judges and legislators alike draw, when they are 'out of norms'. However, legislators are always running out of norms, since it is their job to make them. When judges run out of norms, their decision making becomes more apparent. By leaning over the edges of the legal system, they learn that their decisions, as acts of will, must remain 'inside' the system. This paradoxical aspect of the level of coherence_3 is a necessary requirement of any theory, in that no methodology is self-justifying.

The background theory of a legal system therefore contains the elements explaining and justifying law. It is what must be presupposed in order for a set of norms to make sense as a whole, but also to be a system. I will briefly explore the contours of this background theory, in relating it to freedom, as explored in chapter 4.

As argued above, norms in whatever version limit freedom. In the absence of norms, therefore, there is freedom. Freedom involves the possibility for individuals to act as they please. They act, that is, on their conceptions of freedom. Any external limitation of freedom by a legal norm makes individuals act on a conception about freedom. Conceptions *of* freedom are moral concretisations of freedom; conceptions *about* freedom are legal or political concretisations.

According to this theory of freedom, moral concretisations have a relative priority over the political or legal ones. From this relative priority, it follows that conceptions about freedom can replace conceptions of freedom on the condition of justification. Justification involves giving reasons as to why acting on a conception about freedom has priority over acting on a conception of freedom.

Judges and legislators, so it turns out, can 'run out of norms'. Jurisprudence, as it developed until the date mentioned at the beginning of this chapter, was mainly focused on this 'gap' problem from the perspective of judicial decision making. There is a good deal to say that twentieth-century jurisprudence has been searching for solutions to resolve this gap problem. In this respect, however, legal theory has limited itself to a narrow jurisdictional focus, thereby neglecting the position of the legislator.

The argument set out in the pages above is an attempt to show that at the end of the day, both judges and legislators face gaps in the legal system. It does not make too much sense to consider some types of gaps as 'axiological', thereby suggesting that the judge is trying to avoid the application of the norm that he is called on to apply. Leaving aside from the differences characterising their powers, both legislators and judges make norms, although it is true that these norms are crucially different, depending on whether they stem from a legislative or a judicial source.

My point, however, is less to stress the differences than the similarities. And the crucial similarity is that both judges and legislators can be regarded as legal actors, both creating norms while at the same time being bound to norms of the legal system. Legally unbound legislators belong to the past, just as do mechanically norm-applying judges. Judges makes decisions, and legislators are also bound by the requirements of coherence. Both, that is, have a creative role to play as legal actors. What are the consequences of this?

I wish to draw on one point specifically, that is, the consequence for the position of the judge and the legislator as legal actors. This does not mean that they are ontologically speaking only that. Legislators make policy decisions, more than judges do. But judges do make policy judgments, if for no other reason than because they make decisions. It is on the creative aspect as the common platform of their activity that judges and legislators can be usefully compared, a comparison that gives rise to a different perspective on legal theory compared to the previous one.

Legislators and judges, that is, argue on the level of coherence$_3$, where there are no norms readily available. It is obvious that this will happen more often with the legislator than with the judge. This, however, is not of concern here. What I do want to stress is the connection between judicial and legislative norm creation rather than the differences between them.

Taking freedom seriously means that its reflexive nature should be respected as far as possible. This means that when creating norms, a legislator should not believe that it is creating relations in any ontological sense of the word. If this were the case, the legislator would be operating within something like a Hegelian framework in which surrender to the State is the highest realisation of freedom. According to the terminology used until now, he would be operating according to a theory about freedom. Surrender is in no way an acceptable realisation of freedom.

According to freedom as *principium*, as argued in chapter 4, freedom is the beginning and the *Leitmotiv* of law. This means that since we are *all* free, we are all *equally* free. We are, that is, equal because we are free. In the absence of any argument as to why you could limit my freedom, the extension of our freedom is identical. That is what equality involves. Equality, therefore, is grounded on freedom, not the other way around.

From this interpretation of equality, it follows that the law must be comprised of *general* norms. The reason is that we are all free and therefore we are all equal. This is the same as saying that in freedom we are all equal, or that we are all equally free. Because rulers are humans, and thus equal to all others, any limitation of freedom therefore requires a reason. Since equality follows from freedom, no one has an a priori right to limit another's freedom.

Hobbes, Rousseau and Kant may agree on this point. They support the position that freedom is the proper characteristic of the state of nature, and that within freedom we are equal. After entering into the social contract, we create a state that will act upon us with the help of general norms. The crucial point however, is that their theories, starting from freedom, all collapse into a theory *about* freedom. Having entered into the state, we undergo the effects of our only action on a conception of freedom. We have indeed surrendered to a state.

The contract theories have provided an argument as to why we are to enter into a civil state. The diversity of the argument should not conceal a similar qualitative change in freedom. Entering into the contract for a rational reason suggests that, from the perspective of the subjects, the game is over. All we are required to do is to sit down, shut up, and act according to the norms promulgated. The imposition of norms in the form of a rule is a necessary and sufficient – or exclusionary – reason for action. This is the essence of the contract theories.

Freedom as *principium* therefore is more demanding than 'freedom at the beginning'. Freedom as a *Leitmotiv* indeed suggests that respecting freedom at the beginning is by no means identical to respecting freedom's reflexive nature. The interpretation of freedom in the social contract theories – surrender theories – provides the reason for entering into the state. If freedom is also to count as a *Leitmotiv*, freedom's reflexive nature must be done justice. It is therefore not sufficient to organise the freedom of others. This organisation should be justified in addition to the justification of the organisation itself. Put differently, the institution of the state is one thing, whilst the operationalisation of this institution is quite another. Not every product stemming for the institution is legitimated by the very existence of the institution.

Rulers, therefore, are to give reasons for their limitations of freedom, or why they require legal subjects in order to act on conceptions about freedom replacing conceptions of freedom. Social contract theories make no distinction between legislation as a 'product' and legislation as a 'process'. Once we enter into the state – once we establish the institution – we have exhausted our critical reflective and reflexive potential and we are supposed to do as we are told. The establishment of the institution is a package deal that should be taken as a whole. This is not the case for legisprudence operating according to freedom as *principium* in the double sense of 'beginning' and *Leitmotiv*. According to the latter, any limitation of freedom requires a justification, without which there simply is no *Leitmotiv*. If the only reason for action is 'because a norm tells us to do so', then there is little reason for expecting any additional justification.

This brief sketch of the conceptual relations to which freedom as *principium* gives rise, shows the potential of the level theory of coherence. Coherent legislation as the upshot of freedom as *principium* takes citizens morally seriously in legislative and not only in judicial decision making. The principle of coherence, in other words, allows for system in law, while at the same time it relates law to freedom. This relationship entails the requirement of justification for any limitation of freedom that the law imposes.

The Principle of Alternativity as the Second Principle of Legisprudence

Before starting the argument in this section, it is useful to recall a couple of points from previous chapters. Chapter 2 discussed the social subject, that is, a subject whose consciousness arises in interaction with others. Under this process, the subject's identity (the 'I'-aspect) makes him different from others, while at the same time it is also the locus of his freedom. Chapter 4 has discussed the concept of freedom. Freedom as *principium*, as it was called, means both a beginning and a *Leitmotiv*.

A free subject acts according to conceptions of freedom, that is, his own concretisations of the concept of freedom. In doing so, he keeps others at distance, which is simply another way of saying that through interaction he not only becomes an autonomous subject or agent. Through interaction with others, he also must safeguard his identity. That was called 'freedom as distance'. Freedom as distance was said to be a fine-tuning of freedom as *principium*, in that freedom is the *Leitmotiv* of action. Others, therefore, must be kept at a distance, because the identity of the subject is not fixed once it is 'ready', but is a matter of ongoing differentiation from others.

Interaction is not always conflict-free. While Hobbes and Rousseau, among others, believed that it was the state's job to prevent or resolve conflicts, Chapter 2 pointed to the fact that law is to be regarded as an alternative. Conflicts are most of the time conflicts between free subjects regarding the meaning of the rules governing their social interaction, at least broadly speaking. These rules need not be legal rules, as Hobbes, Rousseau and Kant were tempted to believe. On the contrary, the social practices in which subjects take action have their own rules, without which there would be no practices at all. For this reason, I have called law a 'sub-routine', which is a variant of freedom as distance. Autonomous subjects acting on conceptions of freedom should be able to resolve their conflicts themselves in the first place. Only when this turns out not to be successful can law be called in as a sub-routine, or an alternative.

Freedom as was further argued in chapter 2 is conditioned by the circumstances of human action. These circumstances entail that in order for action to be possible, the subject must make choices. He must, that is, choose according to what conceptions of freedom he is going to act. If no choice is made, no action is possible. Freedom is constitutive of the circumstances of human action in that it makes choice both possible and necessary.

In line with the identification of the circumstances of human action, this study has articulated the circumstances of legislation. Freedom, that is, makes legislation both possible and necessary. As a possibility condition for legislation, freedom is not too big a problem. It is, however, when freedom is also considered a necessary condition for legislation, as Hobbes and Rousseau would have it. They argue that freedom must be regulated by law, since in the absence of law there is chaos, inequality, insecurity, or even a war of all against all. The view expressed in chapter 2 was that freedom makes legislation possible, but not necessary. When the circumstances of legislation obtain, the sovereign should justify why acting on a conception about freedom must be substituted for acting on conceptions of freedom. The reason for this requirement was explained in Chapter 6 where it was argued that the social contract is not a mere proxy to the sovereign that allows him to replace action on conceptions of freedom by conceptions about freedom. The social contract, on the contrary, was interpreted as a trade-off model of justification which requires a sovereign to justify his legislative interventions.

With this in mind, we can now try to get a better hold on the principle of alternativity (PA) as a principle of legisprudence. Like the principle of coherence (PC), the PA is a concretisation of freedom as *principium* in that it requires that an external limitation be justified as an alternative for failing social interaction. That is to say that, since the trade-off model requires that any limitation of freedom be justified, the PA as a principle of legisprudence is an argumentative requirement to justify why an external limitation of freedom is preferable to no limitation.

I will highlight two important aspects of the PA. The first is that it operationalises freedom as *principium*, in that only external limitations that can be justified as alternatives for failing social interaction can be considered legitimate. They can only be legitimate, that is, through legitimation. The second aspect deals with the ethical character of the PA.

The PA and Freedom

Let us begin with the first aspect. Any of a subject's actions under freedom-undetermined is possible only if he makes a choice as to the conception of freedom that he wants to realise. If a limitation is required as a necessary condition for action, it does not automatically follow that conceptions about freedom are preferable to conceptions of freedom. If they were, then we would be adopting the proxy model.

The trade-off model, in contrast to the proxy model, requires a justification for every limitation of freedom, that is, a justification for a conception about freedom being preferable to any alternative conceptions of freedom. So, apart from the justification of the *content* of the limitation of freedom, a justification must be offered as to *why* a limitation of freedom on a conception about freedom is preferable to no limitation of this sort. Put differently, the intervention of the sovereign itself must be justified, since there is no a priori justification for it in the trade-off model. This again does not concern the choice between different conceptions about freedom, as to their content; it only concerns the choice between a conception about freedom instead of a conception of freedom.

What must be justified then is why acting on a conception about freedom is preferable to acting on alternative conceptions of freedom. There may be a temptation to invoke the 'chaos argument' here. Valuable as it may be, in that it is argued that order is preferable to chaos, the argument is of a factual nature. It has, like Hobbes's anthropological thesis or Rousseau's economic thesis, a prima facie force, in that it can be presumed that without external limitations there would be chaos and no one would prefer chaos to order.

It is wrong, however, to say, as Hobbes and Rousseau do, that it is a constituent element of the very nature of human action that, when performed according to conceptions of freedom, it will necessarily end in chaos. That is to say that the mere chance of the outbreak of chaos is not a sufficient argument in order to substitute of conceptions about freedom for conceptions of freedom.

It will be clear from the above that, because of the normative character of freedom undetermined – as argued in chapter 4 – there is a right to be free. What must be argued under the PA is that rules as external limitations are preferable to no rules, or that, in other words, legislative regulation is preferable to or better than self-regulation. Legislative regulation imposes a choice out of the theoretically infinite number of possible concretisations of freedom. In presenting these choices as natural, as strong legalism does, the evaluative nature of the regulatory process is covered with the veil of naturalness, thereby concealing the instrumental character of the rules themselves.

As a matter of fact, rules do seek to achieve a purpose, that is, an end, goal, or value. Under strong legalism, this is unproblematic. The concealed instrumentalist character of strong legalism is, as was argued in Chapter 5, covered by the general proxy of the social contract.

However, the concealment of instrumentalism is a problem under the trade-off model. Unlike under the proxy model, the means does not justify the ends, so to speak. Rules, for Hobbes and Rousseau, are by very definition 'just'. Their very existence entails that the end they purport to realise to be just, so that any rule justifies its end and any end is justified by the fact that it is expressed in a rule.

The PA operationalises freedom undetermined. Freedom is a *principium*, as I have repeatedly said, means that it is the starting-point and the *Leitmotiv* for the organisation of political space. If there is agreement on the former, there might be dispute over the latter.

My claim is that if freedom is to serve as a starting-point, respect for freedom, that is, freedom as a *Leitmotiv*, refers to the requirement to respect as far as possible the reflexive nature of the concept of freedom. And this can only be achieved, so it follows from my claim, if the subject is allowed to act on conceptions of freedom. Only in acting on conceptions of freedom or internal limitations will there be a subject qua subject, that is, a subject of meaning. Meaning is related to the subject, as was argued in Chapter 3, and therefore also emerges from social interaction. Meaning, in other words, is social.

Two objections may be raised against this view. The first is that external limitations provide subjects with meaning, since external limitations provide meaning to social interaction (Ellscheid 1979). In doing so, external limitations structure interaction, and this is the proper task of law. This view is a plausible one, since it relies on the necessity that freedom be limited. It is, however, not acceptable as a whole, in that it presumes that, if freedom is not limited by external limitations, there will be chaos. This is, as I have argued above, a factual argument, which is insufficient in itself to justify external limitations of freedom.

My claim is a more modest one, in so far as it entails the necessity that freedom be limited, not in order to avoid chaos, but in order for action to be possible at all. Since my view starts from freedom as a *principium* in its twofold sense, it cannot be *presumed* that freedom will be better realised according to conceptions about freedom than to conceptions of freedom. If this is the case, there is a need for argumentative support.

The second objection, which is closely connected to the first one, stems from Raz's exclusionary reasons theory (Raz 1990). In Raz's view, if I understand him correctly, law is an exclusionary reason for action that outweighs any first-order reasons for not acting on any reasons other than law itself. With the law as a formal reason for action excluding any other reason, it should always be accepted as preferable to any of these other reasons. Two replies can be formulated at this point.

First, the exclusionary reasons theory, as a supporting qualification to Hart's theory of the internal point of view, no doubt provides a clearer basis for a theory of adjudication than Hart's view on the matter does.

While the reasons for accepting a rule as a norm in Hart may be of a great variety, and not necessarily of a moral nature (Hart 1994: 202 ff.), law as an exclusionary reason may lift all doubt as to the motives for accepting a rule as norm. It simply *is* the reason for action. In my view, however, this can only be the case if it is actually justified or legitimated as being preferable to other reasons for action. This is only done so *in abstracto* under the of exclusionary reasons theory; no particular reasons are given for particular rules. On this view, the theory reads as a variant of strong legalism involving the granting of a proxy to the sovereign.

In addition, this type of justification is not to take place – generally speaking –once the law is there, that is, once a proposition has been transformed into a valid legal rule. In so far as Raz excludes legislation from the domain of legal theory, as most other legal theorists do, his theory is an interesting theory of adjudication. The question, however, is whether it is correct to isolate legislation from a theory that aims to analyse the concept of law in general. It looks then as if the making of law does not belong to the concept of law, and that legal theorising starts from whenever law exists. This is, typically, a strong legalist position, falling foul of all the faults diagnosed in Chapter 5.

The second reply is of a methodological nature, and is closely related to the second part of the first reply. Raz's method amounts to a conceptual analysis of law, deliberately neglecting any substantive or evaluative part of practical philosophy of which his exclusionary reasons theory, as a conceptual analysis, forms a part (Raz 1990: 11). Fruitful as it may seem, it may be wondered whether the exclusionary reasons theory will remain in place when it is asked why an external limitation of freedom is a reason for action for someone, except for the judge qua official who is called to apply it. The argument is similar in its effect to the critique of the Cartesian *cogito* analysed in Chapter 1. For whom, so it was asked, is something certain, based on the idea that certainty does not stand on its own, as truth does?

Leaving aside from the merits of Raz's theory, the question for whom something is a reason for action is, however, not raised, far less answered. Put differently, the legitimation of law – that is, the demonstration of how external limitations of freedom are preferable to internal ones – is left aside. Exclusionary reasons for action are simply legitimate, and require no further legitimation. In relation to this issue, I wonder whether a mere conceptual analysis of law could ever bring up these types of questions, that is, as long as conceptions held by the subject qua subject are not taken into account.

The latter risks jeopardising the consistency of the exclusionary reasons theory. Its promise and purpose is to analyse the logical relations within the concept of law, that is, the method is a *conceptual* one, not a *conceptional* one. If the promise is kept, it can be asked, however, whether Raz's methodological limitation to a conceptual – that is, a content-independent – analysis does not surreptitiously embrace some evaluative statement. It does, in my understanding of the matter, not follow analytically or logically from the concept of law that it is always preferable to follow legal rules than to act on conceptions of freedom. This implicit evaluative statement essentially claims that acting on external limitations is a priori better than acting on internal limitations. This again brings the argumentation back to the track of strong legalism.

Once the implicit character of the evaluative statement comes to the surface, there is a need for a justification. This justification is exactly what the PA requires. According to the PA, the gap between the existence of an external limitation and its being a reason for action must be filled through argument. Something cannot be a reason for action without a subject for whom this is so. That is, reasons for action do not hang in the air, nor are they to be found 'out there'. Their very existence makes them qualify as reasons for action, but this is hardly a sufficient condition for their exclusionary status. It is at best a necessary condition of a trivial character.

On my interpretation, the theory of exclusionary reasons presupposes a symmetrical relationship between the sovereign and his claim to legitimacy on the one hand, and the belief in the legitimacy on the part of the subject on the other. It strikes the balance between a *claim to* and the *belief in* legitimacy. The latter belief is what makes an external limitation a reason for action. To presuppose, however, that this relationship is symmetrical, and so that any of the sovereign's pronouncements provides an exclusionary reason for action, is to hold that any external limitation relies on a proxy, which is, in my view, not correct.

The denial of the symmetrical relationship on which the proxy model relies commits one to the notion that the claim to legitimacy and the belief in legitimacy is of an asymmetrical nature. What does this mean? It means several things. First, contrary to Weber's argument, there is a gap between the claims of authority and the belief in it. For Weber, the existence of law is a reason for believing in it, since legitimacy is exhausted by legality (Weber 1964: 134). Secondly, due to the existence of this gap, there is a need for argumentation in order to fill this gap. Third, because argumentation is of a historical nature, that is, it proceeds through language and is addressed to historical subjects, it can never be supposed to have come to an end. It might stop, in so far as no why-questions are raised any longer, or at least not for the time being. I will come back to this point when analysing the principle of temporality.

The Ethical Dimension of the PA

When discussing the concept of freedom in chapter 4, freedom was identified as distance, as a specification of freedom as *principium*. It was argued in that chapter that freedom as distance not only means distance from other subjects, but also distance from the state and its legislative interventions. Here I will pick up on this idea and argue how it is related to the ethical dimension of the PA. The ethical dimension of the PA refers to the possibility that legislation, far from operating as an alternative for failing social interaction, destroys social interaction altogether.

It should be remembered in this respect that under the proxy model, subjects have consented a priori to any external limitation, whatever its content. Accordingly, any external limitation is considered justified, and this is the essence of the proxy. Under the general proxy model – that is, the model in which no reservation is made for some rights, whether political or other rights – any social relationship can be transformed into a legal one. Put differently, within the general proxy model of which Hobbes and Rousseau were the defenders, there are either no social relations (Hobbes), or they can all be transformed into legal ones (Rousseau and Kant).

According to my interpretation of their theory in connection to Chapter 1, it may be remembered, both philosophers have trouble with the concept of 'relation'. Under Hobbes's nominalist theory, relations have no ontological value. Therefore, prior to the social contract, there is the latent *bellum omnium contra omnes*, and for this reason he argues in favour of the social contract and the surrender to the sovereign by individuals of their capacity to act on conceptions of freedom. Rousseau for his part is subtler in his argument, in that he does not deny that a society existed before there was a state. He criticises Hobbes's idea in saying that war is a form of society – though not the most preferable one. The social contract, for Rousseau, will add to the existing social relations the morality that they were lacking in the state of nature. Kant for his part accepts the existence of social relations in the state of nature, though denies that without a state there will be a war of all against all.

Setting aside the differences, Hobbes, Rousseau and Kant hold that social relations can only be considered normative when they are transformed into legal relations (Kant 1996: § 44). Social relations without legal form or sanctions are 'of a lesser value' than legal relations, if I may say so (ibid.: § 6 ff, § 44).

Their point when it comes to regulation is to rationally argue what the regulation of a political space should look like. Yet, while our philosophers are calling upon the law in order to organise society, their sovereigns are not refraining from issuing external limitations as they please. Apart from not violating rights or constitutional rules, the volume, number, or normative density of external limitations that constrain social interaction in limiting freedom have no ethical consequences. On the contrary, on this view it seems that the more rules there are, the more social relations take on the shape of 'true' relations. The more rules there are, moreover, the less likely it will be that conflicts will develop. In the following pages, I will challenge this overall view on conflict and interaction, which was already criticised in chapter 2, and that underlies strong legalism.

I will challenge this view, by arguing that the legalisation of social relations entails a fundamental change as regards their character. Put briefly, under freedom as *principium*, the subject is initially a subject qua subject, before being a citizen. If he is a citizen, he also remains a subject qua subject or a social subject, the contours of which were articulated in chapter 2. The impact of strong legalism on the subject has an ethical characteristic, and I will briefly comment on some of ethical implications of the juridification of social interaction.

According to the hypothesis that social relations do not exist (Hobbes), or that, if they do exist, they lack true morality (Rousseau), the creation of rules in political space entails the establishment of social relations or their branding as true morality. If so, political space creates social relations in its own deontic language, that is, the language of right and duty. Any relevant social relation then becomes a legal one, expressed in terms of right and duty.

If some social relations can be said to exist, as was read by Rousseau, with Kant in his wake, they are or can be transformed into relations of right and duty. In the absence of any bar to the creation of rules, which is characteristic of the proxy model, any social relation can be transformed into a legal relation. Put more succinctly, under the proxy model, the whole of social interaction can be replaced with schemes of interaction based on the rules of the sovereign, determining rights and duties. The strong legalistic sovereign can even create social relations unknown in social space. It all depends on the sovereign's discretion.

This approach clearly deserves the qualification of strong legalism, of the Shklar version: moral or normative conduct is a matter of rule following, and moral relations are comprised of duties and rights determined by rules (Shklar 1986: 1).

The creation of political space ends in Hobbes's identification of law and morality in his (juridical) positivism, and Rousseau's subordination of morality to law, up to making morality irrelevant for law in his (legal) positivism, exclusively acting on external limitations determining rights and duties (Wintgens 1991a, 1991b).

With this diagnosis in mind, we should remember the analysis contained in chapter 3, where social interaction was claimed to lie at the basis of both meaning and subject. Subjects, so it was argued, acquire their identity from meanings emerging from interaction.

According to the arguments put forward in the previous chapters – that meaning is social in nature, in that it emerges from interaction – social interaction can be considered to be horizontal. Social interaction, in the absence of external limitations, takes place on a horizontal level, where subjects are free from any external constraints by a sovereign. When the idea of the social character of meaning is combined with the theory of freedom sustained in the argument until now, it follows that meaning emerges through interaction of subjects on conceptions of freedom.

Without any external constraint or exercise of power, this interaction is horizontal, in that it is an exchange from different positions on the same – horizontal – level, from which provisional determinations of meaning result. What we learn from Hobbes and Rousseau is that horizontal interaction is not possible or at least problematic, and that the subjects' capacity to act on this level should be surrendered when creating a political space. As a result of that creation, however, a new type of interaction is substituted for horizontal interaction that I propose to call 'vertical' interaction.

If the interactive positions of an A and a B are framed in terms of rights and duties, vertical interaction is substituted for horizontal interaction. A and B speak the language of rights and duties with each other. This replacement means that, for example, B can be forced, with institutional backing, to do what A has the right to. The more rules there are, the more realistic the view becomes that interaction will end up as being exclusively vertical, in that interaction will be limited to the legal enforcement of rights and duties. This, of course, one could object, is a factual situation. I agree, but this is not the point. The point is that any transformation of horizontal into vertical interaction entails an ethical problem.

This ethical problem can be articulated in the following manner. If interaction is transformed from horizontal into a vertical, A and B will end up transforming each other into an object. The rule that mediates their interaction ultimately replaces the interaction with claims of right and duty, and so, on the basis of a rule, A becomes the object of B's right and/or vice versa. A can be forced to do or not to do something and so can B. Their interaction, in short, is limited to a pre-structured scheme of meanings that can be enforced, if necessary with institutional backing.

In the analysis of strong legalism in chapter 5, it was argued that instrumentalism in strong legalism does not only affect the relationship of means to ends. At the same time, it affects the subject, submitted to the rules thus created, in that the subject qua subject disappears – or at least risks disappearing – from the discourse altogether.

The proxy model intervenes in this, in the following way. Under this model, the subject appears only once, that is, at the 'moment' when consenting to the contract. After that, he disappears qua subject, and reappears as the object of rules. In that he is expected, as he promised on entry into the contract, to follow these rules, it is sufficient that the rule determines the content of the external limitation of his freedom. His consent to any particular limitation of freedom is no longer needed during this stage, since the general proxy covers it.

Since the content of the external limitation concerns not the subject but his behaviour, it concludes an abstraction of the subject qua subject. This is simply another formulation of the idea that strong legalism produces a discourse without a subject. Taken as it stands, the subject qua subject is then in constant danger of disappearing.

In addition, this is happening under conditions of increasing vertical interaction, that is, when interaction based on rights and duties is increasingly replacing horizontal interaction. The more rules there are, the more vertical interaction can a priori replace horizontal interaction. This substitution and the subsequent twofold objectivation of the subject – his objectivation resulting from external limitations and the objectivation by fellow subjects who interact with each other on vertical interaction patterns or rules – are reverse sides of the coin called. This problem has been finely articulated by Robert Kagan as 'adversarial legalism', though without being identical to what I am arguing here (Kagan 2001).

The objectivation of the subject jeopardises the ethical dimension of law. This means that the instrumentalisation of law, as it results from strong legalism, erases the ethical dimension set out above. Subjects have a right to act freely according to freedom as *principium*, that is, to act on conceptions of freedom. This is what the reflexive character of the concept of freedom entails. As a result, interaction is horizontal. Any rule or external limitation of freedom risks altering this horizontal feature of interaction, in that interaction under external limitations brings with it a possible transformation into vertical interaction. The more external limitations a sovereign issues, the greater the risk that this will occur, and the greater the jeopardy for the subject qua subject.

The restoration of the ethical dimension of law, and the subsequent rehabilitation of the subject qua subject, requires a specific justification of law itself. The trade-off model, it is argued here, attempts to do so, in that it is necessary to justify why the concretisation of freedom on a conception about freedom outweighs any alternative conceptions of freedom.

This ethical concern is, among other things, what the PA expresses. In order to avoid the subject's dual objectivation, that is, by rules and by other subjects, and its transformation into an object, the PA erects an argumentative bar. This means that any external limitation of freedom must be justified as an alternative for failing social interaction, that is, horizontal interaction on the subjects' conceptions of freedom qua subjects.

A further clarification is necessary in order to properly to understand the PA as a principle of legisprudence. When X is called an alternative for Y, it is taken as a replacement for Y. On this interpretation, it is assumed that the alternative X is preferable to Y, as in the following example. If it is raining and I do not want to get wet, an alternative way to spend my time is playing cards (1).

When the evaluative assumption is omitted, X and Y together form an alternative. So, walking in the rain and playing cards are an alternative, in that playing cards is an alternative for walking in the rain and vice versa (2). If an evaluative assumption is added, depending on its strength – do I absolutely abhor to walk in the rain, or do I not mind when it is only drizzling – I may start playing cards until it stops raining cats and dogs and then go for a walk. So, my dislike of getting wet will be confirmed when the rain is bucketing down, though it can be outweighed, by my need of fresh air, for example, when it is only drizzling (3).

In interpretation (1), X is a substitution for Y, in that X is always preferred. The concept of an alternative is considered a dispositive concept. On X being better than Y, they are mutually exclusive, so that either X or Y, but not both and not both partially, are reasons for action. Interpretation (2) is the descriptive version of (1), that is, without any evaluative statement. It describes the possibilities for action or conceptions of freedom. Interpretation (3) carries out a weighing and balancing of the conceptions of freedom, resulting in a choice that is necessary for action altogether.

With some modification, the example is capable of showing what is meant by 'alternative' as it operates under the PA. If the PA is understood as meaning that acting on a conception about freedom is always preferable to acting on a conception of freedom, the latter automatically outweighs the former. This interpretation fits in with the proxy model; it does not, however, adhere to the trade-off model. Under that model, freedom as *principium* means that the subjects are entitled to act on conceptions of freedom unless and until this actually turns out to be impossible or undesirable.

Over against Hobbes and Rousseau the trade-off model does not presume that things will go wrong if subjects act according to conceptions of freedom. In the absence of that presumption, which is the evaluative assumption in interpretation (1), the alternative to which the PA refers is the description *in abstracto* of acting on conceptions of freedom and acting on conceptions about freedom, which is covered by interpretation (2).

There is, in the trade-off model, an evaluative presumption operating against the background, and that is freedom as *principium*. Under freedom as *principium*, the proxy model is reversed, in that acting on conceptions of freedom is initially, though not a priori, preferable to acting on conceptions about freedom. Being 'initially preferable' does not however mean that it is 'always preferable'. It only means that, according to freedom as principium, it is *prima facie* preferable.

What the PA requires then, in order for the trade-off model to be coherent, is that the outweighing of the alternative be justified. It is important to remember the gap between the claim to legitimacy and the belief in it. Because of this gap, the relation between rulers and the ruled was called 'asymmetrical'. The surplus value, that is, as required by the asymmetric character of the trade-off model, cannot be presumed. In order to fill this gap, the surplus value must be actually realised; this can only be done through justificatory argumentation.

Time in Legislation: The Principle of Temporality

Time is to a large extent resistant to theoretical and philosophical analysis. One of the reasons for this is that time is at odds with truth that is universal, hence not affected by time. Time, that is, has destructive effects on truth (Perelman 1970b). The insensitivity of a legal system to time has another reason. As discussed in Chapter 5, the social contract as the basis of a legal system is a true foundation of it. Foundationalism in general is averse to time, because this negatively influences the truth of the basic principles on which a system is built. However, it was argued in the previous section that time is an essential aspect of coherence. Legal systems, that is, are dynamic in that they change over time. Only 'momentary' legal systems remain unaffected by time.

When analysing the first principle of legislation, that is, the PC a distinction was drawn between consistency and the coherence of a legal system. Consistency was defined as the principle of the identity of the elementary units. Coherence for its part was articulated as 'making sense'. Consistency as a necessary condition for coherence only operates at the level of coherence$_0$, and for momentary legal systems. Momentary legal systems, however, disregard the obvious fact that they are not operating within a socio-temporal vacuum. Judges and legislators, so it was concluded, are legal actors who operate within temporal contexts.

Compared to synchronic coherence, diachronic coherence as the level of coherence$_2$ requires a specific argumentation as to why synchronic coherence is lowered (or even abandoned). Judges can overrule their decisions, while legislators can change their ruling or policy. Legislators can also have good reasons not to change their norms or policies, and here the time dimension may prevent them from doing so, at the cost of making the system incoherent. I think this justifies the claim that time plays an important role when rulers justify their norms on the PC.

While the above analysis of the PC compared the position of the judge with that of the legislator, we shall now leave aside the former and primarily concentrate on the latter. The reason why I will proceed in this manner concerns the very rationality of the legislator on the one hand, and the concept of temporality in a legal system on the one hand. Despite the similarities between the legislator's and the judge's position when dealing with the coherence of their norm setting, there is also a crucial difference between the two. In a word, judicial norm setting puts an end to a conflict. Whether this concrete norm is right or wrong does not matter for the moment, since even a wrong decision – notwithstanding the possibility of an appeal within the chain of legitimation – terminates the conflict.

One might say that once a statute leaves the Parliament, it is legitimate and no longer open to discussion. It is a formally valid norm. This, however, is not the end of the story. According to a commonly accepted theory, the time span of the judge is the past, while the executive branch's is the present, and the legislator's the future. Judges decide about past events, while legislators work on the future. Classical consequences of this theory are that judges cannot rule on cases in general terms, thereby usurping legislative power, while legislators cannot decide for the past without making their ruling retroactive. Much has been said and written about this theme, and I will not engage in repeating it. Instead of focusing on retroactivity and its problems, we shall now focus on the principle of temporality from the point of view of the legislator's rationality.

An attempt was made in the previous chapters to recontextualise the basic tenets of the Modern philosophical project, namely the subject, rationality, and freedom respectively. It was possible to conclude from this recontextualisation in chapter 2 that the subject as it emerges from social interaction in a context with others is a social subject, hence replete with temporality. A similar conclusion followed from the recontextualisation of reason and rationality in chapter 3, where it was argued that only unbounded rationality is a-temporal. Bounded rationality for its part is no longer related to the Cartesian Olympian view on rationality, so that this concept too requires a context in order to make sense for us.

In chapter 4, an attempt was finally made to contextualise freedom, in that the social subject is free in a context with others. According to the social dimension of freedom, it was argued that subjects are free to act according to conceptions of freedom thereby, putting others at a distance. Freedom as distance, as it was called in chapter 4, is a variant of freedom as *principium*. Here again the contextualisation of freedom leads to the conclusion that the circumstances of human action require the subject to act within a context with others. This context for its part is, here as elsewhere, replete with temporality. In this section, an attempt will be made to identify the temporal aspect as developed in the previous chapters as a principle of legislation.

When criticising the Olympian view on rationality in chapter 3, the concept of 'bounded rationality' that Herbert Simon introduced in economic theory was mentioned. Actors are boundedly rational in as far as they have no direct access to reality, including the future. Bounded rationality, as I have argued, refers to limited access to information, techniques, and, more specifically, time. A Cartesian (unbounded) rational actor is not confronted with limits of that kind because rationality is a-temporal or universal, identical for and in every subject. All there is to know can be gathered by the universally rational mind. Mathematics as the proper device of knowledge furthermore provides the a-temporal certainty that brings the Cartesian mind without detours to universal truth or truth unqualified.

Strong legalism, under the auspices of the Modern philosophical project, as was argued in chapter 5, has turned off the switch of time. The validity of law does not suffer from the passing of time, due to the omniscient rational ruler. What may seem true for a Constitution is anything but true for normal legislation.

As social subjects are cursed with bounded rationality, so too are legislators. Their realm of action is the future, but as humans, they face the boundaries of bounded rationality. Minds are limited, and information about the future is scarce. In addition, there is a marginal cost of gathering additional information. Under the conditions of scarcity of means, this involves a constraint which is time. As Elaine Spitz has observed, majority rule presupposes the possibility of future revisions of present-day majority decisions. In contrast, if the proposals of the current majority can be rendered permanent, they threaten to undermine the normative presuppositions of majority rules. Plans for the future must provide for choice. No blueprint can be so comprehensive and so financed or organised that those who inherit it have no viable options over whether to retain it. It is necessary to have the opportunity to revise what has been done. What Spitz refers to is the impossibility of predicting the future in all its details, which is precisely the characteristic of strong legalism. Legislators are, that is, bounded actors, and the fixation of legislation, 'out of time', so to speak, that makes law appear 'just there', paradoxically, installs some arbitrariness.

What the principle of temporality (PT) then amounts to in some more detail is that legislators must argue why a norm or external limitation is necessary now 'all things considered *now*' (ATCN). The ATCN clause indicates that it is the 'right' time to issue a norm. At the same time, it indicates that is only the right time *now*. In this respect according to the PT, the legislator has to argue why he acts now.

There is, however, another aspect to the principle of temporality as a principle of legisprudence that will be clarified in the following pages.

Norms, that is, can and do become obsolete, as is frequently established (Calabresi 1982: 5 ff.). Obsoleteness is an indication of the influence of the time when legislation was enacted; it can be considered from two perspectives.

The first perspective is this. Obsolete rules may rely on distinctions that are now believed to be arbitrary or discriminatory. A distinction between persons that was allowed at the time the rule was issued may after a lapse of time and turn out to amount to discrimination. A distinction is arbitrary and so discriminatory in so far as no rational justification is or actually can be given to support it. From this angle, obsolete rules may be successfully challenged in court in as far as they violate the requirement of equality.

The obsoleteness of an external limitation is an indication of the influence of time. The recognition within the legal system of the possibility of legal challenge in so far as it violates equality does not, however, make it a principle of legislation. The temporality of rules becomes visible within a legal system because of the light shed on it by the principle of equality. The opportunity of legal challenge may be an adequate reaction of the legal system as a reversal of the chain of legitimation.

The second perspective related to obsoleteness is that norms issued at a time and duly justified or legitimated according to the PT ATCN may lose their legitimacy over time. In that setting, the PT in combination with the PC requires that a legislator take the ATCN clause into consideration again. It may be the case that a norm is no longer justified under the PC, so that new action is required. Changing circumstances may require that a norm be changed or on the contrary, be upheld over time.

Speaking more generally, the PT requires that norms not simply be justified under ATCN conditions. Justification under the PT is an ongoing justification, in that legislators must be capable of continuously upholding their rulings. Legislators, as explained above, are boundedly rational. Even if their working field is the future, they cannot overlook it *sub specie aeternitatis*.

The last point is of specific importance, since it highlights the fact that the justification for external limitations is not limited to the moment of its promulgation because of its historical nature. This is simply another formulation of the idea that the gap between the claim to legitimacy and the belief in it can never be supposed to have been conclusively filled. Were this presupposition to arise, then the time switch would be turned off again, which brings us right back on to the track of strong legalism. The result of the historical nature of external limitations or issue under ATCN is that the gap between the claim to legitimacy and the belief in it can never be filled. Ongoing justification is required because of the limited insights of the legislator into the future.

From the basic requirement of the trade-off model that justification must be offered for any trade-off, it is now but a short step to see in what way legitimation in the active sense, that is, legitimation as a process, differs from legitimacy under substantive legitimation models as well as in the proxy model.

Legitimacy under substantive legitimation models as well as under the proxy model is, to use a Dworkinian term, a 'dispositive concept' (Dworkin 1985: 120, 125, 127). A concept is dispositive when it is a matter of all or nothing. So, the concept of a rule is a dispositive concept, in that a rule is valid or not. If it exists, it is valid; if it is not valid, it does not exist. Rousseau might say that legal validity and the existence of a rule are 'correlational', like father and son, or citizen and sovereign (Rousseau 1997a: 111). Under strong legalism, a legally valid norm is at the same time legitimate. It looks as if the term 'legitimate' is of a dispositive nature, which I believe is not the case.

Concepts, that is, are not in themselves 'dispositive' or 'non-dispositive'. Concepts can be used in a dispositive or a non-dispositive manner. This does not work for a concept like 'circle': something is a circle or it is not. Things are different though with a concept like 'legitimacy'. Legitimacy, as I have argued in Chapter 6, is the result of legitimation. In that respect, a norm can be more or less legitimated. The opposite view – that legitimacy is of a dispositive nature – brings us, here as elsewhere, back to the notion of strong legalism.

To consider 'legitimacy' as a dispositive concept is to associate it directly with the proxy model of legitimation. Under strong legalism, 'legitimacy' is used in a dispositive manner. Substantive legitimation models and the proxy model use it in a dispositive manner, thereby presupposing that it is of a dispositive nature. This is, of course, what these models seek to show, that is, that no other use except the dispositive one is correct. In doing so, substantive legitimation models as well as the proxy model tend to a priori bridge the gap mentioned above, up to the point of denying the existence of any gap at all. Put differently, in considering legitimacy as a dispositive concept, substantive legitimation models and the proxy model presuppose the symmetric relationship between the claim to legitimacy and the belief in it, as was pointed out above.

Under the trade-off model of legitimation on the contrary, there is a gap between the former's claim to legitimacy and the latter's belief in it. This means that, in order for the gap to be filled, external limitations must be justified, and this can only be done by leaving the justification open-ended in time. In consequence, the legitimacy of a norm is only temporal ATCN. Under the PT, it must be upheld over time in order to prevent that rules becoming obsolete or otherwise problematic.

The Principle of Necessity of the Normative Density

It is sometimes said that an external limitation on freedom must be necessary in order to be justified. Its necessary character is taken to be the object of its justification. Whilst this may be informative, it is at best a trivial restatement of the PA: whether an external limitation is necessary involves determining whether it is better than having no external limitation. In a less trivial version, the necessity to which the principle of the necessity of normative density (PN) refers is a necessity of normative density that is required if the PA principle turns out to justify an external limitation. In other words, if an external limitation turns out to be justified according to the PA, under the PN the sovereign must justify the necessary normative density of the external limitation. This consists in the normative weight which the sovereign will put on the shoulders of the subject. The normative weight or normative density is what the PN deals with.

On this interpretation, the PN says something different than the PA. Let us first of all consider how the PN is connected to the trade-off model. Taking freedom as principium, under the trade-off model any external limitation should not only be justified as preferable to no external limitation. If freedom is not only the starting-point, but also the *Leitmotiv*, it is but a small step to endorsing the consequence that the less dense or intense the external limitation is, the more room there is for action on internal limitations if, of course, the choice would amount to a choice in favour of action. While the PA says something about whether or not to intervene, the PN deals with the normative impact of the external limitations. What must be justified under the PN is why the normative density of an external limitation is necessary.

In criticising Austin's idea of rules as orders backed by threats, Hart introduced a path-breaking insight to jurisprudence. Although many rules are accompanied by sanctions, it is not true on his analysis that any rule is related to a sanction or that any rule is a coercive order. Some rules, he argues, do not trigger sanctions when transgressed. Apart from the question of what it could mean to contravene a rule holding the conditions for making a valid will, there simply is no sanction for a subject who wishes not to make one. If he makes one, in not following the conditions for a valid will, there simply is no will. So, in the discussion as to nullity as a sanction, my view is that the nullity follows from a declarative judgment that establishes the nullity, without subtracting anything from this act. The will is simply not valid.

Hart's theory of primary and secondary rules, in my view, is a convincing challenge to the Austinian theory of 'orders backed by threats'. The Austinian idea, in a slightly different version, shows up in Kelsen's theory. Its still current appeal to lawyers justifies my treatment of it in some detail here, with a view to showing what kind of problems it generates from the perspective of legisprudence. Its critique will be helpful in further articulating some more aspects of the PN.

Under both Austin's and Kelsen's theory, the standard form of a rule is a conditional formulation of a fact or a set of facts, the non-realisation of which calls for a sanction. This model of 'rule plus sanction' or RS-model is so familiar that it seems to go without saying. However, when freedom is considered as the *principium* in the theory I am setting up, it is easy to see that the RS-model directly intervenes with freedom. Following the transgression of the rule, no further justification is needed in order to impose the sanction.

Two preliminary observations can be made regarding this. First, it could be objected that the imposition of a sanction following the transgression of a rule does not rule out freedom. Freedom remains intact, in that it consists of the freedom not to transgress the rule. If one chooses to transgress the rule, the consequence is known in advance, so that it can be said that the sanction is willed, together with the transgression. Logical as it may sound, this argument, however, misses the point. It does so because of an underlying premise.

The underlying premise is that freedom in this view is *freedom of will*. It is the freedom to follow or not to follow the rule. It is similar to the idea of committing a sin. When committing a sin, one is free to transgress God's rule or not. This concept of freedom does not disappear in the absence of legal rules, that is, when there is so to speak no state. It is intimately connected to substantive legitimation models, under which there are rules and there is freedom that is, however, limited to following or not following them. These rules are of a transcendent or transcendental nature, in that their content is not at the disposal of those who are supposed to abide by them. They must be followed by subjects, whether they wish it or not, but not this time – as a democratic argument would require – because they have contributed to it, or were at least called to do so one way or the other. They are to be followed because they are 'just there'. Freedom is therefore reduced to a binary version of it, that is, to follow or not to follow the rules. Freedom then equals 'free will'.

The second observation expands to this. Even if, under the PA, the concretisation of freedom turns out to make more sense, or even to be the only possibility, then if it is performed according to a conception about freedom, this does not mean that the conception about freedom should reduce the possibilities of action, in that action is reduced to the decision over whether or not to follow the rule. In other words, if the concretisation of freedom on an external limitation is necessarily related to a sanction, then, again freedom is reduced to free will. What is left out of view here is the fact that the limitation of freedom serves a goal or a purpose.

This general modest purpose of a legal system, as has repeatedly been stressed, is freedom as *principium*. Freedom as *principium* results in the law making morality possible. To make morality possible means that subjects should be allowed to act on conceptions of freedom. If there is no freedom, then no morality is possible. In a weaker version, the more freedom is limited to external limitations, the smaller the extension of morality is.

Under the PA, the justification of the external limitation entails, as already been suggested and will be elaborated upon later, that acting on a conception about freedom is preferable to acting on a conception of freedom. 'Being preferable' is an evaluative statement that, in some cases, outweighs any other evaluation. This means that if all actions on conceptions about freedom are always preferable to actions on conceptions of freedom, then there will be no objection to supporting the external limitations with sanctions.

Sanctions prevent the subjects from acting – albeit only temporarily – on conceptions of freedom, because they are, for example, in prison or because they pay a fine that excludes any alternative way of concretising freedom. A consequence of this is that they cannot use these means to realise some alternative conceptions of freedom: money, as a rule of thumb, can be spent only once; when you are in prison, your acting on conceptions of freedom is physically limited.

This second observation thus points to a double external limitation in the RS-model. First, the concretisation of freedom is an external limitation, excluding action on a conception of freedom. Secondly, if the required action is not performed freely, then a second reduction of freedom follows. This second reduction is to a temporal (prison) or material (money) reduction of the reflexive character of freedom.

The first limitation can be justified under the PA, while the second cannot. This second limitation must, however, be justified separately, as the trade-off model requires. As a consequence, a second principle is needed in order to justify the second reduction of freedom included in the external limitation. The requirement of the latter justification is the *raison d'être* of the PN, as I will now argue.

My argument is divided into two parts. In the first part, I will deal with Kelsen's pure theory of law as the paradigmatic instance of the RS-model. I want to argue how Kelsen, in purporting to separate law and morality through his purification of law, beats his head on the very wall of morality. In the second part, I will draw on some consequences of this view that amount, in short, to the requirement to justify the normative impact of an external limitation.

The separation of law from natural law in general and from morality in particular can be said to be the main target of Kelsen's overall enterprise. Law and morality, to stick to this relationship, rely on a different basic norm that is the apex for the identification of a normative system. The parallel operation of both basic norms could bring about the impression that, given their similarity, they are also identical. That this is an illusion is what Kelsen wants to argue. Despite the similarities, he wants to keep law pure, without any conceptual influence of morality, natural law, or whatever.

In doing so, he sets up the legal order as an ensemble of valid rules, regulating human behaviour, promulgated and sanctioned for that purpose by the authorities. In this picture, three distinctions are introduced.

The first distinction is that human behaviour can be regulated in a positive or a negative manner. Positive regulations are those which order, forbid, or permit some behaviour. In the case of permission, rules provide the power to create norms, to impose sanctions or to create exceptions to a general prohibitive rule (Kelsen 1967: 15–17). Negative regulations of behaviour do not include an explicit permission, though they do not explicitly forbid the behaviour either (ibid.: 16, 42–3). Behaviour regulated in this negative way is always permitted.

The second distinction is between the subjective and objective meaning of an act (ibid.: 2–3). This distinction should allow Kelsen to delineate more clearly the juridical or objective meaning of a norm. The act of promulgation of a norm is an act of will. The latter constitutes the subjective meaning of a norm (ibid.: 7–9), in that a number of persons – the rulers – express the will that others should behave in the way that they want.

In the light of the terminology used throughout this book, the subjective meaning of a norm coincides with a conception about freedom. Those who promulgate a norm substitute a conception about freedom for alternative conceptions of freedom. Those subject to the norm, that is, must act on a conception about freedom.

While the subjective meaning of a norm coincides with the content of the act of will, its objective meaning can only be conferred by another – superior – norm. An act, that is, can only have the objective meaning of a norm in so far as a superior norm can be designated as endorsing the newly created norm. Only on that condition can a newly created norm be said to have objective meaning, normative meaning, or to be valid.

Here again, the distinction between conceptions of freedom and conceptions about freedom is elucidating, but from the perspective of legitimacy this time. A norm that relies on a superior norm is valid and legitimate. Because the act of will takes on the objective meaning of a norm, the substitution of a conception about freedom for a conception of freedom is *ipso facto* legitimate. There is, in other words, no need for further legitimation whenever a superior norm can be designated upon which the newly created norm is based.

A third distinction, finally, concerns the difference between legal norms on the one hand and non-legal norms on the other. The former are, in Kelsen's view, always sanctioned norms, while the latter are not. Sanctions are an essential part of a norm, whether directly or indirectly. Sanctions are imposed by the state through its monopoly of violence. It is in the organised nature of the sanction that legal norms crucially differ from moral norms (ibid.: 33 ff.).

The organised nature of sanctions means, to use Hart's terminology, that the legal system contains a number of secondary rules designating a limited number of actors and monopolistically empowering them to impose sanctions. Sanctions are always of a physical nature, or are at least related to physical acts.

The monopoly of violence implies for its part that the acts of will transform violence into a legitimate sanction. The objective meaning of these acts of will logically stems from a norm empowering the designated organ or person to inflict violence. The sanction of norms, together with their subjective and objective meaning, makes them legal norms. Sanctions, that is, are an essential part of the concept of a norm.

Norms deprived of any sanction, logically, are not real norms. Kelsen calls them dependent norms (ibid.: 54 ff.) Norms belonging to this class are only conditions under which other – real – norms, that is, including a sanction, can be created. Within the logic of the Pure Theory of Law, however, they are not to be counted among the norms properly so called because they are not backed by a sanction.

With some mental acrobatics, Kelsen then dodges the issue regarding the claim that dependent norms are legal norms, despite the absence of a sanction. They are according to Kelsen (ibid.: 51) enforceable because they are 'essentially connected with norms that stipulate the coercive acts'. Kelsen however leaves unclarified what this 'essential connection' consists of.

In the light of the analysis of the PN in this section, three remarks are in order here. First, apart from the somewhat bizarre characterisation of the relationship between 'norms without sanction' and 'norms with sanction' as an 'essential connection' in order to keep the Pure Theory consistent, we read from Hart, as from others, that this theoretical description does not fit in with an operational legal order. Any legal order contains rules that are not sanctioned. Although Hart's claim was quite original in the middle of the last century, it now sounds trivial.

Secondly, Paul Amselek has eloquently labelled Kelsen's theory as 'penalistic' (Amselek 1964: 194), a view of the legal system that expresses, so to speak, to the idea of law that is characteristic of 'the man in the street'. Murder, rape, fire-raising and theft, to mention but a few, appeal to the fantasy of most and coincide for them with what law is about. Mergers and acquisitions, takeovers, tax avoidance, or commercial litigation, mainly performed on secondary rules or power rules – and often without sanctions – are not of their concern. The *pars pro toto* view that Kelsen's approach induces is palpably incorrect.

Third, and most importantly, even if Kelsen's view were correct, *quod non*, and even if he had offered some explanation as to what he means by the 'essential connection', it would remain to be seen whether his view were an acceptable one. His view, that is, in connecting law with sanctions transforms law into a social fact. A similar critique could be formulated against Hart, in that for both, law amounts to rules that are 'just there', whether sanctioned or not, but which do not contain any normative bars, and without further justification.

To stay with Kelsen for a moment, regarding his norm that 'what is not forbidden is permitted', there is no limitation on the volume of external limitations of freedom (Kelsen 1967: 42–4). This was already noticed in Hobbes and Rousseau. Subjects can act on conceptions of freedom so long as there are no alternative external limitations, which suggests that any kind content can be law, as Kelsen (ibid.: 198) later on claims.

Logical as it may sound, it embraces the main aspects of strong legalism that were critically diagnosed in Chapter 5, and to which there is no need to return here. With his theory, Kelsen, to be sure, espouses a version of the proxy model, so that the PA is a priori excluded from the scene.

Apart from that, what I do want to stress further is that, in conceptually connecting norms to sanctions, Kelsen's theory must be criticised due to the dual reduction of freedom discussed at the beginning of this section, and that is capable of bringing to light the need for the PN.

We can now focus on some consequences of this view. Strong legalistic legislators, as may be remembered from Chapters 5 and 6, do not give reasons for their external limitations. This is not to say that there are no reasons at all, nor does this imply the denial that rules serve some end, purpose, or value. Most of the time, the end, goal, or value itself does not show up in the ruling activity. Instrumentalism conceals the choice of the rules' ends, goals, or values behind the 'thereness' of the law.

What can be learned from Kelsen in this regard is that, with respect to the implicit goal or target set, or value choice, the best means of realising them is by punishing those who do not follow the external limitation imposed.

What is included in the idea that conceptually connects external limitations to sanctions is that there is no other means of realising the end, goal, or value contained in the conception about freedom expressed by specific external limitations. The following objection to this view may be formulated.

It seems that the only way to realise a pattern of behaviour that is expressed in the external limitation is force, by way of threat or actual exercise. The consequence of this is that if it is already justified on the PA, one reduction of freedom – from acting on conceptions of freedom to acting on conceptions about freedom – of and by itself seems to call for a second reduction of freedom based on a sanction. It looks as if both reductions are analytically – or, in Kelsen's wording, 'essentially' – connected, for which I see no real argument. It is simply included in the concept of a norm or a legal rule.

If a sanction may be an appropriate means of realising some end, goal, or value, it does not follow that it is the only and always the best one. It is here that the trade-off model can be called in again, based as it is on freedom as *principium*. It may be the case that a sanction is the best way of realising the value, end, or goal included in the external limitation. This approach, however, has a price, to which I have referred above: the dual reduction of freedom. If then, freedom as *principium* is taken seriously, as the trade-off model does, the conceptual or essential connection between norm and sanction must be abandoned, since it keeps trace of a substantive model of legitimation.

If then the relationship between an external limitation of freedom and a sanction is not a conceptual one, this means that it must be justified. And this is what the PN requires.

Freedom as *principium*, as it operates under the trade-off model, requires that the goal, end, or value that the external limitation purports to realise entail the least possible impact on freedom itself. In operating a double reduction of freedom, norms with sanctions must therefore be used with caution. They are, that is, not to be banned from regulative discourse altogether. What is meant is that the essential connection between external limitation and sanction simply does not exist, as Kelsen claims, although it may be justifiable that some external limitations may be accompanied by a sanction.

The latter then opens a wider view on the scope of the PN. If under the PA, external limitations must be justified on the grounds that conceptions about freedom are substituted for conceptions of freedom, then sanctions can – but also must – be justified in order to avoid a second reduction of freedom.

Under the PN, the impact or normative density of an external limitation must be shown to be necessary in order to achieve the goal, end, or value. The legal system has, based on freedom as *principium*, the latter as its modest general purpose. On this view, every external limitation of freedom must be justified. On this view, the PN is not satisfied if any external limitation is not justified further and associated with a sanction. Sanctions are one of the many alternatives. The neglect of the PN in legal theory based on strong legalism can be explained by the fact that rules are conceived as purporting to realise ends, goals, or values, without the latter being subject to discussion. This, in essence, is instrumentalism. If instrumentalism is concealed, as in strong legalism, then the legal system as a whole serves some general purpose to the realisation of which every rule is supposed to contribute. The legal system's general purpose cannot be questioned since the proxy that is initially given covers it. Nor can the rules that are part of it be questioned, since their membership of the system, that is, their legal validity, is regarded as a sufficient condition for their legitimacy. Hence, no justification is required.

Under strong legalism, so it has been argued, the ends, goals, or values that the rule purports to realise are simply there, along with the rules that are instruments for realising them. Rules, so to speak, show 'by themselves' the ends, goals, or values at which they aim without further justification. Their incorporation into a rule seems to be understood; their status as a choice is, however, concealed. Therefore, the instrumentalist nature of law – in that law is an instrument to realise ends, goals, or values – is covered with the veil of naturalness or 'thereness' of the law.

I do not deny, however, that law in some sense is an instrument. I do not deny either that, sometimes, a sanction is an appropriate way of achieving an end, goal, or value. What I do, however, deny is that sanction is always the best means of realising an end, goal, or value. This is to say that, under the PN, the RS-model is not an expression of some traits of reality. The RS-model, in other words, is not a theory of reality. This includes the denial that a sanction is necessarily the best way of realising some desirable end, goal, or value. If it is on the contrary held to be so, the relation between a rule and sanction must be justified.

If, under the PA, it turns out that an external limitation is justified, then according to the PN, the normative impact of the external limitation must also be justified. The result of this justification could be that, all things considered, a sanction is to be regarded as the best way for the end, goal, or value to be realised. This means that, apart from sanctions, there are other means of realising a goal, end, or value.

Consider the following example. Imagine as a social purpose that from a certain age upwards people are no longer able to work, and therefore some income must be guaranteed. On the one hand, the purpose can be realised by subjects acting on conceptions of freedom. That is, they can make savings with the bank for the time when they will no longer be able to generate any more income. Suppose that, on the PA, it turns out to be justified to limit freedom, that is, to substitute acting on a conception about freedom for a conception of freedom. A candidate for justification may include the argument that if older people did not make savings during their active lifetime, they are a burden on society which must take care of them.

The purpose can be realised according to a conception about freedom, in that freedom is externally limited and a sanctioned obligation is created in order for subjects to contribute to a common fund administered by a state trust. Under the proxy model of legitimation, this external limitation is justified, in that the proxy requires that subjects will abide by any limitation that has the form of a legal rule.

According to the external limitation, that is, for the matter a rule plus sanction, there is a good chance that the purpose will be realised, and that everyone will contribute to the fund. But is it correct to say that this is the *only* means of achieving the purpose?

The proxy model suggests that it is. The determination of the purpose as well as the choice of the means of realising it is not subject to justification, since it is covered by the general proxy. Suppose the purpose is justified under the PA; this justification does not, however, mean that the choice of the maximum limitation of freedom, that is, a sanction, is justified. The requirement of justification of the latter choice is the essence of the PN.

How is this justification to proceed? Essentially an external limitation is justified under the PN if it argues out all the possible alternatives for realising the goal, end, or value. These alternatives have a weaker normative density than a sanction. Therefore, in order for a sanction to be justified, the external limitation must rule out the alternatives as 'too weak'.

Yet, most of the time there is a range of alternatives to sanctions. I will briefly comment on some of them.

To stay with the example of pension insurance, instead of a rule imposing a sanction, the sovereign could organise a campaign to inform people about the advantages of saving. In addition to that, it could consider allowing a tax deduction, in making savings ostensibly made for that purpose deductible in the annual tax declaration. Information or tax incentives are not associated with a sanction, though they can contribute to the realisation of the purpose.

Arbitrage, mediation, and Alternative Dispute Resolution are other techniques for avoiding an a priori use of sanctions. Management contracts are of the same sort. They leave the actors in the field the possibility to act on conceptions of freedom, while they contribute to the realisation of the goal, end, or value issued in a conception about freedom. Here again, sanctions are not the first and not the best way of doing that. I will say more on this in the next chapter.

What these examples purport to make clear is the *distinction* between the end, goal, or value, in short, the purpose of a rule, and the means of a limitation of freedom. If sanctions automatically accompany external limitations, then no choice is shown to be made between alternative means of realising the purpose. If a choice has been made in favour of a sanction, then the PN requires that this choice result from a weighing and balancing. Weighing and balancing of the means of realising a purpose is a justification of why the means chosen is or are the best way of achieving the purpose. In doing so, the double jeopardy of freedom, discussed earlier in this section, can be warded off.

What the PN, illustrated with the help of the example above, requires is that when alternative means exist a choice must be made. That choice must be justified. Means for realising a purpose are not value free. The choice for a tax measure as an incentive or a sanction will obviously have a different impact on freedom. From freedom as *principium*, it follows that the means with the lowest impact on freedom are to be preferred over any other. The preference is to be justified, in that all alternatives with a lower normative impact must be 'argued out'.

Considering the availability of alternatives, the external limitation with the lowest normative impact or the weakest normative weight – compared to a sanction which is strongest normative impact possible – must be chosen at the outset. This is what the PN requires. Put differently, the requirement of the PN like the PA is that sanctions, and external limitations respectively, are not a priori justified, as they are supposed to be in the proxy model. While the PA requires justification of the purpose, the PN calls for a justification of the means of realising it. Sanctions are only one of the possible means.

The trivial interpretation of the PA, mentioned above, under which the need for an external limitation is taken for granted, will most of the time not do justice to the PN as such. This interpretation, as has been noted, is a mere reformulation of the PA. If, in consequence, the distinction between PA and PN is not made, we will most of the time end up with the need for an external limitation plus sanction as the only possibility. This means that the PN, leaving aside its operation as a trivial interpretation of PA, is also binary in nature. In the absence of any nuance over the extent of the normative impact of external limitations, this interpretation espouses the premises of the proxy model, and so cannot be subscribed to here. The correct interpretation of PN involves a set of alternatives for sanctions, such as, for example, information campaigns or tax incentives, amongst others.

If we abandon the trivial interpretation of the PN that treats it as equivalent to the PA, the proper interpretation of the PN suggests that it deals with the ways of realising a purpose, while the PA deals with the determination of that purpose. The suggestion implies that means and ends are separated. The fact of the matter is that they are but distinct aspects of the same, that is, a concretisation of freedom.

The Principles of Legisprudence in Context

From the analysis in this chapter, some characteristics of the principles of legisprudence can be more clarified. As has been repeated at regular intervals, the principles of legisprudence are concretisations of freedom as *principium*, that is, freedom as the beginning of political organisation and freedom as its *Leitmotiv*. In this respect, they have a normative basis. The normativity of freedom as *principium* was explained in chapter 4. Under freedom as *principium*, external limitations by power holders must be justified. In that sense, the principles of legisprudence concretise this requirement. The principles themselves can be still further concretised, as discussed in Chapter 8, where it will be argued that they entail duties for the legislator.

Given their embedment in freedom as *principium*, it follows that the principles of legisprudence are not elements of a checklist to be marked once their requirements are satisfied. There is no lexical order between them either, which would make one of them more important than others, so that it had to be satisfied before the others.

One of the reasons for this is that the principles are concretisations of freedom as *principium* and are to be used in order to justify the substitution of a conception about freedom for a conception of freedom. In this respect, the four principles have the same vocation. They must all four be respected in order for the external limitation to be justified. They have the same weight and point in the same direction.

This is different from the way in which principles usually show up in legal reasoning. Judges facing a hard case and seeking to avoid discretion, should identify the principles that could decide the case. Dworkin's example of Elmer in Riggs v. Palmer is the best example. Should the murderer of his grandfather who served his time in prison be refused the inheritance to which he was named before he killed the testator on the principle *non bis in idem*? Or should he be refused the inheritance on the principle that no one can profit from his own wrong? The New York Court decided on the last principle, but this does not detract from the fact that the principles point in different directions. The Court, in other words, had to weigh and balance the principles against each other in the context of the legal system as a whole.

The fact that the principles of legisprudence draw on the same source, if I can say so, or point in the same direction – in addition to the obvious fact that legislators by very definition face hard cases – sheds a different light on their weighing and balancing. Three final observations are appropriate here.

First, the equal weight of the principles does not mean that they must or can be observed in an equal manner in each and every case. This points to the method which Lon Fuller has developed. His principles of internal morality have an equal weight, but it is palpable that they do not play an equal role in every situation. Their observation is a matter of aspiration, and not of duty. Were it a matter of duty, then we would find ourselves on the 'checklist track'. The aspirational method Fuller advocates amounts to saying that the ruler should try, as a matter of aspiration, to respect them as much as possible. This method has its limits, in that the failure to respect any of the principles can only lead to law in a Pickwickian sense. There is quite a lot of room for manoeuvre between the latter and the aspiration to do the job as well as possible. Respect for the principles is not a matter of all or nothing; it is a matter of excellence. This is also the case with the principles of legisprudence.

Secondly, as Fuller observes, it may be the case that it is necessary to temporarily or exceptionally deviate from one of the principles of the internal morality of law. In a specific situation, a legislator may have to violate the principle of non-retroactivity, say with an interpretative statute, as an ultimate recourse to prevent too divergent applications of a norm. Retroactive legislation violates the requirement that norms should be applied equally to equal cases, but if for some reason this turns out to be problematic, the violation of the principle of non-retroactivity may prove to be a reasonable solution to the problem.

This, thirdly, sheds light on the appropriate way of understanding the legislator's dealing with the principles of legisprudence. The principles, so I have argued, require a sovereign or a legislator, in order to justify the substitution of a conception about freedom for a conception of freedom. Although this requirement comes in the shape of a duty; it is not a matter of all or nothing. We should remember the argumentation concerning rationality in Chapter 3. There it was argued that rationality in practical matters is not demonstrative but argumentative. Argumentation, over against demonstration, is never conclusive. The exposé relied on Perelman's theory of argumentation. Yet, in addition to the proper nature of argumentation, the legislator as an agent does not look at society from an Olympian point of view. Like any other agent, his rationality is bounded. Bounded rationality as opposed to unbounded rationality is limited by several conditions, like the absence of full information, lack of time, lack of means to gather more of it, and so on.

In this twofold respect – that is, the proper nature of argumentation and the bounded rationality of the legislator – the justification of legislation is open-ended. This is a specific aspect of the principle of temporality, since social circumstances can and do change. A legislator therefore should be capable of upholding his rulings over time, and changing or repealing them in the event that it can no longer justify them according to the principles of legisprudence. The open-ended feature of justification or argumentation and the legislator's bounded rationality fit in with the principle of temporality, but are different from it.

In a similar sense to Fuller's principles, the principles of legisprudence are a framework that allows for 'more or less'. Due to their status as 'principles', they allow for more or less, but it is their framework that interests me here. The framework can be graphically represented as a square, of which the principles are the limits (See Figure on p.282).

External limitations that fall within the square are sufficiently legitimated according to the *four* principles taken together. External limitation falling outside the square is not sufficiently legitimated, or only 'justified' in a Pickwickian sense. The closer a justification is to one of the lines, the better it is legitimated according to the principle. Thus an external limitation right in the middle of the square (X_4) would be equally justified according to all the principles. The further to the left (X_3), the more it would be legitimated according to the PN, the nearer the top (X_7), the more it would be legitimated according to the PA, and so on. Location at one of the corners means that the external limitation is better justified according to the two principles (X_1) whose lines cross at the corner, while less justified according to the other principles, and so on.

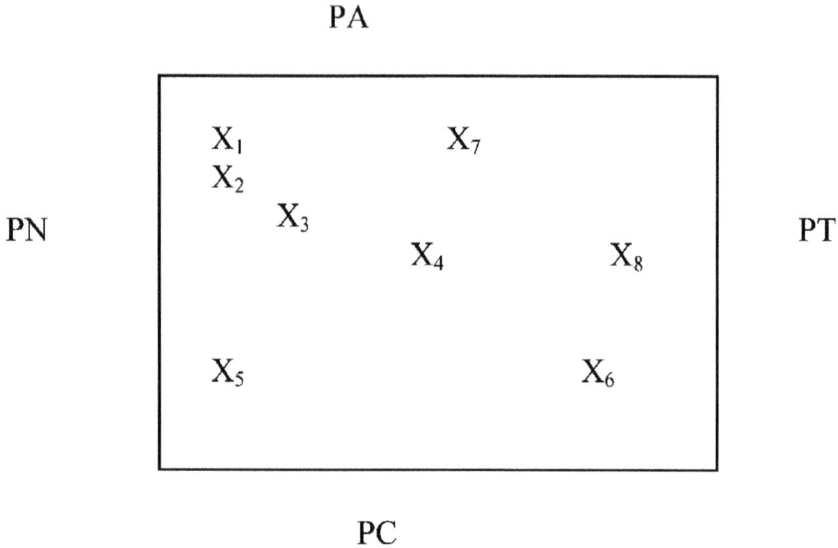

What this scheme illustrates is that, despite the equal weight of the principles, and the fact that they point in the same direction, not all external limitations will be justified in an equal manner. It may be possible, say, that according to the PT, the legislator is arguing that it is urgent to issue the external limitation (X_8), thereby paying less attention to the requirements of the PC. Changing circumstances may mean that an external limitation, say X_4, moves over the square, eventually requiring additional justificatory support in order to remain within the square. The graphical representation of the justification according to the principles of legisprudence has its limits, but it is submitted that it clarifies what the point is: legitimation is a matter of justification according to the principles of legisprudence, without resulting in ultimate legitimacy. The next chapter will explore in greater detail how the legislator deals *in concreto* with the principles and justifications according to them.

As concretisations of freedom as *principium*, the principles form a framework or the context in which justification has to take place. The principles form each other's context. On this idea, it is considered that it will have become clear that 'optimal' legislation is a myth. It refers to an omniscient legislator that acts rationally in the Cartesian sense. A legislator is not, as I repeatedly said before, an optimiser, but a satisfier. It operates within the framework of principles that can never be optimally realised. This is due to their status as principles, the essentially temporal context in which justification occurs, and the limitations on the legislator itself. What we may expect from the legislator is not optimal legislation, whatever this might mean, but satisfactory legislation, that is, legislation sufficiently legitimated according to the principles of legisprudence.

Chapter 8

Legisprudence and the Duties of Power: A Legisprudential Assessment of Rational Legislation

Introduction

The previous chapters have sketched out the contours of legisprudence as a normative theory of rational legislation. It has been argued that legislation is based on principles according to which externally imposed norms must be justified. In this respect, four principles were identified.

These principles are concretisations of freedom as *principium*, that is, freedom as the 'original situation' and as principle. According to freedom as the 'original situation', it has been argued that (1) in the absence of any rational and normative limitation on freedom, we are free. This means that (2) the extension of freedom is undetermined, and that (3) it is under the unlimited extension of freedom that we are all equally free. (4) Equality is the first normative dimension of freedom, in that no one has a right to limit another's freedom without his consent. (5) Consent refers to the self's limitation of freedom or to the reflexive nature of freedom. Freedom, that is, can only be limited by a free subject. (6) Reflexivity or autonomy is therefore the second normative dimension of freedom. Any other limitation is tantamount to domination that violates equality.

According to the above, no one has an a priori right to limit anyone else's freedom, or at least not without a justification. Mutual or multilateral agreement on the limitation of freedom is a necessary condition for it, as well as a sufficient justification. In this respect, the social contract tradition has provided a theoretical framework for the justification of legislation. On the basis of this hypothetical agreement, a sovereign is given the power to limit his subjects' freedom. The multilateral agreement in terms of a social contract to set up a political society involves an a priori submission to the sovereign's norms, whatever their content may be. Chapter 6 identified two versions of the social contract as a legitimation for power, namely, the proxy model and the trade-off model.

According to freedom as *principium*, which is the second meaning of freedom as *principium*, freedom is also the *Leitmotiv* of norm giving. It is on the basis of freedom as *principium* that a norm giver is to justify why freedom is limited, that is, because (1) social interaction is failing, and (2) weaker alternatives are insufficient. In addition, freedom as principle requires that (3) the norm giver justify why he is issuing an external limitation at a certain time, in addition to an upholding of the limitation of freedom over time, and (4) a justification of its relation to the legal system as a whole. These four requirements correspond to the four principles of legisprudence, that is, the principle of alternativity (PA), the principles of normative density (PN), the principle of temporality (PT), and the principle of coherence (PC).

It will be argued in this chapter that the principles of legislation as elaborated in legisprudence can be concretised as duties of the norm giver. These duties are operationalisations of the principles of legisprudence. They operate in the same way as these principles, that is, not in a lexical order, or as a checklist, or a 'cook book', but as a dynamic interactive set.

In the first section, it will be argued that power is related to duties in a sense which is different from Hohfeld's analysis. Given this connection between power and duties, in the next section, the meaning of the 'rationality of the legislator' will be explored, leading to an articulation of the circumstances of legislation. The circumstances of legislation will allow us to delineate the contours of the duties of power. The argument builds on the duty to justify legal norms on the principles of legisprudence. In addition to the fact *that* legislators have to justify their ruling, this chapter will explore the contours of *how* a legislator has to acquit himself of that duty in order to deserve the qualification 'rational', thus showing that practical reason permeates legislation.

The Duties of Power

Primary and Secondary Rules

Western democracies are institutionalised, in that political power is conducted within a framework of law. State power is bound to legal norms that provide the institutional framework for state action (MacCormick 1999: 122). The judicial limitation on state power thus constitutes the core of the rule of law doctrine, in that state action must proceed according to legal norms.

An interesting theory within the context of this section is Rousseau's, referred to in chapter 2. Rousseau's social contract contains only one clause as the necessary and sufficient condition for the existence of a state. That clause is the majority rule. Leaving aside its political meaning, majority rule can also be interpreted as a legal rule, and more specifically as a secondary rule of power. It is a human convention (which is a condition for a rule to be a *legal* rule – Rousseau 1977a: 44). It can be taken to be a rule of recognition of the system, in that all rules can be identified by reference to it. It is also a rule of change, in that no rule can be created or changed. On the basis of the majority rule, legislators can create primary rules of obligation, in addition to supplementary secondary rules of power like rules of adjudication.

The distinction between primary rules of obligation and secondary rules of power already appears in Jhering suggesting that law can be considered from both an anatomical and a physiological point of view. He thereby stresses the idea that apart from its structure, a legal rule has also a function within the legal system (von Jhering 1968: vol. 1, 25 ff.). Léon Duguit (1921: 106–7, 224) and Jean Dabin (1929: 19–21; 1963: 101, 169) for their part distinguish between 'normative' and 'constructive' or 'technical' rules of law. The former require action or that action be desisted from, while the latter ensure the respect and application of the former. Perelman (1976b: 44; 1984d: 71) considers secondary rules a necessary requirement in order for a legal system to elaborate, modify and apply legislative norms.

H.L.A. Hart has proposed a paradigmatic version of an institutionalised legal system as a conjunction of primary norms of obligation and secondary norms of power. This distinction is not wholly unreminiscent of Hohfeld's analysis in his *Fundamental Legal Conceptions*, in which he has identified eight normative concepts in judicial reasoning. The concepts are connected in two groups interchangeably centred on the concepts of 'duty' and 'power'. Hohfeld considers them the 'lowest common denominators of law'(Hohfeld 1913: 58) and the 'basic conceptions of the law – the legal elements that enter into all types of jural interests.' (ibid.: 20).

Hart then argues that norms are not necessarily confined to coercive orders which the sovereign imposed on his political inferiors 'backed by threats' and accompanied by a 'habit of obedience', as Austin thought. Nor are they confined to directions addressed to officials who are authorised to apply sanctions in the event of transgressions. On Hart's account, Austin's legal system is 'primitive', which only contains primary rules (or standards) of obligation and displays a number of defects. In line with Locke (1963c: ch. 9; cf. Kant 1996: 89–90), Hart argues that a social order regulated by mere primary norms means that, from the perspective of a 'mature' legal system, there is *uncertainty* as to what the norms are and consequently what behaviour is expected. In addition, a primitive legal system is *static* in that its norms are inflexible or immune from deliberate change (Hart 1994: 92–3). Finally, a primitive legal system is *inefficient* in that it lacks an agency vested with the power to authoritatively ascertain whether its norms are violated or not (ibid.: 93–4).

A mature legal system in Hart's view includes secondary rules of power that remedy these defects. The class of secondary rules of power contains the rules of adjudication, change and recognition. Secondary rules of power have primary rules of obligation as their object. They are the meta-rules or programme rules of a legal order, in that they make it possible to establish which rules are part of the system, how and by whom they are to be applied and how they can be changed (ibid.: 94). It is maybe too far a stretch to say as Hart does that secondary rules are *all* about primary rules (ibid.). A rule of change, for example, can itself be changed, which is the case for a self-referential application of a secondary rule. More important though is that these are more meta-rules that have primary rules of obligation as their object; although they can also have secondary rules as their object, and may interact with primary rules of obligation. What is more, they may themselves contain obligations.

The functional differentiation between primary and secondary rules referred to by von Jhering (1968: vol. 1, 25 ff.) supplies 'the heart of the legal system' (Hart 1994: 98), thus delineating a legal system from other normative systems. In addition, their union, so it would appear, provides us also with a version of the institutionalisation of power or the rule of law. If this is correct, then there is a question as to whether the 'key to the science of jurisprudence' can also give access to legisprudence as a tool for understanding the position and the function of the legislator in this picture.

The following examples illustrate this problem. Parents have the power to educate their children, that is, to take decisions regarding their school education, to give orders, to threaten punishment, and also to inflict it for disobedience. This power can be identified as a private power, and in this respect it is vested in the same group as the rules conferring the power to make a will or to get married. There is a crucial difference, however, between norms regulating the making of valid wills or marriages and the norms regulating parents' power to educate their children. No one has a duty to make a will or to get married, and do not lose the power when it is not used. Things are different with the power to educate children. Parents cannot escape the duty to exercise this power, and can be legally forced to comply with it.

A second example concerns the power conferred by company regulations on its CEO. Say that a paragraph of the constitutive act of the company confers the power upon the CEO to convene the general assembly, in addition to its mandatory annual meeting. Imagine further that the CEO is informed about dramatic figures in the balance sheet. Can he be held liable for not having convened the general assembly, that is, does he have a duty to exercise this power under the circumstances mentioned, even if no explicit rule compels him to do so? Since he has the right (or the power) to do so, circumstances, so it seems, could put him in a situation where not exercising his power may amount to a breach of a duty. However, this duty or obligation is not expressly imposed by any rule of obligation. It follows from his power to act in that way.

The third example concerns a public official. If a norm empowers a member of the executive to create norms to implement that norm, can the power holder decide not to use this power, claiming that he has no duty to do so? The Belgian Cour de cassation held the power holder responsible for the damages resulting from the failure to implement the norm.[1] If a plaintiff can prove that he suffers loss from this omission, the defendant can be held liable. Other cases similar to this deal with situations where norm givers confer rights upon citizens but neglect to rule about the procedure as how to claim the right. Again, it seems unreasonable for a power holder not to use his power in the absence of an explicit duty or obligation

1 Cass., 20 December 1951; Pasicrisie 1952: I, 204; Cass., 7 March 1963; Pasicrisie 1963: I, 744; Cass., 21 October 1977; Pasicrisie 1978: I, 228; Cass., 23 April 1971; Pasicrisie 1971: I, 752.

to do so. Yet this example is regarded as a tort where the plaintiff must prove the loss and the causal connection with the failure to rule.

The above examples point to the fact that the distinction between secondary rules of power and norms of obligation is far less clear-cut than it seems from an analytical perspective. This does not, however, prove the distinction to be wrong. On the contrary, primary and secondary rules are not mutually exclusive (Singer 1963: 208). The classification of the distinction as 'ideal-typical' is a better candidate than 'analytical'. Hart suggests at some points that there are secondary rules that impose duties, for example, the duty of the judge to exercise his power conferred by a secondary rule, the duty of the judge to hear both parties in a case, the duty to apply the primary rules of obligation, the latter being connected to the ultimate rule of recognition as a 'public, common, standard of correct judicial decision' that must be regarded from an internal point of view (Hart 1994: 116; MacCormick 1991: 102, 104).

There are also other examples, such as the duty of a notary public, bailiff, or municipal official to perform the office to which they are legally empowered. In other words, the conferral of powers on a person to perform some act may be connected with the establishment of a duty for him to perform a definite conventional act (Ziembinski 1976: 303). This means that secondary rules are not merely rules that have primary rules as their object. As a matter of fact, they do interact with one another, as the above examples from case law show. In this respect, it makes sense to speak of the 'duties of power'. Having clarified this first point, I will now turn to the question as to the position and function of the legislator in Hart's legal theory.

Two Readings of the Constitution

Hart is no exception in neglecting the position and function of the legislator in legal theory, placing greater emphasis on adjudication than on legislation.[2] His overall account of the legal system mainly rests on assumptions about common law centred on the position, function and activity of the judge.

The legislator in Hart's work is not however absent. According to the secondary rules of change, he has the power to create new rules and change existing ones. His function, however, remains rather underexposed, though this is not only the case in Hart's theory.

Sovereign legislative power is no longer legally unlimited. Legislative power is conditioned by the rule of law and so is organised and limited by constitutions.

---

2 Raz for his part pushes the latter idea much further saying that 'the existence of norm-creating institutions, though characteristic of modern legal systems, is not a necessary feature of all legal systems … ' (Raz, 1979: 105). What for Raz makes a legal system a system is not the legislature but a set of norm-applying institutions referring to the source-based criteria of the system for the purposes of recognizing the norms to be applied (Raz 1990: 129–48; 1979: 105–11).

Two different ways of reading the constitution can be identified in this respect. The first is the negative or legalistic way; the second is the legisprudential way.

According to the legalistic reading of the constitution, the power holder who does not violate the power conferring norms (for example, by deciding *ultra vires*) cannot be criticised. He acts as the rules of power require him to act. 'Not violating the constitution' can be understood, under the legalistic reading, as a requirement that the legislator follow the procedural rules of the constitution and not stray into the constitutionally protected fields of 'rights', 'immunities', or 'liberties' (for example, freedom of speech or the inviolability of the home).

According to the legisprudential reading of the Constitution, however, 'not violating the rules' is only a necessary condition for the creation, and hence the existence or validity of rules, though not a sufficient one. Is it sufficient for legislators simply 'not to violate the rules' that grant them powers and content themselves with not infringing the constitutional rights of the citizens? Put differently, are legislators free not to act 'competently' according to rules of competence, to issue unreasonable norms or norms that have more negative than positive effects, or not to implement 'rights' that have previously been granted, all of which covered by the cloak of (albeit legally limited) sovereignty? The answer sounds clearly negative.

In the preceding chapters, it was argued that legislators have a duty to justify their norms according to the principles of legisprudence. The argument focused on the fact *that* legislators have a duty to justify their norms. This duty imposes the requirement to justify *why* norms are issued. In the following pages, it will be argued *how* this duty is to be concretised.

Rationality of the Legislator and the Circumstances of Legislation

It is commonplace to presume that legislation is rational because its author is believed to be rational. We do consider legislators rational because the theories – typically the theory of the social contract – in which they appear are rational. Taking these theories as true, legislators are irrefutably presumed to be rational, a quality that is superimposed on the results of their legislative activity. Upon the theory of the social contract, we believe in the rationality of the legislator. According to that theory, the belief in the rationality of the legislator is rationally justified, a view that we shall now challenge.

The concept of rationality involved in this articulation of law and legislation is the Cartesian or Olympian view described and criticised in chapter 3. On this view, rationality is self-revealing in that it can be thought of in a rational way. This self-referring conceptualisation of rationality as a '*Perfektionsbegriff*' (Luhmann 1981: 378–9) is supposed to represent reality. The representational view of reality is the result of the epistemologisation of philosophy throughout the Modern philosophical project. Epistemologised philosophy, as was argued in chapter 3, operates on the presupposition that the concepts used have universal validity, and that what is rational is rational in the same way, for anyone, anywhere, and at any time. Upon this 'monopoly of universality' (Bourdieu 1994: 230), the 'universality of universality' is taken for granted and rationality is considered to be identical in all rational subjects.

The Olympian view on rationality assumes that decision makers have a well-defined problem as well as a full range of alternatives to consider, together with full baseline information, full information regarding the consequences of each alternative, full information regarding the values and preferences of citizens as well as fully adequate time, skill and resources.

This assumption underlies legislative law, which constitutes a special case of decision making in general. One of the upshots of representationalism, with strong legalism in its wake, as discussed in chapter 5, is 'sovereignty', or the 'black box', in the proxy theory of the legitimation of law discussed in chapter 6. Since the concept of sovereignty is a product of 'perfect rationality', the products of sovereignty themselves are supposed to be perfectly rational. Put differently, if the framework of legislation is rational, the product resulting from this framework will be rational too. This belief is supposed to be rational given its justification in the proxy model of the social contract.

The rationality of the legislator, and hence of legislation, operates as a paradigm within classical judge-centred legal theory. It functions as a principle of statutory interpretation in that it presumes that legislators are both technically and socially rational. Technical rationality means, inter alia, that the legislator uses an unambiguous language, avoids antinomies and redundancies, relies on a coherent set of values and respects the Constitution (Ost and van de Kerchove 1987: 100). A socially rational legislator in turn is presumed to strive towards equitable rules and to avoid unfair or absurd results and useless measures. Furthermore, it is presumed to ensure that there is a proportional relationship between means and ends, and that its action not be fundamentally unforeseeable (Ost 1978: 163 ff.).

Because of the patently counterfactual intuition raised by this principle of interpretation, it has been correctly qualified as a fiction (Ziembinski 1978: 177–8; Carbonnier 1972: 271 ff.). This qualification of the rationality of the legislator is a consequence of an epistemological obstacle in the theory of the social contract. An epistemological obstacle is a concept that has an explanatory potential in a theory. The originally explanatory potential of the concept starts producing the opposite effects when it becomes an obstacle. 'Force' in natural science is an example of this. It explains physical reality using Newtonian physics, though it turns into an obstacle when its original explanatory force becomes counterproductive, in that it rather protects acquired knowledge rather than permitting the discovery of new paths. The protective function of the concept then acts more as a brake than as an engine for further explanation.[3]

---

3 The term 'epistemological obstacle' was coined by Gaston Bachelard. Examples of an epistemological obstacle are 'first experiences' that lead too quickly into generalizations (Bachelard 1977: 23) and the belief in unitary knowledge or the presupposition that all

The overprotection of the concept and its development into an epistemological obstacle is the result of an over-evaluation of the theory and its outcomes. This is what happened to the concept of 'rationality' in the theory of the social contract. It became a fiction because the theory in which it appeared was initially fruitful, because the latter overprotects the concept of sovereignty and thus creates an obstacle to its own development and becomes counterproductive. Its counterproductive nature is amply testified by the nearly complete absence of a theory of legislation within the field of jurisprudence.

One of the tools of canonical interpretation according to legal science operating under the auspices of legalism, this fiction is a form of '*Hineininterpretierung*'. It ascribes qualities to rulers and rules which they often obviously lack. Contradictions, for example, do appear in legal systems. They are teased out by way of interpretation, according to the *lex specialis*, *lex superior*, or *lex ulterior* principles. Unconstitutional rules do exist, though they are interpreted as if they were constitutional. Within our pluralistic societies, legislative rules no longer reflect unitary and coherent sets of values, but are rather a patchwork of policies packed up as rules. Legislators cannot foresee every circumstance in which their rules will operate, far less foresee all the effects of their ruling.

The rationality of the legislator and of legislation described above is a variant of rationality as a '*Perfektionsbegriff*' that was analysed and criticised in chapter 3. In response to this, a contextual interpretation of rationality has been proposed, for which support was found in the work of Perelman and Simon, amongst others. Simon's view in particular of 'bounded rationality' is of interest here, in that it contrasts the presuppositions of Olympian rationality with the 'real world' conditions according to which we live. 'We' here is taken to refer to all the actors in contexts of participation, subjects, legislators, judges and other officials alike.

Bounded rationality is a variant of 'rationality in context' in that it refers to the rationality of decision making in context. Rationality in this respect is bounded in two ways. First, it is by its very nature bounded, in that it is limited. These limitations refer to the scarcity of information, attention, skills, knowledge and calculation capacity as well as the limited foreseeability of future consequences, among others. Secondly, rationality is bounded, in that it connected to a context which decisions aim to change. These two aspects of bounded rationality characterise the rationality of legislation according to legisprudence, in that bounded rationality is the main 'circumstance' of legislation as I will explain in the following paragraphs.

---

knowledge fits into a universal whole (ibid.: 83). In legal science, '*Einzelfallgerechtighkeit*', or the first application of a rule that determines its later applications, is another instance of an epistemological obstacle, just as legal certainty.

Circumstances Theories

Hume can be considered the initiator of what we call 'circumstances theories'. He claims that there is a relationship between justice as a concept or as a practice, and the factual circumstances of human life. Hume characterises as the 'circumstances of justice' some factual aspects of human life that incite a type of action. When speaking of the circumstances of justice, Hume is referring to scarce resources, limited generosity, rough equality of capacities and aptitudes, and interdependence, or the fact that human beings depend on external goods and on each other in order to satisfy basic human needs. Because these factors are a 'fact of life', justice is necessary. More specifically, social life requires an organisation that includes the distribution of goods, and satisfies the basic needs of humans.

Humans, however, are also social – that is, they interact with each other. However, our social nature as a source of trouble also contains the key to the solution of the problems thereby caused. Our early education in society gives us an understanding of the resulting advantages. These advantages, so we learn, outweigh the devastating effects of conflict over external goods, the possession of which gives us enjoyment. Social training or socialisation leads to the insight that only a convention can bestow stability on the possession of external goods, and provide peaceful enjoyment of what we may acquire by labour or fortune (Hume 1978: Book III, sect. II, 484–501; 1966: sect. III, part 1, 183–92).

The fact of being social then creates both the *necessity* and the *possibility* of the convention establishing property and safe possession. This fact is called a 'circumstance of justice'. Circumstances of justice make a specific action both necessary and possible in order to achieve peace.

H.L.A. Hart for his part (1994: 193 ff.; Lucas 1966: 1–10) refers to both Hume and Hobbes in his theory of natural law that became famous as the 'minimal content of natural law'. Humans are no angels, nor are they ruthless devils. Minimal protection against the effects of the diabolical side of human nature may be required in order to make life possible. Hart thus suggests that the minimal content of natural law is what is required in order to have a legal system at all. What point is there indeed in having a legal system if it does not contain a minimal protection of property through, for example, a system of torts? In borrowing from Hume and Hobbes, Hart initiated the idea of 'circumstances' within current legal theory, followed by Rawls and Waldron who subsequently provided their own specific interpretation of this idea.

Rawls for his part comes up with a version of the 'circumstances of justice', arguing that they concern the normal conditions under which human cooperation is both possible and necessary. Human cooperation occurs against a background of these circumstances because it is marked by both a conflict and an identity of interests. Principles, therefore, are required that make it possible to choose in which social arrangements to work, and how they will operate.

Objective circumstances are very much similar to what Hart and Hume had referred to, that is, roughly similar physical and mental power, vulnerability to attack, and moderate scarcity. Subjective circumstances of justice obtain because humans have their own plans of life or conceptions of the good as rational long-term plans (and not just whimsy wishes). Subjective circumstances can be articulated as the absence of interest in one another's interest or mutual disinterest (Rawls 1971: 126–30).

Rawls' position is interesting in this respect that he takes sides with the ideal of justice as part of the kingdom of ends. Justice is to be realised by humans who cannot free themselves from the circumstantial elements of life. This displays a great deal of common sense, although it has provoked strong criticism (Sandel 1982: 28–46).

Another version of a 'circumstances theory' is Jeremy Waldron's. Waldron's 'jurisprudence of legislation' considers legislation as the product of political decision making under what he calls the 'circumstances of politics'. Explicitly relying on Rawls' version of the circumstances theory, he, however, adapts it arguing that it is not an initial consensus on the principles of justice that allows for the organisation of society. Societies become organised under the circumstances of politics. The main circumstance of politics – that what makes politics both necessary and possible – is *disagreement*. It is hard to disagree with this original line of thought. Disagreement has nothing perverse, it is not a signal of stupidity or bad character, far less as Hobbes thought, a kind of natural flaw of mankind.

The circumstances of politics obtain because there is a perceived need among the members of a certain group for a common framework, or decision, or course of action on some matter, even in the face of disagreement about what this framework, decision, or action should be (Waldron 1999: 102).

According to this brief characterisation of some 'circumstances theories', it is only a short step to see that bounded rationality is the essential circumstance of legislation according to legisprudence. Bounded rationality is inherent to human decision making that is essentially limited due to the scarcity of information, attention, knowledge and time. Human legislators are no exception to that.

Following Rawls' account of the circumstances of justice, the circumstances of legislation are both objective and subjective. Objective circumstances, according to Rawls, point to some unavoidable facts of human life, while subjective circumstances refer to actors' conceptions of the good as rational long-term plans. The objective circumstances of legislation that occur due to bounded rationality are limitations of rationality (information, attention, knowledge, time). Subjective circumstances obtain since the actors in the process of legislation are conditioned by the circumstances of politics, and this claim is Waldron's trademark. Legislators disagree over long-term plans concerning the organisation of political society conditioned by value pluralism. Value pluralism, it may be remembered from the discussion in chapter 1, is one of the upshots of nominalism. Disagreement is essentially on this point. Disagreement makes politics both necessary and possible. From this perspective, the circumstances of politics can be categorised as the subjective circumstances of legislation. On this view, politics is not separated from legislative law making as strong legalism advocates, but only differentiated from it.

Herculean judges or their doppelgänger in the legislative branch are no real actors; they are by-products of the Cartesian view on rationality. This view claims to provide ontologically true knowledge that represents reality. Whether we like it or not, however, this view no longer fits in with the real world that is exponentially growing ever more complex at an ever increasing pace. The circumstances of legislation point to the contrast between Cartesian rationality and the real world. 'Circumstances', however, should not be taken to simply mean 'facts' occurring in the social world. 'Circumstances', as connected to bounded rationality, point to an essential limitation of rational capacities. Rationality in other words must be contextually interpreted on pain of fostering epistemological obstacles.

As noted above, the irrefutable presumption of the legislator's rationality is one of these obstacles. Under judge-centred legal theory, it operates as a canon of legal reasoning that contributes to preserving the idea of the systematic nature of law. We may call this 'system thinking' in law. Current legal theory, however, is increasingly evolving towards 'problem thinking' that is substituted for system thinking. In focusing on *problems*, legal theorists have become more aware of the importance of rationality in law, following a more general line leading from 'system thinking' to 'problem thinking' in adjudication.[4]

According to this shift, the judge is no longer considered merely as the addressee of the legal norm, as Kelsen wanted it. He is a critical addressee as well, who is expected to solve problems or resolve conflicts in addition to or instead of applying rules. On this thicker view, adjudication is expanded from 'judging' as a theoretical matter, to *decision making* as a *practical* activity. The specificity of 'problem thinking' as a substitute for 'system thinking' has raised the sensitivity for *rational problem solving*. The attention paid to the rationality of judicial decision making and argumentation is a hopeful signal that practical reason in legal reasoning is taken more seriously than it used to be.

When turning our attention to legislation, legisprudence as a new branch of legal theory articulates a different view on the rationality of the legislator. Legisprudence takes legislators to be boundedly rational when dealing with problems concerning the secondary norms of the legal order that empower them to take action. Legisprudence considers bounded rationality the main 'circumstance of legislation'. This means that bounded rationality makes legislation both necessary and possible.

First, even if rationality is of a bounded nature, we are not deprived of some minimum level of rationality that is necessary to orient us in the world. This minimum is what makes decisions possible. However, if rationality were perfect, as the Olympic view suggests, there would be no need to decide anything, since we would be acting according to complete and true knowledge. In this ideal world,

4 For a general overview of how different theories deal with rationality in law, though mainly from the judicial perspective, see MacCormick 1983.

all that remains to be done is to implement truth as an exercise of free will. The moral quality of an act thus consists in its compliance with true norms, which is the characteristic attribute of strong legalism as discussed in chapter 1. It has also been argued that one of the effects of nominalism is that the world is turned into radical contingency. Its subsequent indeterminacy thus favours human action, making it both possible and necessary.

Secondly, the argument runs along the same lines, and indeed corroborates it when we turn from the world's contingency to the essentially limited nature of rationality. Even if, hypothetically speaking, the world were perfectly ordered – as, for example, Descartes believed – and even if we were hypothetically equipped with perfect rationality – as Descartes also believed – even so we would have to rely on the rules of thumb summarised as the provisional morality until the world has been rationally discovered by mechanics, medicine, and so on, before we would *really* know what to do. Had Cartesian morality reached this point, I am afraid that it would have been of the legalistic type. Before reaching that point, however, our rational capacities direct us in a prudential manner, in that they make decisions both possible and necessary.

Bounded rationality points in both directions. Social reality is pretty much complex and consequent upon, I venture to say, the world's ontological contingency. Rationality for its part is limited because of limited information, knowledge, and so on. Without neglecting the crucial differences between individual and collective decision making, the bounded nature of rationality applies in both cases under the contextual interpretation of rationality advocated in chapter 3.

In view of the above considerations, the time has come to put our boundedly rational legislator to work. When creating new or changing existing legislation, legislators deal with facts. It is the facts from which they start in order to change some facet of social reality with the help of their norms. The legislator's must deal with facts in order to make legislation, though this is by no means sufficient to make good legislation. Here as elsewhere, the goal of my ambition is not exhaustiveness. The following pages are therefore limited to a rough attempt to sketch out this aspect of the process of legislative ruling. More specifically, I will explore the way in which a legislator should act throughout his legislative activity with respect to the principles of legisprudence.

Legisprudence and the Duties of the Legislator

The Duty of Relevant Fact Finding

The process of legislation, like judicial ruling, starts with an assessment of facts. Despite the self-evidential nature of this statement, fact finding is probably the most difficult action to theorise about. What, indeed, are facts? And how can they be known? And if we know how they can be known, how do we know which facts are relevant? Questions like these are troublesome, in that they shake up our basic intuition of having a direct access to reality.

However, these questions are of importance when dealing with rationality, since in rational discourse, scientific or otherwise, we do not merely deal with thoughts. We also deal with facts, since our rational discourses, one way or the other, deal with reality 'out there'. Throughout our rational activities, we try to gain a hold on reality and also to gain some rational account of what we do, and how we are doing what we are doing while doing this.

Legislators, like scientists, deal with facts. The scientist, in natural science, for example, tries to explain how facts are related, that is, how they are causally or statistically connected to each other. With a sufficient degree of causal or statistical explanation, we can say that we understand reality, or at least that part of it we have been decrypting in our dealings with it.

Legislators, for their part, interfere with factual reality in that they turn the realisation of some facts or combinations of facts into states of affairs or practices that are a matter of obligation. Other facts, states of affairs, or practices are qualified as undesirable, and so their realization is prohibited. Legislators, that is, intervene in social interaction by acting on facts, states of affairs, or practices. The rationality of laws as the outcome of policy making in this respect consists in their being sustained by a state of affairs (Linde 1975–76: 201). The realisation or non-realisation of some of them is then transformed into a matter of obligation.

Like the scientist, the legislator must clear his path to the facts. If legislation claims some rationality, the external limitations issued by a norm giver must refer to the facts to which they aim to be connected.

Facts are identifiable throughout practices, that is, in the social interaction of which they are part. Society can be roughly characterised as a varied set of practices: the practice of commerce, education, theatre playing, and so on. Facts are therefore an important part of that, though are only seen through the matrix of a practice. To know facts then is to enter into some of the practices in which they are identified or 'dealt with'. Put differently, facts depend for their being known on a context of participation from where they obtain meaning. Knowledge of this meaning involves understanding that practice. This was already referred to in earlier chapters. I think that we can settle on this characterisation of facts in order to be able to articulate norm making.

It may be remembered from the previous chapter that, in contrast with the proxy model, the trade-off model requires any external limitation to be justified. This requirement itself is at the basis of the principles of legisprudence. If an external limitation, as it follows from these principles, must be justified, this justification must be preceded by an adequate analysis of the facts that form the state of affairs on which the external limitation will be superimposed.

If facts depend on their relationship with a context of participation, we can justifiably conclude that their meaning results from the social interaction that characterises that practice. This is merely a specific instance of the more general thesis that meaning is context dependent or depends on interaction. Facts, that is, are not true in themselves; at least, we do not know. If brute facts can be said to exist, our access to them though is mediated by some theoretical setting that endows them with meaning. Meaning, indeed, is 'meaning for someone', not 'meaning *an sich*'.

This means that fact finding depends on grasping the context from which their meaning arises. Meaning as 'meaning for someone' results from social interaction within a context of participation that makes it socially meaningful. Facts, that is, can only be known as meaningful, so that knowing them depends on grasping the context that endows them with meaning. This point was discussed at some length in chapter 2.

This characterisation has some consequences for the legitimation of external limitations. The legitimation of an external limitation that is superimposed on a practice is thus, unsurprisingly, heavily dependent on an account of the facts, that is, of the meanings that constitute the practice at hand. This means that in order for an external limitation to be legitimated, it must 'fit the facts'.

If practices essentially consist of rule following, that is, of interaction on the basis of conceptions of freedom, an external limitation consists of a substitution of a conception about freedom for the conception of freedom to be realised in the practice. This means that the state of affairs resulting from following the rules which the practice consists of is deemed to be undesirable, so that an external limitation seems justified. However, the undesirability of a state of affairs is not a sufficient justification for norm givers to interfere with it. External limitations or norms, that is, must be effectively justified. Therefore, the state of affairs within the practice, as it results from it, must first be adequately described as a condition for the subsequent external limitation that will be superimposed on it in order to be justified.

This analysis serves as a basis for norm givers. The duty of relevant fact finding then involves indicating which facts are relevant for the external limitation which the legislator is issuing, and how they were gathered (hearings, consulting experts, foreign investigations, and so on).

The adequacy of the justification of a norm on the PA depends on the adequacy of the factual analysis. Norms, that is, should be related to a relevant factual basis. This means that the need for justification under the PA imposes duty of adequate fact finding on the norm giver. That is, it imposes a duty on the sovereign to take the facts or the state of affairs of which the practice consists into account as a condition for justification on the PA. In addition to that, the justification on the PA requires that the norm issued be an alternative for failing social interaction. Apart from the required familiarity with the social practice which the legislator is regulating, it is also under a duty to indicate 'where the problem is', that is, what makes social interaction fail. This brings us to the second duty of the legislator.

The Duty of Problem Formulation

The duty of problem formulation is related to an identification of a state of affairs as 'problematic', so that the outcomes of the practice or state of affairs are deemed undesirable. What makes a state of affairs undesirable?

Theories of morality attempt to validate some principle(s) of morality. From this validation, however, it does not follow that external limitations concretising these validated principles, are justified by the principles of legisprudence. Their validation is one thing, whilst the justification of external limitations on the principles of legisprudence that incorporate them is yet another. Legisprudence, that is, is not a theory of morality in the substantive sense. It is a principled, hence normative, theory in that the limitation of freedom according to conceptions about freedom requires justification.

What must be argued for is not that an external limitation incorporates the right morality, whatever that may be. The justification concerns the substitution of a conception about freedom for a conception of freedom. What must be shown is not that a specific moral content is included in the external limitation, but that acting on the external limitation is preferable to acting on a conception of freedom. Legisprudence can therefore be taken to be a meta-theory of morality, in that it allows for the formulation of principles that justify external limitations. It is the latter that make morality possible, without enforcing any substantive moral principle whatsoever.

Nor does legisprudence incorporate a substantive theory of justice, in that the external limitations of freedom seek to realise some distribution of goods that are deemed to be more just than others. This, again, is not to say that legisprudence is not related to justice at all. The relationship is, however, a thinner one and may be articulated as follows.

According to freedom as *principium,* the distribution of goods does matter. Goods, that is, external or externalisable, material or immaterial objects, make up part of the conditions that allow for the realisation of a conception of freedom. Pure spiritual freedom for its part does not require any goods to be realised.

The freedom that freedom as *principium* aims at is freedom of action, and this requires goods to be at the disposal of the acting subject. It is not only that you need, for example, some external goods for food, in order to have, say, the energy to act. Indeed, pure spiritual food will not do the job. From that perspective, goods allow for the realisation of a conception of freedom. Goods need to be distributed, and so legisprudence may be said to incorporate a theory of justice. Again, as is the case with morality, no substantive theory or principle of justice can, on its own merits, claim to be incorporated into the set of external limitations, and so realise one form or another of substantive justice.

If this were the case, then no justification according to the principles of legisprudence would any longer be needed. This justification is needed precisely because legisprudence does not include such a conception. As argued above, law must make morality possible, not the other way around. With freedom as *principium* as the basis of legisprudence, the latter is of a pluralistic nature. This means that legisprudence makes the realisation of different conceptions of freedom possible. Freedom, as argued above, is the moral right to be free in the absence of any external limitation. The realisation of different concretisations of freedom that legisprudence makes possible implies that no specific concretisation is a priori justified. Legisprudence then incorporates a reasonable pluralism of conceptions of freedom.[5]

It does not, however, follow that the external limitations that are to be justified under the principles of legisprudence are, as liberals call it, 'neutral'.[6] The requirement of neutrality seems in a way absurd to me, in that it suggests that neutrality is itself something neutral, something that I fail to see.

The neutrality requirement can be understood in a manner that makes more sense, that is, in a non-dispositive way. According to a non-dispositive reading, it refers to a striving towards as much neutrality as possible. On this view, the requirement of neutrality is yet another version of the PA which holds that an external limitation can only be justified as an alternative for failing social interaction. If this justification does not succeed, the sovereign must refrain from imposing external limitations. Neutrality, at best, includes respect for a reasonable pluralism of conceptions of freedom, not specifically of justice.

On the basis of the above observations, some clarification can now be provided regarding the duty to establish the facts that lead to the identification of a state of affairs as 'problematic', so that it qualifies for an external limitation.

The qualification of a state of affairs as 'problematic' obviously includes a value judgement. This could throw a problematic light on legisprudence, in that, as noted above, it does not allow for value judgements, moral or others, to be rationally incorporated qua value judgements. This does not mean, however, that no value judgements are incorporated into external limitations at all, which would result in the somewhat strange requirement of 'neutrality' pointed to above. This does not mean either that legisprudence as a theory of rational legislation does not itself include a value judgement. On the contrary, freedom as *principium* is the basic value judgement in legisprudence. It only means that value judgements must be made apparent when justification is provided.

It is not necessary for the content of the value, goal, or end to be justified in the process of fact finding. These justifications belong to the domain of ethics in the broad sense, including theories of justice and morality. Their implementation is conditioned by the circumstances of politics as the subjective circumstances of legislation. Political agreements then settle these discussions in what can be called a 'policy' waiting to be transformed into law.

---

5 I borrow the formula 'reasonable pluralism' from John Rawls (1993: 36 ff.) without endorsing, however, the consequences of his theory.

6 See, for example, Ackerman (1983: 10–17), and my critique of this theory (Wintgens, 1992).

Legislators which must cope with both the objective and subjective circumstances of legislation must establish a connection between the external limitation and the value, goal, or end purported to be realised. Under the 'subjective circumstances' of legislation, to use Rawls' terminology, they are *political* actors. Under the objective circumstances of legislation on the contrary, they are *legal* actors. A state of affairs can only be classified as 'problematic' on the strength of the justification of a value judgement. The justification of the external limitation as required under the principles of legisprudence must in turn show how the state of affairs intended to be realised is preferable to the actual one. Again, it is not the justification of the substantive value judgement itself that is the concern of legisprudence; it is the justification of the *relationship* between the value judgement and the state of affairs that it purports to attain. In other words, a legisprudential account of legislation purports to highlight *how* the legislator implements this relationship. This points to another aspect of the legislator's duties.

The Duty to Weigh and Balance Alternatives

A third duty of the sovereign concerns the duty to weigh and balance alternatives. The idea of weighing and balancing was already pointed to in the previous chapter. Legisprudential justification, so it was argued, consists in providing a justification on the principles of legisprudence. The authority of law as a reason for action requires that alternative reasons for action be counterbalanced. Law must be justified as an alternative for failing social interaction. This is one part of weighing and balancing that is ranged under the PA.

Another perspective on weighing and balancing deals with the PN. A justification under the PN involves counterbalancing any of the alternatives with a lower normative density than the external limitation proposed. When focusing on the PN, only one aspect of it was discussed, that is, the requirement that sanctions. This justification entails that any alternative involving no sanction or a less serious sanction must be counterbalanced by arguments in favour of it in order for the sanction to be legitimated.

From this perspective, a particularly rich area is revealed containing a large variety of alternative regulatory techniques alongside rules accompanied by sanctions. These techniques are appropriate for achieving some goals, ends, or values without the use of a sanction. The 'rule plus sanction' (RS)-technique is, so to speak, the technique involving the maximum of normative density, and so it is the least preferable from the perspective of freedom as *principium.*

From the wide variety of possible alternatives to the RS-technique, I will briefly mention five of them. First, the technique of alternative dispute resolution involves avoidance of sanctions in the punitive sense, but also in the sense of constraint. Alternative dispute resolution seeks to deal with conflicts out of court, and so do the techniques of arbitration and mediation. What is characteristic of these techniques is that the participants are closer to the horizontal communication that characterises social interaction, and so these techniques make it possible to solve conflicts in a way that better fits social – horizontal – interaction in general.

The second technique involves using covenants. Covenants qualify as alternatives for the RS-technique in that the social actors, with whom the government makes this covenant, could be forced to achieve the goal, end, or value by imposing a rule with a sanction on them. Instead of doing so, the technique of covenants allows for a determination of the ends, goals, or values to be realised by *all* the parties to the contract, and not only the government.

A characteristic feature of this regulative technique is that the means for realising the goal, end, or value so determined are left to the initiative of the subjects themselves. They have the task of determining the appropriate means for achieving the end, value, or goal determined. Yet, as an alternative, the RS-technique can only be invoked in so far as it turns out that the technique of a covenant does not produce the expected result.

Codes of conduct are a third alternative to sanctioned rules. These codes typically are a form of self-regulation, currently used in economic matters. They are not imposed 'from above', but worked out by social interaction partners 'in the field'. Codes of conduct, or deontological codes of professional organisations, to mention just two, stem from the practices to which they apply. They emerge out of the context of participation which they seek to regulate and that defines the practice itself as a practice.

Fourth, incentives to adopt a specific course of conduct, such as tax incentives, are an alternative regulatory technique in that they do not involve sanctions. The goal, value, or end is achieved through an advantage that is offered when the desired behaviour occurs. If it does not occur, however, no sanction follows. In order for a sanction to be legitimated, it has to be argued that the result of the incentive does not produce the effect that was expected.

A fifth technique involves the issue of licences and certification, and 'labelling'. Granting licences is an appropriate regulatory technique in that it directly contributes to the prevention of some undesired state of affairs or practices. Driving licences or licences to practice medicine are examples of this. Certification is a subclass of the licence technique. Governments or independent agencies can provide certificates for specialisation in certain professions (for example, registered entrepreneurship in building industry), for certain products (for example, medication), for goods or production techniques, or by introducing ISO-standards. Labelling finally has a weak normative density in that a person, product, or service can receive a positive assessment which results in the issue of the label. Bio-friendly products and products not involving child labour are a positive label. Negative labels are conferred upon airway companies that do not satisfy the requirements of safe transportation.

What these techniques have in common is that they do not refer to sanctions or constraints. However, in justifying an RS-regulation, a sovereign must consider that they are all insufficient for realising the goal, end, or value concerned. This is what the duty of weighing and balancing of the alternatives involves.

The Duty of Prospection or the Duty to Take Future Circumstances into Consideration

The duty of prospection requires a sovereign to keep an eye on the circumstances within the practice upon which the external limitation is imposed.[7] Practices are not static wholes. They are, on the contrary, characterised by interaction. The requirement that external limitations be justified then corresponds to a duty to take these changes into consideration. This is, again, to a large extent a matter of fact finding on the basis of the PA. In this respect, two hypotheses can be distinguished.

Under the first hypothesis, the circumstances change *independently* of any external limitations. According to this hypothesis, a legislator finds himself in the position of 'new' facts that he confronts. This activates the three duties that were already commented upon above. A sudden change in the international economic climate like the financial crisis is an example of that.

Under the second hypothesis, which is slightly more complex than the first one, circumstances may have changed as a result of a previous external limitation. This change then will emerge following the fulfilment of the duty of retrospection, which will be discussed briefly below. These changes can be threefold. First, they can be the intended result of the external limitation under assessment. On that hypothesis, the purpose of the external limitation is achieved, in that the intended state of affairs – or the avoidance of an undesirable state of affairs – is achieved.

Secondly, the changes can be the unintended result of the external limitation. Changes as the unintended result call in turn for yet another distinction. First, the change in the circumstances is itself a *negative* effect of the external limitation under assessment. A classic example are the subsidies that were paid to farmers during the initial period of the European Union. Their intended effect was to guarantee an income to the farmers. Following their introduction, however, the latter started to produce as much milk, butter and meat as they could, in order to accumulate as many subsidies as possible. The intended effect was achieved, though it was accompanied by the unintended effect of an overproduction of milk, butter and meat. This overproduction brought about a new situation that had to be tested according to the principles of legisprudence, starting with an assessment of this new state of affairs (PA), problem formulation, selection of alternatives, and so on. This negative side-effect, unintended by definition, could indicate that the duty of prospection was not satisfactorily complied with.

Third, an assessment of the changed circumstances may establish that they are an unintended yet positive effect of the external limitation. This positive effect, like the negative one, is to be tested according to the principles of legisprudence. Indeed, the effect is not characterised as positive. This characterisation can only follow from an assessment of the principles of legisprudence, and the duties corresponding to them.

---

7 'Circumstances' in this context are different from the 'circumstances of legislation'. They are social facts.

Fourth and finally, an insufficient compliance with the duty of prospection may encourage over-quick rule changes. This is not to say that their ruling cannot change; rather it only requires supplementary argumentation as to why change is better than the status quo, or why the latter is preferable to the former. Hasty or frequent changes, even in view of changed circumstances, will not satisfy the requirement of the PC from the perspective of legislation. It is possible to identify a duty of the sovereign to make a reasonable prognosis of whether and in what sense the circumstances could change from this contrast between change and the status quo.

This means that justification according to the PC is satisfactory only if arguments are provided which show that the external limitation is sufficiently resistant to changing circumstances, so that the slightest change does not have immediate repercussions on the external limitation issued. The duty of prognosis requires that the sovereign look far enough into the future in order to be able to argue that not simply any change of the circumstances will result in a rule change. Therefore, the duty of prognosis makes a legal system a more or less stable set of external limitations, and follows from a conjunction of requirements under the PA, the PT and the PC.

The duty of prospection is of course limited to what can reasonably be foreseen. It must be remembered that the legislator is a boundedly rational and not an omniscient actor. However, the duty of prognosis extends to what can be regarded as the foreseeable *effects* of the external limitation issued. From this perspective, the duty of prospection overlaps with the duties of fact finding, problem formulation, and the weighing and balancing of alternatives. Problem formulation depends on adequate fact finding. Since an external limitation purports to remedy a situation that is characterised as problematic, problem formulation embraces a prognosis of the effects that can be expected from the external limitation.

To summarise, the discharge of the duty of prognosis must take into account the effects intended by the external limitation. Only on a naïve account of the matter can external limitations be considered to produce only positive effects. Effects, as I said, can also be unintended. Negative unintended effects come under resort under the duty of prognosis. Accordingly, the weighing and balancing of both the positive and foreseeable negative effects forms, as a matter of duty, part of an adequate prognosis that may justify an external limitation. Whether the duty of prospection has been adequately absolved should be considered in retrospect, which brings us to the duty of retrospection.

The Duty of Retrospection

Closely connected to the duty of prognosis, the duty of retrospection commits the ruler to take into account the past as it has been affected by the external limitation. In its simplest version, a justification according to the PT must be shown to be a response *at a certain point in time* to an undesirable state of affairs justified under the PA.

Under the PT, however, the justification must also stand *over time*. What is justified at $time_1$ will not necessarily withstand the ravages of time. A justification at $time_1$ may have disappeared at $time_2$ and so the rule may become obsolete. Therefore, in contrast to the duty of prognosis, the duty of retrospection therefore commits the legislator to an evaluation of the effects of the external limitation, in order to show whether or not the expected effects according to the duty of prognosis have been achieved. If they have been, the external limitation, justified as it was at $time_1$, is still justified at $time_2$. If not, an additional justification under the simple version of the PT is needed.

If, however, in comparison with the prospection at $time_1$, the effects turn out not to be realised or if the negative effects outweigh the positive ones, the external limitation will no longer be justified according to the PT. The external limitation should then be abolished or changed. Abolition or change raises the complex problem of coherence of a legal system according to the requirements of the PC. Legal systems are much like the Internet: once you drop something on it, it is hard to erase it. Rules in the legal system start living their own lives and hook up with other ones, thus making it hard to eradicate them.

For its part, rule change in the light of the duty of retrospection goes hand-in-hand with the duty of fact finding on a renewed basis. The achievement of the intended state of affairs that corresponds to the purpose of the external limitation must be assessed, and this assessment is in turn, a matter of fact finding.

This assessment means that a refinement of the problem formulation , *casu quo* a wholesale redefinition of the problem, may be needed in order to keep the external limitation in line with the facts that have been newly assessed according to the duty of retrospection. On this point, the duty of problem formulation and the duty of retrospection are consistent with one another. The latter gives raise to a seventh duty, that is, the duty to correct.

The Duty to Correct

The duty to correct of the sovereign consists in a requirement to withdraw or change an external limitation. Boundedly rational sovereigns are not omniscient, nor can they foresee everything or be expected to do so. Even there, they fulfil the duties corresponding to the principles of legisprudence; external limitations can turn out to be unjustified at a certain moment in time. Due to its temporal nature, justification is not peremptorily acquired once it has been successfully established. An external limitation that turns out no longer to apply in that it is no longer justified calls for correction. The duty to correct pushes the legislator back to square one, to the duty of fact finding and the subsequent duties identified in this section.

Having articulated the duties of the sovereign acting under the circumstances of legislation, I want to make three additional observations before ending this section.

First, the concretisation of the principles of legisprudence into duties of the sovereign does not make the latter dispositive or binary in that their fulfilment is a matter of all or nothing. The justification for an external limitation on the principles of legisprudence is obtained from its weighing and balancing in the light of these, both individually and as a whole. This means that the principles themselves must be weighed and balanced against each other throughout the legislative process, since the principles provide context for one another, as was argued in chapter 7.

Second and in connection to this, the chain of the duties of the sovereign as they follow from the principles of legisprudence may look like a lexical scheme, a checklist, or a 'cookbook for good legislation'. Yet, this is only – and unfortunately, some may say – prima facie so. The duties of the sovereign may be distinguished for the purposes of analysis and description. Their normative character follows from their connection with the principles of legisprudence of which they are concretisations. Like the principles of legisprudence, they are not however lexically ordered, nor analytically separated from each other.

Like the principles of legisprudence of which they are concretisations, the duties of the sovereign are intertwined, in that they refer to each other. The fulfilment of one of them activates a 'subsequent' duty that may in turn call for a reactivation of a 'preceding' one. Their intertwinement may be best described as a loop running back and forth. Yet, the more often the sovereign 'runs through the loop', the less adjustments may turn out to be needed. If no readjustments are needed any longer, at any given moment in time, the legislator will at least temporarily be discharged of its duties.

Third, the duties of the legislator identified in this section do not exhaust the complex process of legislation. They merely account for what can be called rational law making under the circumstances of legislation. The rationality of legislation is practical reason in an ongoing process of making legislative ruling more rational.

Assessment of the Duties of the Legislator

It follows from the articulation of the duties of the legislator from a legisprudential perspective that we should now turn to the question as to how the acquittal thereof is to be assessed. The idea of an assessment points to the validity of legal norms issued by the legislator. This problem opens up the wide avenue on which legal theory has hitherto been working, and I will restrict myself in this section to making some remarks that aim to explore the contours of the concept of the 'legisprudential validity' of a norm.

Theories of legal validity can be roughly characterised as normative, factual and axiological theories. Kelsen gives a paradigmatic instance of the first, American and Scandinavian realists of the second, and natural law theories of the third.

It is important to remember the two readings of the Constitution mentioned earlier in this chapter. On a legalistic reading, the legislator suffices with 'not violating the norms of the Constitution'. On a legisprudential reading, as has been argued, 'not violating the norms of the Constitution' is a mere necessary condition in order for legislative norms to be valid, and not a sufficient one. The investigation of the concept of legisprudential validity involves an examination of what counts as a sufficient condition for the validity of a legislative norm, apart from formal validity as its necessary condition.

The concept of the legisprudential validity of a norm comes in the form of mere formal validity in that it limits validity to a matter of all or nothing. Constitutional Courts are at pains to assess legal validity on mere formal grounds. If validity were a matter of all or nothing, it would be relatively easy to declare a norm invalid. The pages-long justifications in support of striking down a legislative norm show that it is anything but an easy job, and that it is certainly not a matter of 'all or nothing'. If it were this easy, one could even wonder why we need a Constitutional Court at all in order to establish whether a norm does or does not violate the Constitution. On a legisprudential reading of the Constitution, we (1) need a Constitutional Court and we (2) should face the fact that it is the *concept* of legal validity that is at stake, not simply the validity of a norm. Different Constitutional Courts at different times and places may have different conceptions of validity. Even within an existing Court there is not necessarily agreement, far less consensus, on which conception prevails. When a Constitutional Court strikes down a legislative norm, the conclusion is that it violates the Constitution. This conclusion, however, is not identical to saying that the legalistic reading of the Constitution wins through.

As argued above, the legisprudential reading of the Constitution, and hence the legisprudential concept of validity, impose duties on the legislator. However, these duties could be understood in a legalistic manner which turns them into a checklist or 'cookbook' for valid rulings. We should stick to the legisprudential track that enabled these duties to be identified, and not fall back on their treatment in a legalistic manner. The idea of a 'duty' of the legislator can only be properly understood in the light of the circumstances of legislation. The circumstances of legislation emerge through the legislator's bounded rationality. This means that the 'optimality' of legislation is nothing but an illusion brought about by the Olympian view on rationality.

A boundedly rational legislator is at best capable of producing 'satisfying' norms, that is, the best possible norms until now. 'Best possible norms until now' satisfy the principles of legisprudence provided that they have considered all things until now or the ATCN-condition referred to in chapter 3. The ATCN-condition changes the perspective on legal validity, since it blurs its 'all or nothing' character. The change in perspective involves to a switch from a legalistic to a legisprudential reading of the constitution.

This switch is, however, more complex than changing clothes. Underlying legislating under the ATCN-condition is an aspirational model of rationality. Following Lon Fuller (1969: 11) saying that 'We can, for example, know what is plainly unjust without committing ourselves to declare with finality what perfect justice would be like ... ', something similar can be said of rationality. Without knowing what 'perfect rationality' is, we can have a view on what is patently not rational.

According to an aspirational model of rationality, a legislator should aspire to the best possible norms of ATCN. And this is how the duties of the legislator articulated in this chapter are to be understood: as aspirational devices to deal with facts as well as possible. The aspirational model of rationality is bounded rationality at work which requires the legislator to comply with its duties as well as possible. The resulting legislative norms then can then be assessed in terms of 'reasonableness'.

Reasonableness, as was argued in chapter 3, is rationality in context. It has no a priori fixed criteria, which could make it vulnerable to the objection that it is vague and therefore inoperative. This objection, however, ranges from the Cartesian or Olympian view on rationality proper through to the legalistic reading of the Constitution according to which rationality operates according to criteria applied in an all-or-nothing manner.

The reasonableness of legislation for its part refers to the process of justification of legislative norms. A norm is reasonable when it is sufficiently justified; it is unreasonable when it is not. 'Reasonableness' is not something that is either lacking or not; it is a matter of degree which can only be negatively assessed in terms of 'shortcoming' (cf. Fuller 1969: 5). Yet a lack of justification makes a norm unreasonable, not in and of itself, but because the process of law making is flawed. The assessment of reasonableness therefore amounts to this. Can a legislator acting reasonably arrive at the legislative norm issued? Would another legislator in similar circumstances arrive at a similar norm?

It is necessary to make a caveat here. The assessment of reasonableness should not be taken to mean that a Constitutional Court enters the political domain mingling with policy issues. Politics and policy are the eminent domain of the legislator. The latter's time perspective is the future, while the Court's is the past. The fact that a norm was issued and *how* this was done is a matter for the past. Nor should a Court enter into the legislator reasons, that is, *why* it issued a norm. The reasons why a legislator issued a norm are a matter for politics. A Constitutional Court should merely confine itself to the process of *how* a legislative norm came into existence, and not its end, content, or merits. The end, content, or merits are internal limits of the Court's spectrum beyond which it should not move without usurping the legislator's position.

Given this separability, the way in which a Constitutional Court assesses the reasonableness of a legislative norm is hence confined to a negative check of the margins of rationality involved in the legislative process. Under this marginal rationality check, the Court scrutinises the boundaries of the rationality of this process, focusing on the arguments which the legislator supplies in support of his norm. The marginal rationality check which a court carries out is quite similar to the way Fuller (1969: 42) considers the examination of his 'principles of internal morality'. They are a matter of duty but are tested on an aspirational basis, that is, not as a violation but as a shortcoming. In this respect, the rationality of legislation is not a matter of 'optimality' but a matter of 'satisficing', to use Simon's terminology (Simon 1997: 295–8), commented upon in chapter 3.

More specifically, with respect to the duties of the legislator identified above, the Constitutional Court's marginal rationality check includes the following aspects: did the legislator rely on sufficiently relevant facts, did it formulate the problem in an adequate manner, and did it satisfactorily identify, weigh and balance alternatives? Moreover, did it take appropriate account of future circumstances and carry out an acceptable retrospective evaluation in view of possible corrections to his norm?

The marginal character of the rationality control performed by a Constitutional Court points to the fact that not all duties are to be complied with in the same way at the same time. Emergency legislation, for example, may be issued following a lower level of fact finding, or weighing and balancing of alternatives. But this lower degree of justification must itself be justified, without which the ensuing norm may be classified as unreasonable. In cases like this, the lower degree of justification must be justified, so that the overall degree of justification is sufficient. The absence of justification for any of the duties or a lower level of compliance with one or more of them results in unreasonable legislation.

References

Aarnio, A. 1987. *The Rational as Reasonable. A Treatise on Legal Justification.* Dordrecht: Kluwer.

Ackerman, B. 1980. *Social Justice in the Liberal State.* New Haven, CT: Yale University Press.

Alchourron, C.E. and Bulygin, E. 1971. *Normative Systems.* Vienna and New York: Springer.

Alexy, R. and Peczenik, A. 1990. 'The Concept of Coherence and its Significance for Discursive Rationality', *Ratio Juris*, 3, Issue Supplement, 130–47.

Ames, V.M. 1955. 'Mead and Husserl on the Self'. *Philosophy and Phenomenological Research*, 15, 320–31.

Amselek, P. 1964. *Méthode phénoménologique et théorie du droit.* Paris: Librairie générale de droit et de jurisprudence.

—— 1994. *Théorie du droit et science.* Paris: P.U.F.

Aquinas, T. 1898. *Quaestiones disputatae et quaestiones duodecimo quodlibetales*, vol. 3, *De veritate*. Turin: Marietti.

—— 1909. *Summa contra gentiles seu de veritate catholicae fidei.* Turin: Marietti.

—— 1910. *Summa Theologica.* Turin: Marietti.

Aristotle 1984a. *The Complete Works of Aristotle*, edited by J. Barnes. Princeton, NJ: Princeton University Press.

—— 1984b. *Physics*, in Aristotle 1984a.

—— 1984c. *Metaphysics*, in Aristotle 1984a.

—— 1984d. *Nichomachean Ethics*, in Aristotle 1984a.

—— 1984e. *Politics*, in Aristotle 1984a.

—— 1984f. *Rhetoric*, in Aristotle 1984a.

Arnaud, A.-J. 1975. *Les juristes face à la société du XIXe siècle* à *nos jours.* Paris: P.U.F.

Arquillière, H.-X. 2006. *L'augustinisme politique. Essai sur la formation des théories politiques du Moyen Age*, 2nd edn. Paris: Vrin.

Atienza, A. 2005. 'Reasoning and Legislation', in Wintgens 2005: 297–317.

Aubenque, P. 1972. *Le problème de l'être chez Aristote. Essai sur la problématique aristotélicienne*, 3rd edn. Paris: P.U.F.

Augustine, A. 32. *De Libero Arbitrio Libri Tres*, in *Patrologia Latina*, vol. 32, 1221–310.

—— 35. *Quaestionum ex Novo Testamento*, in *Patrologia Latina*, vol. 35, 2395–410.

—— 40. *De Diversis Quaestionibus LXXXIII Liber Unus*, in *Patrologia Latina*, vol. 40, 11–100.

—— 42. *Contra Faustum Manichaeum Libri Triginta Tres*, in *Patrologia Latina*, vol. 42, 207–518 <http://www.documentacatholicaomnia.eu/25_10_MPL.html>, published by J.-P. Migne between 1844 and 1855.

Austin, J. 1971. *The Province of Jurisprudence Determined and the Uses of the Study of Jurisprudence*, edited by H.L.A. Hart, 4th edn. London: Weidenfeld & Nicholson.

Bachelard, G. 1977. *La formation de l'esprit scientifique. Contribution à une psychoanalyse de la connaissance objective*. Paris: Vrin.

Baden, E. 1977. *Gesetzgebung und Gesetzesanwendung im Kommunikationsprozeß. Studien zur juristischen Hermeneutik und zur Gesetzgebungslehre*. Baden-Baden: Nomos Verlagsgesellschaft.

Balkin, J. 1993. 'Understanding Legal Understanding: The Legal Subject and the Problem of Legal Coherence', *Yale Law Journal*, 103, 105–76.

Bankowski, Z. and MacCormick, N. 2000. 'Legality without Legalism', in *The Reasonable as Rational. On Legal Argumentation and Justification. Festschrift for Aulis Aarnio*, edited by W. Krawietz et al. Berlin: Duncker &Humblot, 181–95.

—— and Schafer, B. 2007. 'Double-Click Justice: Legalism in the Computer Age', *Legisprudence. International Journal for the Study of Legislation*, 1, 31–49.

Barber, B. 1984. *Strong Democracy. Participatory Politics for a New Age*. London and Berkeley: University of California Press.

Barker, D.C. and Carman, C.J. 2000. 'The Spirit of Capitalism ? Religious Doctrine, Values, and Economic Attitude Constructs', *Political Behavior*, 22, 1–27.

Bastit, M. 1990a. *La naissance de la loi moderne. La pensée de la loi de saint Thomas à Suarez*. Paris: P.U.F.

—— 1990b. 'La loi', *Archives de Philosophie du Droit*, 35, 211–20.

—— 1997. *Les principes des choses en ontologie médiévale (Thomas d'Aquin, Scot, Occam)*. Bordeaux: Bière.

Bender, R. 1978. 'Das "Sandhaufentheorem". Ein Beitrag zur Reglungstechnik in der Gesetzgebungslehre', in *Gesetzgebungstheorie Juristische Logik, Zivil- und Prozessrecht. Gedächtnisschrift für Jürgen Rödig*, edited by U. Klug et al. Berlin: Springer.

Bentham, J. 1948. *A Fragment on Government and an Introduction to the Principles of Morals and Legislation*, edited by W. Harrison. Oxford: Blackwell.

—— 1970. *Of Laws in General*, edited by H.L.A. Hart. London: Athlone.

Berlin, I. 1969. 'Two Concepts of Liberty', in *Four Essays on Liberty*. Oxford: Oxford University Press, 118–72.

Blumenberg, H. 1957. '"Nachahumung der Natur". Zur Vorgeschichte der Idee des schöpferischen Menschen', *Studium Generale*, 10, 266–83.

—— 1983. *The Legitimacy of the Modern Age*, translated by R.M. Wallace. Cambridge, MA: M.I.T. Press.

Blumer, H. 1969. *Symbolic Interactionism. Perspectives and Methods*. Berkeley: University of California Press.

Boehner, P. 1964. *William of Ockham. Philosophical Writings*. Indianapolis, IN: Bobbs Merrill.

BonJour, L. 1985. The Structure of Empirical Knowledge. Cambridge, MA: Harvard University Press.

Bonnes, J.M. and Florijn, N.A. 1995. 'Legisprudentie. Uitvoering van EG–verordeningen: overschrijven verboden!', *RegelMaat*, 9, 115–21.

Borman, T.C. 1993. *Aanwijzingen voor de regelgeving en andere voor de regelgeving relevante aanwijzingen*. Zwolle: W.E.J. Tjeenk Willink.

Bouckaert, B. 1981. *De exegetische school. Een kritische studie van de rechtsbronnen- en interpretatieleer bij de 19de eeuwse commentatoren van de Code Civil*. Antwerp: Kluwer,

Boulnois, O. 1994. *Ce que Dieu n'est pas,* in *La puissance et son ombre. De Pierre Lombard à Luther*, edited by O. Boulnois et al. Paris: Aubier, 9–68.

Bourdieu, P. 1990. 'The Scholastic Point of View', *Cultural Anthropology*, 5, 380–91.

—— 1994. *Raisons pratiques. Sur la théorie de l'action*. Paris: Seuil.

—— 2003. 'Participant Objectivation', *Journal of the Royal Anthropological Institute*, 9, 281–94.

Boutroux, E. 1896. 'La morale. Du rapport de la morale à la science dans la philosophie de Descartes', *Revue de Métaphysique et de Morale*, 4, 502–11.

Brochard, V. 1954. *Etudes de philosophie ancienne et philosophie moderne*. Paris: Vrin.

Broekman, J.M. 1979. *Recht en Anthropologie*. Antwerp and Amsterdam: Standaard Wetenschappelijke Uitgeverij.

Brouwer, P.W. 1990. *Samenhang in het recht. Een analytische studie*. Groningen: Wolters-Noordhoff.

Calabresi, G. 1982. *A Common Law for the Age of Statutes*. Cambridge, MA: Harvard University Press.

Campbell, T.D. 1973. 'Formal Justice and Rule Change', *Analysis*, 33, 113–18.

Canning, J. 1987. *The Political Thought of Baldus de Ubaldis*. Cambridge: Cambridge University Press.

Carbonnier, J. 1972. *Sociologie juridique*. Paris: P.U.F.

Carr, D. 1973. 'The "Fifth Meditation" and Husserl's Cartesianism', *Philosophy and Phenomenological Research*, 34, 14–35.

Cassirer, E. 1902. *Leibniz' System in seinen wissenschaftlichen Grundlagen*. Marburg: Elwert.

—— 1966. *La Philosophie des Lumières*, translated by P. Quillet. Paris: Fayard.

Caton, H. 1975. 'Will and Reason in Descartes' Theory of Error', *The Journal of Philosophy*, 72, 87–104.

Celeyrette, J. and Mazet, E. 2005. 'Jean Duns Scot', in *De la théologie aux mathématiques. L'infini au XIV*[e] *siècle*, edited by J. Biard and J. Celeyrette. Paris: Les Belles Lettres.

Cicero, M.T. 1999. *On the Commonwealth and On the Laws*, edited by J.E.G. Zetzel. Cambridge: Cambridge University Press.

Clark, D.W. 1973. 'William of Ockham on Right Reason', *Speculum*, 48, 13–36.
Clark, E.C. 1883. *Practical Jurisprudence: A Comment on Austin*. Cambridge: Cambridge University Press.
Coing, H. 1989. 'German "Pandektistik" in Its Relationship to the Former "Ius Commune"', *American Journal of Comparative Law*, 37, 9–15.
Comarnescu, P. 1942. 'The Social and Ethical Conceptions of Descartes', *Ethics*, 52, 493–503.
Congar, Y.-M.-J. 1968. *L'Ecclesiologie du haut Moyen-Age*. Paris: Cerf.
Conlisk, J. 1996. 'Why Bounded Rationality?', *Journal of Economic Literature*, 34, 669–700.
Conring, H. 2003. 'Dissertation über die Gesetzgebung oder den vernünftigen Grund, Gesetze zu geben und im besonderen über die Schaffung von Gesetzen im Deutschen Reich [1663]', in Mohnhaupt 2003a, 7–87.
Coons, J.E. 1987. 'Consistency', *California Law Review*, 75, 59–113.
Coppleston, F. 1993a. *A History of Philosophy*, vol. 2, *Medieval Philosophy*. New York: Doubleday.
—— 1993b. *A History of Philosophy*, vol. 3, *Late Medieval and Renaissance Philosophy*. New York: Doubleday.
Cottingham, J. 1976. *Descartes' Conversation With Burman*. Oxford: Clarendon Press.
Courtenay, W. 1990. *Capacity and Volition. A History of the Distinction of Absolute and Ordained Power*. Bergamo: Lubrina.
Courtines, J.-F. 1999. *Nature et empire de la loi. Etudes suaréziennes*. Paris: Vrin.
Cranz, E.F. 1974. 'Cusanus, Luther, and the Mystical Tradition', in *The Pursuit of Holiness in Late Medieval and Renaissance Religion*, edited by C. Trinkaus and H.A. Oberman. Leiden: Brill, 93–102.
Cumming, R. 1955. 'Descartes' Provisional Morality', *Review of Metaphysics*, 9, 207–35.
Cyrul, W. 2005. 'How Rational is Rational Lawmaking?', in Wintgens 2005: 93–103.
d'Entrèves, A.P. 1961. *Natural Law*. London: Hutchinson University Library.
Dabin, J. 1929. *La philosophie de l'ordre juridique positif, spécialement dans les rapports de droit privé*. Paris: Sirey.
—— 1963. *Théorie générale du droit*, 3rd edn. Paris: Dalloz.
Damianus, P. 1972. *Lettre sur la toute-puissance divine*, edited and translated by A. Cantin. Paris: Cerf.
Dauenhauer, B.P. 1982. 'Relational Freedom', *Review of Metaphysics*, 36, 77–101.
de Gaulle, C. 1944. *Le fil de l'épé*. Paris: Berger-Levrault.
de Lagarde, G. 1926. *Recherches sur l'esprit politique de la réforme*. Paris: Picard.
—— 1937. 'Marsile de Padoue et Guillaume d'Occam', *Revue des sciences religieuses*, 17, 167–85 and 428–57.
—— 1946. *La naissance de l'esprit laïque au déclin du Moyen Age*, vol. 5, *Bases de départ de l'Ockhamisme*. Paris: P.U.F.

de Muralt, A. 1966. 'Epoché – Malin Génie – Théologie de la toute–puissance divine. Le concept objectif sans objet. Recherche d'une structure de pensée', *Studia Philosophica*, 26, 159–91.

—— 1970. 'Signification et portée de la pensée de Jean Duns Scot. Introduction, traduction et commentaire à la distinction 17 de l'Opus oxoniense, II', *Studia Philosophica*, 30, 113–49.

—— 1974. 'Pluralité des formes et unité de l'être. Introduction, traduction et commentaire de deux textes de Jean Duns Scot, Sentences, IV, distinction II, question 3; Sentences, II, distinction 16', *Studia Philosophica*, 34, 57–92.

—— 1993a. *L'enjeu de la philosophie médiévale. Etudes thomistes, scotistes, occamiennes et grégoriennes*. Leiden: Brill.

—— 1993b. 'La doctrine médiévale des distinctions', in de Muralt 1993a: 47–89.

—— 1993c. 'La métaphysique occamienne de l'idée', in de Muralt 1993a: 168–255.

—— 1993d. 'La toute-puissance divine, le possible et la non-contradiction', in de Mulralt 1993a: 256–72.

—— 1993e. 'Les consequences de la doctrine occamienne de la toute–-puissance divine. La connaissance d'une chose qui n'existe pas. Commentaire', in de Muralt 1993a: 373–407.

Descartes, R. 1996a. *Œuvres de Descartes*, edited by C. Adam and P. Tannery. Paris: Vrin.

—— 1996b. [Descartes to Mesland] 2 May 1644, in Descartes 1996a: vol. 4, 110–20.

—— 1996c. [Descartes to Elisabeth] 4 August 1645, in Descartes 1996a: vol. 4, 263–8.

—— 1996d. [Descartes Elisabeth] May 1646, in Descartes 1996a: vol. 4, 406–12.

—— 1996e. [Descartes to Elisabeth] September 1646, in Descartes 1996a: vol. 4, 485–94.

—— 1996f. [Descartes to Chanut] 10 November 1647, in Descartes 1996a: vol. 5, 86–8.

—— 1996g. [Descartes and Burman] 16 April 1648, in Descartes 1996a: vol. 5, 144–79.

—— 1996h. 'Discours de la méthode pour bien conduire sa raison et chercher la vérité dans les sciences', in Descartes 1996a: vol. 6, 1–78.

—— 1996i. 'Méditations métaphysiques touchant la première philosophie dans lesquelles l'existence de Dieu et la distinction réelle entre l'âme et le corps de l'homme sont démontrées', in Descartes 1996a: vol. 9, 1–252.

—— 1996j. 'Les p*rincipes de la philosophie*' (first part), in Descartes 1996a: vol. 9, 25–62.

—— 1996k. 'Les passions de l'âme', in Descartes 1996a: vol. 11, 291–497.

—— 1996l. *Règles pour la direction de l'esprit*, translated by J. Sirven. Paris: Vrin.

Dewey, J. 1930. *The Quest for Certainty. A Study of the Relation of Knowledge and Action*. London: Allen & Unwin.

Downes, C. 1965. 'Husserl and the Coherence of the Other Minds Problem', *Philosophy and Phenomenological Research*, 26, 253–9.
Dufour, A. 1991a. *Droits de l'homme, Droit naturel et Histoire. Droit, individu et pouvoir dans l'Ecole du Droit naturel et de l'Ecole du Droit historique*. Paris: P.U.F.
—— 1991b. 'L'influence de la méthodologie des sciences physiques et mathématiques sur les fondateurs de l'Ecole de Droit naturel moderne (Grotius, Hobbes, Pufendorf)', in Dufour 1991a: 93–110.
—— 1991c. 'Savigny et l'Ecole du Droit historique', in Dufour 1991a: 153–63.
—— 1991d. 'Rationnel et irrationnel dans l'Ecole du Droit historique', in Dufour 1991a: 179–94.
—— 1994. 'Le paradigme scientifique dans la pensée juridique moderne', in Amselek 1994: 147–67
Duguit, L. 1921. *Traité de droit constitutionnel*, vol. 1, 3rd edn. Paris: De Bocard.
Dumont, L. 1983. *Essais sur l'individualisme. Une perspective anthropologique sur l'idéologie moderne*. Paris: Seuil.
Duns Scot, 1893. 'Quaestiones in Secundum Librum Sententiarum a Distinctione tertia usque ad decimam quartam', in *Johannis Duns Scoti Opera Omnia*, Paris: Vives.
—— 1894. 'Reportata Parisiensia', in *Johannis Duns Scoti Opera Omnia*. Paris: Vives
Dworkin, R. 1977a. *Taking Rights Seriously*. Cambridge, MA: Harvard University Press.
—— 1977b. 'A Model of Rules I', in Dworkin 1977a: 14–45
—— 1977c. 'Hard Cases', in Dworkin 1977a: 81–130.
—— 1984, 'Rights as Trumps', in *Theories of Rights*, edited by J. Waldron. Oxford: Oxford University Press, 153–67.
—— 1985. *A Matter of Principle*. Cambridge, MA: Harvard University Press.
—— 1986. *Law's Empire*. Cambridge, MA: Harvard University Press.
Edwards, C. 1970. 'The Law of Nature in the Thought of Hugo Grotius', *Journal of Politics*, 32, 784–807.
Ellscheid, G. 1979. 'Die Verrechtlichung sozialer Beziehungen als Problem der praktischen Philosophie', *Neue Hefte fur Philosophie*, 17, 37–61.
Ernoud, A. and Meillet, A. 1994. *Dictionnaire éthymologique de la langue latine. Histoire des mots*, 4th edn. Paris: Klincksieck.
Esser, J. 1972. *Vorverständnis und Methodenwahl in der Rechtsfindung. Rationalitätsgrundlagen Rechtlicher Entscheidungspraxis*, 2nd edn. Frankfurt am Main: Athenäum.
Fallon, R. 1994. 'Reflections on the Hart and Wechsler Paradigm', *Vanderbilt Law Review*, 47, 953–91.
Finnis, J. 1982. *Natural Law and Natural Rights*. Oxford: Clarendon Press.
Foqué, R. and 't Hart, A.C. 1990. *Instrumentaliteit en rechtsbescherming. Grondslagen van een strafrechtelijke waardendiscussie*. Arhem and Antwerp: Gouda Quint and Kluwer.

Frank, J. 1970. *Law and the Modern Mind.* Gloucester, MA: Smith.

Freddoso, A.J. 1991. 'God's General Concurrence With Secondary Causes: Why Conservation is Not Enough', *Philosophy of Religion*, 5, 553–85.

Freund, E. 1890. 'Historical Jurisprudence in Germany', *Political Science Quarterly*, 5, 468–86.

Freund, J. 1974. 'Le droit comme motif et solution de conflits', *Archiv für Rechts- und Sozialphilosophie, Beiheft neue Folge*, 8, 47–62.

—— 1983. *La sociologie du conflit.* Paris: P.U.F.

Friedman, L.M. 1966. 'On Legalistic Reasoning. A Footnote on Weber', *Wisconsin Law Review*, Winter, 148–71.

Fuller, L.L. 1954–55. 'Freedom. A Suggested Analysis', *Harvard Law Review*, 68, 1305–25.

—— 1969. *The Morality of Law*, 2nd edn. New Haven, CT: Yale University Press.

—— 1981. 'The Needs of American Legal Philosophy', in *The Principles of Social Order. Selected Essay of Lon L. Fuller*, edited by K. Winston. Durham, NC: Duke University Press, 249–63.

Gagner, S. 1960. *Studien zur Ideengeschichte der Gesetzgebung.* Uppsala: Almqvist & Wiksells Boktryckeri AB.

Gale, S.G. 1982. 'A Very German Legal Science: Savigny and the Historical School', *Stanford Journal of International Law*, 18, 123–46.

Galilei, G. 1957. 'The Assayer. Selections', in *Discoveries and Opinions of Galileo*, edited by S. Drake. New York: Doubleday & Co.

Gauchet, M. 2006. *Le désenchantement du monde: une histoire politique de la religion.* Paris: Gallimard.

Geach, P.T. 1973. 'Omnipotence', *Philosophy*, 48, 7–20.

Gelasius. 1905. 'Letter of Pope Gelasius to Emperor Anastasius (494)', translated in J.H. Robinson, *Readings in European History.* Boston, MA: Ginn, 72–3.

Gérard, P. 1986. 'Validité juridique et souveraineté', *Archiv für Rechts- und Sozialphilosophie*, 72, 315–35.

—— 1988. 'Antinomie', in *Dictionnaire encyclopédique de théorie et de sociologie juridique*, edited by A.-J.Arnaud. Paris and Brussels: Librairie générale de droit et de jurisprudence and Story-Scientia, 19–23.

Gianformaggio, L. 1990. 'Legal Certainty, Coherence and Consensus: Variations on a Theme by Maccormick', in *Law, Interpretation and Reality. Essays in Epistemology, Hermeneutics, and Jurisprudence*, edited by P. Nerhot. Dordrecht: Kluwer.

Gilson, E. 1952. *Jean Duns Scot. Introduction à ses positions fondamentales.* Paris: Vrin.

—— 1955. *History of Christian Philosophy in the Middle Ages.* New York: Random House.

—— 1960. *Le philosophe et la théologie.* Paris: Arthème Fayard.

—— 1987. *La liberté chez Descartes et la théologie* [1913]. Paris: Vrin.

—— 1999. *The Unity of Philosophical Experience.* San Francisco, CA: Ignatius Press.

Ginascol, F.H. 1959. 'The Question of Universals and the Problem of Faith and Religion', *Philosophical Quarterly*, 37, 319–29.

Gouhier, H. 1937. 'Descartes et la vie morale', *Revue de Métaphysique et de Morale*, 44, 165–97.

Goyard-Fabre, S. 1975. *Le droit et la loi selon Thomas Hobbes*. Paris: Klincksieck.

Grotius, H. 2005. *The Rights of War and Peace*, vol. 1, edited by R. Tuck. Indianapolis, IN: Liberty Fund.

Grua, G. 1956. *La justice humaine selon Leibniz*. Paris: P.U.F.

Guastini, R. 2000. 'On Legal Order: Some Criticisms of the Received View', *Ethical Theory and Moral Practice*, 3: 263–72.

Gusy, C. 1985. 'Das Grundgesetz als normative Gesetzgebungslehre', *Zeitschrift für Rechtspolitik*, 18: 291–9.

Habermas, J. 1973. 'Wahrheitstheorien', in *Wirklichkeit und Reflexion. Festschrift für W. Schulz zum 60. Geburtstag*, edited by H. Fahrenbach. Pfullingen: Neske, pp. 211–65.

—— 1992. *Legitimation Crisis*, translated by T. McCarthy. Cambridge: Polity Press.

—— 1996a. *Between Facts and Norms. Contributions to a Discourse Theory of Law and Democracy*, translated by W. Regh. Cambridge, MA: M.I.T. Press.

—— 1996b. 'Individuation Through Socialization: On George Herbert Mead's Theory of Subjectivity', in *Postmetaphysical Thinking. Philosophical Essays*, translated by W. M. Hohengarten. Cambridge, MA: M.I.T. Press, pp. 149–204.

Haferkamp, H.-P. 2008. 'The Science of Private Law and the State in Nineteenth Century Germany', *American Journal of Comparative Law*, 56, 667–90.

Haggenmacher, P. 1983. *Grotius et la doctrine de la guerre juste*. Paris: P.U.F.

Halpin, A. 1996. 'The Concept of a Legal Power', *Oxford Journal of Legal Studies*, 16: 129–52.

Hampshire, S. 2001. *Justice is Conflict*. Princeton, NJ and Oxford: Princeton University Press,

Hansen, M.H. 2001. *Polis and City-State. An Ancient Concept and its Modern Equivalent*. Copenhagen: Copenhagen Polis Centre.

Hart, H.L.A. 1955. 'Are There Any Natural Rights?', *Philosophical Review*, 64: 175–91.

—— 1968. *Punishment and Responsibility. Essays in the Philosophy of Law*. Oxford: Clarendon.

—— 1982. 'Legal Powers', in *Essays on Bentham. Studies in Jurisprudence and Political Theory*. Oxford: Clarendon Press, pp. 194–219.

—— 1994. *The Concept of Law*, edited by J. Raz and P.A. Bulloch, 2nd edn. Oxford, Clarendon Press.

Hart, H.M. and Sacks, A.M. 1958. *The Legal Process. Basic Problems in the Making and Application of Law*. Tentative Edition.

Hegel, G.W.F. 1955. *Lectures on the History of Philosophy*, vol. 3, *Medieval and Modern Philosophy*, translated by E.S. Haldane and F.H. Simson. Lincoln and London: University of Nebraska Press.

—— 1956. *The Philosophy of History*, translated by J. Sibree. New York: Dover Publications.

—— 1991. *Elements of the Philosophy of Right*, translated by H.B. Nisbet and edited by A.W. Wood. Cambridge: Cambridge University Press.

Heidegger, M. 1950. 'Die Zeit des Weltbildes', in *Holzwege*. Frankfurt am Main: Klosterman, pp. 75–113.

—— 1961. *Nietzsche*, vol. 2. Neske: Pfullingen.

—— 1962. *Die Frage nach dem Ding. Zu Kant's Lehre von den transzendentalen Grundsätzen*. Tübingen: Niemeyer.

—— 1988. *Schelling. Vom Wesen der menschlichen Freiheit* (1809) [1936], in *Gesammtausgabe*, vol. 42, edited by I. Schüssler. Frankfurt am Main: Klostermann.

—— 1993. *Basic Writings*, edited by D.F. Krell, 2nd edn. San Francisco, CA: Harper.

Hintikka, J. 1962. 'Cogito, Ergo Sum: Inference or Performance', *Philosophical Review*, 71: 3–32.

Hobbes, T. 1966a. *The English Works of Thomas Hobbes of Malmesbury*, edited by W. Molesworth, 2nd edn. Aalen: Scientia Verlag.

—— 1966b. *Philosophical Rudiments Concerning Government and Society*, in Hobbes 1966a: vol. 2.

—— 1966c. *Leviathan: or, the Matter, Form, and Power of a Commonwealth, Ecclesiastical and Civil*, in Hobbes, 1966a: vol. 3.

Hoeflich, M.H. 1985. 'John Austin and Joseph Story: Two Nineteenth Century Perspectives on the Utility of the Civil Law for the Common Lawyer', *American Journal for Legal History*, 29: 36–77.

—— 1986. 'Law and Geometry: Legal Science from Leibniz to Langdell', *American Journal of Legal History*, 30: 95–121.

Hohfeld, W.N. 1913. 'Some Fundamental Legal Conceptions as Applied in Judicial Reasoning', *Yale Law Journal*, 23: 16–59.

Hollis, M. 1985. *An Invitation to Philosophy*. Oxford: Blackwell.

Holmes, O.W. 1894–95. 'Privilege, Malice, and Intent', *Harvard Law Review*, 8: 1–14.

Horwitz, M.J. 1977a. *The Transformation of American Law 1780–1860*. Cambridge, MA: Harvard University Press.

—— 1977b. 'The Emergence of an Instrumental Conception of Law', in Horwitz 1977a: pp. 1–30.

—— 1977c. 'The Rise of Legal Formalism', in Horwitz 1977a: pp. 253–266.

Hruschaka, J. 2004. 'The Permissive Law of Practical Reason in Kant's "Metaphysics of Morals"', *Law and Philosophy*, 23: 45–72.

Hume, D. 1966. *An Enquiry Concerning the Principles of Morals, in Enquiries Concerning the Human Understanding and Concerning the Principles of Morals*, edited by L.A. Selby-Bigge. Oxford: Clarendon.

—— 1978. *A Treatise of Human Nature*, edited by L.A. Selby-Bigge, 2nd edn, revised by P.H. Nidditch. Oxford: Oxford University Press.

Hunyadi, M. 1995. *La vertu du conflit. Pour une morale de la médiation*. Paris: Cerf.
Husserl, E. 1970a. *The Crisis of European Sciences and Transcendental Phenomenology. An Introduction to Phenomenological Philosophy*, translated by D. Carr. Evanston, IL: Northwestern University Press.
—— 1970b. 'The Origin of Geometry', in Husserl 1970a: pp. 353–78.
—— 1996. *Méditations cartésiennes. Introduction à la phénoménologie*, translated by G. Pfeiffer and E. Levinas. Paris: Vrin.
Husserl, G. 1955. *Recht und Zeit. Fünf Rechtsphilosophische Essays*. Frankfurt am Main: Klosterman.
Jansen, B. 1929. 'Beiträge zur geschichtlichen Entwicklung der distinctio formalis', *Zeitschrift für katholische Theologie*, 53: 317–44.
Johnson, P.E. 1987. 'Some Thoughts on Natural Law', *California Law Review*, 75: 217–26.
Jouanjan, O. 2005. *Une histoire de la pensée juridique en Allemagne (1800–1918). Idéalisme et conceptualisme chez les juristes allemands du XIXe siècle*. Paris: P.U.F.
Julliard, J. 1985. *La faute à Rousseau. Essai sur les conséquences historiques de l'idee de souveraineté populaire*. Paris: Seuil.
Justinian, 1962. *Digesta Justiniani*, edited by P. Kruger and T. Mommsen. Berlin: Weidman.
Kaeler, L. 1996. 'Weber's Lacuna: Medieval Religion and the Roots of Rationalization', *Journal of the History of Ideas*, 57: 465–85.
Kagan, R.A. 2001. *Adversarial Legalism. The American Way of Law*. Cambridge, MA: Harvard University Press.
Kant, I. 1929. *Critique of Pure Reason*, translated by N.K. Smith. London: MacMillan.
—— 1996. 'Metaphysical First Principles of the Doctrine of Right', in *The Metaphysics of Morals*, translated by M. Gregor. Cambridge: Cambridge University Press, pp. 1–138.
—— 1997. *Groundwork of the Metaphysics of Morals*, translated and edited by M. Gregor. Cambridge: Cambridge University Press.
Kantorowicz, H.U. 1912. 'Volksgeist und historische Schule', *Historische Zeitschrift*, 108: 295–325
Kelley, D.R. 1979. 'Gaius Noster: Substructures of Western Legal Thought', *American Historical Review*, 84: 619–48.
Kelsen, H. 1934. 'Zur Theorie der Interpretation', *Revue Internationale de Théorie du Droit*, 8: 9–17.
—— 1967. *Pure Theory of Law*, translated by M. Knight. Berkeley and Los Angeles: University of California Press.
—— 1991. *General Theory of Norms*, translated by M. Hartney, Oxford: Clarendon.
Kennedy, E.S. 1942. 'Interrelations between Mathematics and Philosophy in the Last Three Centuries', *National Mathematics Magazine*, 16: 290–98.

Kestner, H.E. 2003. 'Betrachtungen zur Gesetzgebungsklugheit, in der die wahren Grundlagen der Rechtswissenschaft aus ihren ursprünglichen Quellen abgeleitet werden [1710]', in Mohnhaupt 2003a: pp. 217–324.

Kiesow, R.M. 1994. 'Science naturelle et droit dans la deuxième moitié du XIXième siècle en Allemagne', in Amselek 1994: pp. 187–210.

Knowles, M.D. 1947. 'Some Recent Advance in the History of Medieval Thought', *Historical Journal*, 9: 22–50.

Kocher, P.H. 1957. 'Francis Bacon on the Science of Jurisprudence', *Journal of the History of Ideas*, 18: 3–26.

Kojève, A. 1981. *Esquisse d'une phénoménologie du droit*. Paris: Gallimard.

Koopmans, T. 1970. 'De rol van de wetgever', in *Honderd jaar rechtsleven*. Zwolle: W.E.J. Tjeenk Willink, pp. 221–35.

Kornhauser, L.A. and Sager, L.G. 1986. 'Unpacking the Court', *Yale Law Journal*, 96: 82–117.

Korobkin, R.B. and Ulen, T.S. 2000. 'Law and Behavioral Science: Removing the Rationality Assumption from Law and Economics', *California Law Review*, 88: 1051–144.

Koyré, A. 1970. *From the Closed World to the Infinite Universe*. Baltimore, MD: John Hopkins University Press.

Kress, K.J. 1984. 'Legal Reasoning and Coherence Theories: Dworkin's Rights Thesis, Retroactivity, and the Linear Order of Decisions', *California Law Review*, 72: 369–402.

—— 1993. 'Coherence and Formalism', *Harvard Journal of Law and Public Policy*, 16: 639–82.

—— 1996. 'Coherence', in *A Companion to Philosophy of Law and Legal Theory*, edited by D. Patterson. Oxford: Blackwell, pp. 533–52.

Kripke, S.A. 1982. *Wittgenstein on Rules and Private Language*. Oxford: Blackwell.

Kubes, V. 1987. *Theorie der Gesetzgebung*. Vienna and New York: Springer.

Laband, P. 1911–14. *Das Staatsrecht des Deutschen Reichs* [1887]. Tübingen: Mohr.

—— 1980. *Abhandlungen, Beiträge und Rezensionen*, vol. 2. Leipzig: Zentralantiquariat der D.D.R.

Lachmayer, F. 1981. 'Legistische Richtlinien als Metanormen des Rechts', in *Gesetzgebung, Kritische* Überlegungen *zur Gesetzgebungslehre und zur Gesetzgebungstechnik*, edited by G.Winkler and B. Schilcher.Vienna: Springer.

Lalande, A. 1983. *Vocabulaire technique et critique de la philosophie*, 14th edn. Paris: P.U.F.

Laplantine, F. 1999. *Je, nous et les autres. Etre humain au-delà des appartenances*. Paris: Le Pommier.

Largeault, J. 1971. *Enquête sur le nominalisme*. Paris and Louvain: Nauwelaerts.

Laurent, F. 1882. *Avant-projet de revision du code civil*, vol. 1. Brussels: Bruylant.

Leff, G. 1956. 'The Fourteenth Century and the Decline of Scholasticism', *Past and Present*, 9: 30–41.

Leibniz, G.W. 1953. *Discourse on Metaphysics*, translated by P.G. Lucas and L. Grint. Manchester: Manchester University Press.

Lindbeck, G. 1959. 'Nominalism and the Problem of Meaning as Illustrated by Pierre D'Ailly on Predestination and Justification', *Harvard Theological Review*, 52: 43–60.

Linde, H. 1975–76. 'Due Process of Lawmaking', *Nebraska Law Review*, 55: 197–255.

Llewellyn, K. 1960. *The Common Law Tradition: Deciding Appeals*. Boston: Little, Brown and Comp.

Lloyd, D. 1981. *The Idea of Law*. London: Penguin.

Lloyd, H.A. 1997. 'Le constitutionalisme', in *Histoire de la pensée politique moderne 1450–1700*, edited by J.H. Burns, translated by J. Ménard and C. Sutte. Paris: P.U.F., pp. 230–69.

Locke, J. 1963a. *The Works of John Locke*. Aalen: Scientia Verlag.

—— 1963b. *A Letter Concerning Toleration, Being a Translation of the Epistola de Tolerantia*, in Locke 1963a: vol. 6.

—— 1963c. *Two Treatises of Government*. Second Treatise, in Locke 1963a: vol. 5.

Lorraine, D. and Stolleis, M. 2008. *Natural Law and Laws of Nature in Early Modern Europe: Jurisprudence, Theology, Moral and Natural Philosophy*. Aldershot: Ashgate.

Löwith, K. 1970. *Meaning in History: The Theological Implications of the Philosophy of History*. Chicago, IL: Chicago University Press.

Lucas, J.R. 1966. *The Principles of Politics*. Oxford: Clarendon Press.

Luhmann, N. 1974. *Grundrechte als Institution. Ein Beitrag zur politischen Soziologie*, 2nd edn. Berlin: Duncker & Humblot.

—— 1981. 'Gerechtigkeit in den Rechtssystemen der modernen Gesellschaft', in *Ausdifferenzierung des Rechts. Beiträge zur Rechtssoziologie und Rechtstheorie*. Francfort on Main: Suhrkamp, 374–418.

—— 1983. *Legitimation durch Verfahren*, 3rd edn. Frankfurt am Main: Suhrkamp.

McCord Adams, M. 1987. *William Ockham*, vol. 1. Notre Dame, IN: Notre Dame University Press.

MacCormick, N. 1978. *Legal Theory and Legal Reasoning*. Oxford: Clarendon Press.

—— 1981. *H.L.A. Hart*. London: Arnold.

—— 1983. 'Contemporary Legal Philosophy: The Rediscovery of Practical Reason', *Journal of Law and Society*, 10: 1–18.

—— 1984. 'Coherence in Legal Justification', in *Theorie der Normen. Festgabe für Ota Weinberger zum 65. Geburstag*, edited by W. Krawietz et al. Berlin: Duncker & Humblot, pp. 37–55.

—— 1989. 'The Ethics of Legalism', *Ratio Juris*, 2: 184–93.

—— 1999. 'My Philosophy of Law', in *The Law in Philosophical Perspectives. My Philosophy of Law*, edited by L.J. Wintgens. Dordrecht: Kluwer, pp. 121–45.

Maine, H.S. 1834. *Ancient Law. Its Connection with the Early History of Society, and Its Relation to Modern Ideas*. New York: Henry Holt.

Marsilius of Padua, 2001. *Defensor Pacis*, translated by A. Gewirth. New York: Columbia University Press.

Mead, G.H. 1962. *Mind, Self & Society from the Standpoint of a Social Behaviorist*, edited by C.W. Morris. Chicago, IL and London: University of Chicago Press.

—— 1972. *Philosophy of the Act*, edited by C.W. Morris et al. Chicago, IL: University of Chicago Press.

—— 1980. *The Philosophy of the Present*, edited by A.E. Murphy. Chicago, IL: University of Chicago Press.

Mecke, C.-E. 2008. 'Objektivität in Recht und Rechtswissenschaft bei G.F. Puchta und R.v. Jhering', *Archiv für Rechts- und Sozialphilosophie*, 94: 147–68.

—— 2009. 'Puchtas und Jherings Beiträge zur heutigen Theorie der Rechtswissenschaft', *Archiv für Rechts- und Sozialphilosophie*, 95: 540–62.

Meijer, K.J. and MacFarlane, D.R. 1996. 'Statutory Coherence and Policy implementation: The Case of Family Planning', *Journal of Public Policy*, 15: 281–98.

Miaille, M. 1976. *Une introduction critique au droit*. Paris: Maspero.

Michaelis, J.D. 1973. *Raisonnement über die protestantischen Universitäten in Deutschland* [1768], vol. 1. Aalen: Scientia Verlag.

Michalski, C. 1927. *Les courants critiques dans la philosophie du XIVe siècle*. Krakow: Imprimerie de l'Université.

Mill, J.S. 1989. 'On Liberty', in *On Liberty and Other Writings*, edited by S. Collini. Cambridge: Cambridge University Press, pp. 1–115.

Modell, A.H. 1993. *The Private Self*. Cambridge, MA: Harvard University Press.

Mohnhaupt, H. 2003a. *Prudentia Legislatoria. Fünf Schriften über die Gesetzgebungsklugheit aus dem 17. und 18. Jarhhundert*. Munich: Beck.

—— 2003b. '"Prudentia"–Lehren in 17. und 18. Jahrhundert', in *Ins Wasser geworfen und Ozeane durchquert. Festschrift für K.W. Nörn*. edited by M. Ascheri. Cologne: Böhlau Verlag, pp. 617–32.

Mollnau, K.A. 1989. 'The Contributions of Savigny to the Theory of Legislation', *American Journal of Comparative Law*, 37: 81–93.

Moody, E.A. 1935. *The Logic of William of Ockham*. London: Sheed & Ward.

—— 1958. 'Empiricism and Metaphysics in Medieval Philosophy', *Philosophical Review*, 67: 145–63.

Morrison, K.F. 1960. *Tradition and Authority in the Western Church 300–1140*. Princeton, NJ: Princeton University Press.

Müller, F. 1996. *Discours de la méthode juridique*, translated by O. Jouanjan. Paris: P.U.F.

Murphy, J.W. 1992. 'Reason, Bounded Rationality, and the *Lebenswelt*: Socially Sensitive Decision Making', *American Journal of Economics and Sociology*, 51: 293–304.

Noll, P. 1972. 'Von der Rechtsprechungswissenschaft zur Gesetzgebungswissenschaft', in *Rechtstheorie als Grundlagenwissenschaft der Rechtstheorie. Jahrbuch für Rechtssoziologie und Rechtstheorie*, edited by H. Albert, N. Luhmann et al. Dusseldorf: Bertelsmann, pp. 524–41.

—— 1973. *Gesetzgebungslehre*. Reinbeck (Hamburg): Rohwolt.
Novak, D. 2000. 'Law: Religious or Secular', *Virginia Law Review*, 68: 569–96.
Nowak, L. 1969. 'De la rationalité du législateur comme élément de l'interprétation juridique', *Logique et Analyse*, 12: 65–86.
Oberman, H.A. 1960. 'Some Notes on the Theology of Nominalism With Attention to its Relation to the Renaissance', *Harvard Theological Review*, 53: 47–76.
—— 1978. 'Fourteenth-Century Religious Thought: A Premature Profile', *Speculum*, 53: 80–93
Ockham, G. 1967. *Scriptum in Liber Primum Sententiarum Ordinatio. Prologus et Distinctio Prima*, edited by G. Gal and S. Brown. St. Bonaventure, NY: Franciscan Institute, St. Bonaventure University.
—— 1970. *Scriptum in Librum Primum Sententiarum Distinctiones II–III*, edited by S. Brown and G. Gal. St. Bonaventure, NY: Franciscan Institute, St. Bonaventure University.
—— 1974. *Summa Logicae*, edited by G. Gal and S. Brown. St. Bonaventure, NY: Franciscan Institute, St. Bonaventure University.
—— 1977. *Scriptum in Librum Primum Sententiarum Ordinatio Distinctiones IV–XVIII*, edited by G.I. Etzkorn. St. Bonaventure, NY: Franciscan Institute, St. Bonaventure University.
—— 1981. *Quaestiones in Librum Secundum Sententiarum (Reportatio)*, edited by G. Gal and R. Wood. St. Bonaventure, NY: Franciscan Institute, St. Bonaventure University.
—— 1984. *Quaestiones Variae*, edited by G.I. Etzkorn et al. St. Bonaventure, NY: Franciscan Institute, St. Bonaventure University.
Ost, F. 1978. 'L'interprétation logique et systématique et le postulat de la rationalité du législateur', in van de Kerchove 1978a: 97–184.
—— and Lenoble, J. 1980. *Droit, mythe et raison. Essai sur la dérive mythologique de la rationalité juridique*. Brussels: Publications des Facultés universitaires Saint-Louis.
—— and van de Kerchove, M. 1987. *Jalons pour une théorie critique du droit*. Brussels: Publications des Facultés universitaires Saint-Louis.
Ozment, S. 1974. 'Mysticism, Nominalism, and Dissent', in *The Pursuit of Holiness in Late Medieval and Renaissance Religion*, edited by C. Trinkaus and H.A. Oberman. Leiden: Brill, pp. 67–92.
Paquier, J. 1927. 'Luther', in Vacant et al. 1903–46, vol. 9, pp. 1146–335.
Pegis, A. 1944. 'Concerning William of Ockham', *Traditio: Studies in Ancient and Medieval History, Thought and Religion*, 2: 465–80.
Percy, W. 1956. 'Symbol as Hermeneutic', *Existentialism. Philosophy and Phenomenological Research*, 16: 522–30.
—— 1958. 'Symbol, Consciousness, and Intersubjectivity', *Journal of Philosophy*, 55: 631–41.
Perelman, C. 1950. 'La quête du rationnel', *Dialectica*, 14: 135–42.
—— 1970a. *Le champ de l'argumentation*. Brussels: Presses University Bruxelles.

—— 1970b. 'De la temporalité comme caractère de l'argumentation', in Perelman 1970a: pp. 41–63.
—— 1970c. 'L'idéal de rationalité et la règle de justice', in Perelman 1970a: pp. 287–301.
—— 1970d. 'La conception de la recherche scientifique de M. Polanyi', in Perelman 1970a: pp. 344–52.
—— 1970e. 'Méthodologie scientifique et philosophie ouverte', *Revue Internationale de Philosophie*, 24: 623–8.
—— 1972a. *Justice et raison*, 2nd edn. Brussels: Editions de l'Université de Bruxelles.
—— 1972b. 'De la justice', in Perelman 1972a: pp. 1–80.
—— 1972c. 'De la méthode analytique en philosophie', in Perelman 1972a: pp. 81–94.
—— 1972d. 'Raison éternelle, raison historique', in Perelman 1972a: pp. 95–103.
—— 1972e. 'Le rôle de la décision dans la théorie de la connaissance', in Perelman 1972a: pp. 121–31
—— 1972f. 'Rapports théoriques de la pensée et de l'action', in Perelman 1972a: pp. 175–83.
—— 1972g. 'Ce qu'une réflexion sur le droit peut apporter au philosophe', in Perelman 1972a: pp. 244–55.
—— 1976a. *Droit, morale et philosophie*, 2nd edn. Paris: Librarie générale de droit et de jurisprudence.
—— 1976b. 'Cinq leçons sur la justice', in Perelman 1976a: pp. 15–66.
—— 1976c. 'Désaccord et rationalité des décisions', in Perelman 1976a: pp. 161–7.
—— 1976d. 'Ce que le philosophe peut apprendre par l'étude du droit', in Perelman 1976a: pp. 191–202.
—— 1984a. *Le raisonnable et le déraisonnable en droit. Au-delà du positivisme juridique*. Paris. Librairie générale de droit et de jurisprudence.
—— 1984b. 'Ontologie juridique et sources du droit', in Perelman 1984a: pp. 34–43.
—— 1984c. 'La sauvegarde et le fondement des droits de l'homme', in Perelman 1984: pp. 49–55.
—— 1984d. 'A propos de l'idée d'un système de droit', in Perelman 1984a: pp. 68–74.
—— 1984d. 'La motivation des décisions de justice, essai de synthèse', in Perelman 1984a: pp. 112–23.
—— and Olbrechts-Tyteca, L. 1976. *Traité de l'argumentation. La nouvelle rhétorique*, 3rd edn. Brussels: Editions de l'Université de Bruxelles.
Pernoud, M.A. 1970. 'Innovation in William of Ockham's References to the "Potentia Dei"', *Antonianum*, 45: 65–97.
Piper, A.M.S. 1986. 'Instrumentalism, Objectivity, and Moral Justification', *American Philosophical Quarterly*, 23: pp. 373–81.
Planiol, M. 1909. *Traité élémentaire de droit civil*, vol. 2, 5th edn. Paris.

Plato, 1943. *Euthyphro; Apology; Crito; Phaedro; Phaedrus*, edited by H.N. Fowler. Cambridge, MA: Harvard University Press.
—— 1946. *The Republic*, books VI–X, translated by P. Shorey. Cambridge, MA: Harvard University Press.
Polin, P. 1971. *La politique de la solitude. Essai sur J.-J. Rousseau*. Paris: Sirey.
Popper, K.R. 1966. *The Open Society and its Enemies*, vol. 1, *The Spell of Plato*, 5th edn. London: Routledge.
—— 1974. 'The Bucket and the Searchlight: Two Theories of Knowledge', in *Objective Knowledge. An Evolutionary Approach*. Oxford: Clarendon Press, pp. 341–61.
Pringsheim, F. 1944. 'The Unique Character of Classical Roman Law', *The Journal of Roman Studies*, 34: 60–64
Puchta, G.F. 1845. *Cursus der Institutionen*, book I, *Encyclopaedie*, 2nd edn. Leipzig: Breitkopf und Härtel.
—— 1851. 'Über die Perioden in der Rechtsgeschichte', in *Kleine Civilistische Schriften*. Leipzig: Breitkopf und Härtel, pp. 135–48.
Pufendorf, S. 1991. *On the Duty of Man and Citizen According to Natural Law*, edited by J. Tully, translated by M. Silverthorne. Cambridge: Cambridge University Press.
—— 1994a. *The Political Writings of Samuel Pufendorf*, edited by C.L. Carr, translated by M.J. Seidler. Oxford: Oxford University Press.
—— 1994b. 'Elements of Universal Jurisprudence in Two Books', in Pufendorf 1994a: pp. 29–92.
—— 1994c. 'On the Law of Nature and of Nations in Eight Books', in Pufendorf 1994a: pp. 93–268.
Putallaz, F.-X. 1983. 'Autour de la connaissance intuitive des non-existents chez Ockham', *Freiburger Zeitschrift für Philosophie und Theologie*, 30: 447–67.
Rawls, J. 1971. *A Theory of Justice*. Cambridge, MA: Harvard University Press.
—— 1993. *Political Liberalism*. New York: Columbia University Press.
Raz, J. 1980. *The Concept of a Legal System. An Introduction to the Theory of Legal System*, 2nd edn. Oxford: Clarendon Press.
—— 1990. *Practical Reason and Norms*. Princeton, NJ: Princeton University Press.
—— 1992. 'The Relevance of Coherence', *Boston University Law Review*, 72: 273–321.
Reimann, M. 1989–90. 'Nineteenth Century German Legal Science', *Boston College Law Review*, 31: 837–97.
Rescher, N. 1974. 'Foundationalism, Coherentism, and the Idea of Cognitive Systematization', *Journal of Philosophy*, 71: 695–708.
Ricoeur, 1975. 'Phenomenology and Hermeneutics', *Nous*, 9: 85–102.
—— 1986a. *Du texte à l'action. Essais d'herméneutique II*. Paris: Seuil.
—— 1986b. 'La fonction herméneutique de la distanciation', in Ricoeur 1986a: pp. 101–17.
—— 1986c. 'La raison pratique', in Ricoeur 1986a: pp. 237–59.

—— 1986d. 'L'intersubjectivité selon Husserl contre l'esprit selon Hegel', in Ricoeur 1986a: pp. 288–302.

—— 1986e. 'Science et idéologie', in Ricoeur 1986a: pp. 303–31.

—— 1990. *Soi-même comme un autre*. Paris: Seuil.

Robinson, J.H. 1905. *Readings in European History*. Boston, MA: Ginn.

Rodis-Lewis, G. 1971. 'Descartes a-t-il eu un professeur nominaliste?', *Archives de Philosophie*, 34: 37–46.

Rorty, R. 1979. *Philosophy and the Mirror of Nature*. Princeton, NJ: Princeton University Press.

Ross, A. 1974. *On Law and Justice*. Berkeley and Los Angeles: University of California Press.

Ross, J.F. 1962. 'Suarez on Universals', *Journal of Philosophy*, 59: 737–8.

Rousseau, J.-J. 1997a. 'Of the Social Contract', in *The Social Contract and Other Later Political Writings*, translated by V. Gourevitch. Cambridge: Cambridge University Press, pp. 41–152.

—— 1997b. 'Discourse on the Origin and Foundations of Inequality Among Men', in *The Discourses and Other Early Political Writings*, translated by V. Gourevitch. Cambridge: Cambridge University Press, pp. 111–88.

Rückert, J. 2004. 'Savigny et la méthode juridique', *Annales de la Faculté de droit de Strasbourg*, 7: 75–95.

Ryle, G. 1988. *The Concept of Mind*. London: Penguin.

Sandel, M.J. 1982. *Liberalism and the Limits of Justice*. Cambridge, MA: Cambridge University Press.

Scheler, M. 1964. 'The Thomist Ethic and the Spirit of Capitalism', *Sociological Analysis*, 25: 4–19.

Schmitt, C. 1934. *Politische Theologie. Vier Kapitel zur Lehre der Souveränität*, 2nd edn. Munich: Duncker & Humblot.

Schneider, H.P. 1966. 'Der Plan einer "Jurisprudentia rationalis" bei Leibniz', *Archiv für Rechts- und Sozialphilosophie*, 52: 553–78.

Schönberger, C. 1997. *Das Parlament im Anstaltstaat. Zur Theorie parlamentarischer Repräsentation in de Staatsrechtslehre des Kaiserreichs (1971–1918)*. Franfurt am Main: Klostermann.

Schwartz Porzecanski, D. 2004. 'Friendship and the Circumstances of Justice According to Aquinas', *The Review of Politics*, 66: 35–54.

Scott, T.K. 1969. 'Ockham on Evidence, Necessity, and Intuition', *Journal of the History of Philosophy*, 7: 27–49.

Sève, R. 1985. 'Discours juridique dans la première moitié du XVIIième siècle. Regards sur la pensée juridique de la France du premier XVIIième siècle', in *L'Etat Baroque*, edited by H. Méchoulan et al. Paris: Vrin, pp. 119–46.

—— 1989. *Leibniz et l'école de droit naturel moderne*. Paris: P.U.F.

Shiner, R. 1992. 'Exclusionary Reasons and the Explanation of Behaviour', *Ratio Juris*, 5: 1–22

Shklar, J.N. 1986. *Legalism. Law, Morals, and Political Trials*, 2nd edn. Cambridge, MA: Harvard University Press.

Sikes, J.G. 1936. 'A Possible Marsilian Source in Ockham', *English Historical Review*, 41: 496–504.
Simmonds, N.E. 2001. 'Protestant Jurisprudence and Modern Doctrinal Scholarship', *Cambridge Law Journal*, 60: 271–300
Simon, H.A. 1978. 'Rationality as a Process and as a Product of Thought', *American Economic Review*, 68: 1–16.
—— 1983. 'Alternative Visions of Rationality', in *Reason in Human Affairs*. Oxford: Blackwell, pp. 3–35.
—— 1997. *Models of Bounded Rationality*. vol. 3. *Empirically Grounded Economic Reason*. Cambridge, MA: M.I.T. Press.
Singer, M. 1963. 'Hart's Concept of Law', *Journal of Philosophy*, 60: 197–220.
Spinoza, B. 1965a. *The Political Works*, edited by A.G. Wernham. Oxford: Clarendon Press.
—— 1965b. 'A Treatise on Religion and Politics', in Spinoza 1965a: pp. 50–255.
—— 1965c. 'A Treatise on Politics', in Spinoza 1965a: pp. 257–445.
Spitz, E.M. 1984. *Majority Rule*. Chatham: Chatham House.
Stichweh, R. 1984. *Die Entstehung des modernen Systems wissenschaftlicher Disziplinen – Physik in Deutschland 1740–1890*. Franfurt am Main: Suhrkamp.
—— 1994. 'Motifs et stratégies de justification employés pour fonder la scientificité de la jurisprudence allemande au XIXe siècle', in Amselek 1994: pp. 169–86.
Strauss, L. 1974. *Natural Right and History*. Chicago, IL: Chicago University Press.
Suarez, F. 1856. *De Legibus ac de Deo Legislatore*, in *Opera Omnia*, vol. 5. Paris: Vivès.
—— 1944. *Selections from Three Works of Francisco Suarez, s.J. De Legibus, ac Deo Legislatore, Defensio Fidei Catholicae, et Apostolicae Adversus Anglicanae Sectae Errores, De Triplici Virtute Theologica, Fide, Spe, et Caritate*, vol. 2, translated by G.L. Williams et al. Oxford: Clarendon (references to this book concern *De Legibus*).
—— 2003. *Des Lois et du Dieu Législateur*, translated by J.-P. Coujou. Paris: Dalloz.
Summers, R.S. 1977. 'Naive Instrumentalism and the Law', in *Law, Morality, and Society. Essays in Honour of H.L.A. Hart*, edited by P.M.S. Hacker and J. Raz Oxford: Clarendon Press, pp. 119–31.
Tapper, C.F.H. 1973. 'Powers and Secondary Rules of Change', in *Oxford Essays on Jurisprudence*, Second Series, edited by A.W.B. Simpson. Oxford: Oxford University Press, pp. 242–77.
Taylor, C. 1985a. *Philosophy and the Human Sciences. Philosophical Papers*, vol. 2. Cambridge: Cambridge University Press.
—— 1985b. 'What's Wrong With Negative Freedom', in Taylor 1985a: pp. 211–29.
—— 1985c. 'Social Theory as Practice', in Taylor 1985a: pp. 91–115.
—— 1995a. *Philosophical Arguments*. Cambridge, MA: Harvard University Press.

—— 1995b. 'Overcoming Epistemology', in Taylor 1995a: pp. 1–19.
—— 1995c. 'Lichtung or Lebensform', in Taylor 1995a: pp. 61–78.
Thibaut, A.F.J. 1814. *Über die Notwendigkeit eines allgemeinen bürgerliches Rechts für Deutschland*. Heidelberg: Mohr und Zimmer.
Thomasius, C. 2003. 'Vorlesungen über die Gesetzesklugheit [1740]', in Mohnhaupt 2003a,: pp. 95–215.
Tierney, B. 2002. 'Natural Law and Natural Rights. Old Problems and Recent Approaches', *Review of Politics*, 64: 389–406.
Tornay, S.C. 1936. 'William of Ockham's Nominalism', *Philosophical Review*, 45: 245–67.
Toulmin, S. 1990. *Cosmopolis: The Hidden Agenda of Modernity*. New York: Free Press.
—— 2001. *Return to Reason*. Cambridge, MA: Harvard University Press.
Ullmann, W. 1955. *The Growth of Papal Government in the Middle Ages: A Study in the Ideological Relation of Clerical to Lay Power*. London: Methuen.
—— 1975. *Law and Politics in the Middle Ages. An Introduction to the Sources of Medieval Political Ideas*. Cambridge: Cambridge University Press.
—— 1979. *Medieval Political Thought*. London: Penguin.
Unger, R.M. 1987. *Social Theory: Its Situation and Its Task. A Critical Introduction to Politics, a Work in Constructive Social Theory*. Cambridge: Cambridge University Press.
Vacant, A. et al. 1903–46. *Dictionnaire de théologie catholique*. Paris: Letouzey & Ané.
van de Kerchove, M. 1978a. *L'interprétation en droit. Approche pluridisciplinaire*, edited by M. van de Kerchove. Brussels: Publications des Facultés universitaires Saint-Louis.
—— 1978b. 'La doctrine du sens clair des textes et la jurisprudence de la Cour de Cassation de Belgique', in van de Kerchove 1978a: pp. 13–50.
—— and Ost, F. 1988. *Le système jurique entre ordre et désordre*. Paris: P.U.F.
Van Gerven, W. 1973. *Het beleid van de rechter*. Antwerp: Standaard Wetenschappelijke Uitgeverij.
Van Hoecke, M. 1988. *Norm, Kontext und Entscheidung. Die Interpretationsfreiheit des Richters*. Louvain and Amersfoort: Acco.
Van Mill, D. 2001. *Liberty, Rationality, and Agency in Hobbes' Leviathan*. Albany: State University Press of New York.
Van Steenberghen, F. 1966. *La philosophie au XIIIième siècle*. Paris and Louvain: Nauwelaerts.
Viandier, A. 1988. *Recherche de légistique comparée*. Berlin: Springer.
Viehweg, T. 1965. *Topik und Jurisprudenz*, 3rd edn. Munich: Beck.
Vignaux, P. 1931. 'Nominalisme', in A Vacant et al. 1903–46: vol. 11: pp. 717–84.
—— 1948. *Nominalisme au XIième siècle*. Montreal: Institut d'Etudes médiévales.
Villey, D. 1958–59. 'Notes de philosophie économique' (unpublished classnotes).
Villey, M. 1942. *La croisade. Essai sur la formation d'une théorie juridique*. Paris: Vrin.

—— 1961. 'Les fondateurs de l'école du droit naturel moderne au XVIIième siècle. Notes de lecture', *Archives de Philosophie du droit*, 6: 73–105.
—— 1962. 'Abrégé du droit naturel classique', in *Leçons d'histoire de la philosophie du droit*. Paris: Dalloz, pp. 109–65.
—— 1989. 'Le droit dans les choses', in *Controverses autour de l'ontologie du droit*, edited by P. Amselek and C. Grzegorczyck. Paris: P.U.F., pp. 11–26.
—— 2003. *La formation de la pensée juridique moderne*, 2nd edn. Paris: P.U.F.
von Gerber, C.F.W. 1851. *Zur Karakteristik der Deutschen Rechtswissenschaft*. Tübingen: Laupp & Siebeck.
—— 1880. *Grundzüge des Deutschen Staatsrechts*. Leipzig: Tauchnitz.
von Jhering, R. 1857. 'Unsere Aufgabe', *Jahrbücher für die Dogmatik des heutigen römischen und deutschen Privatrechts*, 1: 1–52.
—— 1968. *Geist des römischen Rechts auf den verschiedenen Stufen seiner Entwicklung*, 9th edn. Aalen: Scientia Verlag.
von Savigny, F.C. 1815a. 'Rezension von Gönner Ueber Gesetzgebung und Rechtswissenschaft unserer Zeit', *Zeitschrift für geschichtliche Rechtswissenschaft*, 1: 373–423.
—— 1815b. 'Über den Zweck dieser Zeitschrift', *Zeitschrift für geschichtliche Rechtswissenschaft*, 1: 1–17.
—— 2002. *On the Vocation of Our Age for Legislation and Jurisprudence*, translated by A. Hayward. Union, NJ: The Lawbook Exchange.
Waaldijk, C. 1994. *Motiveringsplichten van de wetgever*. Lelystad: Koninklijke Vermande.
Waldron, J. 1999. *Law and Disagreement*. Oxford: Oxford University Press.
—— 2000. '"Transcendental Nonsense" and System in the Law', *Columbia Law Review*, 100: 16–53.
Warrender, H. 1962. 'Obligations and Rights in Hobbes', *Philosophy*, 37: 352–75.
Watt, J.A. 1993. 'Pouvoir spirituel et pouvoir temporel', in *Histoire de la pensée politique médiévale 350–1450*, edited by J.H. Burns and translated by J. Ménard. Paris: P.U.F., pp. 347–99.
Weber, M. 1964. *The Theory of Social and Economic Organisation*, edited by A. M. Henderson, translated by T. Parsons. New York: Free Press.
—— 1992. *The Protestant Ethic and the Spirit of Capitalism*, translated by T. Parsons. London: Routledge.
Wellschmied, K. 1952. 'Zur Inleidinge tot de Hollandsche Rechts-Geleerdheid des Hugo Grotius', *Tijdschrift voor Rechtsgeschiedenis*, 20: 389–440.
Welzel, H. 1962. *Naturrecht und Materiale Gerechtigkeit*, 4th edn. Göttingen: Vandenhoeck & Ruprecht.
Wieacker, F. 1995. *The History of Private Law in Europe With Particular Reference to Germany*, translated by T. Weir. Oxford: Clarendon Press.
Wilhelm, W. 2003. *Zur juristischen Methodenlehre im 19. Jahrhundert. Die Herkunft der Methode Paul Labands aus der Privatrechtswissenschaft*, 2nd edn. Frankfurt am Main: Klostermann.

Wilks, M. 1963. *The Problem of Sovereignty in the Late Middle Ages: the Papal Monarchy with Augustinus Triumphus and the Publicists*. Cambridge: Cambridge University Press.

Winch, P. 1965. 'Universalisability of Moral Judgments', *The Monist*, 49: 198–214.

—— 1990. *The Idea of a Social Science and its Relation to Philosophy*, 2nd edn. London: Routledge.

Windscheid, B. 1904. 'Die Geschichtliche Schule in der Rechtswissenschaft', in *Gesammelte Reden und Abhandlungen*. Leipzig: Duncker & Humblot.

Wintgens, L.J. 1991a. 'Law and Morality: a Critical Relation', *Ratio Juris*, 4: 177–201.

—— 1991b. *Rechtspositivisme en wetspositivisme. Een rechtstheoretische en rechtsfilosofische analyse*. Brussels: Story-Scientia.

—— 1992. 'Possibilités et limites du langage libéral', *Archives de Philosophie du droit*, 37: 205–26.

—— 1993. 'Rhetoric, Reasonableness, and Ethics. An Essay on Perelman', *Argumentation*, 7: 451–60.

—— 2000. *Droit, principes et théories. Pour un positivisme critique*. Brussels: Bruylant.

—— 2002. *Legisprudence. A New Theoretical Approach to Legislation*. Oxford: Hart Publishing.

—— 2005. *The Theory and Practice of Legislation: Essays in Legisprudence*. Aldershot: Ashgate.

—— 2006a. 'Le projet philosophique moderne: l'histoire standard et la *quaestio originis*', in *L'architecture du droit*, edited by D. de Béchillon et al. Paris: Economica, pp. 1003–19.

—— 2006b. 'Legisprudence as a New Theory of Legislation', *Ratio Juris*, 19: 1–25.

—— 2007. *Legislation in Context: Essays in Legisprudence*. Aldershot: Ashgate.

—— 2010. 'Modern Science as Freedom. An Essay on the Mechanisation of the Worldview, Religion, and the Epistemologisation of Philosophy', *Rechtstheorie*, 41: 199–232.

—— 2011. 'Two Readings of Modernity', *Rechtstheorie*, 42, forthcoming.

—— and Lindemans, J.-F. 1986. 'Kelsen et le problème des lacunes dans l'ordre juridique', *Revue Interdisciplinaire d'Etudes Juridiques*, 16: 105–21.

Wittgenstein, L. 1969. *The Blue and Brown Books: Preliminary Studies for the Philosophical Investigations, Generally Known as The Blue and Brown Books*. Oxford: Blackwell.

—— 1976. *Philosophical Investigations*, translated by G.E.M. Anscombe. Oxford: Blackwell.

Wolter, A.B. 1962. 'The Realism of Scotus', *Journal of Philosophy*, 59: 725–36.

Wood, J.E. 1967. 'Christianity and the State', *Journal of the American Academy of Religion*, 35: 257–70.

Xanthaki, H. 2010. 'Drafting Manuals and Quality of Legislation: Positive Contribution Towards Certainty in the Law or Impediment to the Necessity for Dynamism of Rules?', *Legisprudence. International Journal for the Study of Legislation*, 4: 111–28.

Zamboni, M. 2007. *The Policy of Law. A Legal Theoretical Framework*. Oxford: Hart Publishing.

Ziembinski, Z. 1970. 'La notion de rationalité du législateur', *Archives de Philosophie du droit*, 23: 175–87.

—— 1976. *Practical Logic*. Dordrecht: Reidel Publishing.

Zuckerman, C. 1975. 'The Relationship of Theories of Universals to Theories of Church Government in the Middle Ages. A Critique of Previous Views', *Journal of the History of Ideas*, 36: 579–94.

Index

For Product Safety Concerns and Information please contact our EU
representative GPSR@taylorandfrancis.com
Taylor & Francis Verlag GmbH, Kaufingerstraße 24, 80331 München, Germany

www.ingramcontent.com/pod-product-compliance
Ingram Content Group UK Ltd.
Pitfield, Milton Keynes, MK11 3LW, UK
UKHW022018230926
702UK00029B/1987